I0414374

THE UNIVERSITY OF MICHIGAN
CENTER FOR CHINESE STUDIES

MICHIGAN PAPERS IN CHINESE STUDIES

Chang Chun-shu, James Crump, and
Rhoads Murphey, Editors

Ann Arbor, Michigan

Chinese Paintings in Chinese Publications, 1956-1968:

An Annotated Bibliography and An Index to the Paintings

by

E. J. Laing

Michigan Papers in Chinese Studies

No. 6

1969

Copyright 1969

by

Center for Chinese Studies
The University of Michigan
Ann Arbor, Michigan 48104

ISBN 978-0-89264-124-6 (hardcover)
ISBN 978-0-89264-006-5 (paper)
ISBN 978-0-472-12789-4 (ebook)
ISBN 978-0-472-90185-2 (open access)

Contents

Foreword and Acknowledgments

Among the many contributions to scholarly endeavor in the field of Chinese painting made by Dr. Osvald Sirén were his "Annotated Lists of Paintings and Reproductions of Paintings by Chinese Artists." These "Annotated Lists" were published as a part of his Chinese Painting, Leading Masters and Principles (The Ronald Press Company, New York, 1956-58, 7 volumes).

Since 1956, the publication of reproductions of Chinese paintings has continued at a great pace throughout the world. The Chinese themselves have issued many of these publications. A few private Chinese collectors, living in Hong Kong, Japan and elsewhere, have made their paintings accessible for study through illustrated catalogues of their collections. The bulk of the Chinese publications, however, are the result of government sponsorship both on Mainland China and on Taiwan.

On the Mainland, an extensive publication program had reached the stage where several of the museums established after 1948 (such as those in Shanghai, Suchou, Tientsin and Liao-ning) had produced illustrated catalogues of their painting collections, sometimes with color plates of excellent quality. All this was brought, regrettably, to a sudden and complete halt by the Great Cultural Revolution in 1966.

On Taiwan, the National Palace and Central Museums published a three volume descriptive catalogue of the collection of calligraphy and painting in that Museum in 1956 (Ku-kung shu-hua lu 故宮書畫錄); this was followed in 1959 by the large and handsomely illustrated six volumes of Ku-kung ming-hua san-pai chung 故宮名畫三百種 Three Hundred Masterpieces of Chinese Painting in the Palace Museum. More recently (1966), the National Palace Museum started a ten volume work reproducing paintings in the collection (Ku-kung ming-hua 故宮名畫). In addition, the National Palace Museum is currently issuing two excellent periodicals devoted to scholarly articles on the materials in the Museum's collection: The National Palace Museum Bulletin and Ku-kung chi-k'an 故宮季刊 The National Palace Museum Quarterly. Undoubtedly, this publication program will be continued.

Both on the Mainland and on Taiwan, there has been a tendency to extract the maximum use out of a single large group of photographic plates: the plates may all be reproduced in a single work, then one or more selections from and re-arrangements of this corpus of material will be made and published in different formats with different titles.

All of these publications have provided a tremendous flood of pictorial material (both new and old) for art historians and students of Chinese painting. The very bulk of the materials published over the last decade or so and the inevitable duplication of some paintings in several books has given rise to a pressing need for these published materials to be reviewed and presented in a systematic fashion. Thus, in 1965, Professor Richard Edwards suggested that the task of reviewing these publications in the form of an annotated bibliography accompanied by an index to the paintings reproduced in these books be undertaken. Dr. Edwards' constant interest in this project and his frequent assistance has been invaluable. Professor James Cahill has been equally enthusiastic in his support of the project. In addition to providing pieces of valuable information, he has also lent volumes from his personal library.

Several libraries throughout the country have been utilized in the course of completing this project; particular gratitude is due to Mr. Raymond Tang, Curator of the Chinese Collection of the Asia Library at the University of Michigan for his efforts on behalf of this project. Many thanks are extended to Mr. Wu T'ung and to Mrs. Yiu-fong T. Dew for their willing and competent assistance in checking the materials and in working on specific problems. To Miss Louise Ripple fell the task of proof-reading; her invariable good humor during the long hours spent in this tedious work was much appreciated. Sincere gratitude, appreciation and thanks are due to R. Laing for his unlimited patience and for assistance in innumerable ways.

The entire project could not have been completed without the assistance of a grant from the American Council of Learned Societies and a Research Grant-in-aid from Wayne State University. The interest and cooperation of the Center for Chinese Studies at the University of Michigan is, of course, gratefully acknowledged.

BIBLIOGRAPHY

Notes on the Bibliography

The Bibliography includes publications issued between 1956 and August, 1968 which reproduce Chinese paintings now in Chinese public or private collections. The great majority of these publications were produced in Mainland China, Taiwan, Hong Kong or Japan. The two exceptions are the Western publications <u>Art Treasures of the Peking Museum</u> by François Fourcade and the Skira catalogue <u>Chinese Art Treasures</u>, both of which were included because they contain illustrations of paintings exclusively in Chinese museums.

Each publication included in the Bibliography has been provided (in addition to the usual bibliographical data) with a detailed physical description of the publication itself: the amounts of text, the number of plates in color and in monochrome, and a general evaluation of the quality of the reproductions. The great disparity in the actual sizes of Chinese paintings and the need to reproduce heterogeneously sized paintings in a standard size to fit a given publication inevitably leads to great differences in the clarity of the reproductions within one book. This and other reasons inherent in the nature of reproduction processes, made it impossible to establish and abide by a simple, standardized scale of judgment in the evaluation of the plates. The evaluations, then, are given with qualifications whenever possible. It is hoped that these annotations will prove helpful to the librarian and scholar alike. The title by which each work is referred to in the Index is included at the end of each entry.

ANNOTATED BIBLIOGRAPHY

<u>Art Treasures of the Peking Museum</u>, by François Fourcade, translated by Norbert Guterman. Harry N. Abrams, Inc., New York, 1965; fifty tipped-in color plates reproducing paintings. There are fifteen pages of introductory text for the section on painting. The captions for each painting give the artist's name, the title of the painting, its format, medium and size. In addition, there are several paragraphs devoted to each painting providing comments about the artist and the painting, sometimes including full or partial translations of inscriptions or colophons. The quality of the reproductions varies, although generally accurate, details are sometimes blurred; at least seven of the paintings have been reproduced elsewhere, some in more satisfactory color plates, some in monochrome. PM.

Chan Tzu-ch'ien 展子虔 , by Wang Po-min 王伯敏 , Jen-min mei-shu ch'u-pan-she, Shanghai, 1958; Chung-kuo hua-chia ts'ung-shu series, 14 pp. text, 6 monochrome plates, paperbound. The plates are small and of rather poor quality. Chan Tzu-ch'ien.

Chang Seng-yu 張僧繇 , by Wu Shih-ch'u 吳詩初 , Jen-min mei-shu ch'u-pan-she, Shanghai, 1963; Chung-kuo hua-chia ts'ung-shu series, 33 pp. text, 14 monochrome plates, paperbound. The plates, reproducing only one painting, are small and of rather poor quality. Chang Seng-yu.

Chao Chi 趙佶 [Emperor Hui-tsung], by Teng Pai 鄧白 , Jen-min mei-shu ch'u-pan-she, Shanghai, 1958; Chung-kuo hua-chia ts'ung-shu series, 20 pp. text, 16 monochrome plates, paperbound. The plates are small and of rather poor quality. Chao Chi.

Chao Chih-ch'ien hua-chi 趙之謙畫集 (A collection of paintings by Chao Chih-ch'ien), T'ien-ching mei-shu ch'u-pan-she, Tientsin, 1960; 8 loose color plates in a paper envelope. The color is somewhat bright; however, details of the paintings are adequately visible. CC-c hua-chi.

Che-chiang ku-tai hua-chia tso-p'in hsüan-chi 浙江古代畫家作品 選集 (Selected works of ancient artists of Chekiang Province), compiled by Wang Po-min 王伯敏 and Huang Yung-ch'üan 黃湧泉 , Che-chiang jen-min ch'u-pan-she, Hangchou, 1958; 104 plates reproducing 102 paintings from the T'ang dynasty on, 6 color plates, hardbound. The text includes a five page history of painting in South China as well as notes on the artists whose paintings are reproduced. The reproductions are of mediocre quality, being often blurred or indistinct; the color plates are dark and muddy; some fifty-seven of the paintings found herein have been reproduced elsewhere. Che-chiang.

Ch'en Hung-shou 陳洪綬 , by Huang Yung-ch'üan 黃湧泉 , Jen-min mei-shu ch'u-pan-she, Shanghai, 1958; Chung-kuo hua-chia ts'ung-shu series, 48 pp. text, 18 monochrome plates, paperbound. The plates are small and of poor quality. Ch'en Hung-shou.

Ch'en Hung-shou Hua-ts'e 陳洪綬畫册 (An album of paintings by Ch'en Hung-shou), published by the Nanking Museum, Wen-wu ch'u-pan-she, Peking, 1959; 12 monochrome plates, paperbound. The one page introduction to the artist and the album is by Hsü Pang-ta 徐邦達 . The quality of the reproduction is adequate. CH-s Hua-ts'e, A.

Ch'en Hung-shou Hua-ts'e 陳洪綬畫册 (An album of paintings by Ch'en Hung-shou) in the collection of the Palace Museum, Peking, Wen-wu

ch'u-pan-she, Peking, 1964; 8 loose color plates in a cardboard wrapper.
A one page explanation consists of a brief biography of the artist, some
comments on his style and on later artists who were influenced by his
work. The color reproduction is good, the details of the paintings are
clear and precise. CH-s Hua-ts'e, B.

Chin Tung-hsin Hua-hsüan　金冬心畫選　(An album of paintings by
Chin Tung-hsin [Chin Nung]), Chung-kuo ku-tien i-shu ch'u-pan-she,
Peking, 1958, 1959; 12 loose monochrome plates in a paper envelope.
The one page of text consists of the artist's biography. The plates are
small and have a pronounced greyish cast, details are often indistinct.
CT-h Hua-hsüan.

Chinese Art Treasures, Chung-hua wen-wu　中華文物　, A Selected
Group of Objects from the Chinese National Palace Museum and the Chinese
National Central Museum, Taichung, Taiwan; exhibited in the United States
by the Government of the Republic of China, 1961-1962, Skira, Geneva,
1961. The text includes a preface by Wang Shih-chieh　王世杰　, a
two-and-a-half page foreword, an eleven page introduction to the collection
of Chinese art in the National Palace and Central Museums, a map of
China, a chronology, a select bibliography, and a list of titles of paintings
and objects in Chinese. A total of 116 paintings are reproduced, six in
color; there are extensive notes on each painting. Although small in
scale, the reproductions are quite accurate and the color excellent. CAT.

Chinese Cultural Art Treasures, National Palace Museum Illustrated
Handbook, The National Palace Museum, 2nd edition, Taipei, 1966. The
text on painting (pp. 69-78) by Li Lin-ts'an　李霖燦　. Fifty-eight
paintings or sections thereof are reproduced, ten are in color; of these
fifty-eight paintings, all but about ten have been previously reproduced in
Palace Museum publications. The quality of the monochrome plates is
uneven, some reproductions are too light, others lack detail; the color
reproductions of early paintings tend to be reddish in tone; those of later
paintings, somewhat flat. CCAT.

Ch'ing Chu Ta Shan-shui hua-niao ts'e　清朱奔山水花鳥冊　(An
album of landscapes, flowers and birds by Chu Ta of the Ch'ing dynasty),
in the Shanghai Museum, Shanghai Museum, Shanghai, n.d.; 8 monochrome
plates, paperbound. A one page introduction consists of a brief biography
of the artist and a few comments about the album. The quality of the reproduction varies, some plates are adequate, others are too light and
fuzzy. CT Shan-shui hua-niao.

Ch'ing Chü Lien Erh-shih-ssu-fan hua hsin feng hua-ts'e 清居廉二
十四番花信風畫册 (An album of paintings of flowers of the
four seasons by Chü Lien of the Ch'ing dynasty), Wen-wu ch'u-pan-she,
Peking, 1961; 8 loose color plates in a cardboard wrapper. There is a
one page introduction to the artist and the album, including a list of
flowers representative of each season. In general, the colors in the
reproductions are inaccurate, being too harsh and often muddy.
CL Erh-shih-ssu-fan.

Ch'ing-hsiang Shu-hua-kao chüan Ch'ing Shih-t'ao hui 清湘書畫
稿卷清石濤繪 (A draft scroll of painting and calligraphy
by Ch'ing-hsiang, painted by the Ch'ing dynasty artist Shih-t'ao [Tao-chi,
t. Shih-t'ao, h. Ch'ing-hsiang]), in the collection of the Palace Museum,
Peking, Chao-hua mei-shu ch'u-pan-she, Peking, 1961; Chung-kuo ku-tai
hui-hua hsüan-chi series, 15 monochrome plates in a paper wrapper. The
introductory paragraph by Hsü Pang-ta 徐邦達 consists of a short
biography of the artist and brief comments about the scroll. The quality
of the reproduction is good. C-h Shu-hua.

Ch'ing-jen-hua ssu fu 清人畫四幅 (Four paintings by Ch'ing
artists), n. p., Chung-kuo ku-tien i-shu ch'u-pan-she, 1959; 4 color
plates in a paper envelope. A list of contents and brief notes are on the
back of the envelope. The reproductions are very poor, the printing is
unclear and the colors are dull and blurred. Ch'ing-jen-hua.

Ch'ing Shih-t'ao Fang Mi Tien shan-shui 清石濤仿米顛山水
(Landscape after "Crazy Mi" by Shih-t'ao [Tao-chi] of the Ch'ing dynasty),
To-yün hsüan, Shanghai, n. d.; reproduced as a hanging scroll in color on
paper with silk mounting. The quality of the reproduction is good.
S-t Fang Mi Tien.

Ch'ing Shih-t'ao Hsi-yü ch'iu-sung t'u 清石濤細雨虬松圖
(Fine rain and twisted pine by Shih-t'ao [Tao-chi] of the Ch'ing dynasty),
To-yün hsüan, Shanghai, n. d.; reproduced as a hanging scroll in color
on paper with silk mounting. The quality of the reproduction is good.
S-t Hsi-yü.

Ch'ing Shih-t'ao Hua-yang shan-chü t'u 清石濤華陽山居圖
(Dwelling in the Hua-yang Mountains by Shih-t'ao [Tao-chi] of the Ch'ing
dynasty), To-yün hsüan, Shanghai, n. d.; reproduced as a hanging scroll
in color on paper with silk mounting. The quality of the reproduction is
good. S-t Hua-yang.

Ch'ing Shih-t'ao Shan-shui 清石濤山水 (Landscape by Shih-t'ao [Tao-chi] of the Ch'ing dynasty), To-yün hsüan, Shanghai, n.d.; reproduced as a hanging scroll in color on paper with silk mounting. The quality of the reproduction is good. S-t Shan-shui.

Ch'ing Shih-t'ao T'ing-ch'üan t'u 清石濤聽泉圖 (Listening to the spring by Shih-t'ao [Tao-chi] of the Ch'ing dynasty), To-yün hsüan, Shanghai, n.d.; reproduced as a hanging scroll in color on paper with silk mounting. The quality of the reproduction is good. S-t T'ing-ch'üan.

Chou Fang 周昉, by Wang Po-min 王伯敏, Jen-min mei-shu ch'u-pan-she, Shanghai, 1958; Chung-kuo hua-chia ts'ung-shu series, 16 pp. text, 10 monochrome plates, paperbound. The plates are small and of rather poor quality. Chou Fang.

Chu Ta 朱耷, by Hsieh Chih-liu 謝稚柳, Jen-min mei-shu ch'u-pan-she, Shanghai, 1958, 1961; Chung-kuo hua-chia ts'ung-shu series, 16 pp. text, 12 monochrome plates, paperbound. The 1961 edition was used for indexing; the same plates are found in the 1958 edition, but in a slightly different order and not numbered. The plates are small and of fair quality. Chu Ta.

Chu Ta Shu-hua ho-ts'e 朱耷書畫合冊 (An album of calligraphy and painting by Chu Ta), Shanghai Museum publication number 4, n.d.; 16 color plates (7 of painting, 9 of calligraphy) in one ts'e. The reproduction tends to be rather light. CT Shu-hua ho-ts'e, A.

Chu Ta Shu-hua ho-ts'e 朱耷書畫合冊 (An album of calligraphy and painting by Chu Ta), Shanghai Museum publication number 5, n.d.; 17 color plates (7 of calligraphy, 10 of painting) in one ts'e. The reproduction is somewhat light. CT Shu-hua ho-ts'e, B.

Chü Ch'ao tso-p'in hsüan-chi 居巢作品選集 (Selected works by Chü Ch'ao), Ling-nan mei-shu ch'u-pan-she, Canton, 1962; 12 color reproductions of folding fan paintings, each mounted on cardboard, in a cardboard box. A one page introduction by Teng Pai 鄧白. The quality of the reproduction is good. CC tso-p'in.

Chü Ku-ch'üan hua-ch'ung hsüan-chi 居古泉花虫選輯 (Selected flower and insect paintings by Chü Ku-ch'üan [Chü Lien]), Jen-min mei-shu ch'u-pan-she, Shanghai, 1959; 8 loose color plates in a paper wrapper. A one page introduction by Huang Tu-wei 黃苗維 gives a brief biography of Chü and comments about his influence on the Ling-nan School.

The reproductions tend to be too light and are sometimes blurred.
CK-c hua-ch'ung.

Chü Lien shan-mien hua-hsüan 居 廉 扇 面 畫 選   (Selected fan
paintings by Chü Lien), Ling-nan mei-shu ch'u-pan-she, Canton, 1963;
13 color plates loose in a box. A one page preface by Teng Pai 鄧 白
presents Chü's biography and some characteristics of his art. The reproduction is good if somewhat light. CL shan-mien.

Chung-hua mei-shu t'u-chi 中華美術圖集   Art of China,
Chung-hua ts'ung-shu wei-yüan-hui, Taipei, three volumes (ts'e) on
painting, 1955-1956; reproductions of paintings in the National Palace
Museum collection. Vol. I: 45 paintings, T'ang to Sung; Vol. II: 46
paintings, Yüan; Vol. III: 95 paintings, Ming and Ch'ing. The contents
for each volume are in Chinese and in English; the Chinese text accompanying each painting gives the artist's biography, medium, and measurements
of the painting; the English text provides a brief biographical sketch of the
artist. The reproductions, all monochrome, are decidedly dark and details are often lacking in clarity. The majority of the paintings in these
three volumes have been repeatedly reproduced, but at least fifteen paintings have seldom or never been published. CH mei-shu.

Chung-hua ming-hua hsüan-ts'ui 中華名畫選梓   (A collection
of Chinese paintings), Chung-hua ts'ung-shu wei-yüan-hui, Taipei, 1957;
10 loose color plates in a paper envelope reproducing paintings in the
National Palace Museum collection. Information such as the title, the
artist and the size of the painting is found (in Chinese and in English) on
the back of each reproduction. The quality of reproduction ranges from
mediocre to poor. CH ming-hua.

Chung-kuo chin-pai-nien hui-hua chan-lan hsüan-chi 中國近百
年繪畫展覽選集   (Selections from an exhibition of
the last century of Chinese painting), Wen-wu ch'u-pan-she, Peking,
1959; 96 plates of which 12 are in color. The table of contents gives the
artist, title, measurements and collection for each painting reproduced;
a six page introduction by Cheng Chen-to 鄭 振 鐸 surveys the de-
velopments in Chinese painting during the last century, mainly through
brief biographies of the forty-one artists represented in the exhibition.
The monochrome plates are mediocre, the color plates tend to be blurred.
CK chin-pai-nien.

Chung-kuo hua 中國畫 (Chinese Painting), Chung-kuo ku-tien mei-shu
ch'u-pan-she and Jen-min mei-shu ch'u-pan-she, Peking, 1957-1960. The

following issues of this journal have been indexed: I-II (1957, 1958); IV-XV (1959, 1-12); XVI-XXI (1960, 1-6). Each issue has both mono-chrome and color plates; many paintings published here are not repro-duced elsewhere, unfortunately, the quality of the reproductions leaves much to be desired in terms of clarity and accuracy. CK hua.

Chung-kuo ku-hua chi 中國古畫集 Collection of Ancient Chinese Paintings, Book I, Hong Kong, 1956; 60 monochrome plates of paintings in the collection of S. M. Siu (Hsiao Shou-min 蕭壽民) in one ts'e. There is a one page preface by S. M. Siu in Chinese and in English; the following information is given, in English, for each painting reproduced: artist, dates, date of the painting, measurements. In addition, a brief biography of the artist is given in Chinese. The reproductions are quite small and entirely too dark to be satisfactory. CK ku-hua, A.

Chung-kuo ku-hua chi 中國古畫集 Collection of Ancient Chinese Paintings, Hong Kong, 1966; 263 monochrome plates reproducing paintings in the collection of S. M. Siu (Hsiao Shou-min 蕭壽民), hardbound. All 60 paintings found in the previous entry are again reproduced in this volume. The table of contents is given in Chinese and in English; for each painting Mr. Siu has provided notes in Chinese and in English on the artist and on prior collectors. The reproductions are too dark and unclear. CK ku-hua, B.

Chung-kuo ku-tai hui-hua hsüan-chi 中國古代繪畫選集 (A selection of ancient Chinese paintings), Jen-min mei-shu ch'u-pan-she, Peking, 1963; 108 monochrome plates reproducing paintings from the Warring States Period through the Ch'ing dynasty. The text consists of a one page introduction by the editors, a twenty-two page foreword by Cheng Chen-to 鄭振鐸 on the history of Chinese painting and six pages of explanations for the plates giving artist, title and artist's biog-raphy; a title caption accompanies each plate. About half of the scroll paintings reproduced here have been published previously; of the remain-der, many are paintings apparently now in Mainland museum collections and have not appeared in other books of reproductions. The quality of the plates ranges from adequate to mediocre; frequently the reproductions are too dark. CK ku-tai.

Chung-kuo li-tai shu-hua hsüan 中國歷代書畫選 Selections of Chinese Paintings and Calligraphy, Chung-hua ts'ung-shu wei-yüan-hui, Taipei, n.d.; 60 loose monochrome plates in a paper envelope reproducing calligraphy and painting in the National Palace Museum collection. Cap-tions are given in Chinese and in English; there is also a separate list of contents in Chinese and in English. All of the fifty paintings reproduced

8

herein have been published before. The reproductions tend to be somewhat dark and indistinct. CKLTSHH.

Chung-kuo shu-hua 中 國 書 畫   Chinese Painting and Calligraphy,
I, edited by Chu Hsing-chai 朱 省 齋 , Chinese Painting and Calligraphy
Press, Hong Kong, 1961, paperbound. A journal devoted to Chinese art,
it contains reproductions of paintings as well as essays on painting and
calligraphy with text in both Chinese and English; only one issue has been
published to date. The reproductions are adequate. CK shu-hua.

Fei Hsiao-lou ch'uan-shen chia-p'in 費 曉 樓 傳 神 佳 品
(Distinguished examples of portraiture by Fei Hsiao-lou [Fei Tan-hsü]),
by Huang Yung-ch'üan 黃 湧 泉 and Sun Yüan-ch'ao 孫 元 超 ,
Jen-min mei-shu ch'u-pan-she, Peking, 1959; 12 pp. text, including
two pages of explanations of plates, 33 monochrome plates, paperbound.
The reproductions being small and indistinct are quite poor. FH-1 p'in.

Fei Hsiao-lou Shih-nü hua   費 曉 樓 仕 女 畫 (An album of paintings
of ladies by Fei Hsiao-lou [Fei Tan-hsü]), Chung-kuo ku-tien i-shu ch'u-
pan-she, Peking, 1959; 12 loose monochrome plates in a paper envelope.
A one-and-one-half page introduction by Huang Yung-ch'üan 黃 湧 泉
provides a brief biography of Fei, his artistic accomplishments and his
relationship to earlier artists. The reproductions are adequate although
the ground tends to be a smeared grey. FH-1 Shih-nü.

Fei Tan-hsü 費 丹 旭 , by Huang Yung-ch'üan 黃 湧 泉 , Jen-min
mei-shu ch'u-pan-she, Shanghai, 1962; Chung-kuo hua-chia ts'ung-shu
series, 46 pp. text (including a nien-piao), 16 monochrome plates. The
plates are small and rather blurred. Fei Tan-hsü.

Fu Shan hua-chi 傅 山 畫 集 (A collection of paintings by Fu Shan),
compiled by the Institute for the Protection of Cultural Relics of Chin-
tz'u (in T'ai-yüan) Shansi, Jen-min mei-shu ch'u-pan-she, Shanghai,
1965; 30 plates, of which 29 are in color, in one ts'e, reproducing paintings in the Palace Museum, Peking, the Shanghai Museum and the Tientsin Art Museum. A two page foreword by the editors gives a biography
of Fu Shan; four pages of plate explanations provide the size and medium
of each painting, inscriptions and other pertinent data. The reproductions
are generally excellent. FS hua-chi.

Fu Shan shu-hua hsüan 傅 山 書 畫 選   (Selected calligraphy and
painting by Fu Shan), compiled by the Shansi Committee for the Preservation of Cultural Relics, the Institute for the Protection of Cultural
Relics of Chin-tz'u (in T'ai-yüan), Shansi and the Shansi Provincial

Museum, Jen-min mei-shu ch'u-pan-she, Peking, 1962; 26 monochrome plates in one ts'e (11 plates of painting, 17 of calligraphy). A one page foreword consists of a brief biography of Fu Shan; there are two pages of plate explanations giving transcriptions of the calligraphy but no explanations for the paintings. The reproductions tend to lack contrast and are often somewhat indistinct. FS shu-hua.

Han-ch'üeh t'u chüan Sung Ts'ui Po hui 寒雀圖卷宋崔白繪 (Handscroll of cold sparrows by Ts'ui Po of the Sung dynasty), in the collection of the Palace Museum, Peking, Chung-kuo ku-tien i-shu ch'u-pan-she, Peking, 1959; 7 loose monochrome plates in a paper envelope. A one page explanation by Hsü Pang-ta 徐邦達 giving the artist's biography and the provenance of the painting; a paragraph provides the size of the painting, the medium, information about the seals on the painting and the colophon by Wen P'eng. The reproduction is adequate, although somewhat gray. Han-ch'üeh.

Hsiao Ch'ih-mu Shan-shui chüan 蕭尺木山水卷 (A landscape handscroll by Hsiao Ch'ih-mu [Hsiao Yün-ts'ung]), Chung-kuo ku-tien i-shu ch'u-pan-she, Peking, 1959; 6 loose monochrome plates in a paper envelope. There is one page of notes by Ch'in Ling-yün 秦嶺云 on the artist and the painting. The reproduction is adequate. HC-m Shan-shui.

Hsin-lo shan-jen hua-chi 新羅山人畫集 (A collection of paintings by Hsin-lo shan-jen [Hua Yen]), Jen-min mei-shu ch'u-pan-she, Shanghai, 1962; 42 plates, 10 in color, paperbound. There is a three page introduction to Hua Yen and his work by Ho T'ien-chien 賀天健. The reproductions tend to be too light, some are out of focus. H-l s-j hua-chi.

Hsin-lo shan-jen Ling-mao hua-ts'e 新羅山人翎毛畫冊 (An album of paintings of birds by Hsin-lo shan-jen [Hua Yen]), n. p. , n. d. ; ten paintings reproduced in color on silk, mounted as an album. The reproductions are somewhat stiff, the color is rather bright. H-l s-j Ling-mao.

Hsü Hsi yü Huang Ch'üan 徐熙與黃筌 , by Teng Pai 鄧白 , Jen-min mei-shu ch'u-pan-she, Shanghai, 1958; Chung-kuo hua-chia ts'ung-shu series, 22 pp. text, 10 monochrome plates. The plates are small and of fair quality. HH/HC.

Hsü-ku Hua-kuo 虛谷華果 (Flowers and fruits by Hsü-ku), To-yün hsüan, Shanghai, 1959; 4 loose color plates in a paper envelope. The quality of the reproductions is very poor. H-k Hua-kuo.

Hsü Wei 徐渭 , by Ho Lo-chih 何樂之 , Jen-min mei-shu ch'u-pan-she, Shanghai, 1959; Chung-kuo hua-chia ts'ung-shu series, 35 pp. text, including an explanation of the plates, 12 monochrome plates, paperbound. The plates are small and rather poor. Hsü Wei.

Hu-chia shih-pa po 胡笳十八拍 (Eighteen songs for a foreign flute, Lady Wen-chi's return to China), edited by the Nanking Museum, Jen-min mei-shu ch'u-pan-she, Shanghai, 1961; 18 color plates, paperbound. There is a two page introduction by Hsü Hsin-nung 許華農 ; the appropriate poem is written next to each illustration. The color is rather flat and details sometimes unclear. Hu-chia shih-pa po.

Hua Yen Hua-niao ts'e 華嵒花鳥冊 (An album of flowers and birds by Hua Yen), in the collection of the Palace Museum, Peking, Wen-wu ch'u-pan-she, Peking, 1964; 8 loose color plates in a cardboard wrapper. A one page introduction gives some information about the artist and the album. The color in the reproductions is rather bright. HY Hua-niao.

Hua Yen Tsa-hua ts'e Ch'ing Hua Yen hui 華嵒雜畫冊清華嵒繪
(An album of miscellaneous paintings by Hua Yen of the Ch'ing dynasty), in the collection of the Palace Museum, Peking, Chao-hua mei-shu ch'u-pan-she, Peking, 1961; Chung-kuo ku-tai hui-hua hsüan-chi series, 12 monochrome plates in a paper wrapper. A paragraph of introduction by Hsü Pang-ta 徐邦達 contains comments on the artist and the album. The quality of the reproduction is good. HY Tsa-hua.

Huang Kung-wang yü Wang Meng 黃公望與王蒙 , by P'an T'ien-shou 潘天壽 and Wang Po-min 王伯敏 , Jen-min mei-shu ch'u-pan-she, Shanghai, 1958; Chung-kuo hua-chia ts'ung-shu series, 20 pp. text, 18 monochrome plates, paperbound. The plates are small and rather **poor**. HK-w/WM.

Hung-jen K'un-ts'an 弘仁髡殘 , by Cheng Hsi-chen 鄭錫珍 , Jen-min mei-shu ch'u-pan-she, Shanghai, 1963; Chung-kuo hua-chia ts'ung-shu series, 39 pp. text, 20 monochrome plates, paperbound. The plates are small and fair in quality. Hung-jen K'un-ts'an.

I-yüan chi-chin 藝苑集錦 (Assembled elegances from the garden of art), compiled by the Tientsin Art Museum, T'ien-ching mei-shu ch'u-pan-she, Tientsin, 1959; 60 plates, 10 in color, hardbound. The three page foreword is by Chang Ying-hsüeh 張映雪 ; the five page table of contents includes brief biographical information about the artists and measurements of the paintings. About ten of the paintings have been reproduced elsewhere. The reproduction varies considerably, all monochrome plates have a yellowish ground. I-yüan chi-chin.

Jen Po-nien hua-chi　任伯年畫集　(A collection of paintings by Jen Po-nien [Jen I]), compiled by Ts'ai Jo-hung 蔡若虹, Jen-min mei-shu ch'u-pan-she, Peking, 1960; 166 paintings, 35 in color. In addition to a one page foreword, there is a twelve page preface by Ts'ai Jo-hung; the table of contents lists the date of each painting; the paintings are arranged in two subject categories: figures; flowers and birds. The color reproduction is somewhat harsh, some plates are unclear. JP-n hua-chi.

Jen Po-nien hua-hsüan　任伯年畫選　(Selected paintings by Jen Po-nien [Jen I]), Jen-min mei-shu ch'u-pan-she, Peking, 1962; 10 color plates reproducing 14 paintings, loose in a paper wrapper. The plates are taken from Jen Po-nien hua-chi; there is one paragraph of explanation on the cover. The plates are quite clear but the color is somewhat strong. JP-n hua-hsüan.

Jen Po-nien hua-niao ssu fu　任伯年花鳥四幅　(Four flower and bird paintings by Jen Po-nien [Jen I]), Chung-kuo ku-tien i-shu ch'u-pan-she, n.p., 1959; 4 loose color plates in a paper envelope. There is a short explanation on the cover. The reproduction is poor, the printing is clear, but the colors are muddy. JP-n hua-niao.

Jen Po-nien hua-niao ts'ao-ch'ung ts'e 任伯年花鳥草虫册 (An album of paintings of flowers, birds, grasses and insects by Jen Po-nien [Jen I]), To-yün hsüan, Shanghai, 1959; 8 color plates each mounted on silk, in a cardboard folder. The color is somewhat strong. JP-n ts'ao-ch'ung.

Jen Po-nien Hua-ts'e　任伯年畫册　(An album of paintings by Jen Po-nien [Jen I]), Jung-pao chai hsin-chi, Peking, 1954; 8 color plates in a t'ao. A single page of text provides a brief biography of the artist. The quality of the color reproduction is extremely poor. JP-n Hua-ts'e, A.

Jen Po-nien hua-ts'e　任伯年畫册　(An album of paintings by Jen Po-nien [Jen I]), T'ien-ching mei-shu ch'u-pan-she, Tientsin, 1958; 17 loose color plates reproducing 21 paintings. JP-n hua-ts'e, B.

Jen Po-nien k'o-t'u hua-kao 任伯年課徒畫稿 (Practice sketches by Jen Po-nien [Jen I]), Jung-pao chai hsin-chi, Peking, 1960; 8 color prints in a paper envelope. One paragraph giving the artist's biography is on the back of the envelope. The reproduction is relatively accurate. JP-n k'o-t'u.

12

Kao Ch'i-p'ei Hua-ts'e 高其佩畫册 (An album of paintings by Kao Ch'i-p'ei), edited by Wang Tun 王敦 , of the Nanking Museum, Wen-wu ch'u-pan-she, Peking, 1959; 8 monochrome plates, paperbound. A two page foreword consists of a brief biographical sketch of the artist and comments on each album leaf. The reproduction is adequate although a little too grey. KC-p Hua-ts'e.

Kao Feng-han 高鳳翰 , by Li Chi-t'ao 李既匋 , Jen-min mei-shu ch'u-pan-she, Shanghai, 1963; Chung-kuo hua-chia ts'ung-shu series, 34 pp. text, 16 monochrome plates, paperbound. The plates are small and of fair quality. Kao Feng-han.

K'o Chiu-ssu shih-liao 柯九思史料 (Historical data on K'o Chiu-ssu), by Tsung Tien 宗典 , Jen-min mei-shu ch'u-pan-she, Shanghai, 1963; 207 pp. text, 40 monochrome illustrations, including examples of K'o's calligraphy, colophons and seals. The illustrations are small and somewhat blurred. KC-s shih-liao.

Ku-hsien shih-i t'u chüan Ming Chin Tsung shu Tu Chin hui 古賢詩意圖卷明金琮書杜菫繪 (Illustrations to ancient poems, written by Chin Tsung, painted by Tu Chin of the Ming dynasty), in the collection of the Palace Museum, Peking, Chao-hua mei-shu ch'u-pan-she, Peking, 1961; Chung-kuo ku-tai hui-hua hsüan-chi series, 36 loose monochrome plates in a cardboard wrapper. The single page of notes by Hsü Pang-ta 徐邦達 gives brief biographical information about the artists and about the subject of each illustration. The reproduction is good. Ku-hsien shih-i.

Ku K'ai-chih 顧愷之 , by P'an T'ien-shou 潘天壽 , Jen-min mei-shu ch'u-pan-she, Shanghai, 1958, 1961; Chung-kuo hua-chia ts'ung-shu series, 33 pp. text, 26 monochrome plates, paperbound. The plates are small and fair to poor in quality. Ku K'ai-chih.

Ku K'ai-chih yen-chiu 顧愷之研究 (A study of Ku K'ai-chih), by Ma Ts'ai 馬采 , Jen-min mei-shu ch'u-pan-she, Shanghai, 1958; 87 pp. text, 50 monochrome plates. Despite their small size, the plates are clear enough to be useful. KK-c yen-chiu.

Ku K'ai-chih yen-chiu tzu-liao 顧愷之研究資料 (Materials for the study of Ku K'ai-chih), by Yü Chien-hua 俞劍華 , Lo Shu-tzu 羅尗子 and Wen Chao-t'ung 溫肇桐 , Jen-min mei-shu ch'u-pan-she, Peking, 1962; 231 pp. text, 38 monochrome plates. The plates are small and range in quality from fair to poor. KK-c tzu-liao.

Ku-kung chi-k'an　故宮季刊　The National Palace Museum Quarterly,
Taipei, 1966-.　The following issues have been indexed: Vol. I: 1-4.
NPM Quarterly.

Ku-kung chu-p'u　故宮竹譜　(Bamboo paintings in the Palace
Museum, I), the National Palace and Central Museums, Taipei, 1962;
10 monochrome plates in one ts'e.　Two pages of plate explanations include measurements, inscriptions, signatures, artists' seals.　The reproductions are rather light and some are blurred.　KKCP.

Ku-kung ming-hua　故宮名畫　Select Chinese Painting in the
National Palace Museum, projected ten volume series, compiled by the
Editorial Committee of the National Palace Museum, Wang Shih-chieh
王　世　杰,　, editor-in-chief, Taipei, 1966-, hardbound.　Volumes
I-VI have been indexed.　Vol. I: 43 plates, 4 in color, T'ang, Five Dynasties and Northern Sung;　Vol. II: 39 plates, 5 in color, Northern
Sung; Vol. III:　54 plates, 5 in color, Southern Sung; Vol. IV: 52 plates,
5 in color, Southern Sung; Vol. V: 48 plates, 4 in color, Yüan; Vol. VI:
53 plates, 5 in color, Yüan.　Each volume contains a foreword in Chinese,
a table of contents in Chinese and in English; the notes accompanying each
painting give the title, artist, size, medium, format, and a short biography of the artist in Chinese and English.　Although many of the paintings
contained in this series have been reproduced before, each volume has
about four to six previously unpublished paintings.　The quality of the
reproduction is adequate, although the monochrome plates have a yellowish
background tone in which details are sometimes lost; the color plates vary
in quality, some are quite good, others unclear or dull.　KKMH.

Ku-kung ming-hua san-pai chung　故宮名畫三百種　Three Hun-
dred Masterpieces of Chinese Painting in the Palace Museum, selected and
compiled by the Editorial Committee of the Joint Board of Directors of the
National Palace Museum and the National Central Museum, Wang Shih-chieh
王　世　杰,　, editor-in-chief. National Palace Museum and National
Central Museum, Taichung, 1959; six ts'e in two t'ao, reproductions of
300 paintings, 37 in color.　Text portions include an introduction by Wang
Shih-chieh in Chinese and in English and an essay by Lo Chia-lun 羅　家
倫　in English; the table of contents is in Chinese and in English; the caption for each painting gives a brief biography of the artist, the measurements
of the painting, its medium and format and additional notes in both Chinese
and English; there is an index in ts'e six in English.　The reproductions
are of large format and, in general, are excellent, although occasionally
a print will be somewhat faint; the color reproductions are good.　All but
a handful of the paintings reproduced herein were published during the
1930's in Palace Museum publications.　300 M.

Ku-kung po-wu-yüan so ts'ang Chung-kuo li-tai ming-hua chi 故宮博
物院所藏中國歷代名畫集 (A col-
lection of paintings of successive dynasties in China in the collection of
the Palace Museum), Jen-min mei-shu ch'u-pan-she, Peking, 1964-1965,
2nd edition, 5 volumes, hardbound. There is a foreword to the second
edition and a nine page preface by Cheng Chen-to 鄭振鐸 (dated
1958, taken from the first edition) presenting a survey of literature on
Chinese painting. Vol. I: 76 paintings, T'ang, Five Dynasties and Sung;
Vol. II: 105 paintings, Sung; Vol. III: 110 Yüan dynasty paintings; Vol.
IV: 161 Ming dynasty paintings; Vol. V: 73 Ch'ing dynasty paintings. All
of the reproductions are in monochrome; although generally acceptable,
many plates lack clarity of detail. CKLTMHC.

Ku-kung po-wu-yüan ts'ang-hua 故宮博物院藏畫 (Paintings
in the Palace Museum [Peking]), Volume II, Sui-T'ang, Jen-min mei-shu
ch'u-pan-she, Peking, 1964 (no other volumes of this series have appeared
to date); 44 tipped-in plates including 28 in color reproducing 15 paintings,
hardbound; generally the whole painting is reproduced in monochrome with
one or more details in color. The caption for each painting gives the
artist's biography and a few notes about the painting. There are two
appendices, one reproducing the colophons for each painting, the other
giving the written records of each painting. In general, the quality of
the reproductions, which are of large size, varies. Some plates are excellent, but others are too dark, or the colors unclear or the whole painting indistinct. KKPWY ts'ang-hua.

Ku-kung po-wu-yüan ts'ang hua-niao-hua hsüan 故宮博物院
藏花鳥畫選 (Selected flower and bird paintings in the
Palace Museum [Peking]), Wen-wu ch'u-pan-she, Peking, 1965; 100 tipped-
in color plates, hardbound. A three page foreword provides some comments on the history of bird and flower painting; captions give title, artist,
format, medium, measurements, the date of the painting and a brief biography of the artist. A separate folder lists the contents in English. The
color reproduction is excellent and only a few of the paintings have been
previously reproduced. KKPWY hua-niao.

Kuang-tung ming-chia shu-hua hsüan-chi 廣東名家書畫選集
(A collection of selected calligraphy and painting by famous artists of
Kuangtung), Ta-kung pao, Hong Kong, 1960; 64 monochrome plates of
calligraphy and painting, hardbound. The text portion includes a preface by the editors, a one page sketch of the history of painting in Kuang-
tung, three and one-half pages of biographies of the painters whose works
are reproduced in the book; the table of contents is in Chinese and in

English. Most of the paintings have not been reproduced before; however, the plates are small, often too faint or unclear and leave much to be desired. Kuang-tung shu-hua.

Kuang-tung ming-hua-chia hsüan-chi 廣東名畫家選集 (A collection of selected paintings by famous Kuangtung artists), Chinese Artist's Association, Kuangtung Branch, Canton, 1961; 108 tipped-in color plates, hardbound. There is a one-and-one-half page foreward by the editorial committee; commentary accompanying each plate provides the artist's biography, the medium of the painting, its size and occasional notes on the painting. A separate pamphlet contains the introduction and contents in English. The color reproductions are large and of excellent quality. Kuang-tung hua-chia.

Kung Hsien 龔賢 , by Liu Kang-chi 劉綱紀 , Jen-min mei-shu ch'u-pan-she, Shanghai, 1962; Chung-kuo hua-chia ts'ung-shu series, 37 pp. text, 18 monochrome plates, paperbound. The plates are small and of fair quality. Kung Hsien.

Kuo Hsi 郭熙 , by Chang An-chih 張安治 , Jen-min mei-shu ch'u-pan-she, Shanghai, 1959, 1963; Chung-kuo hua-chia ts'ung-shu series, 26 pp. text, 14 monochrome plates, paperbound. The plates are small and of poor quality. Kuo Hsi.

Li Kung-lin 李公麟 , by Chou Wu 周蕪 , Jen-min mei-shu ch'u-pan-she, Shanghai, 1959, 1961; Chung-kuo hua-chia ts'ung-shu series, 31 pp. text, 16 monochrome plates, paperbound. The plates are small and of poor quality. Li Kung-lin.

Li Shan Hua-hui ts'e 李鱓花卉冊 (An album of flower paintings by Li Shan), in the Chinese History Museum, Wen-wu ch'u-pan-she, Peking, 1964; 10 color plates in a cardboard wrapper. There is a one page explanation. The reproduction is good. LS Hua-hui.

Li Shan Hua-hui ts'e-yeh 李鱓花卉冊頁 (Album leaves of flowers by Li Shan), in the collection of the Palace Museum, Peking, Chao-hua mei-shu ch'u-pan-she, Peking, 1961; 8 monochrome plates in a paper folder, Chung-kuo ku-tai hui-hua hsüan-chi series. The one page of notes by Hsü Pang-ta 徐邦達 consists of a brief biography of Li Shan and comments about each album leaf. The reproduction is adequately clear. LS ts'e-yeh.

Li-tai jen-wu-hua hsüan-chi 歷代人物畫選集 (Selected figure paintings of various dynasties), Jen-min mei-shu ch'u-pan-she, Shanghai, 1959; 74 paintings reproduced in monochrome in one ts'e. The text includes a one page introduction, a table of contents and captions (giving artist and title only) for each painting. About three-fourths of the paintings reproduced in this book have been published elsewhere, sometimes with greater accuracy. The plates here tend to lack contrast, details are often obliterated. Li-tai jen-wu.

Liang Sung ming-hua ts'e 兩宋名畫冊 Album Paintings of the North and South Sung Dynasties, Wen-wu ch'u-pan-she, Peking, 1963; 60 tipped-in color plates, hardbound. Reproductions of paintings in the Szechuan Provincial Museum, the Palace Museum, Peking, the Shanghai Museum, the Tientsin Art Museum, the Liao-ning Provincial Museum and the Suchou Committee for the Preservation of Historical Relics. The twelve pages of text by Chang Heng 張珩 include artist's biographies, the measurements, location, and provenance of each painting as well as some stylistic comments. Plates 1-59 are reproduced with greater fidelity in Sung-jen hua-ts'e; the last painting is reproduced in monochrome in the Su-chou po-wu-kuan ts'ang-hua chi. Liang Sung.

Liao-ning sheng po-wu-kuan ts'ang-hua chi 遼寧省博物館藏畫集 (A collection of paintings in the Liao-ning Provincial Museum), Wen-wu ch'u-pan-she, Peking, 1962; 142 paintings reproduced in monochrome in 2 ts'e in 1 t'ao. Notes on the paintings are by Yang Jen-k'ai 楊仁愷 and Tung Yen-ming 董彥明 and include artist, title, format, medium, size, a brief description of the painting, names of colophon authors, signature of artist, and where the painting is recorded. The reproductions tend to be soft and lacking clarity of detail; 14 Sung and Yüan album leaves are reproduced in color in Sung Yüan shan-shui chi ts'e, a few paintings are also found in I-yüan chi-chin, but the majority of the paintings reproduced here are not published elsewhere. Liao-ning.

Lo P'ing Jen-wu shan-shui ts'e-yeh 羅聘人物山水冊頁 (Album-leaf paintings of figures and landscapes by Lo P'ing), in the collection of the Palace Museum, Peking, Chao-hua mei-shu ch'u-pan-she, Peking, 1962; Chung-kuo ku-tai hui-hua hsüan-chi series, 12 monochrome plates in a paper wrapper. The introductory paragraph by Hsü Pang-ta 徐邦達 gives a brief biography of the artist, the size of the album and some comments on the album. The reproduction is good. LP Jen-wu.

Lo-tsai hsüan chen-ts'ang hua 樂在軒珍藏畫 , Lok Tsai
Hsien Collection of Chinese Paintings, Volume One, Ming Dynasty,
(Huang Pao-hsi 黄寶熙 collection) n. p. , Hong Kong, n. d. ; 12
color plates, mounted on cardboard in a t'ao. The explanation of plates
is in Chinese and in English; captions are given in Chinese and in English
on the reverse of each plate. The color reproduction is excellent.
Lo-tsai hsüan.

Ma Yüan yü Hsia Kuei 馬遠與夏珪 , by Teng Pai 鄧白
and Wu Fu-chih 吳芾之 , Jen-min mei-shu ch'u-pan-she, Shanghai,
1958; Chung-kuo hua-chia ts'ung-shu series, 26 pp. text, 16 monochrome
plates, paperbound. The plates are small and rather poor. MY/HK.

Mei Ch'ing Fang-ku shan-shui hua-ts'e 梅清仿古山水畫冊
(An album of landscapes after old masters by Mei Ch'ing), Shanghai Museum publication number 7, n. p. , n. d. ; 24 color plates in one ts'e. The
reproduction is adequate. MC Fang-ku.

Mei Ch'ing Huang-shan t'u ts'e 梅清黄山圖冊 (An album
of landscapes of Huang-shan by Mei Ch'ing), in the collection of the Palace
Museum, Peking, Wen-wu ch'u-pan-she, Peking, 1960; 15 monochrome
plates, paperbound. The reproduction is somewhat unclear.
MC Huang-shan.

Mei Ch'ü-shan hua-chi 梅瞿山畫冊 (A collection of paintings
by Mei Ch'ü-shan [Mei Ch'ing]), Jen-min mei-shu ch'u-pan-she, Shanghai,
1960, 1962; 46 monochrome plates, paperbound. A two page foreword
consisting of a general appreciation of Mei Ch'ing's work is by Ho T'ien-
chien 賀天健 . The reproduction is uneven, some plates
are too light or are blurred, some are too dark. MC-s hua-chi.

Mi Fei yü Mi Yu-jen 米芾與米友仁 , by Sun Tsu-pai
孫祖白 , Jen-min mei-shu ch'u-pan-she, Shanghai, 1962; Chung-
kuo hua-chia ts'ung-shu series, 76 pp. text, 10 monochrome plates, paperbound. The plates are small and rather poor. MF/MY-j.

Ming Ch'ing shan-mien chi-chin 明清扇面集錦 (A collec-
tion of fan paintings of the Ming and Ch'ing dynasties), Jen-min mei-shu
ch'u-pan-she, Hopei, 1959; 22 loose color plates in a paper envelope
reproducing paintings in the collection of Hui Hsiao-t'ung 惠孝同 .
There is a one page preface by Hui. The quality of the color reproduction
is abysmally poor. Shan-mien chi-chin.

18

Ming Ch'ing shan-mien-hua hsüan-chi　明清扇面畫選集
(A collection of selected fan paintings of the Ming and Ch'ing dynasties),
Jen-min mei-shu ch'u-pan-she, Shanghai, 1959; 100 color plates mounted
on cardboard, loose in a t'ao, reproducing paintings which belong to the
Shanghai Committee for the Preservation of Historical Relics. A separate
booklet contains a foreword and the explanation that the paintings were
collected between 1949 and 1959; a brief discussion about the techniques
of painting on gold paper is included. The booklet concludes with a list
of the paintings reproduced in this set and their artists. The quality of
the color reproduction is generally excellent. Shan-mien-hua.

Ming Ch'iu Ying Shan-shui　明仇英山水　　(Landscape by Ch'iu
Ying of the Ming dynasty), Jung-pao chai hsin-chi, Peking, 1955; reproduced as a hanging scroll in color on silk with a silk mounting. There is
a short biography of Ch'iu on the reverse of the scroll. The reproduction
of the brushwork is quite stiff and the color slightly harsh. CY Shan-shui.

Ming Hsü Tuan-pen Hua-ts'e　明徐端本畫册　　(An album of
paintings by Hsü Tuan-pen [Shih Chung] of the Ming dynasty), in the Shanghai Museum, published by the Shanghai Museum, Shanghai, n.d.; 20 monochrome plates, paperbound. There is one paragraph of notes. The reproduction is good. HT-p Hua-ts'e.

Ming Kuo Hsü Hua-ts'e　　明郭詡畫册　　(An album of paintings
by Kuo Hsü of the Ming dynasty) in the Shanghai Museum, published by
the Shanghai Museum, Shanghai, n.d.; 8 monochrome plates, paperbound.
There is one paragraph of biographical and introductory notes. The
reproduction is good. KH Hua-ts'e.

Ming Lan Ying Hsia-ching shan-shui　明藍瑛夏景山水
(Summer landscape by Lan Ying of the Ming dynasty), Jung-pao chai hsin-
chi, Peking, 1955; reproduced as a hanging scroll in color on paper with
silk mounting. There is a short biography of the artist on the back of the
scroll. The reproduction is rather harsh and dry. LY Hsia-ching.

Ming Lan Ying T'ing-ch'üan t'u　　明藍瑛聽泉圖
(Listening to the spring by Lan Ying of the Ming dynasty), Jung-pao chai
hsin-chi, Peking, 1955; an album leaf reproduced as a hanging scroll in
color on paper with silk mounting. There is a short biography of the
artist on the back of the scroll. The reproduction is adequate.
LY T'ing-ch'üan.

Ming Shen Chou Liang Chiang ming-sheng t'u ts'e 明 沈周 兩 江 名勝圖册 (An album depicting scenic spots in the Chiang and Che area by Shen Chou of the Ming dynasty), To-yün hsüan, Shanghai, n. d. (c. 1965); 10 paintings printed in color on silk, mounted and bound as an album. The color is somewhat bright, the general accuracy is questionable. SC Liang Chiang.

Mu-fei ts'ang-hua k'ao-p'ing 木扉藏畫考評 A Study of Some Ming and Ch'ing Paintings in the Mu-fei Collection (belonging to Cheng Te-k'un 鄭德坤), by Ch'eng Hsi 程曦 , published by Ch'eng Hsi and Cheng Te-k'un, Hong Kong, 1965; 53 monochrome illustrations, paperbound. Seventy pages of text give extensive details about the paintings reproduced; there is a list of illustrations in English. The illustrations are small and the quality varies, larger paintings are sometimes indistinct, smaller paintings are sometimes quite clear. Mu-fei.

The National Palace Museum Bulletin, Taipei, 1966-; a bi-monthly journal devoted to scholarly articles on objects in the National Palace Museum, Taipei. Reproductions appear in color and in monochrome, details of paintings are sometimes provided; reproductions in general are excellent. The following issues have been indexed: Vol. I (1966) 1-6; Vol. II (1967) 1-6. NPM Bulletin.

Ni Tsan 倪瓚 , by Cheng Cho-lu 鄭拙盧 , Jen-min mei-shu ch'u-pan-she, Shanghai, 1961; Chung-kuo hua-chia ts'ung-shu series, 29 pp. text, including an explanation of the plates, 11 monochrome plates, paperbound. The plates are small and fair to poor in quality. Ni Tsan.

Ni Yün-lin 倪雲林 [Ni Tsan], by Cheng Ping-shan 鄭秉珊 , Jen-min mei-shu ch'u-pan-she, Shanghai, 1958; Chung-kuo hua-chia ts'ung-shu series, 18 pp. text, 12 monochrome plates, paperbound. The plates are small and of fair quality. Ni Yün-lin.

Pa-ta shan-jen hua-chi 八大山人畫集 (A collection of paintings by Pa-ta shan-jen [Chu Ta]), Jen-min mei-shu ch'u-pan-she, Shanghai, 1959; 28 monochrome plates, paperbound. There is a two page foreword by Shao Lo-yang 邵洛羊 . About half of the paintings have been reproduced before; the reproductions here tend to be greyish and are sometimes unclear. P-t s-j hua-chi.

Pa-ta shan-jen Hua-ts'e 八大山人畫册 (An album of paintings by Pa-ta shan-jen [Chu Ta]), Jung-pao chai hsin-chi, Peking,

1959; 8 loose color plates in a paper envelope. There is a brief biography
of Chu Ta on the cover. The reproductions are very poor.
P-t s-j Hua-ts'e, A.

Pa-ta shan-jen Hua-ts'e 八 大 山 人 畫 冊   (An album of
paintings by Pa-ta shan-jen [Chu Ta]), Chao-hua mei-shu ch'u-pan-she,
Peking, 1961; 9 monochrome plates in one ts'e. There is a one page introduction. The reproduction is adequate. P-t s-j Hua-ts'e, B.

Shang-hai po-wu-kuan ts'ang-hua 上 海 博 物 館 藏 畫
(Paintings in the Shanghai Museum), Jen-min mei-shu ch'u-pan-she,
Shanghai, 1959; 100 tipped-in color plates, hardbound. The text portions
include a one page introduction , a table of contents; captions give the
title and artist, the medium and size of the painting, a brief biography
of the artist, some comments on his style and where the painting is recorded. At least 26 paintings are reproduced in other publications, but
not necessarily in color. The color reproductions are excellent and the
format large. Shang-hai.

Shen Chou Hua-ts'e 沈 周 畫 冊   (An album of paintings by
Shen Chou) in the Suchou Museum, Wen-wu ch'u-pan-she, Peking, 1963;
12 color plates loose in a cardboard wrapper. There is one page of explanation. The reproduction is good. SC Hua-ts'e.

Shen Chou Tung-chuang t'u ts'e 沈 周 東 莊 圖 冊   (An album
of paintings of Tung-chuang by Shen Chou), edited by the Nanking Museum,
Wen-wu ch'u-pan-she, Peking, 1966; 21 monochrome plates in a cardboard wrapper. There is a one page explanation. The reproduction is
good. SC Tung-chuang.

Shen Shih-t'ien 沈 石 田   [Shen Chou], by Cheng Ping-shan
鄭 東 珊   , Jen-min mei-shu ch'u-pan-she, Shanghai, 1958;
Chung-kuo hua-chia ts'ung-shu series, 28 pp. text, including explanation
of plates, 14 monochrome plates, paperbound. The plates are small and
rather poor. Shen Shih-t'ien.

Shen Shih-t'ien hua-chi 沈 石 田 畫 集   (A collection of paintings by Shen Shih-t'ien [Shen Chou]), edited by Wu Su 吳　蘇   , n.p. ,
Taipei, 1965; 57 monochrome plates, paperbound. The text consists of
a one page introduction. The reproductions are somewhat dim and consist mainly of album leaves which were published originally during the
1920's and 1930's. SS-t hua-chi.

Shih-t'ao hua-chi　石濤畫集　(A collection of paintings by Shih-t'ao [Tao-chi]), Jen-min mei-shu ch'u-pan-she, Shanghai, 1960; 68 paintings reproduced in monochrome, paperbound. There is a three page introduction by Hsieh Chih-liu　謝稚柳　and a table of contents. The reproductions are mediocre in quality. S-t hua-chi.

Shih-t'ao Shan-shui ts'e-yeh　石濤山水冊頁　(Album leaf landscape paintings by Shih-t'ao [Tao-chi]) in the Canton Art Museum, Jen-min mei-shu ch'u-pan-she, Peking, 1962; 8 color plates in one ts'e. There is one page of text. The reproductions are adequate to good. S-t Shan-shui ts'e-yeh.

Shih-t'ao shan-shui wu-shang miao-p'in　石濤山水無上妙品　(Unparalleled examples of landscapes by Shih-t'ao [Tao-chi]), edited by Kuo Ch'ang-wei　郭昌偉　, Ya-yün chai, Taipei, n.d.; 28 paintings reproduced in monochrome in one ts'e. This book is essentially a reprint, with fewer illustrations, of volume two of the catalogue of Chang Ta-ch'ien's collection (Ta-feng t'ang ming-chi　大風堂名蹟　). The reproductions are somewhat dark and lack clarity of detail. S-t miao-p'in.

Ssu-ching shan-shui t'u chüan Sung Liu Sung-nien hui　四景山水圖卷宋劉松年繪　(A handscroll depicting landscapes of the four seasons painted by Liu Sung-nien of the Sung dynasty) in the collection of the Palace Museum, Peking, Chao-hua mei-shu ch'u-pan-she, Peking, 1961; Chung-kuo ku-tai hui-hua hsüan-chi series, 10 monochrome plates loose in a paper envelope. There is one paragraph of explanation by Hsü Pang-ta　徐邦達　. The reproductions tend to be too dark. Ssu-ching.

Su-chou po-wu-kuan ts'ang-hua chi　蘇州博物館藏畫集　(A collection of paintings in the Suchou Museum), Wen-wu ch'u-pan-she, n.p., 1963; 118 monochrome plates reproducing 82 paintings from the Sung dynasty on, in one ts'e. The text consists of a one-and-one-half page preface by Hsieh Hsiao-ssu　謝孝思　, a table of contents, and sixteen pages of detailed notes on the paintings by Hsieh. The reproductions in general tend to be too soft, so that much detail, especially in larger paintings, is lost; very few of the paintings are published elsewhere. Su-chou.

Sung Chang Hsün-li Chiang-t'ing lan-sheng　宋張訓禮江亭覽勝　(Enjoying the scenery from a river pavilion by Chang Hsün-li of the Sung dynasty), Jung-pao chai hsin-chi, Peking, 1956; a fan reproduced as a hanging scroll in color on silk with a silk mounting.

A note about the artist is on the back of the scroll. The reproduction
is poor. CH-l Chiang-t'ing.

Sung Chang Tse-tuan Ch'ing-ming shang-ho t'u chüan　宋張擇端
　　清明上河圖卷　　　　　　(The Ch'ing-ming Festival on the
river by Chang Tse-tuan of the Sung dynasty), Chung-kuo ku-tien i-shu
ch'u-pan-she, Peking, 1958; 44 loose monochrome plates in a paper
cover. There is a nine page introduction by Hsü Pang-ta 徐邦達 .
The reproduction is adequate. CT-t Ch'ing-ming.

Sung Chao Ch'ang Chieh-tieh t'u chüan　宋趙昌蛺蝶圖卷
(A handscroll of butterflies by Chao Ch'ang of the Sung dynasty) in the
collection of the Palace Museum, Peking, Wen-wu ch'u-pan-she, Peking,
1960; 5 loose plates in a cardboard wrapper, 2 color plates (the painting)
and three monochrome plates (the colophons). The color is adequate although slightly flat. CC Chieh-tieh.

Sung Chao Meng-chien Shui-hsien t'u chüan　宋趙孟堅水仙圖卷
(A handscroll of narcissi by Chao Meng-chien of the Sung dynasty), edited
by the Tientsin Art Museum, Wen-wu ch'u-pan-she, Peking, 1961; 25
loose monochrome plates in a cardboard wrapper. There is a one page
introduction by Han Shen-hsien 韓慎先 . The reproduction is
adequate. CM-c Shui-hsien.

Sung Ch'en Chü-chung Ssu-yang t'u　宋陳居中四羊圖
(Four goats by Ch'en Chü-chung of the Sung dynasty), Jung-pao chai hsin-
chi, Peking, 1958; an album leaf reproduced as a hanging scroll in color
on silk with silk mounting. The reproduction is poor. CC-c Ssu-yang.

Sung Hsiao Chao Ch'iu-shan hung-shu　宋蕭照秋山紅樹
(Red trees in autumn mountains by Hsiao Chao of the Sung dynasty),
Jung-pao chai hsin-chi, Peking, 1956; a fan reproduced as a hanging
scroll in color on silk with silk mounting. A short note about the artist
is on the back of the scroll. The color is cloudy and the brushwork
appears crude and stiff. HC Ch'iu-shan.

Sung Hsüan-ho Liu-ya lu-an　宋宣和柳鴉蘆雁　　(Four
magpies in a bare willow and four geese on the shore by Hsüan-ho [Em-
peror Hui-tsung] of the Sung dynasty), Shanghai Museum, Shanghai, n.d.;
reproduced as a handscroll in color on paper with paper mounting. The
color tends to be dull and flat. H-h Liu-ya.

Sung hua shih fu　宋畫十幅　　(Ten Sung dynasty paintings),
Palace Museum, Peking, n.d.; 10 leaves in color mounted as an album.

A separate page lists the artist and the title of each leaf in Chinese, Russian, English and French. All ten paintings are reproduced more accurately in Sung-jen hua-ts'e, I-XIX, the color here is somewhat dark and details are unclear. Sung hua shih fu.

Sung Hui-ch'ung Sha-t'ing yen-shu　宋 惠 崇 沙 汀 烟 樹
(A sandy beach and misty trees by Hui-ch'ung of the Sung dynasty), Jung-pao chai hsin-chi, Peking, 1957; an album leaf reproduced as a hanging scroll in color on silk with a silk mounting. The reproduction is poor. H-c Sha-t'ing.

Sung-jen hua-hsüan　宋 人 畫 選　(A selection of paintings by Sung dynasty artists), compiled by Hsieh Chih-liu 謝 稚 柳　, Jen-min mei-shu ch'u-pan-she, Shanghai, 1958; 10 loose color plates in a cardboard wrapper, table of contents on the flap. Eight paintings have been reproduced with greater clarity in Sung-jen hua-ts'e, I-XIX. Here the plates have a pronounced pinkish overtone, in some plates the colors are muddy and the details fuzzy. Sung-jen hua-hsüan.

Sung-jen hua-ts'e 宋 人 畫 冊　Sung Dynasty Album Paintings, compiled by Cheng Chen-to 鄭 振 鐸　, Chang Heng 張 珩 and Hsü Pang-ta 徐 邦 達　, Chung-kuo ku-tien i-shu ch'u-pan-she, Peking, 1957; 100 tipped-in color plates reproducing paintings in the Palace Museum, Peking, hardbound. The plates are divided into two sections but are numbered consecutively. The table of contents and captions are in Chinese; there is a four page foreword by Cheng Chen-to and twelve pages of explanations giving the provenance of each painting and including comments on its style, the artist and former attributions. English versions of Cheng's foreword, the table of contents and the annotated list of paintings are in a separate fourteen page booklet. The quality of the reproductions is excellent. Sung-jen hua-ts'e, A.

Sung-jen hua-ts'e 宋 人 畫 冊　Paintings of the Sung Dynasty (960-1279 A.D.), selected and reproduced by the Palace Museum, Peking, n.d.; 100 color plates in ten albums each in a t'ao. This ten volume set reproduces the same paintings as the previous entry, but in a different order. Each plate is provided with a Chinese label; additional accompanying text for each album varies, some albums are provided with a loose pamphlet which gives the title of each painting in Chinese and in English or another Western language, some albums also have protective tissue sheets for each plate giving the same information.

What is here considered a continuation of this series are the 90 paintings issued under the same title but only in sets of 10 loose color plates in

24

paper envelopes numbered XI to XIX (Wen-wu ch'u-pan-she, Peking, volumes XI-XIII, 1958; volumes XIV-XVI, 1959; volumes XVII-XIX, 1962). This continuation reproduces paintings in the Palace Museum, Peking, the Shanghai Museum, the Tientsin Art Museum and the Szechuan Provincial Museum. There is no list of contents for volumes XI-XIV; volumes XV-XIX have the contents listed on the back of each envelope; artist and title captions are provided on each plate in the series. The quality of the reproduction in the ten album portion is excellent; volumes XI-XIX are generally good, but sometimes unclear. Sung-jen hua-ts'e, B.

Sung-jen Pai-hua t'u 宋人百花圖 (One hundred flowers by a Sung dynasty artist) in the collection of the Palace Museum, Peking, Wen-wu ch'u-pan-she, Peking, 1958; 46 monochrome plates in a paper envelope. The reproduction is somewhat too grey. Sung-jen Pai-hua t'u.

Sung-jen Wang-hsien ying-chia t'u 宋人望賢迎駕圖 (Greeting the emperor at the village by a Sung artist), Shanghai Museum, Shanghai [1959], reproduced as a single large plate in color on paper. The details of the drawing are quite clear, but the colors are rather dark in tone. Wang-hsien ying-chia.

Sung Kuo Hsi Ch'i-shan hsing-lü t'u 宋郭熙溪山行旅圖 (Travelers in the mountains by Kuo Hsi of the Sung dynasty), Jung-pao chai hsin-chi, Peking, 1956; a fan reproduced as a hanging scroll in color on silk with silk mounting. The reproduction is poor. KH Ch'i-shan.

Sung Li Sung Hsi-hu t'u 宋李嵩西湖圖 (West Lake by Li Sung of the Sung dynasty), Shanghai Museum, Shanghai, n.d.; handscroll reproduction in color on paper. An accompanying booklet has explanations in Chinese, French, English and German. The quality of the reproduction is adequate. LS Hsi-hu.

Sung Li T'ang Sung-hu tiao-yin 宋李唐松湖釣隱 (Fishing under a pine-covered cliff by Li T'ang of the Sung dynasty), Jung-pao chai hsin-chi, Peking, 1957; a fan reproduced as a hanging scroll in color on silk with silk mounting. The reproduction is poor. LT Sung-hu.

Sung Li Tung Hsüeh-chiang mai-yü 宋李東雪江賣魚 (A fisherman selling fish on a snowy river by Li Tung of the Sung dynasty), Jung-pao chai hsin-chi, Peking, 1958; a fan reproduced as a hanging scroll on silk with a silk mounting. The reproduction is poor. LT Hsüeh-chiang.

Sung Liang K'ai Pa kao-seng ku-shih t'u chüan 宋梁楷八高僧故實圖卷 (Illustrations to events in the lives of eight famous monks by Liang K'ai of the Sung dynasty), Shanghai Museum, Shanghai, n.d.; reproduced as a handscroll in color on paper with paper mounting. A separate pamphlet contains explanations in Chinese, English, French and German. While the drawing is reproduced quite clearly, the color tends to be muddy. LK Pa kao-seng.

Sung Liu Sung-nien Ch'iu-ch'uang tu I　宋劉松年秋窗讀易
(Reading the I Ching by an autumn window by Liu Sung-nien of the Sung dynasty), Jung-pao chai hsin-chi, Peking, 1957; a fan reproduced as a hanging scroll in color on silk with a silk mounting. The reproduction is poor. LS-n Ch'iu-ch'uang.

Sung Ma Yüan Shui t'u　宋馬遠水圖　(Twenty views of billowing water by Ma Yüan of the Sung dynasty) in the collection of the Palace Museum, Peking, Wen-wu ch'u-pan-she, Peking, 1958; 15 loose monochrome prints in a paper envelope. The quality of the reproduction is adequate. MY Shui.

Sung-tai hua-niao　宋代花鳥　960-1279 (Sung dynasty flower and bird paintings), Wen-wu ch'u-pan-she, Peking, 1964; 20 color postcards in a cardboard folder. The titles are listed on one flap of the folder and on the reverse of each card. Reproductions of fans and album leaves previously reproduced with greater fidelity in Sung-jen hua-ts'e. SSHN.

Sung-tai shan-shui　宋代山水　960-1279 (Sung dynasty landscapes), Wen-wu ch'u-pan-she, Peking, 1964; 20 color postcards in a cardboard folder. The titles are listed on one flap of the folder and on the reverse of each card. Reproductions of fans and album leaves previously reproduced with greater fidelity in Sung-jen hua-ts'e. STSS.

Sung Wang Shen Yü-lou ch'un-ssu　宋王詵玉樓春思
(A man in a pavilion on a river bank by Wang Shen of the Sung dynasty), Jung-pao chai hsin-chi, Peking, 1956; a fan reproduced as a hanging scroll in color on silk with a silk mounting. The reproduction is poor. WS Yü-lou.

Sung Yang Wu-chiu Hsüeh-mei t'u　宋楊無咎雪梅圖
(Plum blossoms and bamboo in snow by Yang Wu-chiu [Yang Pu-chih] of the Sung dynasty) in the collection of the Palace Museum, Peking, Wen-wu ch'u-pan-she, Peking, 1960; 20 loose monochrome plates in a cardboard wrapper. The reproduction is good although slightly greyish. YW-c Hsüeh-mei.

Sung Yüan shan-shui chi-ts'e Liao-ning sheng po-wu-kuan ts'ang-hua chi
chih i 宋元山水集册遼寧省博物館藏畫集之一
(A collection of Sung and Yüan dynasty landscapes, Paintings in the Liao-
ning Provincial Museum, collection one), Liao-ning mei-shu ch'u-pan-
she, Liao-ning, 1960; 14 color plates mounted as an album. A separate
sheet gives explanations of each painting. All Sung dynasty leaves are
reproduced in better color in Sung-jen hua-ts'e XI-XIX and in monochrome
in Liao-ning sheng po-wu-kuan ts'ang-hua. The reproductions in this
volume have a pronounced reddish tone. Sung Yüan shan-shui.

Tan-tang Shan-shui ts'e-yeh 檐當山水册葉   (Album leaves
of landscapes by Tan-tang [P'u-ho]) in the collection of Ch'en Shu-t'ung
陳叔通   , Jen-min mei-shu ch'u-pan-she, Peking, 1962; 22
color plates in a ts'e. There is a one page foreword. The background of
the paintings is a uniform creamy-yellow tone, so that the reproductions
lack contrast and are sometimes quite blurred. T-t ts'e-yeh.

Tan-tang shu-hua chi 檐當書畫集   (A collection of calligraphy
and painting by Tan-tang[P'u-ho]), compiled by the Yünnan Provincial
Museum, Wen-wu ch'u-pan-she, n.p. , 1963; 64 monochrome plates in
one ts'e, reproducing painting and calligraphy in private collections, in
the Liang Chiang Culture Hall and the Yünnan Provincial Museum. In
addition to a one-and-one-half page foreword, there is a one page appen-
dix with P'u-ho's nien-p'u. The quality of the reproduction is quite good,
although some plates are too light, others have a definite greyish cast.
T-t shu-hua.

T'ang Han Huang Wu-niu t'u   唐韓滉五牛圖   (Five water
buffaloes by Han Huang of the T'ang dynasty) in the collection of the Palace Museum, Peking, Wen-wu ch'u-pan-she, Peking, 1959; 5 loose color
plates in a paper envelope with 18 monochrome plates of colophons. The
reproduction is very good. HH Wu-niu.

T'ang-jen Wan-shan shih-nü t'u 唐人紈扇仕女圖   (Ladies
with embroidered fans by a T'ang dynasty artist) in the collection of the
Palace Museum, Peking, Wen-wu ch'u-pan-she, Peking, 1958, 1961; 9
loose color plates in a paper envelope. The accuracy of the reproduction
is questionable, the colors appear to be too dark and dull.
T'ang-jen Wan-shan.

T'ang Liu-ju hua-chi 唐六如畫集   (A collection of paintings
by T'ang Liu-ju [T'ang Yin]), I-shu hua-pao-she, Canton, 1962; 40 mono-

chrome plates, paperbound. The two page foreword consists of T'ang's biography and an introduction to his art by Sun Tsu-pai 孫祖白 . The reproductions are mediocre. TL-j hua-chi.

T'ang Sun Wei Kao-i t'u chüan 唐孫位高逸圖卷 (The four great scholars by Sun Wei of the T'ang dynasty) n. p., n. d.; reproduced as a scroll in color on paper with paper mounting. The colors are muddy and dull, although details of the drawing are clear. SW Kao-i.

T'ang Sung Yüan Ming Ch'ing hua-hsüan 唐宋元明清畫選 (Selected paintings of the T'ang, Sung, Yüan, Ming and Ch'ing dynasties), I-shu hua-pao-she, Canton, 1963; 108 plates including 7 in color. The text portions consist of a table of contents and eight pages giving explanations of the plates, including artist, title, format, and size of the painting and a brief biography of the artist. There is a ten page postscript by Hsieh Chih-liu 謝稚柳 presenting a general survey of the history of Chinese art and including notes on some of the paintings reproduced in this volume. About twenty-two paintings have been previously reproduced; the quality of the reproductions is mediocre, monochrome plates are somewhat light and lacking detail, the color plates appear rather bright. TSYMC hua-hsüan.

T'ang-tai jen-wu hua 唐代人物畫 (Figure painting of the T'ang dynasty), by Liu Ling-ts'ang 劉凌滄 , Chung-kuo ku-tien mei-shu ch'u-pan-she, Peking, 1958; 76 pp. text, 78 illustrations and plates, including 4 color plates. The illustrations include details of scrolls as well as paintings at Tun-huang. The monochrome plates are quite small; the color plates are mediocre in quality. T'ang-tai jen-wu.

T'ang Wu-tai Sung Yüan ming-chi 唐五代宋元名迹 (Famous relics of the T'ang, Five Dynasties, Sung and Yüan dynasties), compiled by Hsieh Chih-liu 謝稚柳 , Ku-tien wen-hsüeh ch'u-pan-she, Shanghai, 1957; 107 monochrome plates reproducing 35 paintings, hardbound. The text consists of a table of contents and captions for each painting giving title, artist and a paragraph on the artist and the painting. Some eleven of the paintings have been published elsewhere with greater accuracy. In general, the reproductions are somewhat dark. TWSY ming-chi.

T'ang Yen Li-pen Pu-nien t'u 唐閻立本步輦圖 (Emperor T'ai-tsung in a sedan chair by Yen Li-pen of the T'ang dynasty) in the collection of the Palace Museum, Peking, Wen-wu ch'u-pan-she, Peking, 1959; 3 color plates reproducing the painting and 8 monochrome plates reproducing the colophons, loose in a cardboard folder. There is a one page explanation. The reproduction, although somewhat flat in color tone, is accurate in details. YL-p Pu-nien.

Tao-chi Hua-ts'e 道濟畫冊 (An album of paintings by Tao-chi) in the collection of the Palace Museum, Peking, Wen-wu ch'u-pan-she, Peking, 1960; 15 monochrome plates, paperbound. There is a one page explanation about the artist and the paintings. Although somewhat grey-ish, the reproductions are adequate. T-c Hua-ts'e.

Tao-chi Su-kuo hua-ts'e 道濟蔬果畫冊 (An album of fruits and vegetables by Tao-chi), Shanghai Museum publication number 3, n.d.; 10 color plates in one ts'e. The reproduction tends to be somewhat un-clear. T-c Su-kuo.

T'ien-ching shih i-shu po-wu-kuan ts'ang-hua chi 天津市藝術博 物館藏畫集 (A collection of paintings in the Tientsin Art Museum), Wen-wu ch'u-pan-she, Peking, 1959; 96 monochrome plates in a ts'e. There is a preface of four pages by Chang Ying-hsüeh 張映雪 consisting of general comments, a table of contents gives the era, the artist, title, medium and size of each painting. Hsü chi 續集 (Supplement) Wen-wu ch'u-pan-she, Peking, 1963; 151 monochrome plates in a ts'e. The reproductions in both volumes tend to be soft and lacking contrast, details are often lost. Although some paintings are reproduced elsewhere, the majority appear in these two volumes for the first time. T'ien-ching.

T'ien-yin t'ang ming-hua hsüan 天隱堂名畫選 Tien Yin Tang Collection, One Hundred Masterpieces of Chinese Painting, selected and compiled by Tien Yin Tang (Chang Pe-chin), 2 volumes. Volume I, (n.p., Tokyo, 1963) contains 100 monochrome reproductions in one ts'e in a t'ao, a one page preface in Chinese and in English, a table of contents in Chi-nese and English; accompanying each painting are notes in Chinese and in English giving title, artist and comments about the painting. Volume II (n.p., Tokyo, 1965) consists of the 18 album leaves by Sung and Yüan artists formerly in the Chuang-t'ao ko 壯陶閣 collection, 3 are reproduced in color; prefaces by Chang Ta-ch'ien 張大千 and Chang Pe-chin in Chinese, the latter also in English, contents in Chinese and in English. The quality of the reproduction in both volumes is very good, although larger paintings tend to be a little indistinct. Tien Yin Tang.

Ts'ang-chou ch'ü t'u chüan Ming Shen Chou hui 滄州趣圖卷明沈 周繪 (A handscroll of scenery of Ts'ang-chou painted by Shen Chou of the Ming dynasty) in the collection of the Palace Museum, Peking, Chao-hua mei-shu ch'u-pan-she, Peking, 1961; Chung-kuo ku-tai hui-hua hsüan-chi series, 36 monochrome plates in a paper wrapper. There is one paragraph of notes by Hsü Pang-ta 徐邦達 . The reproduction is good. Ts'ang-chou.

Wang Fu 王紱 , by Yü Chien-hua 俞劍華 , Jen-min mei-shu ch'u-pan-she, Shanghai, 1961; Chung-kuo hua-chia ts'ung-shu series, 55 pp. text, 12 monochrome plates, paperbound. The plates are small and rather poor. Wang Fu.

Wang Mien 王冕 , by Hung Jui 洪瑞 , Jen-min mei-shu ch'u-pan-she, Shanghai, 1962; Chung-kuo hua-chia ts'ung-shu series, 41 pp. text, 6 monochrome plates, paperbound. The plates are small and fair to poor in quality. Wang Mien.

Wang Shih-ku 王石谷 [Wang Hui], by Hu P'ei-heng 胡佩衡 , Jen-min mei-shu ch'u-pan-she, Shanghai, 1958, 1963; Chung-kuo hua-chia ts'ung-shu series, 40 pp. text, including notes on the plates, 19 monochrome plates, paperbound. The plates are small and fair to poor in quality. Wang Shih-ku.

Wang Shih-ku Hua-hsüan 王石谷畫選 (An album of selected paintings by Wang Shih-ku [Wang Hui]), Chung-kuo ku-tien i-shu ch'u-pan-she, Peking, 1958, 1959; 18 monochrome plates loose in a paper envelope. One paragraph of text consists of a brief biography of the artist. The reproductions are mediocre. WS-k Hua-hsüan.

Wang Wei 王維 , by Ho Lo-chih 何樂之 , Jen-min mei-shu ch'u-pan-she, Shanghai, 1959; Chung-kuo hua-chia ts'ung-shu series, 26 pp. text, 9 monochrome plates, paperbound. The plates are small and rather poor. Wang Wei.

Wen Cheng-ming 文徵明 , by Chang An-chih 張安治 , Jen-min mei-shu ch'u-pan-she, Shanghai, 1959; Chung-kuo hua-chia ts'ung-shu series, 17 pp. text, 13 monochrome plates, 2 color plates, paperbound. The plates are small and rather poor. Wen Cheng-ming.

Wen T'ung Su Shih 文同蘇軾 , by Yü Feng-pien 于鳳編 , Jen-min mei-shu ch'u-pan-she, Shanghai, 1960, 1962; Chung-kuo hua-chia tsung-shu series, 35 pp. text, 10 monochrome plates, paperbound. The plates are small and rather poor. Wen T'ung Su Shih.

Wen-wu 文物 (Cultural relics), the continuation of Wen-wu ts'an-k'ao tzu-liao, Peking, 1959-1966. The following issues have been indexed:

1959: 1-12; 1960: 1-9 (numbers 10-12 never published); 1961: 1-12; 1962: 1-12; 1963: 1-12; 1964: 1-12; 1965: 1-12; 1966: 1-5. WW.

Wen-wu ching hua 文 物 精 華 (Cultural treasures), Wen-wu ch'u-pan-she, Peking. Vol. I, 1959; Vol. II, 1963; Vol. III, 1964. WWCH.

Wen-wu ts'an-k'ao tzu-liao 文 物 參 考 資 料 (Materials for cultural history), Peking, 1950-1958. The following issues of this journal have been indexed: 1950: 1-7, 9-10, 12; 1951: 1-12; 1952: 3-4; 1953: 1-8, 11; 1954: 2-12; 1955: 1-12; 1956: 1-12; 1957: 1-12; 1958: 1-12. WW.

Wu Chen 吳 鎮 , by Cheng Ping-shan 鄭 秉 珊 , Jen-min mei-shu ch'u-pan-she, Shanghai, 1958; Chung-kuo hua-chia ts'ung-shu series, 18 pp. text including notes on the plates, 14 monochrome plates, paperbound. The plates are small and rather poor. Wu Chen.

Wu Li 吳 歷 , by Shao Lo-yang 邵 洛 羊 , Jen-min mei-shu ch'u-pan-she, Shanghai, 1962; Chung-kuo hua-chia ts'ung-shu series, 22 pp. text including notes on the plates, 15 monochrome plates, 1 color plate, paperbound. The plates are small and fair in quality. Wu Li.

Wu Tao-tzu 吳 道 子 , by Wang Po-min 王 伯 敏 , Jen-min mei-shu ch'u-pan-she, Shanghai, 1958; Chung-kuo hua chia ts'ung-shu series, 15 pp. text, 7 monochrome plates, paperbound. The plates are small and fair in quality. Wu Tao-tzu.

Yang-chou pa-chia hua-chi 揚 州 八 家 畫 集 (A collection of paintings by eight Yang-chou artists) in the Nanking Museum, Wen-wu ch'u-pan-she, Peking, 1959, 1960, 1961; 12 monochrome plates. A three page preface on Yang-chou and the artists and notes on each painting by Hsü Hsin-nung 許 莘 農 . The reproductions are a little indistinct, but most of the paintings reproduced herein have not been published before. Yang-chou pa-chia.

Yüan Chang Hsün Shuang-kou-chu t'u chüan 元 張 遜 雙 鈎 竹 圖 卷 (A handscroll of outline bamboo, rocks and pines by Chang Hsün of the Yüan dynasty), Wen-wu ch'u-pan-she, Peking, 1964; 19 monochrome plates in a cardboard wrapper. There is a one page explanation. The reproduction is good. CH Shuang-kou.

Yüan Chao Meng-fu Jen-chi t'u 元 趙 孟 頫 人 騎 圖 (An official on horseback by Chao Meng-fu of the Yüan dynasty) in the collection of the Palace Museum, Peking, Wen-wu ch'u-pan-she, Peking, 1959;

11 loose color plates in a cardboard wrapper. Although the details of the painting are quite clear, the color seems rather flat. CM-f Jen-chi.

<u>Yüan Chao Meng-fu shu Yen-chiang tieh-chang shih</u> 元 趙 孟 頫 書 煙 江 疊 嶂 詩 (Chao Meng-fu's calligraphy of the "Misty River and Layered Mountains" poem [including the paintings by Shen Chou and Wen Cheng-ming]), edited by the Liao-ning Provincial Museum, Wen-wu ch'u-pan-she, Peking, 1962; 36 monochrome plates reproducing the calligraphy and the painting in one <u>ts'e</u>. There is a one page postscript by Yang Jen-k'ai 楊 仁 愷 . The reproduction is adequate. Yen-chiang tieh-chang.

<u>Yüan-jen hua-ts'e</u> 元 人 畫 册 (Album-leaf paintings by Yüan masters), Vols. I, II, Wen-wu ch'u-pan-she, Peking, 1959; each volume consists of 10 loose color plates in a cardboard wrapper. The reproduction is good. Yüan-jen hua-ts'e.

<u>Yüan Jen Jen-fa Chang Kuo chien Ming-huang t'u</u> 元 任 仁 發 張 果 見 明 皇 圖 (The Taoist sorcerer Chang Kuo-lao before the Emperor Ming-huang by Jen Jen-fa of the Yüan dynasty) in the collection of the Palace Museum, Peking, Wen-wu ch'u-pan-she, Peking, 1962; 2 color plates reproducing the painting and 3 monochrome plates reproducing the colophons loose in a cardboard wrapper. Accompanying the plates is a three page leaflet of notes. The reproduction is good. JJ-f Chang Kuo.

<u>Yüan Wu Chen Shan-shui chen-chi</u> 元 吳 鎮 山 水 真 蹟 The Reproduction of Wu Chen's Landscape Paintings Yuen Dynasty (1280-1354 A.D.), edited by Lo T'ien-pi 勞 天 庇 , South East Printing Press, Hong Kong, 1963; 23 monochrome plates, hardbound. The painting belongs to Hsiao Su (Siu So 蕭 蘇). In addition to the painting, Wu Chen's inscription is reproduced along with poems by Emperor Ch'ienlung and a colophon by Chang T'ai-k'ai. There is a one page preface by Lo and a one page biography of Wu Chen, both in Chinese and in English; a two page appendix reproduces the entry for this painting as found in <u>Shih-ch'ü pao-chi</u> 石 渠 寶 笈 . The quality of the reproduction is somewhat light but adequate. WC Shan-shui.

<u>Yün Nan-t'ien Hua-hui ts'e</u> 惲 南 田 花 卉 册 (An album of flower paintings by Yün Nan-t'ien [Yün Shou-p'ing]), Hua-p'ien ch'u-pan-she, Shanghai, 1957; 8 color plates in a cardboard wrapper. The color is somewhat flat, and the background a monotonous creamy-yellow tone. YN-t Hua-hui.

<u>Yün Shou-p'ing Hua-ts'e</u>　恽壽平畫册　　(An album of paintings by Yün Shou-p'ing) in the collection of the Palace Museum, Peking, Wen-wu ch'u-pan-she, Peking, 1961; 10 monochrome plates, paperbound. There is a one page introduction to the artist and the paintings. The reproduction is adequate. YS-p Hua-ts'e.

INDEX

Guide to the Index

Only those paintings reproduced in the publications listed in the Bibliography are covered in the Index. It is expected that the Index will be used in conjunction with Osvald Sirén's "Annotated Lists." For this reason, the Index is arranged according to Sirén's general scheme: by dynasty and then by artist in alphabetical order. Anonymous paintings are listed by subject matter at the end of each dynastic list.

Brief biographical information is given in the Index for each artist. For the sources of biographical information (and for additional paintings not found in the Index), reference is given to the volume and page where this artist and his works are found in Sirén's "Annotated Lists" (see example below). In some cases, the artist's dates given in the Index will vary from those found in Sirén's "Annotated Lists." Unless otherwise noted, these new dates have been taken from Kuo Wei-ch'ü 郭　味蕖 , Sung Yüan Ming Ch'ing shu-hua-chia nien-piao 宋元明清書畫家年表 (An annual chronology of Sung, Yüan, Ming and Ch'ing dynasty calligraphers and artists, Jen-min mei-shu ch'u-pan-she, Peking, 1962). For those artists not mentioned in Sirén's "Annotated Lists," the biographical sources are indicated in the Index by the same alphabetical key employed by Sirén and includes a new entry: "W" (see example below). For the sake of convenience, a key to these biographical sources and their code letters is provided before the Index proper.

The paintings for each artist are arranged in two main categories: dated and undated works. The dated paintings are listed in chronological order. The undated paintings are listed first by order of appearance in Sirén's "Annotated Lists" (the subject matter of a few paintings has warranted exceptions to this); these are followed by the remaining undated paintings arranged according to museum (beginning with the National Palace Museum, Taipei and the Palace Museum, Peking, then other Chinese museums in alphabetical order, then non-Chinese museums); then those paintings in private collections, with Chinese collections first, in alphabetical order; and finally, those paintings in unknown locations according to the title of the book in which they are reproduced. The anonymous paintings, categorized according to subject matter, are listed first according to the order of appearance in the anonymous paintings sections of Sirén's "Annotated Lists;" then those paintings listed elsewhere in Sirén's "Annotated Lists" (according to dynasty and artist in alphabetical order); then those paintings which have multiple attributions to artist or period, but which are not in Sirén's "Annotated Lists;" and finally by the same museum, private collection and unknown location arrangement as used for listing the works of specific artists. For paintings which have been reproduced under multiple attributions or as by anonymous artists of different periods, the entire entry is repeated under as many headings in the Index as appropriate (see example below).

Many of the paintings reproduced between 1956 and 1968 were also reproduced prior to 1956 and were listed by Sirén. Every effort has been made to collate these reproductions; to indicate that a painting has been listed by Sirén, the title used by Sirén has been retained (in some cases, lengthy descriptive titles have been shortened) and the abbreviation "AL" ("Annotated Lists") appears at the end of the title portion of the entry. When it has been possible to determine that Sirén listed a single painting under more than one title, all titles are included in the Index entry. For those paintings which have been reproduced under multiple attributions or as by anonymous artists of different periods and which are listed somewhere else in Sirén's "Annotated Lists," the name of the artist or the appropriate anonymous list under which this painting will be found in Sirén's "Annotated Lists," has also been noted (see example below).

The Index includes references to each place a specific painting is reproduced in the books listed in the Bibliography. Many short titles for these books have been used throughout the Index; a key to these short titles is provided before the Index proper. An asterisk after a plate number signifies a color reproduction.

Examples

Artist entries

LI TUNG 李東 . Active during the reign of emperor Li-tsung (1225-1264). (H. 4; M. p. 195.)

Li Tung is not included in Sirén's "Annotated Lists." Li's biography will be found in chüan 4 of H: Hsia Wen-yen, T'u-hui pao-chien and on page 195 of M: Sun Tao-kung, Chung-kuo hua-chia jen-ming ta tz'u-tien.

HUANG CH'ÜAN 黄筌 , t. Yao-shu 要叔 . B. c. 900, d. 965, from Ch'eng-tu, Szechuan, served as tai-chao under Meng Ch'ang of the Later Shu dynasty (935-965), painted flowers and birds, Buddhist and Taoist subjects. (CP, II, AL, 28-29.)

Huang Ch'üan is listed by Sirén. Additional biographical information and sources as well as the paintings by Huang listed by Sirén will be found on pages 28-29 of the "Annotated Lists" (AL) in volume II of Sirén's Chinese Painting, Leading Masters and Principles (CP).

Painting entries

Under Huang Ch'üan:

> Four crows in a bare willow and two ducks on the water in snow, album leaf, Nat. Pal. Mus., Taipei, (AL). CKLTMHC, II.79 (as anon. Sung); KKMH, II.17* (as Huang Ch'üan).

AL: indicates that this painting is listed by this title in Sirén's "Annotated Lists" under Huang Ch'üan. CKLTMHC, II.79 (as anon. Sung): this painting (sometimes given to Huang Ch'üan) is published as an anonymous Sung work on plate 79 of volume II of Ku-kung po-wu-yüan so ts'ang Chung-kuo li-tai ming-hua chi. KKMH, II.17* (as Huang Ch'üan): this same painting is published as being by Huang Ch'üan in color (*) on plate 17 of volume II of Ku-kung ming-hua. Because this painting is published both as a work by Huang Ch'üan and as an anonymous Sung work, it is listed twice in the Index: once under Huang Ch'üan as above and again under anonymous Sung, Flowers and Birds:

> Four crows in a bare willow and two ducks on the water in snow, album leaf, Nat. Pal. Mus., Taipei, (AL, Huang Ch'üan). CKLTMHC, II.79 (as anon. Sung); KKMH, II.17* (as Huang Ch'üan).

AL, Huang Ch'üan: indicates that this painting is listed by this title in Sirén's "Annotated Lists" under Huang Ch'üan. The painting does not appear in Sirén's anonymous Sung List.

The same system of multiple entries and cross-references to Sirén's "Annotated Lists" has been employed in the Index for all anonymous paintings assigned to more than one period.

Key to Biographical Sources

A	Chang Yen-yüan	張 彥 遠
	Li-tai ming-hua chi	歷 代 名 畫 記
B	Chu Ching-hsüan	朱 景 玄
	T'ang-ch'ao ming-hua lu	唐 朝 名 畫 錄
C	Huang Hsiu-fu	黃 休 復
	I-chou ming-hua lu	益 州 名 畫 錄
D	Liu Tao-ch'un	劉 道 醇
	Sheng-ch'ao ming-hua p'ing	聖 朝 名 畫 評

E   Liu Tao-ch'un
     Wu-tai ming-hua pu-i   劉道醇   五代名畫補遺

F   Kuo Jo-hsü
     T'u-hua chien-wen chih   郭若虛   圖畫見聞志

G   Hsüan-ho hua-p'u   宣和文畫譜

H   Hsia Wen-yen
     T'u-hui pao-chien   夏文彥   圖繪寶鑑

I   P'ei-wen-chai shu-hua p'u   佩文齋書畫譜

J   Li E
     Nan-Sung-yüan hua-lu   厲鶚   南宋院畫錄

K   Lu Chün
     Sung Yüan i-lai hua-jen
     hsing-shih lu   魯駿   宋元以來畫人姓氏錄

L   P'eng Yün-ts'an
     Hua-shih hui-chuan   彭蘊燦   畫史彙傳

M   Sun Tao-kung
     Chung-kuo hua-chia jen-ming
     ta tz'u-tien   孫韜公   中國畫家人名大辭典

N   Chiang Shao-shu
     Wu-sheng shih-shih   姜紹書   無聲詩史

O   Hsü Ch'in
     Ming-hua lu   徐沁   明畫錄

P   Chou Liang-kung
     Tu-hua lu   周亮工   讀畫錄

Q   Chang Keng
     Kuo-ch'ao hua cheng lu   張庚   國朝畫徵錄

R   Feng Chin-po
     Kuo-ch'ao hua-shih   馮金伯   國朝畫識

S   Hu Ching
     Kuo-ch'ao yüan hua-lu   胡敬   國朝院畫錄

T   Chiang Pao-ling
     Mo-lin chin-hua   蔣寶齡   墨林今話

U   Ch'in Tsu-yung
     T'ung-yin lun-hua   秦祖永   桐陰論畫

V	Chung-kuo jen-ming ta tz'u-tien	中 國 人 名 大 辭 典
W	Wang Chao-yung	汪 兆 鏞
	Ling-nan hua cheng lüeh	嶺 南 畫 徵 畧
X	Saitō Ken	齋 藤 謙
	Shinagaka Jimmei Jiten	支 那 畫 家 人 名 辭 典

Abbreviations used in the Index

AL: "Annotated Lists" in CP.

CP: Osvald Sirén, Chinese Painting, Leading Masters and Principles, The Ronald Press, New York, 1956-1958, Volumes II and VII.

WWKLWYH: Wen-wu kuan-li wei-yüan-hui 文 物 管 理 委 員 會
Committee for the Preservation of Cultural Relics.

WWPKWYH: Wen-wu pao-kuan wei-yüan-hui 文 物 保 管 委 員 會
Committee for the Protection of Cultural Relics.

* Color reproduction.

Key to Short Titles used in Index

The following short titles used in the Index are here arranged in strict alphabetical order regardless of capitals or hyphens.

300 M.	Ku-kung ming-hua san-pai chung
CAT	Chinese Art Treasures
CCAT	Chinese Cultural Art Treasures
CC Chieh-tieh	Sung Chao Ch'ang Chieh-tieh t'u chüan
CC-c hua-chi	Chao Chih-ch'ien hua-chi
CC-c Ssu-yang	Sung Ch'en Chü-chung Ssu-yang t'u
CC tso-p'in	Chü Ch'ao tso-p'in hsüan-chi
Che-chiang	Che-chiang ku-tai hua-chia tso-p'in hsüan-chi
Ch'ing-jen-hua	Ch'ing-jen-hua ssu fu
CH-l Chiang-t'ing	Sung Chang Hsün-li Chiang-t'ing lan-sheng
CH mei-shu	Chung-hua mei-shu t'u-chi
CH ming-hua	Chung-hua ming-hua hsüan-ts'ui
CH Shuang-kou	Yüan Chang Hsün Shuang-kou-chu t'u chüan
CH-s Hua-ts'e, A	Ch'en Hung-shou Hua-ts'e (1959)
CH-s Hua-ts'e, B	Ch'en Hung-shou Hua-ts'e (1964)
C-h Shu-hua	Ch'ing-hsiang Shu-hua-kao chüan Ch'ing Shih-t'ao hui

CK chin-pai-nien	Chung-kuo chin-pai-nien hui-hua chan-lan hsüan-chi
CK-c hua-ch'ung	Chü Ku-ch'üan hua-ch'ung hsüan-chi
CK hua	Chung-kuo hua
CK ku-hua, A	Chung-kuo ku-hua chi (1956)
CK ku-hua, B	Chung-kuo ku-hua chi (1966)
CK ku-tai	Chung-kuo ku-tai hui-hua hsüan-chi
CKLTMHC	Ku-kung po-wu-yüan so ts'ang Chung-kuo li-tai ming-hua chi
CKLTSHH	Chung-kuo li-tai shu-hua hsüan
CK shu-hua	Chung-kuo shu-hua
CL Erh-shih-ssu-fan	Ch'ing Chü Lien Erh-shih-ssu-fan hua hsin feng hua-ts'e
CL shan-mien	Chü Lien Shan-mien hua-hsüan
CM-c Shui-hsien	Sung Chao Meng-chien Shui-hsien t'u chüan
CM-f Jen-chi	Yüan Chao Meng-fu Jen-chi t'u
CT-h Hua-hsüan	Chin Tung-hsin Hua-hsüan
CT Shan-shui hua-niao	Ch'ing Chu Ta Shan-shui hua-niao ts'e
CT Shu-hua ho-ts'e, A	Chu Ta Shu-hua ho-ts'e (Shanghai Museum publication number 4)
CT Shu-hua ho-ts'e, B	Chu Ta Shu-hua ho-ts'e (Shanghai Museum publication number 5)
CT-t Ch'ing-ming	Sung Chang Tse-tuan Ch'ing-ming shang-ho t'u chüan
CY Shan-shui	Ming Ch'iu Ying Shan-shui
FH-l p'in	Fei Hsiao-lou ch'uan-shen chia-p'in
FH-l Shih-nü	Fei Hsiao-lou Shih-nü hua
FS hua-chi	Fu Shan hua-chi
FS shu-hua	Fu Shan shu-hua hsüan
Han-ch'üeh	Han-ch'üeh t'u chüan Sung Ts'ui Po hui
HC Ch'iu-shan	Sung Hsiao Chao Ch'iu-shan hung-shu
HC-m Shan-shui	Hsiao Ch'ih-mu Shan-shui chüan
H-c Sha-t'ing	Sung Hui-ch'ung Sha-t'ing yen-shu
HH/HC	Hsü Hsi yü Huang Ch'üan
H-h Liu-ya	Sung Hsüan-ho Liu-ya lu-an
HH Wu-niu	T'ang Han Huang Wu-niu t'u
H-k Hua-kuo	Hsü-ku Hua-kuo
HK-w/WM	Huang Kung-wang yü Wang Meng
H-l s-j hua-chi	Hsin-lo shan-jen hua-chi
H-l s-j Ling-mao	Hsin-lo shan-jen Ling-mao hua-ts'e
HT-p Hua-ts'e	Ming Hsü Tuan-pen Hua-ts'e
HY Hua-niao	Hua Yen Hua-niao ts'e
HY Tsa-hua	Hua Yen Tsa-hua ts'e Ch'ing Hua Yen hui

JJ-f Chang Kuo	Yüan Jen Jen-fa Chang Kuo chien Ming-huang t'u
JP-n hua-chi	Jen Po-nien hua-chi
JP-n hua-hsüan	Jen Po-nien hua-hsüan
JP-n hua-niao	Jen Po-nien hua-niao ssu fu
JP-n Hua-ts'e, A	Jen Po-nien Hua-ts'e (1954)
JP-n hua-ts'e, B	Jen Po-nien hua-ts'e (1958)
JP-n k'o-t'u	Jen Po-nien k'o-t'u hua-kao
JP-n ts'ao-ch'ung	Jen Po-nien hua-niao ts'ao-ch'ung ts'e
KC-p Hua-ts'e	Kao Ch'i-p'ei Hua-ts'e
KC-s shih-liao	K'o Chiu-ssu shih-liao
KH Ch'i-shan	Sung Kuo Hsi Ch'i-shan hsing-lü t'u
KH Hua-ts'e	Ming Kuo Hsü Hua-ts'e
KKCP	Ku-kung chu-p'u
KK-c tzu-liao	Ku K'ai-chih yen-chiu tzu-liao
KK-c yen-chiu	Ku K'ai-chih yen-chiu
KKMH	Ku-kung ming-hua
KKPWY hua-niao	Ku-kung po-wu-yüan ts'ang hua-niao-hua hsüan
KKPWY ts'ang-hua	Ku-kung po-wu-yüan ts'ang-hua
Ku-hsien shih-i	Ku-hsien shih-i t'u chüan Ming Chin Tsung shu Tu Chin hui
Kuang-tung hua-chia	Kuang-tung ming-hua-chia hsüan-chi
Kuang-tung shu-hua	Kuang-tung ming-chia shu-hua hsüan-chi
Liang Sung	Liang Sung ming-hua ts'e
Liao-ning	Liao-ning sheng po-wu-kuan ts'ang-hua chi
Li-tai jen-wu	Li-tai jen-wu-hua hsüan-chi
LK Pa kao-seng	Sung Liang K'ai Pa kao-seng ku-shih t'u chüan
Lo-tsai hsüan	Lo-tsai hsüan chen-ts'ang hua
LP Jen-wu	Lo P'ing Jen-wu shan-shui ts'e-yeh
LS Hsi-hu	Sung Li Sung Hsi-hu t'u
LS Hua-hui	Li Shan Hua-hui ts'e
LS-n Ch'iu-ch'uang	Sung Liu Sung-nien Ch'iu-ch'uang tu I
LS ts'e-yeh	Li Shan Hua-hui ts'e-yeh
LT Hsüeh-chiang	Sung Li Tung Hsüeh-chiang mai-yü
LT Sung-hu	Sung Li T'ang Sung-hu tiao-yin
LY Hsia-ching	Ming Lan Ying Hsia-ching shan-shui
LY T'ing-ch'üan	Ming Lan Ying T'ing-ch'üan t'u
MC Fang-ku	Mei Ch'ing Fang-ku shan-shui hua-ts'e
MC Huang-shan	Mei Ch'ing Huang-shan t'u ts'e
MC-s hua-chi	Mei Ch'ü-shan hua-chi
MF/MY-j	Mi Fei yü Mi Yu-jen
Mu-fei	Mu-fei ts'ang-hua k'ao-p'ing

MY/HK	Ma Yüan yü Hsia Kuei
MY Shui	Sung Ma Yüan Shui t'u
NPM Bulletin	The National Palace Museum Bulletin
NPM Quarterly	Ku-kung chi-k'an
PM	Art Treasures of the Peking Museum
P-t s-j hua-chi	Pa-ta shan-jen hua-chi
P-t s-j Hua-ts'e, A	Pa-ta shan-jen Hua-ts'e (1959)
P-t s-j Hua-ts'e, B	Pa-ta shan-jen Hua-ts'e (1961)
SC Hua-ts'e	Shen Chou Hua-ts'e
SC Liang Chiang	Ming Shen Chou Liang Chiang ming-sheng t'u ts'e
SC Tung-chuang	Shen Chou Tung-chuang t'u ts'e
Shang-hai	Shang-hai po-wu-kuan ts'ang-hua
Shan-mien chi-chin	Ming Ch'ing shan-mien chi-chin
Shan-mien-hua	Ming Ch'ing shan-mien-hua hsüan-chi
SS-t hua-chi	Shen Shih-t'ien hua-chi
Ssu-ching	Ssu-ching shan-shui t'u chüan Sung Liu Sung-nien hui
S-t Fang Mi Tien	Ch'ing Shih-t'ao Fang Mi Tien shan-shui
STHN	Sung-tai hua-niao
S-t Hsi-yü	Ch'ing Shih-t'ao Hsi-yü ch'iu-sung t'u
S-t hua-chi	Shih-t'ao hua-chi
S-t Hua-yang	Ch'ing Shih-t'ao Hua-yang shan-chü t'u
S-t miao-p'in	Shih-t'ao shan-shui wu-shang miao-p'in
S-t Shan-shui	Ch'ing Shih-t'ao Shan-shui
S-t Shan-shui ts'e-yeh	Shih-t'ao Shan-shui ts'e-yeh
STSS	Sung-tai shan-shui
S-t T'ing-ch'üan	Ch'ing Shih-t'ao T'ing-ch'üan t'u
Su-chou	Su-chou po-wu-kuan ts'ang-hua chi
Sung Yüan shan-shui	Sung Yüan shan-shui chi-ts'e
SW Kao-i	T'ang Sun Wei Kao-i t'u
T'ang-jen Wan-shan	T'ang-jen Wan-shan shih-nü t'u
T'ang-tai jen-wu	T'ang-tai jen-wu hua
T-c Hua-ts'e	Tao-chi Hua-ts'e
T-c Su-kuo	Tao-chi Su-kuo hua-ts'e
T'ien-ching	T'ien-ching shih i-shu po-wu-kuan ts'ang-hua chi
Tien Yin Tang	T'ien-yin t'ang ming-hua hsüan
TL-j hua-chi	T'ang Liu-ju hua-chi
Ts'ang-chou	Ts'ang-chou ch'ü t'u chüan Ming Shen Chou hui
TSYMC hua-hsüan	T'ang Sung Yüan Ming Ch'ing hua-hsüan
T-t shu-hua	Tan-tang shu-hua chi

41

T-t ts'e-yeh	Tan-tang Shan-shui ts'e-yeh
TWSY ming-chi	T'ang Wu-tai Sung Yüan ming-chi
Wang-hsien ying-chia	Sung-jen Wang-hsien ying-chia t'u
WC Shan-shui	Yüan Wu Chen Shan-shui chen-chi
WS-k Hua-hsüan	Wang Shih-ku Hua-hsüan
WW	Wen-wu ts'an-k'ao tzu-liao, Wen-wu
WWCH	Wen-wu ching-hua
WS Yü-lou	Sung Wang Shen Yü-lou ch'un-ssu
Yang-chou pa-chia	Yang-chou pa-chia hua-chi
Yen-chiang tieh-chang	Yüan Chao Meng-fu shu Yen-chiang tieh-chang shih
YL-p Pu-nien	T'ang Yen Li-pen Pu-nien t'u
YN-t Hua-hui	Yün Nan-t'ien Hua-hui ts'e
YS-p Hua-ts'e	Yün Shou-p'ing Hua-ts'e
YW-c Hsüeh-mei	Sung Yang Wu-chiu Hsüeh-mei t'u

INDEX

Painters of the T'ang Period and Earlier

Chan Tzu-ch'ien	Liang Ling-tsan	
Chang Hsüan	Lu Hung	
Chang Seng-yu	Lu Leng-chia	
Ch'en Hung	Tai I	
Chou Fang	Tai Sung	
Han Huang	Wang Wei	
Han Kan	Wei Yen	
Ku K'ai-chih	Wu Tao-tzu	
Li Chao-tao	Yen Li-pen	
Li Chen	Yü Hsi	
Li Ssu-hsün		

CHAN TZU-CH'IEN 展子虔 . From Po Hai (Ts'ang-chou), Hopei,
active in the Sui dynasty (581-609), painted Buddhist figures, scenes with
men and horses, landscapes. (CP, II, AL, 14.)
>   A river-view in spring, handscroll, Palace Museum, Peking, (AL).
>   Chan Tzu-ch'ien, 1-3; CK hua, I. 1-2; CK ku-tai, 8; KKPWY
>   ts'ang-hua, II. 1-4*.
>   Study of classics, album leaf, attributed, Nat. Pal. Mus., Taipei,
>   (AL). 300 M., 34 (as anon. T'ang in style of Chan Tzu-ch'ien);
>   CKLTMHC, II. 71 (as anon. Sung).
>   Landscape, handscroll, copy by Emperor Hui-tsung. Chan Tzu-
>   ch'ien, 4 (section).

CHANG HSÜAN 張萱 . A native of Ch'ang-an, active in the K'ai-
yüan era (713-741), painted figures in palace gardens or on horseback.
(CP, II, AL, 14-15.)
>   An empress of T'ang and her retinue returning from a journey, (AL).
>   T'ang-tai jen-wu, p. 31.
>   Ladies preparing silk, handscroll, copy by the Emperor Hui-tsung,
>   Museum of Fine Arts, Boston, (AL). Chao Chi, 9-11; Li-tai
>   jen-wu, 21; T'ang-tai jen-wu, pp. 28-30.
>   Emperor Ming-huang playing a flute, album leaf, attributed, Nat.
>   Pal. Mus., Taipei. 300 M., 15; KKMH, II. 3.
>   Lady Kuo-kuo on a spring outing, copy by Emperor Hui-tsung, hand-
>   scroll, Liao-ning Provincial Museum. Chao Chi, 12-13; Liao-
>   ning, I. 36-38; Li-tai jen-wu, 20; T'ang-tai jen-wu, pl. 7*; WW,
>   1955. 5. 10; 1961. 12 inside back cover.

CHANG SENG-YU 張僧繇 . From Wu (Kiangsu), active 500-550,
landscapes, snow-scenes, Buddhist and Taoist figures. (CP, II, AL, 15.)
>   The five planets and twenty-eight constellations, handscroll, Abe col-
>   lection, Ōsaka Museum, (AL). Chang Seng-yu, 1-14 (as Chang
>   Seng-yu); T'ang-tai jen-wu, pp. 39, 40 (sections, as Liang Ling-
>   tsan).

CH'EN HUNG 陳閎 . A native of K'uei-chi, Chekiang, introduced
at court in the K'ai-yüan period (713-741), painted portraits of the emperors Hsüan-tsung and Su-tsung (756-763), illustrations of imperial
hunting parties. (CP, II, AL, 16.)
>   Meritorious military and civil officials, handscroll, Nelson Gallery
>   of Art, Kansas City, (AL). Li-tai jen-wu, 8 (two figures).

CHOU FANG 周昉 , t. Chung-lang 仲朗 and Ching-yüan 景元 .
A native of Ch'ang-an, active c. 780-810, painted pictures of court ladies.
(CP, II, AL, 16-17.)

Ladies occupied with embroidery, handscroll, attributed, Palace
Museum, Peking, (AL). Chou Fang, 5-10 (as anon. T'ang);
KKPWY ts'ang-hua, II, 9-15* (as Chou Fang); T'ang-jen Wan-
shan* (as anon. T'ang); T'ang-tai jen-wu, pp. 46,47 (sections,
as Chou Fang); WW, 1957.1.35-37 (as Chou Fang).

A barbarian envoy bringing a white antelope in tribute, album leaf,
Nat. Pal. Mus., Taipei, (AL). 300 M., 18; CCAT pl. 90;
KKMH, I.4.

Two ladies seated on the ground in the act of writing a poem, album
leaf, Nat. Pal. Mus., Taipei, (AL). CKLTMHC, II.70 (as anon.
Sung).

Listening to music, handscroll, Nelson Gallery of Art, Kansas City,
(AL). Chou Fang, 3-4 (as anon. T'ang).

Listening to music, handscroll, Ueno collection, Tokyo, (AL). Li-
tai jen-wu, 7; T'ang-tai jen-wu, p. 44.

Two ladies playing double-sixes, handscroll, Nat. Pal. Mus., Taipei, (AL). KKMH, II.5.

Two ladies playing double-sixes, handscroll, Freer Gallery of Art,
Washington, D.C., (39.37), (AL). TWSY ming-chi, 9 (as anon.
N. Sung).

Ladies wearing flowered hats, handscroll, attributed, Liao-ning Provincial Museum. Chou Fang, 1-2; CK ku-tai, 17 (section); Liao-
ning, I, 13-15; T'ang-tai jen-wu, pl. 10*; WW, 1955.5.9 (section);
1958.6.26 (section).

HAN HUANG 韓 滉 , t. T'ai-cn'ung 太 冲 . B. 723, d. 787,
from Ch'ang-an, painted figures and buffaloes. (CP, II, AL, 17.)

Four scholars in a garden, handscroll, Palace Museum, Peking,
(AL). CK hua, I.3-4; KKPWY ts'ang-hua, II, 16-18*; Li-tai
jen-wu, 10; T'ang-tai jen-wu, p. 50.

The Wu-niu t'u, five water buffaloes, handscroll, attributed, Palace
Museum, Peking, (AL). CK ku-tai, 12; CK shu-hua, I.1-5;
HH Wu-niu*; KKPWY ts'ang-hua, II.19-21*; T'ang-tai jen-wu,
p. 51; TWSY ming-chi, 1; WW, 1960.1.4-5.

HAN KAN 韓 幹 . From Ch'ang-an, active in the T'ien-pao era
(742-756), painted horses. (CP, II, AL, 17-18.)

A groom on horseback, leading another saddled horse, Nat. Pal. Mus.,
Taipei, (AL). 300 M., 16; CAT, 3; CKLTMHC, I.3; CK shu-hua,
I.6; KKMH, II.4; T'ang-tai jen-wu, p. 34; WW, 1955.7.1 (33).

A horse tied to a pole, called The Shining Light of Night, album leaf,
Lady David collection, London, (AL). CK ku-tai, 11; T'ang-tai
jen-wu, p. 36; WW, 1958.6.27.

KU K'AI-CHIH 顧 愷 之 , t. Ch'ang-k'ang 長 康 , h. Hu-
t'ou 虎 頭 . B. c. 344, d. c. 406, from Wu-hsi, Kiangsu, painted portraits and figures, landscapes. (CP, II, AL, 18.)

> The Nymph of the Lo River, handscroll, Palace Museum, Peking,
> (AL). CK ku-tai, 5 (two sections, as Ku K'ai-chih); Ku K'ai-
> chih, 25-26 (two sections, as Ku K'ai-chih); KK-c tzu-liao, 10-
> 26 (as an anon. copy); KK-c yen-chiu, 1 (as Ku K'ai-chih); Li-
> tai jen-wu, 2 (two sections, as Ku K'ai-chih); WW, 1958.6.21
> (section, as anon. Sung copy).
> The Nymph of the Lo River, handscroll, Freer Gallery of Art, Wash-
> ington, D.C., (AL). KK-c yen-chiu, 3 (five sections).
> The Nymph of the Lo River, handscroll, Liao-ning Provincial Museum.
> KK-c tzu-liao, 27-29 (three sections, as an anon. copy); KK-c
> yen-chiu, 2 (five sections, as Ku K'ai-chih); Liao-ning, I.1-12
> (as Ku K'ai-chih in caption, anon. Sung copy in notes); WW, 1961.
> 6. cover (section, as anon. Sung copy).
> Admonitions of the Instructress to the Ladies of the Palace, handscroll,
> British Museum, London, (AL). Ku K'ai-chih, 1-10; KK-c tzu-
> liao, 1-9; KK-c yen-chiu, 4; Li-tai jen-wu, 1 (two scenes); T'ang-
> tai jen-wu, pp. 4, 5 (sections).
> Admonitions of the Instructress to the Ladies of the Palace, handscroll,
> Palace Museum, Peking. KK-c yen-chiu, 5 (seven sections, as
> Ku K'ai-chih); WW, 1961.6.8-9 (three sections, as anon. Sung
> copy).
> Lieh-nü t'u, four groups of famous women, handscroll, Palace Mu-
> seum, Peking, (AL). Ku K'ai-chih, 11-24 (as anon. Sung copy);
> KK-c tzu-liao, 35-37 (three sections, as anon. Sung copy); KK-c
> yen-chiu, 6 (six sections, as Ku K'ai-chih); Li-tai jen-wu, 3 (as
> Ku K'ai-chih); WW, 1958.6.22-24 (sections, as anon. Sung copy).
> Making a ch'in, handscroll, Palace Museum, Peking. KK-c tzu-liao,
> 38 (one section, as anon. Sung copy).
> Portrait of Vimalakīrti, once attributed to Ku, Tōfuku-ji, Kyōto.
> KK-c tzu-liao, 30.

LI CHAO-TAO 李 昭 道 . Active c. 670-730, son of Li Ssu-hsün,
painted landscapes. (CP, II, AL, 18-19.)

> Travellers in the mountains in spring, Nat. Pal. Mus., Taipei, (AL).
> 300 M., 4.
> The Lo-yang Tower, album leaf, Nat. Pal. Mus., Taipei, (AL).
> KKMH, I.3.
> A dragon-boat race, fan, attributed, Palace Museum, Peking, (AL).
> Sung-jen hua-ts'e, A.100* (as anon. Sung); B. VI.3* (as anon.
> Sung).

Horsemen by a lake, Nat. Pal. Mus., Taipei. 300M., 32 (as anon. T'ang); KKMH, II.2 (as Li Chao-tao).

LI CHEN 李真 or Li Shen 李紳 . Active c. 780-804; said to have followed Kōbō Daishi from China to Japan and to have painted in temples in Kyōto. (CP II, AL, 19.)

> Portrait of the patriarch Pu-k'ung chin-kang (Amoghavajra), Tōji, Kyōto, (AL). T'ang-tai jen-wu, p. 48.

LI SSU-HSÜN 李思訓 , t. Chien-chien 建見 . B. 651, d. 716, member of the imperial T'ang family, painted landscapes. (CP, II, AL, 19.)

> Chiang-fan lou-ko t'u. Boats on the river, Nat. Pal. Mus., Taipei, (AL). 300 M., 3*; CKLTMHC, I.2; KKMH, I.2; WW, 1961.6.14.

LIANG LING-TSAN 梁令瓚 . From Szechuan; active during the K'ai-yüan era (713-741); calligrapher, painted figures. (M. p. 391.)

> The five planets and twenty-eight constellations, handscroll, Abe collection, Ōsaka Museum, (AL, Chang Seng-yu). Chang Seng-yu, 1-14 (as Chang Seng-yu); T'ang-tai jen-wu, pp. 39, 40 (sections, as Liang Ling-tsan).

LU HUNG 盧鴻 , or Lu Hung-i 盧鴻一 , t. Hao-jan 顥然 or 浩然 . From Yu-chou, Hopei, active in the K'ai-yüan era (713-741). (CP, II, AL 19.)

> Ts'ao-t'ang shih-chih, handscroll, Nat. Pal. Mus., Taipei, (AL). 300 M., 5-14; CAT, 4 (first section); CH mei-shu, I; CKLTMHC, I.4.

LU LENG-CHIA 盧稜伽 or 楞伽 . From Ch'ang-an, active c. 730-760, executed wall-paintings in Buddhist temples and did other religious pictures. (CP, II, AL, 20.)

> Buddhist arhats with worshippers, album leaves, Palace Museum, Peking, (AL). KKPWY ts'ang-hua, II.26-31* (six leaves); WW, 1960.1.2 (leaf five).

TAI I 戴嶧 . Eighth century, younger brother of Tai Sung, painted buffaloes. (CP, II, AL, 20.)

> Two fighting water-buffaloes, album leaf, Nat. Pal. Mus., Taipei, (AL, under Tai Sung). KKMH, I.5.

TAI SUNG 戴嵩 . Eighth century, pupil of Han Huang, painted buffaloes. (CP, II, AL, 20.)

Two fighting water-buffaloes, handscroll, signed, Nat. Pal. Mus.,
Taipei, (AL). 300 M., 19.

WANG WEI 王 維 , t. Mo-ch'i 摩 詰 . B. 699, d. 759, from T'ai-
yüan, also known by his official title Yu-ch'eng 右 丞 , poet and land-
scape-painter, also did Buddhist and Taoist pictures. (CP, II, AL, 21.)
River scenery with cottages and a boat in snow, (AL). Wang Wei, 9.
Sharply outlined mountains and bare trees, attributed, Nat. Pal. Mus.,
Taipei, (AL; also listed as Pointed mountains and bare trees by a
river in snow under anon. before Sung). 300 M., 31* (as anon.
T'ang).
Master Fu delivering the classics, handscroll, Abe collection, Ōsaka
Museum, (AL). Li-tai jen-wu, 6; T'ang-tai jen-wu, p. 37; Wang
Wei, 7-8.
Clearing after snowfall on hills by a river, handscroll, Ogawa col-
lection, Kyōto, (AL). Wang Wei, 1-6.

WEI YEN 韋 偃 or 鷃 . From Ch'ang-an, lived in Szechuan,
active late seventh-early eighth century, painted horses, pine trees and
stones. (A. 10; B; C. 3; G. 13; H. 2; I. 47; M. p. 270.)
Two riders, album leaf, attributed, Nat. Pal. Mus., Taipei.
300 M., 17*.

WU TAO-TZU 吳 道 子 , also called Wu Tao-hsüan 吳 道 玄 . From
Yang-chai, Honan, active c. 720-760, served at court during the reign of
the emperor Hsüan-tsung, executed wall-paintings in Buddhist and Taoist
temples in Ch'ang-an and Lo-yang, also painted landscapes. (CP, II, AL,
22.)
Kuan-yin standing on waves (rubbing) (AL). T'ang-tai jen-wu, p. 22;
Wu Tao-tzu, 1.
A soaring devil, engraving, (AL). T'ang-tai jen-wu, p. 17.
The birth and presentation of Buddha, handscroll, Abe collection,
Ōsaka Museum, (AL). CK ku-tai, 10 (section); Li-tai jen-wu,
5; T'ang-tai jen-wu, pp. 18, 19; Wu Tao-tzu, 2-7.
Sou-shan t'u. Demons fighting wild animals. T'ang-tai jen-wu, pp.
23, 24 (sections).

YEN LI-PEN 閻 立 本 . D. 673, from Wan-nien, Shensi, son of
Yen Pi and brother of Yen Li-te; served at court under emperors T'ai-
tsung (627-649) and Kao-tsung (650-683), President of the Board of Works
in 657, one of the two prime-ministers in 668; leading figure painter.
(CP, II, AL, 23.)
Portraits of thirteen emperors, handscroll, Museum of Fine Arts,

Boston, (AL)   CK ku-tai, 9 (one section); Li-tai jen-wu, 4 (two sections); T'ang-tai jen-wu, pp. 6, 10-14.

Western barbarians bringing tribute, handscroll, Nat. Pal. Mus., Taipei, (AL). 300 M., 1*; CAT, 1 (section); KKMH, I.1.

Hsiao I securing the Lan-t'ing manuscript, handscroll, Nat. Pal. Mus., Taipei, (AL). 300 M., 2; CKLTMHC I.1; KKMH, II.1; T'ang-tai jen-wu, p. 13; WW, 1965.12. p. 14.

Emperor T'ai-tsung in a sedan chair greeting three envoys from Tibet, handscroll, colophon by Chang Yu-chih in which he says the painting was done by Yen and mounted in the year 641; nineteen other colophons, Palace Museum, Peking. KKPWY ts'ang-hua, II.5-8*; WW 1959.7.3; YL-p Pu-nien*.

YÜ HSI 于錫 . T'ang dynasty, painted flowers and birds, chickens and dogs. (A.10; G.15; H.2; I.48; M. p. 7.)

Two pheasants with plum blossoms and bamboo, S. M. Siu collection, Hong Kong. CK ku-hua, B.1.

Painters of the Five Dynasties

Chao Kan	趙	幹	Kuan T'ung	關	同
Chao Yen	趙	巖	Kuo Chung-shu	郭	忠 恕
Ching Hao	荊	浩	Li P'o	李	頗
Ch'iu Wen-po	丘 文	播	Li Sheng	李	昇
Chou Hsing-t'ung	周 行	通	Li Tsan-hua	李 贊	華
Chou Wen-chü	周 文	矩	Sun Wei	孫	位
Chü-jan	巨	然	T'ang Hsi-ya	唐 希	雅
Hsü Hsi	徐	熙	T'eng Ch'ang-yu	滕 昌	祐
Hu Kuei	胡	瓌	Tiao Kuang-yin	刁 光	胤
Huang Chü-ts'ai	黃 居	寀	Tung Yüan	董	源
Huang Ch'üan	黃	筌	Wang Ch'i-han	王 齊	翰
Juan Kao	阮	郜	Wei Hsien	衛	賢
Ku Hung-chung	顧 閎	中	Yen Wen-kuei	燕 文	貴
Kuan-hsiu	貫	休			

CHAO KAN 趙幹 . From Nanking, member of the Academy of Painting in the reign of Li Hou-chu (961-975) painted landscapes. (CP, II, AL, 24.)

Early snow over the river, handscroll, signed, Nat. Pal. Mus., Taipei, (AL). 300 M., 50; CAT, 12 (two sections); CCAT, pl. 93 (section); CK ku-tai, 22 (section); CKLTMHC, I.12; NPM Quarterly, I.2, pls. XIII A-B (sections).

Fishing in the winter, signed, S. M. Siu collection, Hong Kong. CK ku-hua, B.3.

CHAO YEN 趙巖 , original name Chao Lin 趙霖 , t. Ch'iu-yen 秋巘 . D. 922, son-in-law of the emperor T'ai-tsu of the Posterior Liang dynasty (907-912), painted figures and horses. (CP, II, AL, 24-25.)

Pa-ta ch'un-yu t'u. Eight gentlemen riding on horseback in spring, attributed, Nat. Pal. Mus., Taipei, (AL). 300 M., 53; CAT, 11* (section); CKLTMHC, I.9; KKMH, II.8*.

CHING HAO 荊浩 , t. Hao-jan 浩然 , h. Hung-ku-tzu 洪谷子 From Ch'in-shui, Honan, active late ninth-early tenth centuries, painted landscapes, teacher of Kuan T'ung. (CP, II, AL, 25.)

The K'uang-lu Mountain, Nat. Pal. Mus., Taipei, (AL). 300 M., 37; CCAT, pl. 91; CK ku-tai, 20; CKLTMHC, I.6; KKMH, I.10; NPM Bulletin, II.6. p. 5.

CH'IU WEN-PO 丘文播 , also named Ch'iu Ch'ien 丘潛 . From Kuang-han in Shu (Szechuan), active c. 933-965, painted Buddhist and Taoist figures, landscapes, buffaloes. (CP, II, AL, 25.)

A literary meeting, Nat. Pal. Mus., Taipei, (AL). 300 M., 56 (as Ch'iu Wen-po); CKLTMHC, II.35 (as anon. Sung); KKMH, II.18 (as Ch'iu Wen-po).

CHOU HSING-T'UNG 周行通 , nick-named Chou Hu 周胡 . From Ch'eng-tu, Szechuan, active during the Posterior Shu period (933-965), painted figures and animals. (CP, II, AL, 25.)

A sheep and bamboo, album leaf, signed, S. M. Siu collection, Hong Kong. CK ku-hua, B.38.2.

CHOU WEN-CHÜ 周文矩 . From Chü-jung, Kiangsu, served as tai-chao at the court of Li Hou-chu, ruler of the Southern T'ang dynasty (961-975), painted figures. (CP, II, AL, 26.)

The parting of Su Wu and Li Ling, handscroll, attributed, Nat. Pal. Mus., Taipei, (AL). CAT, 9; KKMH, II.14*.

Ming-huang of T'ang playing chess, handscroll, attributed, Nat. Pal.
Mus. , Taipei, (AL). 300 M., 51*; CKLTMHC, I. 10.

Three women washing children in tubs, fan, Freer Gallery of Art,
Washington, D. C. (35. 8), (AL). TWSY ming-chi, 91 (as anon.
S. Sung).

A fairy riding on a flying feng-bird, fan, attributed, Palace Museum,
Peking, (AL). PM, 23* (as anon. Sung); Sung hua shih fu, 4* (as
anon. Sung); Sung-jen hua-ts'e, A. 1* (att. to Chou Wen-chü);
B. I. 1* (as anon. Sung).

A concubine mounting a horse, handscroll, Tso Hai collection. CK
hua, XI. 10-11*.

Emperor Li Yü watching chess in front of a "double screen", handscroll, attributed. CK hua, VII. 14; CK ku-tai, 26; Li-tai jen-
wu, 14 (section); NPM Bulletin, I. 2. 4 (section).

CHÜ-JAN 巨 然 . Active c. 960-980, a monk of the K'ai-yüan temple in Nanking, later settled in K'ai-feng, painted landscapes, followed
Tung Yüan. (CP, II, AL, 26-27.)

Landscape in snow, attributed by Tung Ch'i-ch'ang, Nat. Pal. Mus. ,
Taipei, (AL). 300 M. , 133 (as anon. Sung); CH mei-shu, I (as
Chü-jan); CKLTMHC, I. 19 (as Chü-jan); KKMH II. 13 (as Chü-
jan).

Mountain stream between wooded shores, Nat. Pal. Mus. , Taipei,
(AL). 300 M. , 48 (as Chü-jan); CKLTMHC, II. 25 (as anon.
Sung); KKMH, II. 12 (as Chü-jan).

Topped hills in vertical layers, Nat. Pal. Mus. , Taipei, (AL).
300 M. , 44; CAT, 15; CCAT, pl. 92; CKLTMHC, I. 18; CKLTSHH;
CH mei-shu, I; KKMH, I. 14.

River landscape in autumn, Nat. Pal. Mus. , Taipei, (AL). 300 M. ,
45 (as Chü-jan); CKLTMHC, III. 46 (as Wu Chen); KKMH, II. 11
(as Chü-jan).

Pavilions under pine-trees by a mountain stream, Nat. Pal. Mus. ,
Taipei, (AL). 300 M. , 49 (as Chü-jan); CKLTMHC, III. 39 (as
Sheng Mou).

River scenery, handscroll, J. D. Ch'en collection, Hong Kong, (AL).
TWSY ming-chi, 4-7.

Mountain landscape with a temple in a gully, Nat. Pal. Mus. , Taipei,
(AL, anon. Sung). 300 M. , 47 (as Chü-jan); CKLTMHC, II. 69
(as anon. Sung); KKMH, I. 16 (as Chü-jan).

Two mountain peaks, path through tree-covered valley, Nat. Pal.
Mus. , Taipei. 300 M. , 46; CH mei-shu, I; CK ku-tai, 28;
CKLTMHC, I. 17; KKMH, I. 15; WW, 1955. 7. 2 (34).

Ten-thousand gullies, wind in the pines, a mountain landscape with
men in elaborate pavilions along rapids, Shanghai Museum.

CK hua, XV.9; Shang-hai, 1*; TSYMC hua-hsüan, 4; WW, 1961.
1.39.

Hermitage in the mountains, J.D. Ch'en collection, Hong Kong. WW,
1964.3.18.

Fishermen in boats on a mountain inlet, signed, colophons by Yü
Chi and two others, S.M. Siu collection, Hong Kong. CK ku-
hua, A.2; B.4.

HSÜ HSI 徐 熙 . From Nanking, active under the Southern T'ang dynasty, died before 975, painted flowers and birds. (CP, II, AL, 27.)

A pheasant among peonies and magnolia flowers, Nat. Pal. Mus.,
Taipei, (AL). 300 M., 54*.

A rich composition of flowering shrubs and trees, handscroll, attributed, (AL). HH/HC, 2-3.

Dragonfly and bean flower, fan, attributed, Palace Museum, Peking.
Sung-jen hua-ts'e, A.2* (att. to Hsü Hsi); B, VI.8* (as anon.
Sung).

Duck and lotus, album leaf, signed, S.M. Siu collection, Hong Kong.
CK ku-hua, B.38.1.

Three pigeons and flowering plant, album leaf, attributed. HH/HC, 1.

Bamboo and rocks in snow, attributed. TSYMC hua-hsüan, 11 (as
anon. Sung); TWSY ming-chi, 3 (as Hsü Hsi).

HU KUEI 胡 瓌 (Hu Huai). A Khitan painter active during the Posterior T'ang dynasty (923-935), painted horses and Mongolian landscapes.
(CP, II, AL, 28.)

Four Mongols on horseback holding falcons, album leaf, Nat. Pal.
Mus., Taipei, (AL). CAT, 8 (as Hu Kuei); CKLTMHC, II.80
(as anon. Sung); KKMH, II.7 (as Hu Kuei).

Three Mongols on horseback on a sandy plain, album leaf, Nat. Pal.
Mus., Taipei, (AL). 300 M., 30; CAT, 7; KKMH, I.6.

Banquet scene in a Khitan camp, handscroll. CK ku-tai, 19 (section);
Li-tai jen-wu, 12 (two sections); T'ang-tai jen-wu, pp. 52-53;
WW, 1959.6.34 (section).

HUANG CHÜ-TS'AI 黃 居 寀 , t. Po-luan 伯 鸞 . B. 933, d.
after 993, son of Huang Ch'üan, served as <u>tai-chao</u> under the Later Shu
dynasty (929-966) and under the emperor Kao-tsung of Sung, painted
flowers, birds and landscapes. (CP, II, AL, 28.)

Ten doves on a large branch, album leaf, Nat. Pal. Mus., Taipei
(AL). CKLTMHC, II.74 (as anon. Sung).

A pheasant and small birds by dry jujube shrubs, Nat. Pal. Mus.,
Taipei, (AL). 300 M., 57*; CAT, 16; CK ku-tai, 33; CKLTMHC,

I. 27; HH/HC, 10; KKMH, I. 20; WW, 1955. 7. 4 (36).

Sparrows fighting among reeds, fan, attributed, Palace Museum, Peking, (AL). Sung-jen hua-ts'e, A. 39* (as anon. Sung); B.III. 9* (as anon. Sung).

Crab and fading lotus, fan, attributed, Palace Museum, Peking. Sung hua shih fu, 9* (as anon. Sung); Sung-jen hua-ts'e, A. 4* (att. to Huang Chü-ts'ai); B.I. 5* (as anon. Sung).

Flower and butterfly, fan, attributed, Chang Pe-chin collection. Tien Yin Tang, II. 1*.

HUANG CH'ÜAN 黄筌 , t. Yao-shu 要叔 . B. c. 900, d. 965, from Ch'eng-tu, Szechuan, served as tai-chao under Meng Ch'ang of the Later Shu dynasty (935-965), painted flowers and birds, Buddhist and Taoist subjects. (CP, II, AL, 28-29.)

Four crows in a bare willow and two ducks on the water in snow, album leaf, Nat. Pal. Mus. , Taipei, (AL). CKLTMHC, II. 79 (as anon. Sung); KKMH, II. 17* (as Huang Ch'üan).

Studies from nature, birds and insects, handscroll, inscribed and signed, Palace Museum, Peking, (AL). CK ku-tai, 23; HH/HC, 6-8; KKPWY hua-niao, 1*.

Two cranes under bamboos, Abe collection, Ōsaka Museum, (AL), HH/HC, 9.

Ducks among reeds, album leaf, attributed, Palace Museum, Peking, (AL). Sung-jen hua-ts'e, A. 3* (att. to Huang Ch'üan); B.II. 4* (as anon. Sung).

Ducks on a snowy bank under bamboo and plum, album leaf, attributed, Nat. Pal. Mus. , Taipei. CKLTMHC, II. 24 (as anon. Sung).

Oriole on an apple branch, fan, attributed, Nat. Pal. Mus. , Taipei. NPM Bulletin , I. 2 cover*.

Pear blossom and bird, S. M. Siu collection, Hong Kong. CK ku-hua, A. 1; B. 2.

A deer under a gnarled tree, attributed. HH/HC, 4-5.

JUAN KAO 阮郜 . Painted illustrations, figures, ladies. (G. 6; H. 2; I. 49; M. p. 117.)

Female Immortals in Elysium, handscroll, three inscriptions. WWCH, II. 17-23.

KU HUNG-CHUNG 顧閎中 . From Chiang-nan, served as tai-chao at the court of the emperor Hsüan-tsung of the Southern T'ang dynasty (943-960), painted figures. (CP, II, AL, 29.)

Han Hsi-tsai's night revels, handscroll, Palace Museum, Peking, (AL). CK hua, XVI. 6-7, 10-13, 16-17, 19; XVII. 8, 10-11,

14-15, 18-19; CK ku-tai, 18 (section); Li-tai jen-wu, 13; NPM
Bulletin, I.2.1-2 (sections); WW, 1958.6.31 (section).

Han Hsi-tsai's night revels, handscroll, Nat. Pal. Mus., Taipei.
KKMH, I.17*.

KUAN-HSIU 貫休 . Family name Chiang 姜 , personal name Hsiu
休 . t. Te-yin 德隱 and Te-yüan 德遠 . h. Ch'an-yüeh 禪月
B. 832, d. 912, from Chin-hua, Chekiang, a Ch'an monk, also famous as
a poet, painted Buddhist figures. (CP, II, AL, 29-30.)

Arhat seated behind a rock, Imperial Household collection, Tokyo,
(AL). Che-chiang, 3; T'ang-tai jen-wu, p. 56.

Arhat wrapped in a heavy robe seated on a rock, Imperial Household
collection, Tokyo, (AL). Li-tai jen-wu, 11 (section).

An arhat behind a rock, side view, Imperial Household collection,
Tokyo, (AL). T'ang-tai jen-wu, p. 56.

KUAN T'UNG 關同 or 關仝 . From Ch'ang-an, active in Nanking
during the Posterior Liang dynasty (907-923), painted landscapes. (CP,
II, AL, 30.)

Steep mountains with a waterfall, Nat. Pal. Mus., Taipei, (AL).
300 M., 38; CKLTMHC, I.8; KKMH, I.11.

The western mountains at sunset, fan, attributed, Palace Museum,
Peking, (AL). Sung-jen hua-ts'e, B.XV* (as anon. Sung).

Travellers at the mountain pass, attributed, Nat. Pal. Mus., Taipei.
300 M., 39; CAT, 13; CKLTMHC I.7; KKMH, II.9.

An autumnal mountain, attributed, Nat. Pal. Mus., Taipei. 300 M.,
40.

KUO CHUNG-SHU 郭忠恕 , t. Shu-hsien 恕先 . From Loyang,
a scholar, served in the Confucian Temple during the Posterior Chou dynasty (951-959) and the Sung dynasty; painted landscapes, boundary paintings and figures. (CP, II, AL, 30.)

Hsüeh-chi chiang-hsing t'u. Two large junks with high masts, Nat.
Pal. Mus., Taipei, (AL). 300 M., 52; CK ku-tai, 29; CKLTMHC,
I.20; KKMH, II.16; WW, 1955.7.3 (35).

A hostel in the mountains, travellers with bullock carts approach-
ing and leaving, fan, attributed, Palace Museum, Peking, (AL).
Sung-jen hua-ts'e, A.82* (as anon. Sung); B.VII.6* (as anon.
Sung); STSS* (as anon. Sung).

Flying herons and a riverside pavilion, fan, attributed, Nat. Pal.
Mus., Taipei. KKMH, I.18.

LI P'O 李頗 or 坡 or Po 波 . From Nan-ch'ang, worked during
the Southern T'ang dynasty (937-975), painted bamboo. (F.2; G.20;

H. 2; I. 49; M. p. 188.)
> Bamboo in the wind, attributed, Nat. Pal. Mus., Taipei. 300 M.,
> 41; KKCP, I. 1; KKMH, I. 12; NPM Quarterly, I. 4, pl. 15.

LI SHENG 李昇 , t. Chin-nu 錦奴 . From Ch'eng-tu, active
under the Former Shu dynasty (908-925), worked in the style of Wang
Wei. (CP, II, AL, 31.)
> The Yo-yang Palace, fan, signed, Nat. Pal. Mus., Taipei. KKMH,
> I. 19.

LI TSAN-HUA 李贊華 , known as Prince of Tung-tan 東丹王 .
Original name: Yeh-lü T'u-yü 耶律突欲 . Eldest son of the first
Liao emperor, T'ai-tsu (907-926), in 931 he emigrated to China and was
given the family name Li and the personal name Tsan-hua by the emperor
Ming-tsung of the Posterior T'ang dynasty (926-933), painted Khitan chief-
tans and horses. (CP, II, AL, 31.)
> A Khitan soldier in front of his horse, album leaf, Nat. Pal. Mus.,
> Taipei, (AL). 300 M., 36 (as Li Tsan-hua); CKLTMHC, II. 96
> (as anon. Sung).

SUN WEI 孫位 (also called Yü 遇). From K'uei-chi, Chekiang,
active in the capital, went to Shu in 880, settled in Ch'eng-tu, did temple
wall-paintings, dragons and water. (CP, II, AL, 32.)
> Kao-i t'u. The four great scholars, handscroll, Shanghai Museum,
> (AL). Che-chiang, 1-2*; CK ku-tai, 13 (section); Li-tai jen-wu,
> 9 (section); SW Kao-i*; T'ang-tai jen-wu, pp. 54, 55; TSYMC
> hua-hsüan, 1; WW, 1965. 8. pl. 1.

T'ANG HSI-YA 唐希雅 . From Chia-hsing, active during the
Southern T'ang dynasty (961-975), a calligrapher, painted bamboo and
trees, birds, animals, grasses and insects. (F. 4; G. 17; H. 3; I. 49;
M. p. 325.)
> Dove in an old tree, fan, signed, Nat. Pal. Mus., Taipei. KKMH,
> II. 15.
> Three birds on a willow branch, album leaf, attributed, S. M. Siu
> collection, Hong Kong. CK ku-hua, B. 37. 1.

T'ENG CH'ANG-YU 滕昌祐 , t. Sheng-hua 勝華 . From
Kiangsu, followed the emperor Hsi-tsung of T'ang to Shu in 880, died
after 930 at the age of 85, painted flowers and birds. (CP, II, AL, 32.)
> Peony flowers, Nat. Pal. Mus., Taipei, (AL). CKLTSHH; CH mei-
> shu, I; KKMH, I. 21.

TIAO KUANG-YIN 刁光胤 or Tiao Kuang 刁光 . From Ch'ang-an,

moved to Shu in the T'ien-fu era (901-903), died at the age of 80, painted flowers, birds and animals. (CP, II, AL, 32.)

    Ten fan pictures, Nat. Pal. Mus., Taipei, (AL). 300 M., 20-29; KKMH, II. 6 (1-10).

TUNG YÜAN 董源 or 董元 , t. Shu-ta 叔達 , h. Pei-yüan 北苑 . From Nanking, served as an assistant director of the imperial parks under the Southern T'ang dynasty (937-975), painted landscapes. (CP, II, AL, 32-33.)

    Pavilion on the Mountain of the Immortals, Nat. Pal. Mus., Taipei, (AL). 300 M., 43* (as Tung Yüan); CAT, 14 (as Tung Yüan); CH mei-shu, I (as Tung Yüan); CKLTMHC, II. 18 (as anon. Sung); CKLTSHH (as Tung Yüan); KKMH, II. 10 (as Tung Yüan).

    Lung-su chiao-min t'u. Mountain landscape with winding waters, boats and figures, Nat. Pal. Mus., Taipei, (AL). 300 M., 42; CH mei-shu, I; CKLTMHC, I. 11; KKMH, I. 13; TSYMC hua-hsüan, 3.

    Travellers' inn by a stream in the mountains, Ōgawa collection, (AL). CK shu-hua, I. 7.

    Hsiao-hsiang t'u. River landscape with fishermen drawing their nets and people in boats, handscroll, Palace Museum, Peking, (AL). CK hua, XII. 12-13, 15; CK ku-tai, 24.

    River view: high mountains at the side, Chang Ta-ch'ien collection, (AL). TWSY ming-chi, 2.

    Awaiting a crossing at the foot of mountains in summer, handscroll, attributed, Liao-ning Provincial Museum. Liao-ning, I. 16-21.

WANG CH'I-HAN 王齊翰 . From Nanking, served as a tai-chao at the court of Li Hou-chu (961-975), painted Buddhist and Taoist figures. (CP, II, AL, 33.)

    K'an-shu t'u. Examining books (or Ear-picking), handscroll, (AL). TSYMC hua-hsüan, 2.

WEI HSIEN 衛賢 . From K'aifeng, a court painter in Nanking in the time of the Southern T'ang dynasty (937-975), painted houses, trees and figures. (CP, II, AL, 33.)

    Kao-shih t'u. A scholar in a pavilion at the foot of steep mountains, attributed, Palace Museum, Peking, (AL). CK hua, II. 1; CK ku-tai, 21.

    Water wheel, handscroll, signed. WW, 1966. 2. 3.

YEN WEN-KUEI 燕文貴 or Yen Kuei 燕貴 . From Wu-hsing, Chekiang, served as a soldier, retired in the reign of T'ai-tsung (976-997) became a tai-chao in the Painting Academy, painted landscapes and figures. (CP, II, AL, 34.)

Three Immortals seated in a cave, attributed, Nat. Pal. Mus. , Taipei, (AL). 300 M. , 72.

Towering mountains rising over a river, Nat. Pal. Mus. , Taipei,
(AL). 300 M. , 71; CCAT, pl. 95; CKLTMHC, I.26; KKMH, II.26.

Temple among autumn peaks, signed, Nat. Pal. Mus. , Taipei. Che-
chiang, 4; KKMH, I.32.

Travellers in autumn mountains, returning boats, handscroll, signed,
Chang Pe-chin collection. Tien Yin Tang, I.1.

Returning home after snowfall, attributed, S. M. Siu collection, Hong
Kong. CK ku-hua, B.5.

River landscape, handscroll. TWSY ming-chi, 10-12.

Paintings by anonymous artists active before the Sung period

Buddhist and Taoist

Arhat with a tiger, Nat. Pal. Mus. , Taipei. CKLTMHC, I.13 (as
anon. Five Dyn.)

Buddhist images and donors, Shanghai Museum. WW, 1962.12.3
(as anon. T'ang).

Landscapes

Pointed mountains and bare trees by a river in snow, Nat. Pal. Mus. ,
Taipei, (AL; also listed as Sharply outlined mountains and bare
trees under Wang Wei). 300 M. , 31* (as anon. T'ang).

Mountain landscape with travellers, known as Emperor Ming-huang's
journey to Shu, Nat. Pal. Mus. , Taipei, (AL). 300 M. , 35* (as
anon. T'ang); CAT, 2* (section, as anon. T'ang); CKLTMHC, II.1
(as anon. Sung); KKMH, I.7 (as anon. T'ang); NPM Quarterly,
I.2.pl. XXVIII (as anon. T'ang); WW, 1961.6.15 (as anon. T'ang).

Horsemen by a lake, Nat. Pal. Mus. , Taipei. 300 M. , 32 (as anon.
T'ang); KKMH, II.2 (as Li Chao-tao).

Figures and Animals

Yu-ch'i t'u. Seven men on horseback riding through a landscape, Nat.
Pal. Mus. , Taipei, (AL). KKMH, I.8 (as anon. T'ang).

Fisherman in straw mantle standing among snow-covered reeds, Nat.
Pal. Mus. , Taipei, (AL). 300 M. , 60*; KKMH, II.19 (both as
as anon. Five Dyn.).

Palace ladies seated around a table making music,
Nat. Pal. Mus. , Taipei, (AL; also listed as Palace musicians,

under anon. Sung). 300 M. , 204* (as anon. Yüan); CAT, 10 (as
anon. Five Dyn.); CCAT, pl. 12 (as anon. Five Dyn.); CKLTMHC,
II. 15 (as anon. Sung); KKMH, I. 22 (as anon. Five Dyn.); WW,
1955. 7. 8 (40) (as anon. Sung).

Deer in an autumn grove of colored trees, Nat. Pal. Mus. , Taipei,
(AL). 300 M. , 58*; CAT, 5; CKLTMHC, I. 16; KKMH, II. 20
(all as anon. Five Dyn.).

Deer in an autumn grove, Nat. Pal. Mus. , Taipei, (AL). 300 M. ,
59; (CAT, 6); CH mei-shu, I; CK ku-tai, 25; CKLTMHC, I. 15;
CKLTSHH; KKMH, I. 24* (all as anon. Five Dyn.).

Study of classics, album leaf, Nat. Pal. Mus. , Taipei, (AL, Chan
Tzu-ch'ien). 300 M. , 34 (as anon. T'ang in style of Chan Tzu-
ch'ien); CKLTMHC, II. 71 (as anon. Sung).

Ladies occupied with embroidery, handscroll, Palace Museum, Peking,
(AL, Chou Fang). Chou Fang, 5-10 (as anon. T'ang); KKPWY
ts'ang-hua, II, 9-15* (as Chou Fang); T'ang-jen Wan-shan* (as
anon. T'ang); T'ang-tai jen-wu, pp. 46, 47 (sections, as Chou
Fang); WW, 1957. 1. 35-37 (as Chou Fang).

Listening to music, handscroll, Nelson Gallery of Art, Kansas City,
(AL, Chou Fang). Chou Fang, 1-2 (as anon. T'ang).

A lady accompanied by three servants "washing the moon", Nat. Pal.
Mus. , Taipei, (AL, anon. Sung). CH mei-shu, I; CKLTMHC,
I. 14; CKLTSHH; KKMH, I. 23* (all as anon. Five Dyn.).

Copy of Ku K'ai-chih's Nymph of the Lo river, album leaf, Nat. Pal.
Mus. , Taipei. 300 M. , 33*; CKLTMHC. I. 5; KKMH, I. 9 (all
as anon. T'ang).

Gentlemen riders on an outing, handscroll, Palace Museum, Peking.
KKPWY ts'ang-hua, II. 32-35* (as anon. T'ang).

One hundred horses, handscroll, Palace Museum, Peking. KKPWY
ts'ang-hua, II. 36-38* (as anon. T'ang).

Tribute bearers, handscroll, Nanking Museum. WW, 1960. 7. 1 (as
anon. Six Dyn.).

Palaces and Buildings

Palaces and gardens, Palace Museum, Peking. KKPWY ts'ang-hua,
II. 22-23*; WW, 1961. 6. inside front cover (both as anon. T'ang).

Figures in palace and garden complex, handscroll, Palace Museum,
Peking. KKPWY ts'ang-hua, II. 24-25* (as anon. T'ang).

Painters of the Sung Dynasty

Ai Hsüan	Fan K'uan
Chang Chi	Feng Ta-yu
Chang Hsün-li	Ho Ch'üan
Chang Mao	Hsi-chin chü-shih
Chang Sheng-wen	Hsia Kuei
Chang Tse-tuan	Hsiao Chao
Chang Tun-li	Hsiao Yung
Chao Ch'ang	Hsü Ch'ung-chü
Chao Fu	Hsü Ch'ung-ssu
Chao Ling-jang	Hsü Tao-ning
Chao Meng-chien	Hsü Yü-kung
Chao Po-chü	Hui-ch'ung
Chao Po-su	Hui-tsung of Sung, Emperor
Chao Ta-heng	
Ch'ao Pu-chih	I Yüan-chi
Ch'en Ch'ing-po	Jih-kuan
Ch'en Chü-chung	Kao K'o-ming
Ch'en K'o-chiu	Kao-tsung of Sung, Emperor
Ch'en Tsung-hsün	Kung Su-jan
Ch'i Hsü	Kuo Hsi
Chia Shih-ku	Li An-chung
Chiang Ts'an	Li Ch'eng
Ch'iao Chung-ch'ang	Li Kung-lin
Chu Huai-chin	Li Sung
Chu Jui	Li T'ang
Chu Kuang-p'u	Li Ti
Chu Shao-tsung	Li Ts'ung-hsün
Chu Wei-te	

58

Li Tung	Su Han-ch'en
Li Wei	Su Shih
Liang K'ai	Ts'ui Ch'üeh
Liang Shih-min	Ts'ui Po
Lin Ch'un	Wang Chü-cheng
Liu Sung-nien	Wang Hsi-meng
Liu Ts'ai	Wang Hsiao
Liu Tsung-ku	Wang Ning
Lou Kuan	Wang Shen
Lu Tsung-kuei	Wang T'ing-yün
Ma Ho-chih	Wen (Jih-kuan)
Ma Hsing-tsu	Wen T'ung
Ma K'uei	Wu Ping
Ma Lin	Wu Tsung-yüan
Ma Shih-jung	Wu Yüan-chih
Ma Yüan	Yang Mei-tzu, Empress Yang
Mao I	Yang Pu-chih
Mi Fei	Yao Yüeh-hua
Mi Yu-jen	Yang Wei
Mou I	Yen Su
Mu-ch'i	Yen Tz'u-p'ing
P'u-an	Yen Tz'u-yü
Ssu-ma Huai	
Su Ch'uo	

AI HSÜAN　艾宣　. From Nanking, member of the Academy of Painting during the reign of emperor Shen-tsung (1068-1085), painted flowers and birds. (CP, II, AL, 37.)

Two flowering poppy plants, fan, Nat. Pal. Mus., Taipei, (AL).
KKMH, II.35.

CHANG CHI 張激 . Unidentified.

The White Lotus Society meeting, handscroll, the colophons by Li Chieh, Chang Chi and Chao Ling-shih were all inscribed by Fan Tun in 1161, Liao-ning Provincial Museum. Liao-ning, I. 24-35.

CHANG HSÜN-LI 張訓禮 , see Chang Tun-li 張敦禮 .

CHANG MAO 張茂 , t. Ju-sung 如松 . From Hangchou, active in Kuang-tsung's reign (1190-1193), painted landscapes, birds and flowers. (CP, II, AL, 37.)

Two ducks in water, fan, signed, Palace Museum, Peking, (AL). Sung-jen hua-ts'e, A. 30*; B. VI. 9*.

CHANG SHENG-WEN 張勝溫 . Active at the beginning of the 13th century in the South. (CP, II, AL, 37.)

Buddhas, Lohans and Bodhisattvas, long handscroll, inscription dated 1180, Nat. Pal. Mus., Taipei, (AL). 300 M., 124-126 (sections); CAT, 45 (sections); CKLTMHC, I. 76 (four sections); NPM Quarterly, I. 2, pl. XXV (section).

CHANG TSE-TUAN 張擇端 , t. Cheng-tao 正道 . From Tung-wu, active at the beginning of the 12th century in K'aifeng and Hangchou, painted landscapes, boats, carriages, bridges. (CP, II, AL, 38.)

The Ch'ing-ming Festival at K'aifeng, handscroll, Palace Museum, Peking, (AL). CK ku-tai, 39 (two sections); CT-t Ch'ing-ming; WWCH, I, pp. 9-28.

Boat race on the Chin-ming Lake, album leaf, signed, Tientsin Art Museum. I-yüan chi-chin, 1* (as anon. Sung); Liang Sung, 16* (att. to Chang Tse-tuan); Sung-jen hua-ts'e, B. XVI* (as anon. Sung); WW, 1960. 7. 5 (as anon. Sung).

CHANG TUN-LI 張敦禮 (Hsün-li 訓禮). Of the two painters named Chang Tun-li active in the Sung period, the younger changed his name to Hsün-li when, in the reign of emperor Kuang-tsung (1190-1194), tun became taboo, painted landscapes and figures. (CP, II, AL, 38.)

Scholars drinking wine and examining pictures in a garden, attributed, Nat. Pal. Mus., Taipei, (AL). CKLTMHC, I. 53.

Fishing boat in a spring landscape, fan, attributed, Palace Museum, Peking. Sung-jen hua-ts'e, A. 31* (att. to Chang Hsün-li); B. IX. 2* (as anon. Sung); STSS (as anon. Sung).

Cowherd returning home, album leaf, S. M. Siu collection, Hong Kong. CK ku-hua, B. 37. 5.

Enjoying the scenery from a river pavilion, fan, attributed, composition identical to the painting in the Liao-ning Provincial

Museum given to Chu Huai-chin. CH-l Chiang-t'ing*.

CHAO CH'ANG 趙昌 , t. Ch'ang-chih 昌之 . From Kuang-han, Szechuan, active at the beginning of the 11th century, painted flowers and birds. (CP, II, AL, 39.)

> Flowers of the New Year's Day, Nat. Pal. Mus., Taipei, (AL). 300 M., 55.
> Butterflies, grasshoppers and water plants, handscroll, Palace Museum, Peking, (AL). CC Chieh-tieh*.
> A branch of white jasmine, fan, once attributed to Chao Ch'ang, Sugahara collection, Kamakura, (AL). NPM Quarterly, I. 2, pl. XII B.
> Eggplant, S. M. Siu collection, Hong Kong. CK ku-hua, B. 6.

CHAO FU 趙黻 or 趙芾 . From Chen-chiang, Kiangsu, active in the Shao-hsing era (1131-1162). (CP, II, AL, 39.)

> Returning to the village after rain, album leaf, signed, S. M. Siu collection, Hong Kong. CK ku-hua, B. 37. 11.
> Autumn river and mountains, album leaf, S. M. Siu collection, Hong Kong. CK ku-hua, B. 38. 5.

CHAO LING-JANG 趙令穰 , t. Ta-nien 大年 . Active c. 1070-1100, member of the imperial Sung family, painted landscapes. (CP, II, AL, 40-41.)

> River scenery with floating mist, handscroll, signed, dated 1100, Museum of Fine Arts, Boston, (AL). CK ku-tai, 35.
> A village by the water in mist, fan, attributed, Palace Museum, Peking, (AL). Sung-jen hua-ts'e, A. 78* (as anon. Sung); B. VI. 2* (as anon. Sung).
> Orange grove and birds, fan, attributed, Nat. Pal. Mus., Taipei. KKMH, I. 39.
> River village on an autumn morning, handscroll. TWSY ming-chi, 21-22.

CHAO MENG-CHIEN 趙孟堅 , t. Tzu-ku 子固 , h. I-chai 彜齋 . B. 1199, d. 1267, a relative of the imperial Sung family, lived near Hai-yen, Chekiang, Han-lin member in 1260, retired after the fall of the Sung dynasty, painted narcissi, plum blossoms, epidendrum and bamboo. (CP, II, AL, 41.)

> The three friends of cold winter, album leaf, artist's seals, Nat. Pal. Mus., Taipei, (AL). 300 M., 131; CAT, 67; CKLTMHC, I. 75; KKMH, III. 27.
> Narcissi, handscroll, poem, signed, (AL, Tōsō, 102). Che-chiang, 18.
> Three friends of winter: pine, bamboo and plum, fan, artist's seal, Shanghai Museum. Liang Sung, 47*; Sung-jen hua-ts'e, B. XVII*.

Narcissus plants, handscroll, inscribed and signed, Tientsin Art
Museum. CM-c Shui-hsien; T'ien-ching, I. 1-5; WW, 1958. 10. 19.
Narcissi, inscribed, signed, three colophons, S. M. Siu collection,
Hong Kong. CK ku-hua, A. 13; B. 31.

CHAO PO-CHÜ 趙伯駒   , t. Ch'ien-li 千里 . A descendant of
the first Sung emperor, active in K'aifeng and Hangchou, painted land-
scapes and architectural motifs. (CP, II, AL, 42.)
Mountains in spring, Nat. Pal. Mus. , Taipei, (AL). CKLTMHC,
II. 39 (as anon. Sung).
A fairy riding on a dragon, attributed, Nat. Pal. Mus. , Taipei, (AL).
CKLTMHC, II. 38 (as anon. Sung).
An imperial palace of the Han period, fan, after Li Chao-tao, Nat.
Pal. Mus. , Taipei, (AL). CAT, 42; CKLTMHC, I. 52; KKMH,
III. 9; NPM Quarterly, I. 2, pl. XXIX*.
The A-fang Palace, Nat. Pal. Mus. , Taipei, (AL). CKLTMHC, II. 4
(as anon. Sung); CH mei-shu, I (as Chao Po-chü).
Rocky mountains along a river in autumn, handscroll, signed (?),
Palace Museum, Peking, (AL). CK hua, XIII. 10-11, 14-15,
18-19, 21; CK ku-tai, 47 (section).
A sea deity listening to a discourse, Nat. Pal. Mus. , Taipei. 300 M. ,
107 (as Chao Po-chü); CKLTMHC, II. 37 (as anon. Sung).

CHAO PO-SU 趙伯驌   , t. Hsi-yüan 希遠 . B. 1124, d. 1182,
younger brother of Chao Po-chü. (CP, II, AL, 42.)
A warrior returning from the hunt, album leaf, attributed, Palace
Museum, Peking. Sung-jen hua-ts'e, A. 19* (att. to Chao Po-su);
B. V. 1* (as anon. Sung).

CHAO TA-HENG 趙大亨   . Active mid-twelfth century, a servant
of Chao Po-chü. (CP, II, AL, 43.)
Immortals on the P'eng-lai Island, Nat. Pal. Mus. , Taipei, (AL).
CKLTMHC, II. 54 (as anon. Sung).
Resting in a pavilion under fruit trees, fan, signed, Liao-ning Provincial Museum. Liang Sung, 14*; Liao-ning, I. 41; Sung-jen hua-
ts'e, B. XVIII*; Sung Yüan shan-shui, 5*.

CH'AO PU-CHIH 晁補之 , t. Wu-chiu 无咎 , h. Kuei-lai-tzu
歸來子 . B. 1053, d. 1110, from Chü-yeh, Shantung; literary writer,
poet and official, painted figures, trees and animals. (CP, II, AL, 43.)
Lao-tzu riding on a buffalo, signed, Nat. Pal. Mus. , Taipei, (AL).
300 M. , 87; CH mei-shu, I.

CH'EN CH'ING-PO 陳清波 . From Ch'ien-t'ang, Chekiang, tai-chao in the Painting Academy in the Pao-yu era (1253-1258), painted landscapes. (CP, II, AL, 43.)

A spring morning, landscape with palaces and figures, fan, signed, dated i-wei 1235 or 1295, Palace Museum, Peking, (AL). Che-chiang, 15; Sung-jen hua-ts'e, A. 62*; B. X. 3*.

CH'EN CHÜ-CHUNG 陳居中 . Tai-chao in the Academy at Hangchou in the Chia-t'ai era (1201-1204), painted horses and camp scenes. (CP, II, AL, 43-44.)

A man on horseback, leading another horse by a rope, album leaf, Nat. Pal. Mus., Taipei, (AL). NPM Bulletin, I. 3, cover*.
Wen-chi preparing to return to China, Nat. Pal. Mus., Taipei, (AL). 300 M., 116; CAT, 48; CKLTMHC, I. 60; KKMH, IV. 19; WW, 1959. 6. 33 (detail).
Tending horses by the willow stream, fan, attributed, Palace Museum, Peking, (AL). Sung-jen hua-ts'e, A, 27* (att. to Ch'en Chü-chung); B. I. 8* (as anon. Sung).
Deer hunting on the plain, album leaf, attributed, Nat. Pal. Mus., Taipei. CKLTMHC, II. 72 (as anon. Sung).
Four goats, album leaf, artist's seal, Palace Museum, Peking. CC-c Ssu-yang*; Sung-jen hua-ts'e, A. 26*; B. IV. 4*.
A large herd of horses bathing in a stream, handscroll, signed, Liao-ning Provincial Museum. Liao-ning, II. 64-65 (as anon. Ming).
Eighteen Songs for a Foreign Flute, Lady Wen-chi's return to China, handscroll. WW, 1959. 5. 55.

CH'EN K'O-CHIU 陳可久 . Tai-chao in the Painting Academy during the Pao-yu era (1253-1258), painted fish, flowers and trees of the four seasons, studied Hsü Hsi. (H. 4.)

Fish swimming in spring stream, album leaf, attributed, Palace Museum, Peking. Sung-jen hua-ts'e, A. 65* (att. to Ch'en K'o-chiu); B. III. 10* (as anon. Sung).

CH'EN TSUNG-HSÜN 陳宗訓 . From Hangchou, tai-chao in the Academy during the Shao-ting era (1228-1233), painted figures (CP, II, AL, 44.)

Three children playing in a courtyard, fan, attributed, Palace Museum, Peking. Sung-jen hua-ts'e, A. 66* (att. to Ch'en Tsung-hsün); B. VIII. 5* (as anon. Sung).

CH'I HSÜ 祁序 , also named Ch'i Yü 祁嶼 . From Chiang-nan, 10th century, painted flowers, birds, water-buffaloes and cats. (CP, II, AL, 45.)

A boy leading a buffalo, signed, Nat. Pal. Mus., Taipei, (AL). 300
   M., 70; KKMH, I.31.
Buffalo and herdboy, signed, S.M. Siu collection, Hong Kong. CK
   ku-hua, B.9.

CHIA SHIH-KU 賈師古 . From K'aifeng, chih-hou in the Painting
Academy in Hangchou, active c. 1130-1160, painted Buddhist and Taoist
figures. (CP, II, AL, 45.)
   Kuanyin seated on a rock, signed, Nat. Pal. Mus., Taipei, (AL).
      KKMH, III.7.
   Temple by the cliff pass, album leaf, signed, Nat. Pal. Mus., Taipei.
      CAT, 38 (as Chia Shih-ku); CKLTMHC, II.53 (as anon. Sung);
      KKMH, IV.4 (as Chia Shih-ku).

CHIANG TS'AN 江參 , t. Kuan-tao 貫道 . From Wu-hsing, Che-
kiang, active during first half of the 12th century, painted landscapes.
(CP, II, AL, 45-46.)
   The Lu Mountain, after Fan K'uan, signed, Nat. Pal. Mus., Taipei,
      (AL). 300 M., 101; CH mei-shu, I; CKLTSHH.
   Thousand miles of mountains and river, long handscroll, signed,
      Nat. Pal. Mus., Taipei, (AL). 300 M., 100; CKLTMHC, I.42;
      NPM Bulletin, I.3, figs. 1, 3, 5, 8 (details).
   A richly wooded mountain in autumn, a homestead by a river, attribu-
      ted, Nat. Pal. Mus., Taipei, (AL, anon. Yüan). CKLTMHC,
      I.43 (as Chiang Ts'an); NPM Bulletin, I.3, figs. 2, 4, 6, 7 (as
      Chiang Ts'an); KKMH, VI.41 (as anon. Yüan).

CH'IAO CHUNG-CH'ANG 喬仲常 . From Ho-chung, Shansi, active
in the first half of the 12th century, followed Li Kung-lin in religious pictures, also painted secular figures and landscapes. (CP, II, AL, 46.)
   Illustrations to Su Tung-p'o's (later) fu-poem The Red Cliff, hand-
      scroll, signed, colophon by Chao Te-lin dated 1123, John M.
      Crawford collection, New York, (AL). TWSY ming-chi, 23-33.

CHU HUAI-CHIN 朱懷瑾 . From Ch'ien-t'ang, Chekiang; tai-chao
in the Painting Academy during the Pao-yu era (1253-1258), painted landscapes and figures, followed Hsia Kuei. (CP, II, AL, 47.)
   Boats on a river in autumn, high rocky shores, fan, signed, (signa-
      ture also read as Chu Wei-te 朱惟德 , otherwise unrecord-
      ed), Liao-ning Provincial Museum, (AL). Liang Sung, 46* (as
      Chu Wei-te); Liao-ning, I.63 (as Chu Huai-chin); Sung-jen hua-
      ts'e, B.XVIII* (as Chu Wei-te); Sung Yüan shan-shui, 10* (as
      Chu Huai-chin).

CHU JUI 朱銳 . From Hopei, <u>tai-chao</u> in Painting Academy in K'ai-feng and in Hangchou, painted landscapes and figures. (CP, II, AL, 48.)

    Illustration to Su Tung-p'o's <u>fu</u>-poem The Red Cliff, handscroll, formerly att. to Chu Jui, now given to Wu Yüan-chih, Nat. Pal. Mus., Taipei, (AL). 300 M., 132 (as Wu Yüan-chih); CAT, 46 (sections, att. to Wu Yüan-chih); CKLTMHC, II.2 (as anon. Sung).

    An ox-cart crossing a mountain stream, album leaf, signed, Shanghai Museum, (AL). Liang Sung, 5*; Sung-jen hua-ts'e, B.XIV*.

    Travellers in snowy mountains, album leaf, signed, S.M. Siu collection, Hong Kong. CK ku-hua, B.37.8.

CHU KUANG-P'U 朱光普 , t. Tung-mei 東美 . From K'aifeng, moved to Hangchou at the fall of the Northern Sung, a member of the Painting Academy in Hangchou, painted farm scenes. (H.4; J.3; I.51; M. p.92.)

    A man in a pavilion by a river, fan, attributed, Liao-ning Provincial Museum. Liang Sung, 36* (as anon. Sung); Liao-ning, I.40 (as Chu Kuang-p'u); Sung-jen hua-ts'e, B.XVIII* (as anon. Sung); Sung Yüan shan-shui, 3* (as Chu Kuang-p'u).

CHU SHAO-TSUNG 朱紹宗 . A member of the Painting Academy, painted figures, flowers and birds, especially cats and dogs. (H.4; J.8; I.51; M. p.92.)

    Butterflies among chrysanthemums, fan, signed Chu___, Palace Museum, Peking. Sung-jen hua-ts'e, A.69* (att. to Chu Shao-tsung); B.V.8* (as anon. Sung).

CHU WEI-TE 朱惟德 , see Chu Huai-chin 朱懷瑾 .

FAN K'UAN 范寬 , original name Fan Chung-cheng 范中正 , t. Chung-li 仲立 . From Hua-yüan, Shensi, active c. 990-1030, painted landscapes. (CP, II, AL, 48-49.)

    Men with donkeys approaching a stream at the foot of steep mountains, Nat. Pal. Mus., Taipei, (AL). 300 M., 65.

    Sitting in contemplation by a stream at the foot of cloudy mountains, Nat. Pal. Mus., Taipei, (AL). 300 M., 67; CH mei-shu, I; CKLTMHC, I.25; KKMH, II.23.

    Travellers among mountains and streams, Nat. Pal. Mus., Taipei, (AL). 300 M., 64; CAT, 18; CCAT pl. 94; CH mei-shu, I; CK ku-tai, 30; CKLTMHC, I.23; CKLTSHH; KKMH, I.27; NPM Quarterly, I.2, pls. XVI-XVII.

    Snow-covered mountains, Nat. Pal. Mus., Taipei, (AL). 300 M., 66; CKLTMHC, I.24; KKMH, II.22.

A waterfall in autumn among leafy trees, Nat. Pal. Mus., Taipei,
(AL). 300 M., 68; CH mei-shu, I; KKMH, I. 28.

River in snow, travellers crossing a bridge, fan, signed, Chang Pe-
chin collection, (AL). Tien Yin Tang, II. 2.

Ch'ün-feng hsüeh-chi t'u. Clearing after snow on the mountains, album
leaf, Nat. Pal. Mus., Taipei, (AL). KKMH, II. 24.

Calligraphy and painting of the Lan-t'ing, handscroll, S. M. Siu collection, Hong Kong. CK ku-hua, B. 7.

Travellers in autumn mountains, album leaf, S. M. Siu collection,
Hong Kong. CK ku-hua, B. 37. 3.

FENG TA-YU 馮大有 , h. I-chai 怡齋 . Lived in Suchou,
painted lotus flowers. (H. 4; I. 51; M. p. 529.)

Lotus and mandarin ducks, fan, attributed, Nat. Pal. Mus., Taipei.
KKMH, III. 26.

HO CH'ÜAN 何筌 . Unidentified.

Visitors arriving at a country estate, fan, signed, dated hsin-mao,
Palace Museum, Peking. Liang Sung, 45* (as Ho Ch'üan); Sung-
jen hua-ts'e, B. XI* (as anon. Sung).

HSI-CHIN CHÜ-SHIH 西金居士 , real name was Chin Ta-shou 金
大受 . Lived at Ch'e-ch'iao in Ch'ing-yüan, Chekiang, active at the
close of the Southern Sung period in Ning-po, Chekiang, painted Buddhist
figures. (CP, II, AL, 50.)

One of ten pictures of arhats: arhat seated on a platform, a servant
peeling fruit, National Museum, Tokyo, (AL). Che-chiang, 17.

HSIA KUEI 夏珪 , t. Yü-yü 禹玉 . From Ch'ien-t'ang, Chekiang,
tai-chao in the Painting Academy, c. 1190-1225, painted landscapes. (CP,
II, AL, 50-51.)

Far-reaching clear views over streams and mountains, handscroll,
Nat. Pal. Mus., Taipei, (AL). 300 M., 115; CAT, 57 (sections),
CCAT, pl. 101 (section); CH mei-shu, I; CKLTMHC, I. 70; MY/
HK, 12-13 (sections); NPM Quarterly, I. 2. pl. VI (section);
WW, 1960. 7. 32 (section).

Looking for plum-blossoms, Nat. Pal. Mus., Taipei, (AL). MY/HK,
15.

Entertaining a guest in a mountain pavilion under a large tree, Nat.
Pal. Mus., Taipei, (AL). KKMH, IV. 17.

The willow dyke of the West Lake, Nat. Pal. Mus., Taipei, (AL).
300 M., 114; Che-chiang, 12; KKMH, III. 22; MY/HK, 16.

High cliffs by a river, attributed, Nat. Pal. Mus., Taipei, (AL).
CKLTMHC, I. 68.

Two men seated on a high river-bank under a projecting pine, album
leaf, attributed, Nat. Pal. Mus., Taipei, (AL). CAT, 58; CK
ku-tai, 51; CKLTMHC, I. 69.

Rain-storm over a pavilion among trees by a river, signed, ex-Kawa-
saki collection, (AL). MY/HK, 14 (section).

River view with an anchored boat, Iwasaki collection, Tokyo, (AL).
MY/HK, 11.

Twelve river views, handscroll, signed, Nelson Gallery of Art, Kansas City, (AL). Che-chiang, 13 (section); MY/HK, 8-10.

Temples in a mountain, fan, attributed, Palace Museum, Peking,
(AL). Liang Sung, 30* (as anon. Sung); Sung-jen hua-ts'e, B.XI*
(as Hsia Kuei).

Misty mountains, fan, attributed, Palace Museum, Peking, (AL).
Sung-jen hua-ts'e, A. 51* (as Hsia Kuei); B. VII. 1* (as anon. Sung).

Man seated on a terrace under pines looking at clouds, album leaf,
Nat. Pal. Mus., Taipei. CKLTMHC, II. 86 (as anon. Sung).

Gazing at a waterfall, fan, signed, Nat. Pal. Mus., Taipei. KKMH,
III. 23; NPM Bulletin, II. 5, cover*.

Fishing   on a cold stream, fan, signed, Nat. Pal. Mus., Taipei.
KKMH, IV. 18.

A hamlet below mountain peaks, fan, signed, Palace Museum, Peking.
Sung-jen hua-ts'e, A. 47*; B. VI. 10*; STSS*.

Scholar's study by a pond, album leaf, signed, Palace Museum, Peking. Sung-jen hua-ts'e, A. 48* (as Hsia Kuei); B. VIII. 1* (as
anon. Sung).

A ch'in player by a stream, fan, attributed, Palace Museum, Peking.
Sung-jen hua-ts'e, A. 49* (att. to Hsia Kuei); B. IX. 1* (as anon.
Sung).

Distant peaks, two scholars and servant looking across a misty valley,
album leaf, attributed, Palace Museum, Peking. PM, 2* (att. to
Hsia Kuei); Sung-jen hua-ts'e, A. 50* (att. to Hsia Kuei); B. IX. 6*
(as anon. Sung).

Two scholars conversing on a ledge overlooking rooftops and a valley,
album leaf, attributed, Palace Museum, Peking. Liang Sung, 28*;
Sung-jen hua-ts'e, B. XI*.

Travellers on muleback, fan, signed, Chang Pe-chin collection. Tien
Yin Tang, II. 7.

Travellers on a bridge leading to a village, fan, signed, S. M. Siu
collection, Hong Kong. CK ku-hua, A. 8; B. 24.

A fisherman's house by a river, album leaf, signed, S. M. Siu collection, Hong Kong. CK ku-hua, B. 37. 10.

Landscape after rain, travellers on a bridge, S. M. Siu collection,
Hong Kong. CK ku-hua, B. 25.

HSIAO CHAO 蕭照　．From Hu-tse, Shansi, <u>tai-chao</u> in the Painting
Academy in Hangchou, c. 1130-1160, pupil of Li T'ang, landscapes and
figures. (CP, II, AL, 52.)
 A high tower in the mountains overlooking a dark view, signed, Nat.
  Pal. Mus., Taipei, (AL, also listed as River landscape). 300 M.,
  103; CKLTMHC, I. 54; KKMH, III. 6.
 Red trees in autumn mountains, fan, attributed, Liao-ning Provincial
  Museum. HC Ch'iu-shan*; Liang Sung, 20* (as anon. Sung); Liao-
  ning, I. 39 (as Hsiao Chao); Sung-jen hua-ts'e, B. XVIII* (as anon.
  Sung); Sung Yüan shan-shui, 4* (as Hsiao Chao).
 Three scenes illustrating events in the reign of T'ai-tsu, three paint-
  ings mounted in handscroll with sections of text, Tientsin Art
  Museum. T'ien-ching, II. 1-6.
 Four scenes illustrating events in the reign of T'ai-tsu, handscroll,
  total of 12 sections, possibly part of preceding painting. TWSY
  ming-chi, 65-81 (sections 4, 5, 6, 8).
 Pavilion and terrace among plum and bamboo, album leaf, signed,
  S. M. Siu collection, Hong Kong. CK ku-hua, B. 38. 4.

HSIAO YUNG 蕭溶　．Served as a high official at the court of the em-
peror Hsing-tsung of the Liao dynasty (1030-1055), painted birds. (CP,
II, AL, 52.)
 Pheasants on a rock by a stream, signed, Nat. Pal. Mus., Taipei,
  (AL). 300 M., 94; CH mei-shu, I; CKLTSHH; KKMH, I. 43.

HSÜ CH'UNG-CHÜ 徐崇矩　．From Nanking, grandson of Hsü Hsi,
11th century, painted birds and flowers. (CP, II, AL, 52.)
 Bird on smartweed, fan, attributed, Palace Museum, Peking. KKPWY
  hua-niao, 4* (as anon. Sung); Sung-jen hua-ts'e, A. 5* (att. to
  Hsü Ch'ung-chü); B. I. 2* (as anon. Sung); STHN* (as anon. Sung).

HSÜ CH'UNG-SSU 徐崇嗣　．From Nanking, grandson of Hsü Hsi,
11th century, painted birds and flowers. (CP, II, AL, 52.)
 Long-tailed bird on a branch of loquat tree, fan, attributed, Nat.
  Pal. Mus., Taipei. CKLTMHC, II. 73 (as anon. Sung).

HSÜ TAO-NING 許道寧　．From Ho-chien, Hopei, active during the
first half of the 11th century, painted landscapes. (CP, II, AL, 53.)
 Mountain pass in snow, after Li Ch'eng, signed, Nat. Pal. Mus.,
  Taipei, (AL). 300 M., 75*; KKMH, I. 34.
 Snowy peaks in mist, fishermen's cottages on the shore, inscribed
  with the painter's name and a non-existent date, Nat. Pal. Mus.,
  Taipei, (AL). CAT, 19; KKMH, II. 30.

Old leafless trees on bare cliffs, Nat. Pal. Mus., Taipei, (AL).
CKLTMHC, II. 11 (as anon. Sung).

A returning boat in storm, fan, attributed, Palace Museum, Peking,
(AL). Sung-jen hua-ts'e, A. 94* (as anon. Sung); B. III. 8* (as
anon. Sung); STSS* (as anon. Sung).

Blue mountains and white clouds, fan, attributed, Palace Museum,
Peking, (AL). Sung-jen hua-ts'e, A. 95* (as anon. Sung); B. III. 1*
(as anon. Sung).

A homeward-bound boat, a man seated on the shore, fan, attributed,
Chang Pe-chin collection. Tien Yin Tang, II. 3.

HSÜ YÜ-KUNG 徐禹功 . Unidentified.

Plum blossoms and bamboo in snow, handscroll, signed, dated <u>hsin-yu</u> (1141?), colophons by Yang Pu-chih, Chao Meng-chien (dated
1257), Chang Yü (dated 1349) and others, Liao-ning Provincial
Museum. Liao-ning, I. 55-56.

HUI-CH'UNG 惠崇 . From Chien-yang, Fukien, a monk-painter
active at the beginning of the 11th century, painted water fowl and landscapes. (CP, II, AL, 53-54.)

Dawn over streams and mountains in spring, handscroll, Palace Museum, Peking, (AL). CK hua, XXI. 16-19.

Two mandarin ducks on a beach in autumn, album leaf, attributed,
Nat. Pal. Mus., Taipei, (AL). 300 M., 69* (as Hui-ch'ung);
CAT, 22 (att. to Hui-ch'ung); CH mei-shu, I (as Hui-ch'ung);
CKLTMHC, II. 101 (as anon. Sung); CKLTSHH (as Hui-ch'ung);
KKMH, I. 29 (as Hui-ch'ung).

Two geese on a river shore, fan, attributed, Nat. Pal. Mus., Taipei,
(AL). KKMH, II. 25*.

Birds on an autumn bank, album leaf, attributed, Nat. Pal. Mus.,
Taipei. KKMH, I. 30.

Sandy beach and misty trees, album leaf, attributed, Liao-ning Provincial Museum. H-c Sha-t'ing*; Liang Sung, 10* (as anon. Sung);
Liao-ning, I. 23 (as Hui-ch'ung); Sung-jen hua-ts'e, B. XVIII* (as
anon. Sung); Sung Yüan shan-shui, 1* (as Hui-ch'ung).

Two geese under a willow, signed, S. M. Siu collection, Hong Kong.
CK ku-hua, B. 8.

EMPEROR HUI-TSUNG OF SUNG 宋徽宗 , Chao Chi 趙佶 .
B. 1082, d. 1135, reigned from 1101-1126, specialized in birds and flowers. (CP, II, AL, 54-55.)

A large flock of cranes flying among rooftops, handscroll, signed,
dated 1112. TSYMC hua-hsüan, 7.

Imperial eagle on a roost, inscribed, signed, dated 1114. TWSY
ming-chi, 34.

Three mynah birds fighting, signature and seal of the emperor, (AL).
Chao Chi, 16.

A white heron, two ducks and some lotus plants at a lake shore, handscroll, the emperor's signature and seal, Nat. Pal. Mus., Taipei, (AL). CKLTMHC, I.37.

Streams and mountains in autumn hues, the emperor's signature and
seal, Nat. Pal. Mus., Taipei, (AL). 300 M., 91; CAT, 32;
CKLTMHC, I.35; KKMH, II.37.

A white goose resting on a shore and a red polygonum plant, the emperor's seal, Nat. Pal. Mus., Taipei, (AL). 300 M., 90* (as
Hui-tsung); CH mei-shu, I (as Hui-tsung); CKLTMHC, II.3 (as
anon. Sung); CKLTSHH (as Hui-tsung); KKMH, I.42 (as Hui-tsung).

Two small birds in a leafless blossoming wax-tree, inscription and
poem by the emperor, Nat. Pal. Mus., Taipei, (AL). 300 M.,
89; CCAT, pl. 98; Chao Chi, 2; CH mei-shu, I; CKLTMHC, I.36;
KKMH, II.38*.

Twelve scholars of the Sung period at a festival meal in a garden,
poem by the emperor and his signature, Nat. Pal. Mus., Taipei,
(AL). 300 M., 92; CAT, 31; CKLTMHC, I.34; KKMH, I.41.

A scholar seated under a large tree playing the ch'in to two visitors,
the emperor's signature, Palace Museum, Peking, (AL). Chao
Chi, 14; Li-tai jen-wu, 19; PM, 21*; WW, 1957.3*.

A pheasant perched on the branch of a blossoming shrub, inscription
by the emperor, Palace Museum, Peking, (AL). Chao Chi, 3;
CK hua, I.12*; CK ku-tai, 45; KKPWY hua-niao, 2*.

Four magpies in a bare willow and four ducks on the shore, handscroll,
signature and seals of the emperor, Shanghai Museum, (AL).
H-h Liu-ya*; WW, 1963.10.18 (section).

Two small birds on bamboo branches extending from a rock, handscroll, signature and seal of the emperor, John M. Crawford
collection, New York, (AL). TWSY ming-chi, 40.

Returning fishing boats on a snowy river, handscroll, seal and signature of the emperor, (AL). Chao Chi, 4-8.

A five-colored parakeet on the branch of a blossoming apricot-tree,
handscroll, a poem and colophon by the emperor, Museum of
Fine Arts, Boston, (AL). Chao Chi, 1.

Ladies preparing newly woven silk, after Chang Hsüan, handscroll,
Museum of Fine Arts, Boston, (AL). Chao Chi, 9-11; Li-tai
jen-wu, 21.

Loquats, bird and butterfly, fan, signed, Palace Museum, Peking.
KKPWY hua-niao, 3*; Sung-jen hua-ts'e, A.8*; B.I.3*.

A white-eye on a blossoming plum branch, album leaf, signed, Palace Museum, Peking. Liang Sung, 2*; Sung-jen hua-ts'e, B. XII*;
STHN*.

Lady Kuo-kuo on a spring outing, after Chang Hsüan, handscroll,
Liao-ning Provincial Museum. Chao Chi, 12-13; Liao-ning,
I. 36-38; Li-tai jen-wu, 20; T'ang-tai jen-wu, pl. 7*; WW, 1955.
5. 10; 1961. 12 inside back cover.

Two birds on plum blossom and cedar branches, album leaf, signed,
Szechuan Provincial Museum. Liang Sung, 1*; Sung-jen hua-
ts'e, B. XVI*.

The five poisonous creatures, signed, S. M. Siu collection, Hong Kong.
CK ku-hua, A. 4; B. 14.

Peach blossoms, bamboo and birds, handscroll, inscribed and signed,
S. M. Siu collection, Hong Kong. CK ku-hua, B. 15.

Copy of a landscape by Chan Tzu-ch'ien, handscroll. Chan Tzu-ch'ien,
4 (section).

Rare birds, handscroll. CK shu-hua, I. 11-16.

Butterflies, birds and flowers, handscroll, emperor's signature.
TWSY ming-chi, 35-39.

I YÜAN-CHI 易元吉 , t. Ch'ing-chih 慶之 . From Ch'ang-sha,
Hunan, summoned twice in the Chih-p'ing era (1064-1067) to the capital
where he executed some wall-paintings in the palace, died while occupied
in this work, painted flowers, birds and particularly monkeys. (CP, II,
AL, 55-56.)

A monkey seated on the ground, holding a kitten in its bosom while the
mother cat is murmuring angrily, handscroll, Nat. Pal. Mus.,
Taipei, (AL). 300 M., 73*; CAT, 25; CKLTMHC, I. 30; KKMH,
II. 27; NPM Quarterly, I, 2, XI. A.

Three monkeys on a juniper tree, fan, Nat. Pal. Mus., Taipei.
KKMH, I. 33.

Monkey reaching for a spider, fan, attributed, Palace Museum, Peking. Sung hua shih fu, 6* (as anon. Sung); Sung-jen hua-ts'e,
A. 7* (att. to I Yüan-chi); B. III. 2* (as anon. Sung).

Three monkeys in an oak tree, fan, attributed, Chang Pe-chin collection. Tien Yin Tang, II. 5.

JIH-KUAN 日觀 , see Wen 溫 .

KAO K'O-MING 高克明 . From Chiang-chou, Shansi, tai-chao in
the Painting Academy from c. 1008 to 1053, painted landscapes and
figures. (CP, II, AL, 56.)

Snow over the mountains along the river, handscroll, signed and dated
1035, John M. Crawford collection, New York, (AL). TWSY
ming-chi, 13-14.

Autumn grove and water birds, fan, attributed, Nat. Pal. Mus., Taipei, (AL, Leafy trees on the shore and flocking birds?). KKMH,
II. 29.

Village market on pine-covered cliff, fan, attributed, Nat. Pal. Mus.,
Taipei. CKLTMHC, II. 76 (as anon. Sung).

EMPEROR KAO-TSUNG OF SUNG 宋高宗 , Chao Kou 趙構 . B.
1107, d. 1187, son of the emperor Hui-tsung and the first emperor of the
Southern Sung dynasty, painted figures, landscapes and flowers. (CP,
II, AL, 56.)

River landscape with a fishing-boat, fan, poem by the emperor, Palace Museum, Peking, (AL). Sung-jen hua-ts'e, A. 16* (as anon.
Sung); B. II. 8* (as anon. Sung).

Fisherman awaking in his boat, album leaf, poem, Nat. Pal. Mus.,
Taipei. KKMH, III. 1.

KUNG SU-JAN 宮素然 . A Taoist nun from Chen-yang, Kueichou,
active at the beginning of the 12th century. (CP, II, AL, 57.)

Chao-chün on her way to Mongolia under the escort of Mongol horsemen, handscroll, signed, Abe collection, Ōsaka Museum, (AL).
Li-tai jen-wu, 22; WW, 1964. 3. 3.

KUO HSI 郭熙 , t. Shun-fu 淳夫 . From Wen-hsien in Hoyang
(Honan), probably born shortly after 1020, active c. 1060-1075, served
as i-hsüeh in the Painting Academy, painted landscapes, followed Li
Ch'eng; author of Lin-ch'üan kao-chih chi. (CP, II, AL, 57-58.)

Early spring, signed, dated 1072, Nat. Pal. Mus., Taipei, (AL).
300 M., 76; CAT, 20; CCAT, pl. 96; CKLTMHC, I. 21; KKMH,
I. 35; Kuo Hsi, 1; NPM Quarterly, I. 2, pl. XXI*, XXIII A; WW,
1955. 6. 14.

Mountain path in snow, signed, dated 1072, Nat. Pal. Mus., Taipei,
(AL). 300 M., 78; CH mei-shu, I; CKLTMHC, I. 22; KKMH,
II. 32; Kuo Hsi, 13.

Rock, twisted trees, distant river view, short handscroll, signed,
dated 1078, Palace Museum, Peking. CK hua, XIV. 10-11; CK
ku-tai, 34; Kuo Hsi, 4; WWCH, III. 14.

Village in a mountain valley, signed, Nat. Pal. Mus., Taipei, (AL).
300 M., 77; KKMH, I. 36; Kuo Hsi, 11.

Tortuous old cedar-trees in front of snowy mountains. Nat. Pal. Mus.,
Taipei, (AL). CH mei-shu, I; CKLTSHH; KKMH, II. 31.

A steep cliff, temple buildings and willows in mist by a bay, signed,
Nat. Pal. Mus. , Taipei, (AL). 300 M. , 79.

A bay with rocky shores in autumn, inscribed with the artist's name,
Nat. Pal. Mus. , Taipei, (AL). Kuo Hsi, 12.

Fishing boats at the shore, two others approaching, fan, attributed,
Palace Museum, Peking, (AL). Sung-jen hua-ts'e, A. 43* (as
anon. Sung); B II. 6* (as anon. Sung).

Ku-mu yao-shan t'u, Shanghai Museum, (AL). Kuo Hsi, 14; WW,
1962. 12. 4; WWCH, III. 11*.

Autumn in the valley of the Yellow River, section of a handscroll,
attributed, Freer Gallery of Art, Washington, D. C. , (AL). Kuo
Hsi, 5-10 (as Kuo Hsi); TWSY ming-chi, 15-20 (as Wang Shen).

Snowy river gorge, attributed, Shanghai Museum. CK hua, XI. 13;
Kuo Hsi, 2-3; Shang-hai, 2*; TSYMC hua-hsüan, 5; WWCH, III. 13.

A mountain village, attributed. WWCH, III. 12.

Travellers in the mountains, fan, attributed. KH Ch'i-shan*.

LI AN-CHUNG 李安忠 . Member of the Academy of Painting both
in K'aifeng and in Hangchou, c. 1117-1140, painted flowers and birds,
particularly quails. (CP, II, AL, 58.)

Two quails among chrysanthemums and thorny shrubs, album leaf,
attributed, Nat. Pal. Mus. , Taipei, (AL). CKLTMHC, II. 102
(as anon. Sung).

Bird on a branch, fan, signed, Nat. Pal. Mus. , Taipei, (AL). CAT,
34; KKMH, III. 8*.

Butterflies, fan, attributed, Palace Museum, Peking. Sung-jen hua-
ts'e, A. 21* (att. to Li An-chung); B. VI. 4* (as anon. Sung);
STHN* (as anon. Sung).

LI CH'ENG 李成 , t. Hsien-hsi 咸熙 . B. 919, d. 967, from
Ying-ch'iu, Shantung, painted landscapes. (CP, II, AL, 59.)

Bare trees by a snowy cliff, album leaf, attributed, Nat. Pal. Mus. ,
Taipei, (AL). 300 M. , 62; KKMH, I. 25.

Old pine-trees on a low shore in water, Nat. Pal. Mus. , Taipei, (AL).
300 M. , 63.

Old pine-trees on snowy rocks; a fisherman in a boat, attributed, Nat.
Pal. Mus. , Taipei, (AL). CAT, 17 (att. to Li Ch'eng); CKLTMHC,
II. 9 (as anon. Sung).

Old cedar trees by a swirling stream, Nat. Pal. Mus. , Taipei, (AL).
300 M. , 61 (as Li Ch'eng); CKLTMHC, II. 10 (as anon. Sung);
KKMH, II. 21 (as Li Ch'eng).

Reading the stone tablet, inscribed with the artist's name; figures
by Wang Hsiao, Abe collection, Ōsaka Museum, (AL). CK ku-
tai, 27.

Two fishing boats on a river, fan, attributed, Nat. Pal. Mus., Tai-
pei, (AL, River landscape with two fishing-boats?). KKMH, I.26.
Small wintry grove, short handscroll, attributed, Liao-ning Provin-
cial Museum. Liao-ning, I.22.
Old trees in a wintry grove, album leaf, S.M. Siu collection, Hong
Kong. CK ku-hua, B.37.2.

LI KUNG-LIN 李 公 麟 , t. Po-shih 伯 時 , H. Lung-mien chü-
shih 龍 眠 居 士 . B. 1049, d. 1106, from Shu-ch'eng, Anhui, painted
figures, horses and landscapes. (CP, II, AL, 60-61.)
Illustrations to Chiu ko, Songs of the Nine Spirits, by Ch'ü Yüan, hand-
scroll, signed, (AL). Li Kung-lin, 1-3 (sections); WW, 1964.3.7
(last section, as anon. Sung).
Kuo Tzu-i receiving the homage of the Uighurs, handscroll, signed,
Nat. Pal. Mus., Taipei, (AL). 300 M., 85; CAT 29 (sections);
CKLTMHC, I.33; Li Kung-lin, 4-7.
A great number of horses brought out to pasture, after Wei Yen, long
handscroll, Palace Museum, Peking. (AL). Li Kung-lin, 15-16;
WW, 1961.6.2 (section).
Shan-chuang t'u. Dwelling in the mountains, handscroll, Nat. Pal.
Mus., Taipei, (AL). CH mei-shu, I.
Vimalakīrti seated on the floor of a raised platform, Victor Hauge
collection, Tokyo, (AL). KK-c tzu-liao, 31; Li Kung-lin, 8;
Li-tai jen-wu, 17.
Five tribute horses, handscroll, (AL). CK ku-tai, 38; Li Kung-lin,
9-13.
Lady Kuo-kuo and her sister setting forth on an outing, handscroll,
Nat. Pal. Mus., Taipei. CCAT, pl.97 (section); KKMH, II.36.
The Lotus Society meeting, handscroll, Shanghai Museum. Li-tai
jen-wu, 18 (two sections).
Three men gathered around a large rock on which is placed a tree
branch. Li Kung-lin, 14.

LI SUNG 李 嵩 . From Hangchou, tai-chao in the Painting Academy
c. 1190-1230, did boundary paintings and figures. (CP, II, AL, 62.)
The knick-knack peddlar, fan, signed, dated 1210, Nat. Pal. Mus.,
Taipei. CAT, 50; KKMH, IV.11; NPM Bulletin, I.4.1, 10, 11;
NPM Quarterly, I.2.XXIV.
Knick-knack peddlar, short handscroll, signed, dated 1211, (AL).
WW, 1958.6.3 (section).
A scholar listening to a lady playing a p'i-p'a, Nat. Pal. Mus., Tai-
pei, (AL). CKLTMHC, II.50 (as anon. Sung); KKMH, III.15*
(as Li Sung).

The Lantern Festival, Nat. Pal. Mus., Taipei, (AL). CKLTMHC,
II. 51 (as anon. Sung); KKMH, IV. 10 (as Li Sung).

An arhat seated on a bench and two acolytes, Nat. Pal. Mus., Taipei,
(AL). CH mei-shu, I; CKLTSHH.

Palace scenery; some figures burning incense on a terrace, fan, signed
ch'en Li, Nat. Pal. Mus., Taipei, (AL). CKLTMHC, I. 63.

A palace overlooking a stormy sea, fan, signed, Nat. Pal. Mus., Taipei, (AL). CAT, 51; CKLTMHC, I. 62; NPM Bulletin, II. 3, p. 8.

A view over the West Lake in Hangchou, handscroll, signed, Shanghai
Museum, (AL). Che-chiang, 10; LS Hsi-hu*; TSYMC hua-hsüan,
8.

Boating by plum trees and cliffs, fan, signed, Nat. Pal. Mus., Taipei.
CKLTMHC, II. 89 (as anon. Sung).

Dragon boat, album leaf, signed, Nat. Pal. Mus., Taipei. NPM Bulletin, I. 4. 6.

An imperial audience, album leaf, signed, Nat. Pal. Mus., Taipei.
NPM Bulletin, I. 4. 7.

Flower basket, album leaf, signed, Nat. Pal. Mus., Taipei. NPM
Bulletin, I. 4. 9; II. 6 cover*.

Skeleton puppet show, fan, signed, Palace Museum, Peking. Che-
chiang, 11*; Sung-jen hua-ts'e, A. 58*; B. IV. 10*.

Flower basket, album leaf, signed, Palace Museum, Peking. KKPWY
hua-niao, 11*; Sung-jen hua-ts'e, A. 59*; B. IV. 9*.

Three scholars in a pavilion over water under a misty mountain cliff,
fan, signed, Palace Museum, Peking. Sung-jen hua-ts'e, XV*
(as anon. Sung).

Exchanging New Year's greetings, signed, Nat. Pal. Mus., Taipei.
WW, 1955. 7. 7 (39).

Watching a waterfall under the pines, album leaf, S. M. Siu collection,
Hong Kong. CK ku-hua, B. 38. 6.

An arhat, S. M. Siu collection, Hong Kong. CK ku-hua, B. 29.

LI T'ANG 李 唐 , t. Hsi-ku 晞古 . B. in the 1050's, d. after
1130, from Ho-yang, Honan, tai-chao in the Painting Academy in K'aifeng
and in Hangchou, painted landscapes and figures. (CP, II, AL, 62-63.)

Pine-trees in a rocky valley by a turbulent stream, signed, dated
1124, Nat. Pal. Mus., Taipei, (AL). 300 M., 95; CAT, 36;
CCAT, pl. 99; CH mei-shu, I; CKLTMHC, I. 47; KKMH, III. 2;
TSYMC hua-hsüan, 6.

The virtuous brothers Po I and Shu Ch'i in the wilderness picking
herbs, handscroll, signed, Palace Museum, Peking. (AL).
CK hua, I. 13; CK ku-tai, 42; Li-tai jen-wu, 24; WW, 1960. 7. 4.

The village doctor, Nat. Pal. Mus., Taipei, (AL). 300 M., 99 (as
Li T'ang); CH mei-shu, I (as Li T'ang); CKLTMHC, II. 33 (as

anon. Sung); CKLTSHH (as Li T'ang); KKMH, III. 3 (as Li T'ang).
High mountains and tall trees along a river, handscroll, Nat. Pal.
    Mus. , Taipei, (AL). 300 M. , 98; CAT, 37 (sections); CKLTMHC,
    I. 50.
Storm over snow-covered mountains by a river, Nat. Pal. Mus. , Tai-
    pei, (AL). CKLTMHC, I. 48.
Landscapes of the four seasons, short handscrolls mounted as an al-
    bum, Nat. Pal. Mus. , Taipei, (AL). KKMH, IV. 2.
Clear stream and a hermit fisherman, Nat. Pal. Mus. , Taipei, (AL).
    300 M. , 96; CKLTMHC, I. 51.
River-view in snow, Nat. Pal. Mus. , Taipei, (AL). 300 M. , 97;
    CKLTMHC, I. 49; KKMH, IV. 1.
Six pictures illustrating episodes from the history of Wen, Duke of
    Chin, handscroll, Private collection, New York, (AL). TWSY
    ming-chi, 41-57.
Tending buffaloes, fan, attributed, Palace Museum, Peking, (AL).
    Sung-jen hua-ts'e, A. 80* (as anon. Sung); B. III. 4* (as anon. Sung).
Men conversing in a hall, album leaf, attributed, Palace Museum,
    Peking, (AL). Sung-jen hua-ts'e, A. 90* (as anon. Sung); B. X. 1*
    (as anon. Sung).
Wen-chi returning to China, album leaf, Nat. Pal. Mus. , Taipei.
    CCAT, pl. 132.
Island peak with temples, album leaf, Nat. Pal. Mus. , Taipei.
    CKLTMHC, II. 105 (as anon. Sung).
Boat returning to shore in storm, fan, signed, Palace Museum, Pe-
    king. PM, 3*.
Fishing under a pine-covered cliff, fan, attributed, Liao-ning Pro-
    vincial Museum. Liang Sung, 41* (as anon. Sung); Liao-ning,
    I. 79 (as anon. Sung); Sung-jen hua-ts'e, B. XIX* (as anon. Sung);
    Sung Yüan shan-shui, 11* (as anon. Sung); LT Sung-hu*.
Herdboy leading water buffalo under willow trees, fan, attributed,
    Chang Pe-chin collection. Tien Yin Tang, II. 4*.
Fishermen in a boat, riverside huts and boats, S. M. Siu collection,
    Hong Kong. CK ku-hua, A. 5; B. 17.
Ships anchored at night by a village, album leaf, signed, S. M. Siu
    collection, Hong Kong. CK ku-hua, B. 37. 6.

LI TI 李 迪 . B. c. 1100, d. after 1197, from Hoyang, Honan, a
member of the Painting Academy in K'aifeng and Vice-director of the Academy in Hangchou, painted flowers, bamboo, birds, dogs and landscapes.
(CP, II, AL, 63-64.)
    Two herd-boys on buffaloes returning home through a rain-storm,
        signed and dated 1174, Nat. Pal. Mus. , Taipei, (AL). 300 M. ,

104*; CAT, 40; CKLTMHC, I. 55; KKMH, IV. 5.

Cat, album leaf, signed, dated 1174, Nat. Pal. Mus. , Taipei. CAT, 39.

A winter bird in a snowy tree, signed, dated 1187, Shanghai Museum, (AL). Shang-hai, 3*; WW, 1963. 10. 19.

A hawk chasing a pheasant, a pair of hanging scrolls, signed, dated 1196, Palace Museum, Peking. KKPWY hua-niao, 8*.

A large dog walking with lowered head, album leaf, signed, dated 1197, Palace Museum, Peking, (AL). Sung-jen hua-ts'e, A. 57*; B. II. 10*.

Two chickens, album leaf, signed, dated 1197, Palace Museum, Peking, (AL). KKPWY hua-niao, 9*; Sung hua shih fu, 2*; Sung-jen hua-ts'e, A. 56*; B. II. 9*.

A bird bathing, album leaf, attributed, Nat. Pal. Mus. , Taipei. NPM Bulletin, II. 3. cover*.

A dog among rocks and flowers, album leaf, S. M. Siu collection, Hong Kong. CK ku-hua, B. 38. 3.

LI TS'UNG-HSÜN 李從訓 . From Hangchou, tai-chao in the Painting Academy in both K'aifeng and Hangchou, painted figures, flowers and birds. (CP, II, AL, 64.)

Two pheasants in an old pine by a waterfall, album leaf, signed, S. M. Siu collection, Hong Kong. CK ku-hua, B. 37. 4.

LI TUNG 李東 . Active during the reign of emperor Li-tsung (1225-1264). (H. 4; M. p. 195.)

A fisherman selling fish to a woman in a pavilion along a snowy river, fan, signed, Palace Museum, Peking. LT Hsüeh-chiang*; PM, 4* (as anon. Sung); Sung-jen hua-ts'e, A. 63* (as Li Tung); B. VII. 9* (as Li Tung).

LI WEI 李瑋 , t. Kung-chao 公炤 . From Ch'ien-t'ang, Chekiang, son-in-law of the emperor Jen-tsung (1032-1063), specialized in bamboos. (CP, II, AL 65.)

A bamboo garden with pavilions and figures, signed, Museum of Fine Arts, Boston, (AL). Che-chiang, 5.

LIANG K'AI 梁楷 , h. Feng-tzu 風子 . From Tung-p'ing, Shantung, tai-chao in the Painting Academy in Hangchou c. 1201-1204, left the Academy and devoted himself to Ch'an Buddhism, painted landscapes, Buddhist and Taoist figures. (CP, II, AL, 65-66.)

The top of a bare willow-tree; two birds in flight, fan, signed, Palace Museum, Peking, (AL). KKPWY hua-niao, 10*; PM, 30*; Sung-jen hua-ts'e, A. 60*; B. IX. 5*.

San-kao. Three old scholars under a pine-tree, fan, signed, Palace
Museum, Peking, (AL). Sung-jen hua-ts'e, A. 61*; B. IX. 4*.

An old Immortal in a loose open gown, album leaf, signed, Nat. Pal.
Mus. , Taipei, (AL). 300 M. , 118; CAT, 63; CCAT, pl. 102;
CKLTMHC, I. 61; KKMH, IV. 23; Li-tai jen-wu, 26.

The sixth Ch'an patriarch Hui-neng cutting a bamboo pole, signed,
National Museum, Tokyo, (AL). Li-tai jen-wu, 27.

Four magpies: two flying and two seated on a tree stump, fan, signed,
Palace Museum, Peking. WW, 1966. 4. 39.

Illustrations to events in the lives of eight famous monks, long handscroll, eight paintings of which four are signed, separated by
sections of text, Shanghai Museum. CK ku-tai, 52 (sections);
LK Pa kao-seng*.

T'ao Ch'ien in his garden, signed, S. M. Siu collection, Hong Kong.
CK ku-hua, A. 12; B. 26.

Po I and Shu Ch'i, signed, S. M. Siu collection, Hong Kong. CK ku-
hua, B. 27.

The returning fisherman, signed, S. M. Siu collection, Hong Kong.
CK ku-hua, B. 28.

LIANG SHIH-MIN 梁師閔 or 梁士閔 , t. Hsün-te 循德
From K'aifeng, active in the Hui-tsung reign, governor of Chung-chou,
painted landscapes, specialized in flowers and bamboos. (CP, II, AL,
66.)

River-view in winter, handscroll, signed, Palace Museum, Peking,
(AL). CK ku-tai, 43.

LIN CH'UN 林椿 . From Ch'ien-t'ang, Chekiang, tai-chao in the
Painting Academy c. 1174-1189, painted flowers and birds. (CP, II, AL,
66.)

Ten magpies on a cliff and in a pine-tree, signed, Nat. Pal. Mus. ,
Taipei, (AL). 300 M. , 106.

A bird on a branch of a peach-tree, album leaf, signed, Palace Museum, Peking, (AL). CK ku-tai, 54; KKPWY hua-niao, 7*;
Sung hua shih fu, 1*; Sung-jen hua-ts'e, A. 23*; B. VII. 2*; STHN*.

A pair of peacocks, fan, attributed, Nat. Pal. Mus. , Taipei, (AL).
CKLTMHC, II. 92 (as anon. Sung).

A branch of li-chih tree with fruits, fan, signed, Nat. Pal. Mus. ,
Taipei, (AL). CKLTMHC, I. 64.

Camellia blossoms after snow, fan, attributed, Nat. Pal. Mus. , Taipei. NPM Bulletin, I. 6. cover*.

Grapes and insects, fan, signed, Palace Museum, Peking. KKPWY
hua-niao, 6* (as Lin Ch'un); Sung-jen hua-ts'e, A. 22* (as Lin

Ch'un); B. VIII. 4* (as anon. Sung); STHN* (as Lin Ch'un).

Bird on snowy plum blossoms and bamboo, fan, signed, Palace Museum, Peking. Liang Sung, 15*; Sung-jen hua-ts'e, B. XIII*; STHN*.

Birds on hibiscus and bamboo, handscroll. Che-chiang, 7* (section).

LIU SUNG-NIEN 劉 松 年 . From Ch'ien-t'ang, Chekiang; entered the Painting Academy in the Shun-hsi era (1174-1189); became a tai-chao in the Shao-hsi period (1190-1194); active in the reign of Ning-tsung (1195-1224) painted figures and landscapes. (CP, II, AL, 67-68.)

An arhat leaning against a tree, two monkeys picking fruit for him, signed, dated 1207, Nat. Pal. Mus., Taipei, (AL). CAT, 49; Che-chiang, 9; CKLTMHC, I. 56; WW, 1955. 7. 6 (38).

Drunken monk writing, signed, dated 1210, Nat. Pal. Mus., Taipei. 300 M., 109; CCAT, pl. 100; CKLTMHC, I. 58; KKMH, IV. 8.

Fishermen by cliffs, album leaf, signed, dated 1210, S. M. Siu collection, Hong Kong. CK ku-hua, B. 37. 7.

Two women on a terrace making silk thread, signed, Nat. Pal. Mus., Taipei, (AL). KKMH, III. 13.

A celestial girl offering flowers to a Bodhisattva and some monks, album leaf, seal, Nat. Pal. Mus., Taipei, (AL). 300 M., 110 (as Liu Sung-nien); CKLTMHC, II. 95 (as anon. Sung); NPM Bulletin, I. 4. 4 (as Liu Sung-nien).

Two men and a servant in a pavilion, Nat. Pal. Mus., Taipei, (AL). CKLTMHC, I. 59.

Five scholars on a garden terrace examining books and writings, Nat. Pal. Mus., Taipei, (AL). CH mei-shu, I (as Liu Sung-nien); CKLTMHC, II. 5 (as anon. Sung); CKLTSHH (as Liu Sung-nien); KKMH, III. 14 (as Liu Sung-nien).

The Lan-t'ing gathering, handscroll, (AL). Che-chiang, 8 (section); Li-tai jen-wu, 23 (section).

Three men discussing the Tao under pine-trees, fan, attributed, Palace Museum, Peking, (AL). Sung-jen hua-ts'e, A. 89* (as anon. Sung); B. VII. 4* (as anon. Sung).

Mending clothes, signed, Nat. Pal. Mus., Taipei. KKMH, IV. 9.

Huang Ch'u-p'ing changing stones into sheep, album leaf, signed, Nat. Pal. Mus., Taipei. NPM Bulletin, I. 4. 2, 3.

A lohan seated on a rock, Nat. Pal. Mus., Taipei. CKLTMHC, I. 57.

Landscapes of the four seasons, handscroll, Palace Museum, Peking. CK hua, VIII. 15* (Spring, Autumn); CK ku-tai, 46 (Summer); Ssu-ching*.

Reading the I Ching by an autumn window, fan, signed, Liao-ning Provincial Museum. Liang Sung, 40*; Liao-ning, I. 57; LS-n Ch'iu-ch'uang*; Sung-jen hua-ts'e, B. XVIII*; Sung Yüan shan-shui, 9*.

LIU TS'AI 劉宷 , t. Tao-yüan 道源 or Hung-tao 宏道 . Lived in K'aifeng; active in the reign of Shen-tsung (1068-1085), painted fish. (CP, II, AL, 68.)

> Swimming fish and falling blossoms, handscroll, attributed, Palace Museum, Peking, (AL). CK ku-tai, 36.
>
> Fishes playing among aquatic plants, fan, attributed, Palace Museum, Peking, (AL). Sung-jen hua-ts'e, A. 6* (att. to Liu Ts'ai); B.I. 4* (as anon. Sung).

LIU TSUNG-KU 劉宗古 . From K'aifeng; tai-chao in the Painting Academy during the Hsüan-ho era (1119-1125); still active during the Shao-hsing era (1131-1162); figures. (H. 4; I. 51; J. 2; M. p. 658.)

> Ladies enjoying the moonlight on a terrace, fan, attributed, Palace Museum, Peking. Sung-jen hua-ts'e, A. 10* (att. to Liu Tsung-ku); B. VIII. 8* (as anon. Sung).

LOU KUAN 樓觀 . From Ch'ien-t'ang, Chekiang; chih-hou in the Painting Academy in Hangchou c. 1265-1274, painted landscapes, flowers and birds. (CP, II, AL, 69.)

> River landscape with two moored boats, fan, attributed, National Museum, Tokyo, (AL). Che-chiang, 16*.

LU TSUNG-KUEI 魯宗貴 . From Ch'ien-t'ang, Chekiang; tai-chao in the Painting Academy in Hangchou c. 1228-1233, painted flowers, bamboos, birds and animals. (CP, II, AL, 70.)

> A pheasant and a quail on a rock, signed, Nat. Pal. Mus., Taipei, (AL). Che-chiang, 14; KKMH, IV. 24.
>
> Summer flowers, fan, attributed, Palace Museum, Peking. Sung-jen hua-ts'e, A. 64* (att. to Lu Tsung-kuei); B. X. 9* (as anon. Sung); STHN* (as anon. Sung).
>
> Birds in spring, inscribed with the two characters Ch'ao-hsü 巢虛 , Chang Pe-chin collection. Tien Yin Tang, I. 2.

MA HO-CHIH 馬和之 . From Ch'ien-t'ang, Chekiang; chin-shih in the Shao-hsing era (1131-1162); still active in the reign of Hsiao-tsung, painted landscapes and figures. (CP, II, AL, 71-72.)

> A bay at the foot of misty mountains, album leaf, signed, Nat. Pal. Mus., Taipei, (AL). CH mei-shu, I; KKMH, IV. 3.
>
> A falcon in an old tree by a rock, album leaf, signed, Nat. Pal. Mus., Taipei, (AL). 300 M., 102; CH mei-shu, I; CKLTMHC, I. 40; KKMH, III. 5.
>
> A house-boat under a willow-tree, signed, Nat. Pal. Mus., Taipei, (AL). Che-chiang, 6; CKLTMHC, I. 39; KKMH, III. 4*.

The Red Cliff, handscroll, Palace Museum, Peking, (AL). CK ku-
tai, 49; PM, 22* (section); WW, 1956.1.

A thatched pavilion by the river, fan, attributed, Nat. Pal. Mus.,
Taipei. NPM Bulletin, II.4, cover*.

An illustration to a chapter on filial piety in the Li Chi, Nat. Pal. Mus.,
Taipei. CCAT, pl. 131.

A man sitting on a riverbank listening to autumn sounds in the moonlight, fan, attributed, inscription by Chao Meng-fu, Liao-ning
Provincial Museum. Liang Sung, 8*; Liao-ning, I.54; Sung-jen
hua-ts'e, B. XVIII*; Sung Yüan shan-shui, 2*.

Illustrations to the Twelve Odes of T'ang, handscroll with text between
each painting, Liao-ning Provincial Museum. Liao-ning, I.42-54.

Man in a pavilion under a willow, signed, S.M. Siu collection, Hong
Kong. CK ku-hua, A.9; B.16.

MA HSING-TSU 馬 興 祖 . Son of Ma Fen; tai-chao in the Painting
Academy in Hangchou in the Shao-hsing era (1131-1162). (CP, II, AL, 72.)

A small bird on the stalk of lotus plant and a dragonfly, album leaf,
attributed, Palace Museum, Peking. (AL). Sung-jen hua-ts'e,
A.18* (att. to Ma Hsing-tsu); B.IV.2* (as anon. Sung); STHN*
(as anon. Sung).

MA K'UEI 馬 逵 . Son of Ma Shih-jung; active c. 1180-1220, painted
landscapes, figures, flowers and birds. (CP, II, AL, 72.)

Boating by a willow bank, fan, attributed, Nat. Pal. Mus., Taipei.
KKMH, IV.16.

MA LIN 馬 麟 . Son of Ma Yüan, d. after 1246; chih-hou in the Painting Academy, painted landscapes, flowers and birds. (CP, II, AL, 73-74.)

Two branches of a blossoming plum-tree, signed, poem by Yang Mei-
tzu, her seal dated 1216, Palace Museum, Peking, (AL). KKPWY
hua-niao, 12*; NPM Bulletin, II.2, p. 14.

A garden pavilion and blossoming trees, fan, signed, Nat. Pal. Mus.,
Taipei, (AL). CAT, 61*; CKLTMHC, I.72; KKMH, III.25; NPM
Quarterly, I.2. pl. XXX*.

Listening to the wind in the pine-trees, signed, Nat. Pal. Mus.,
Taipei, (AL). 300 M., 117; CAT, 60; CKLTMHC, I.71; KKMH,
III.24.

An orchid plant, fan, attributed, Palace Museum, Peking, (AL). Sung-
jen hua-ts'e, A.84* (as anon. Sung); B.VII.7* (as anon. Sung).

Two birds on the branch of a thorny shrub in front of a trunk in snow,
album leaf, signed, inscribed by Yang Mei-tzu, Nat. Pal. Mus.,
Taipei, (AL). KKMH, IV.22.

Fragrant spring after rain, album leaf, signed, Nat. Pal. Mus. , Taipei, (AL). CAT, 59; KKMH, IV. 20; NPM Bulletin, II. 2, p. 13.

Bamboo and plum blossoms reflected in a stream, album leaf, attributed, Nat. Pal. Mus. , Taipei. CCAT, pl. 102 (as Ma Lin); CH
mei-shu, I (as Ma Lin); CKLTMHC, II. 93 (as anon. Sung); KKMH,
IV. 21* (as Ma Lin).

Three Taoist divinities on an excursion, Nat. Pal. Mus. , Taipei.
CKLTMHC, II. 47 (as anon. Sung).

Two men standing in front of a waterfall, signed, Palace Museum,
Peking. CK hua, XII. 14; PM, 1*.

Peacocks and red plum blossoms, album leaf, signed Ma ___, attributed to Ma Lin, Palace Museum, Peking. KKPWY hua-niao, 5*
(as anon. Sung); Sung-jen hua-ts'e, A. 53* (att. to Ma Lin); B. IX. 7*
(as anon. Sung).

Oranges, fan, signed, Palace Museum, Peking. Sung-jen hua-ts'e,
A. 52*; B. X. 2*; STHN*.

A willow-lined lake and river scene, handscroll, signed, Liao-ning
Provincial Museum. Liao-ning, I. 58-62.

Scholar with a staff and a servant in a landscape, fan, signed, Shanghai Museum. Liang Sung, 23* (as Ma Lin); Sung-jen hua-ts'e,
B. XIII* (as anon. Sung).

Cottages under bare trees, snowy hills, fan, attributed, Chang Pe-
chin collection. Tien Yin Tang, II. 9.

An egret on a snowy tree, album leaf, signed, S. M. Siu collection,
Hong Kong. CK ku-hua, B. 37. 12.

MA SHIH-JUNG　馬世榮　. Son of Ma Hsing-tsu; tai-chao in the Painting Academy in the Shao-hsing era (1131-1162), painted landscapes, figures,
flowers and birds. (CP, II, AL, 74.)

Landscape with high pavilions, fan, attributed, Palace Museum, Peking, (AL). Sung-jen hua-ts'e, A. 32* (att. to Ma Shih-jung);
B. X. 5* (as anon. Sung).

MA YÜAN　馬遠 , t. Ch'in-shan　欽山 . From Ho-chung, Shansi;
son of Ma Shih-jung; tai-chao in the Painting Academy in the Shao-hsi
era (1190-1194); still active at the beginning of the emperor Li-tsung's
reign (1225-1264). (CP, II, AL, 74-76.)

A man returning over a snow-covered field, album leaf, signed, Nat.
Pal. Mus. , Taipei, (AL). CAT, 53; CCAT, pl. 101; KKMH,
IV. 15.

Spring time in the mountains, album leaf, signed, poem by Yang Mei-
tzu, Nat. Pal. Mus. , Taipei, (AL). 300 M. , 113; CAT, 52;
CKLTMHC, I. 67; KKMH, III. 19; NPM Bulletin, II. 2, p. 11.

Portrait of Confucius, album leaf, signed, Palace Museum, Peking, (AL). Liang Sung, 21*; Sung-jen hua-ts'e, B. XIX. *.

Wild geese over the peaks in autumn, fan, attributed, Nat. Pal. Mus., Taipei, (AL). KKMH, III. 21.

Pine-trees in the wind on a temple terrace by a river, album leaf, signed, Nat. Pal. Mus., Taipei, (AL). KKMH, III. 20.

Two men under pine-trees on a terrace overlooking a misty valley, Nat. Pal. Mus., Taipei, (AL). CKLTMHC, II. 42 (as anon. Sung).

Mountains and tall pine-trees by a cottage in snow, signed, Nat. Pal. Mus., Taipei, (AL). CKLTMHC, II. 44 (as anon. Sung).

An old hermit asleep in a boat in autumn, artist's seal, Nat. Pal. Mus., Taipei, (AL). 300 M., 112; MY/HK, 6.

A feast of lanterns, signed, colophon by Ch'ien-lung, Nat. Pal. Mus., Taipei, (AL). 300 M., 111; CH mei-shu, I; CKLTMHC, I. 65; KKMH, IV. 13; WW, 1960. 7. 30 (section).

A feast of lanterns, attributed, Nat. Pal. Mus., Taipei, (AL). CAT, 56 (as anon. Sung); KKMH, III. 18 (as Ma Yüan); NPM Bulletin, II. 2, inside cover (as Ma Yüan).

Three herons on the rocks by a river in winter, signed, Nat. Pal. Mus., Taipei, (AL). CKLTMHC, I. 66.

Looking at the moon, Nat. Pal. Mus., Taipei, (AL). CH mei-shu, I; CKLTSHH.

A man on a projecting cliff drinking wine in the moonlit night, attributed, Nat. Pal. Mus., Taipei, (AL). KKMH, IV. 12.

Twenty views of billowing water, handscroll, attributed, Palace Museum, Peking, (AL). CK hua, I. 14; II. 3; MY Shui.

Ta ko t'u. Peasants singing as they return from their work, signed, Palace Museum, Peking, (AL). CK hua X. 12; CK ku-tai, 50; MY/HK, 1; WW, 1960. 7. 3.

Ducks on the water below a blossoming tree, album leaf, signed, Palace Museum, Peking, (AL). Sung-jen hua-ts'e, A. 44* (as Ma Yüan); B. IV. 7* (as anon. Sung).

The three old men on the mountainside, album leaf (?), attributed, (AL). MY/HK, 3.

Mountains along a river in snow and mist, handscroll, inscription by Empress Yang, (AL). MY/HK, 4-5.

An angler on a wintry lake, handscroll, National Museum, Tokyo, (AL). MY/HK, 2.

Ssu hao. The Four Old Recluses in the Shang mountains, handscroll, signed, Art Museum, Cincinnati, (AL). TWSY ming-chi, 83-85.

Apricot blossoms, album leaf, signed, Nat. Pal. Mus., Taipei. CAT, 54; KKMH, IV. 14; NPM Bulletin, II. 2, p. 6.

Playing the lute in moonlight, attributed, Nat. Pal. Mus., Taipei. CAT, 55; KKMH, III. 17.

Man in pavilion in snow, servant walking along riverside under plum
tree, album leaf, attributed, Nat. Pal. Mus., Taipei. CKLTMHC,
II. 85 (as anon. Sung).

White roses, album leaf, signed, Palace Museum, Peking. Sung-jen
hua-ts'e, A. 45*; B. IV. 8*.

Burning incense by a mountain brook, fan, attributed, Palace Museum,
Peking. CK shu-hua, I, cover* (as Ma Yüan); Sung-jen hua-ts'e,
A. 46* (att. to Ma Yüan); B. VII. 10* (as anon. Sung).

Scholar and servant on a terrace, a flying crane, fan, signed, Palace
Museum, Peking. Sung-jen hua-ts'e, B. XIII*.

Pavilion among willow trees on a moonlit night, fan, signed, Shanghai
Museum. Liang Sung, 22*; Sung-jen hua-hsüan, 1*; Sung-jen
hua-ts'e, B. XIV*; STSS*.

Scholar leaning on a pine over a pool, a servant with a ch'in, signed,
Shanghai Museum. Shang-hai, 4*; TSYMC hua-hsüan, 9.

Composing poetry on a spring outing, handscroll, attributed, Nelson
Gallery of Art, Kansas City. TWSY ming-chi, 86-90 (erroneously
titled "Elegant Gathering in the Western Garden").

Scholar and servant approaching a bridge, a homestead among bamboo,
fan, signed, Chang Pe-chin collection. Tien Yin Tang, II. 6.

A man on a mountain terrace playing a lute and looking at a waterfall,
signed, S. M. Siu collection, Hong Kong. CK ku-hua, A. 6; B. 22.

Three friends of winter, signed, S. M. Siu collection, Hong Kong. CK
ku-hua, A. 7; B. 23.

Passing the summer in a pavilion in a bamboo grove, album leaf,
signed, S. M. Siu collection, Hong Kong. CK ku-hua, B. 37. 9.

Man and boy in a pavilion by a lotus pond, album leaf, signed. Li-tai
jen-wu, 25.

Man in a pavilion by the river, snow scene. MY/HK, 7.

MAO I 毛益 . From K'un-shan, Kiangsu; son of Mao Sung; tai-chao
in the Painting Academy in the Ch'ien-tao era (1165-1173), painted flowers,
birds, animals, especially cats and dogs. (CP, II, AL, 76-77.)

Chickens in a garden with day lilies and rocks, album leaf, S. M. Siu
collection, Hong Kong. CK ku-hua, B. 38. 8.

MI FEI 米芾 , originally Mi Fu 米黻 , t. Yüan-chang 元章 ,
h. Nan-kung 南宮 , Lu-men chü-shih 鹿門居士 , Hsiang-
yang man-shih 襄陽漫士 , Hai-yüeh wai-shih 海嶽外史 .
B. 1051, d. 1107; from Hsiang-yang, Hupeh, painted landscapes; author
of Hua shih. (CP, II, AL, 77.)

Misty mountains, signed, dated 1078, S. M. Siu collection, Hong Kong.
CK ku-hua, A. 3; B. 13.

Verdant mountains and pine-trees rising through the mist, signed,
Nat. Pal. Mus., Taipei, (AL). 300 M., 88*; CAT, 28; CH mei-
shu, I; KKMH, I.40.

MI YU-JEN 米友仁 , t. Yüan-hui 元暉 . B. 1074, d. 1153; son of
Mi Fei; also known by his boyhood name Hu-erh 虎兒 , painted landscapes (CP, II, AL, 78.)

Rocks in mist by a stream, album leaf, inscription dated 1134, Abe
collection, Ōsaka Museum, (AL). MF/MY-j, 10.

Mountains in clouds and mist, handscroll, done before 1135, Nat. Pal.
Mus., Taipei. CAT, 35 (section); CKLTMHC, I.38.

Cloudy mountains, signed, dated 1140, S.M. Siu collection, Hong Kong.
CK ku-hua, B.18.

Cloudy mountains, ink play, handscroll, signed, Palace Museum, Peking. MF/MY-j, 7-8; WW, 1961.6.21.

Strange views of the Hsiao and Hsiang, trees on a shore, low mountains
in the background, handscroll, attributed, Palace Museum, Peking. CK ku-tai, 41 (section); MF/MY-j, 3-6; WW, 1961.6.3
(section).

Cloudy mountains and river, handscroll. MF/MY-j, 9; TWSY ming-
chi, 58.

Fishermen in a mountain river, handscroll. TWSY ming-chi, 59-61.

MOU I 牟益 , t. Te-hsin 德新 and Te-ts'ai 德彩 . B. 1178,
d. after 1240, painted figures. (CP, II, AL, 78.)

Tao-i t'u. Preparing clothes for warriors, handscroll, inscribed and
dated 1240, Nat. Pal. Mus., Taipei, (AL). 300 M., 119; CAT,
62 (sections); CKLTMHC, I.73.

MU-CH'I 牧谿, or 牧溪 , h. of the monk Fa-ch'ang 法常 .
B. 1177, d. 1239; from Szechuan, lived near Hangchou; pupil of the priest
Wu-chun (d. 1249), painted landscapes, figures, flowers, birds and ani-
mals. (CP, II, AL, 78-80.)

Various kinds of birds, vegetables and flowers, handscroll, signed,
dated 1265, Nat. Pal. Mus., Taipei, (AL). 300 M., 120-123;
CKLTMHC, I.74.

An arhat in meditation encircled by a snake, artist's seal, Seikadō,
(AL). Li-tai jen-wu, 28.

A monkey with her baby on a pine branch, a crane in a bamboo grove,
two of the set of three paintings in Daitoku-ji, signed, (AL). WW,
1965.8, pls. 5-6.

Fruits, birds and fish, handscroll, colophon by Shen Chou, Palace
Museum, Peking. WW, 1964.3.4-6.

P'U-AN 樸菴 . Unidentified.
    Two men running from a boat toward trees in rain, album leaf, sign-
        ed, Shanghai Museum. Liang Sung, 38*; Sung-jen hua-ts'e,
        B. XVII*.

SSU-MA HUAI 司馬槐 , t. Tuan-heng 端衡 . Active during the
Shao-hsing era (1131-1162); son of Ssu-ma Kuang. (M. p. 70.)
    Bare trees on a river bank, handscroll. TWSY ming-chi, 62-64.

SU CH'UO 蘇焯 . Son of Su Han-ch'en; tai-chao in the Painting Academy during the Lung-hsing era (1163-1164); Buddhist and Taoist figures.
(H. 4; I. 51; J. 4; M. p. 731.)
    Two sheep on a hill, album leaf, signed, S. M. Siu collection, Hong
        Kong. CK ku-hua, B. 38. 7.

SU HAN-CH'EN 蘇漢臣 . From K'aifeng; tai-chao in the Painting
Academy in the reign of emperor Hui-tsung (1101-1125); still active at the
beginning of Hsiao-tsung's reign (c. 1163), painted figures, especially
children. (CP, II, AL, 80-81.)
    A peddler with a wheel-barrow and six children playing together,
        attributed, Nat. Pal. Mus., Taipei, (AL). CKLTMHC, I. 45;
        KKMH, III. 10.
    The Dragon-boat Festival, five children with masks at play, Nat. Pal.
        Mus., Taipei, (AL). CKLTMHC, I. 46.
    Two small children in a garden playing with crickets, Nat. Pal. Mus.,
        Taipei, (AL). 300 M., 108; CAT, 41; CCAT, pl. 14*; CH mei-
        shu, I; CK ku-tai, 40; CKLTMHC, I. 44; CKLTSHH; KKMH, IV. 6.
    The hundred children enjoying spring, fan, signed, Palace Museum,
        Peking, (AL). Sung-jen hua-ts'e, A. 85* (as anon. Sung); B. I. 7*
        (as anon. Sung).
    Ladies looking at the moon under wu-t'ung trees, fan, attributed, Pal-
        ace Museum, Peking, (AL). Sung-jen hua-ts'e, A. 76* (as anon.
        Sung); B. VIII. 6* (as anon. Sung).
    Six gentlemen playing football, fan, attributed, Nat. Pal. Mus., Tai-
        pei. KKMH, IV. 7*.
    Children playing, one chasing butterflies, one holding a fan, album
        leaf, signed, Tientsin Art Museum. I-yüan chi-chin, 2* (as anon.
        Sung); Liang Sung, 7* (as Su Han-ch'en); Sung-jen hua-ts'e, B.XVI*
        (as anon. Sung).
    Children at play with hobby-horse and lotus leaf, fan, attributed, Chang
        Pe-chin collection. Tien Yin Tang, II. 8*.

SU SHIH 蘇軾 , t. Tzu-chan 子瞻 , h. Tung-p'o chü-shih 東坡居士 .
B. 1036, d. 1101; from Mei-shan, Szechuan; official, poet, calligrapher,

painter and art critic. (CP, II, AL, 81.)

>A twisted old tree and some bamboo shoots by a large stone, hand-scroll, attributed to Su Shih by Liu Liang-tso, (AL). CK ku-tai, 37; Wen T'ung Su Shih, 2.
>Dry tree, bamboo and stone, handscroll. WW, 1965.8. pl.3.

TS'UI CH'ÜEH 崔慤 , t. Tzu-chung 子中 . Brother of Ts'ui Po; active during the second half of the 11th century, painted flowers and birds. (CP, II, AL, 83.)

>Two quail by rocks, S.M. Siu collection, Hong Kong. CK ku-hua, B.11.

TS'UI PO 崔白 , t. Tzu-hsi 子西 . From Hao-liang, Anhui; i-hsüeh in the Painting Academy at the beginning of the Hsi-ning era (1068-1077), specialized in birds and flowers, (CP, II, AL, 83-84.)

>Two magpies in a wind-swept tree and a rabbit, signed and dated 1061, Nat. Pal. Mus., Taipei, (AL). 300 M., 81; CAT, 23*; CCAT, pl. 13*; CKLTMHC, I.29; KKMH, II.33; WW, 1955.6.13.
>A goose and some reeds on a low shore, signed, Nat. Pal. Mus., Taipei, (AL). 300 M., 80* (as Ts'ui Po); CKLTMHC, II.22 (as anon. Sung).
>A wild goose resting on a rushy beach, attributed, Nat. Pal. Mus., Taipei, (AL). CKLTMHC, II.21 (as anon. Sung); KKMH, I.37* (as Ts'ui Po).
>A heron and bamboos in wind, signed, Nat. Pal. Mus., Taipei, (AL). CH mei-shu, I; CKLTMHC, I.28; CKLTSHH.
>Seven sparrows on a dry branch and one descending from the air, handscroll, signed, Palace Museum, Peking, (AL). CK hua, XIV.12-13; CK ku-tai, 32; Han-ch'üeh; WW, 1956.1.
>Bamboo and quail, signed, S.M. Siu collection, Hong Kong. CK ku-hua, B.10.

WANG CHÜ-CHENG 王居正 , also known by the name Han-ko 憨哥 . From Ho-tung, Shansi; active probably about the middle of the 11th century, painted figures. (CP, II, AL, 84.)

>A woman spinning thread assisted by a man-servant, handscroll, Chang Ta-ch'ien collection, (AL). Li-tai jen-wu, 16; WW, 1961.2.3.

WANG HSI-MENG 王希孟 . Active in the Hsüan-ho period (1119-1125) in the Imperial Academy; died at the age of twenty. (CP, II, AL, 84.)

>A thousand li of rivers and mountains, handscroll, signed, painted when the artist was eighteen years old, Palace Museum, Peking, (AL). CK ku-tai, 44 (two sections).

WANG HSIAO 王曉 . From Ssu-chou, Anhui; active during the second
half of the 10th century, painted figures, flowers and birds. (CP, II, AL,
84.)
>   Reading a stone tablet. The figures in Li Ch'eng's landscape, Abe
>   collection, Ōsaka Museum, (AL). CK ku-tai, 27.

WANG NING 王凝 . From Chiang-nan; 11th century; tai-chao in the
Painting Academy, painted birds and flowers. (CP, II, AL, 85.)
>   A mother hen walking with some chickens on its back, signed, Nat.
>   Pal. Mus., Taipei, (AL). 300 M., 74*; KKMH, II.28.

WANG SHEN 王詵 , t. Chin-ch'ing 晉卿 . From T'ai-yüan,
Shansi; active in the second half of the 11th century; son-in-law of the
emperor Ying-tsung, painted landscapes. (CP, II, AL, 85-86.)
>   The Land of the Immortals, handscroll, signed, dated 1064 or 1124,
>   Nat. Pal. Mus., Taipei, (AL). 300 M., 86; CAT, 30 (sections);
>   CKLTMHC, I.32.
>   Fishermen's village under snow, handscroll, Palace Museum, Peking,
>   (AL). CK hua, I.5-11; WW, 1961.6.2-3.
>   Dense fog over the river, handscroll, attributed, Shanghai Museum,
>   (AL). WW, 1962.12.5 (section).
>   Boating on a lotus lake, fan, attributed, Palace Museum, Peking (AL).
>   Sung-jen hua-ts'e, B.XV* (as anon. Sung).
>   Autumn in the valley of the Yellow River, section of a handscroll,
>   usually att. to Kuo Hsi, Freer Gallery of Art, Washington, D.C.,
>   (AL, Kuo Hsi). Kuo Hsi, 5-10 (as Kuo Hsi); TWSY ming-chi,
>   15-20 (as Wang Shen).
>   Garden and two-storied pavilion, two ladies on the balcony, album
>   leaf, attributed, Nat. Pal. Mus., Taipei. CKLTMHC, II.90
>   (as anon. Sung).
>   A man in a pavilion on a river bank, misty mountains, fan, attributed,
>   Liao-ning Provincial Museum. Liang Sung, 17* (as anon. Sung);
>   Liao-ning, I.76 (as anon. Sung); Sung-jen hua-ts'e, B.XVIII* (as
>   anon. Sung); Sung Yüan shan-shui, 6* (as anon. Sung); WS Yü-lou*.
>   A parrot on a tree, signed, S.M. Siu collection, Hong Kong. CK ku-
>   hua, B.12.

WANG T'ING-YÜN 王庭筠 , t. Tzu-tuan 子端 , h. Huang-hua
shan-jen 黃華山人 . B. 1151, d. 1202; from Ho-tung, Shansi;
nephew of Mi Fei; a Han-lin member under the Chin dynasty, painted landscapes, bamboos and old trees. (CP, II, AL, 86.)
>   Four stalks of bamboo, signed, dated 1194, S.M. Siu collection, Hong
>   Kong. CK ku-hua, A.10; B.32.
>   A tree trunk and a bamboo, handscroll, colophon by the painter, Fujii
>   Yūrinkan, Kyōto, (AL). NPM Quarterly, I.4, pl. 3.

WEN 溫 , usually called Tzu Wen 子溫 , t. Chung-yen 仲言 , h. Jih-kuan 日觀 and Chih-kuei-tzu 知歸子 . From Hua-t'ing, Kiangsu; active late 13th century; lived as a monk in the Ma-nao temple near Hangchou, specialized in grapevines. (CP, II, AL, 86.)

> Grapevine, signed, dated 1303, S. M. Siu collection, Hong Kong. CK ku-hua, A. 11; B. 30.

WEN T'UNG 文同 , t. Yü-k'o 與可 , h. Chin-chiang tao-jen 錦江道人 , Hsiao-hsiao hsien-sheng 笑笑先生 and Shih-shih hsien-sheng 石室先生 . B. 1018, d. 1079; from Tzu-t'ung, Szechuan; served as magistrate of Hu-chou, Chekiang, hence known as Wen Hu-chou 文湖州 , poet, calligrapher, painted bamboo. (CP, II, AL, 87.)

> A branch of bamboo, seals of the painter, Nat. Pal. Mus., Taipei, (AL). 300 M., 83; CAT, 27; CKLTMHC, I. 31; KKMH, I. 38; NPM Quarterly, I. 4, pl. 2; Wen T'ung Su Shih, 1.
> A bamboo branch bent in a sharp angle, album leaf, signed, Nat. Pal. Mus., Taipei, (AL). 300 M., 84; KKMH, II. 34.
> Ink bamboo, handscroll, signed. WW, 1965. 8, pl. 4.

WU PING 吳炳 . From Pi-ling (Wu-chin), Kiangsu; tai-chao in the Painting Academy in the reign of Kuang-tsung (1190-1194), painted flowers and birds. (CP, II, AL, 87.)

> Insects and butterflies on grasses, album leaf, attributed, Nat. Pal. Mus., Taipei, (AL, Butterflies among tall grass?). CKLTMHC, II. 103 (as anon. Sung).
> Lotus blossom on the water, fan, attributed, Palace Museum, Peking. KKPWY hua-niao, 13* (as anon. Sung); PM, 36* (as anon. Sung); Sung-jen hua-ts'e, A. 20* (att. to Wu Ping); B. I. 9* (as anon. Sung); STHN* (as anon. Sung).

WU TSUNG-YÜAN 武宗元 , originally Tsung-tao 宗道 , h. Tsung-chih 總之 . D. 1050, from Pai-po, Honan, painted Buddhist and Taoist figures. (CP, II, AL, 88.)

> The celestial rulers of Taoism and their attendants in a long procession, handscroll, C. C. Wang collection, New York, (AL). CK ku-tai, 31 (section); T'ang-tai jen-wu, p. 25 (section); WW, 1956. 2. 54-55 (section).
> The celestial rulers of Taoism and their attendants in a long procession, handscroll, ex-Hsü collection, Peking, (AL). Li-tai jen-wu, 15 (three sections).

WU YÜAN-CHIH 武元直 , t. Shan-fu 善夫 . From Pei-p'ing, active during the Ming-ch'ang era (1190-1196) of the Chin State; painted landscapes. (H. 4; I. 52; M. p. 223.)

Illustration to Su Tung-p'o's <u>fu</u>-poem The Red Cliff, handscroll, formerly att. to Chu Jui, now given to Wu Yüan-chih, Nat. Pal.
Mus., Taipei, (AL, Chu Jui). 300 M., 132 (as Wu Yüan-chih);
CAT, 46 (sections, att. to Wu Yüan-chih); CKLTMHC, II.2 (as
anon. Sung).

EMPRESS YANG 楊后 , Yang Mei-tzu 楊妹子 . B. 1162, d. 1232,
consort of Emperor Ning-tsung. See: Chiang Chao-shen, "The Identity of
Yang Mei-tzu and the Paintings of Ma Yüan", <u>The National Palace Museum
Bulletin</u>, vol. II, no. 2 (May 1967) pp. 1-15; no. 3 (July 1967) pp. 8-13.
  Two orioles on branches of cherry tree, album leaf, seal dated 1213,
    inscribed. TSYMC hua-hsüan, 10*.

YANG PU-CHIH 楊補之 ; t. Wu-chiu 無咎 , h. T'ao-ch'an lao-
jen 逃禪老人 and Ch'ing-i ch'ang-che 清夷長者 . B. 1097,
d. 1169; from Nan-ch'ang, Kiangsi,. painted plum blossoms. (CP, II, AL,
88.)
  Ink plum blossoms, signed, dated 1158, S.M. Siu collection, Hong
    Kong. CK ku-hua, B.19.
  A spray of bamboo, album leaf, colophons, Nat. Pal. Mus., Taipei.
    300 M., 93; CKLTMHC, I.41; KKMH, II.39.
  Plum blossoms and bamboo in snow, handscroll, numerous colophons
    from Yüan dynasty on, Palace Museum, Peking. YW-c Hsüeh-mei.
  Ink plum blossoms, fan, signed, Tientsin Art Museum. Liang Sung,
    6*; Sung-jen hua-ts'e, B.XIX*.
  Four plum blossom studies, handscroll. CK ku-tai, 48.

YAO YÜEH-HUA 姚月華 . A woman; painted flowers, birds and animals. (I.52.)
  Chrysanthemums in a vase, fan, attributed, poem by Emperor Ning-
    tsung, Palace Museum, Peking. Sung-jen hua-ts'e, A.54* (att.
    to Yao Yüeh-hua); B.IX.10* (as anon. Sung).

YANG WEI 楊威 . From Chiang-chou, Szechuan, 11th century; painted farm scenes. (G.3; I.51; M. p. 582.)
  Peasants at work, fan, attributed, Palace Museum, Peking. Sung-jen
    hua-ts'e, A.9* (att. to Yang Wei);·B.VI.1* (as anon. Sung).

YEN SU 燕肅 , t. Mu-chih 穆之 . D. 1040; from I-tu, Shantung;
also known as Yen Lung-t'u because of his service in the Lung-t'u Pavilion; President of the Board of Rites in the reign of the emperor Chen-
tsung (998-1022), painted landscapes. (CP, II, AL, 89.)
  Mountains in snow along a river, attributed, Nat. Pal. Mus., Taipei,
    (AL). 300 M., 82.

YEN TZ'U-P'ING 閻次平. Son of the painter Yen Chung; entered the Painting Academy c. 1164, became a <u>chih-hou</u> and was still active in 1181, painted landscapes, specialized in water-buffaloes. (CP, II, AL, 89.)

> Landscape with water and pavilion, know as The four contentments, Nat. Pal. Mus., Taipei, (AL). 300 M., 105.
>
> A homestead on a rocky shore among large pine-trees, fan, signed, Nat. Pal. Mus., Taipei, (AL). CKLTMHC, II.77 (as anon. Sung); KKMH, III.11 (as Yen Tz'u-p'ing).
>
> Herding buffalo, four album leaves (?), Nanking Museum. CK hua, XIX.16-17.

YEN TZ'U-YÜ 閻次于 . Younger brother of Yen Tz'u-p'ing; <u>chih-hou</u> in the Painting Academy c. 1164, painted landscapes. (CP, II, AL, 90.)

> A promontory with cottages and trees, album leaf, signed, Freer Gallery of Art, Washington, D.C. (35.10), (AL). TWSY ming-chi, 82.

Paintings by anonymous artists attributed to the Sung Period

Taoist and Buddhist

White-robed Kuanyin seated on a bench before a screen, Nat. Pal. Mus., Taipei, (AL). CKLTMHC, II.68.

Sakyamuni Buddha on a pedestal, Nat. Pal. Mus., Taipei, (AL). CAT, 66; CKLTMHC, II.48.

A sea deity listening to a discourse, Nat. Pal. Mus., Taipei. 300 M., 107 (as Chao Po-chü); CKLTMHC, II.37 (as anon. Sung).

Three Taoist divinities on an excursion, att. to Ma Lin, Nat. Pal. Mus., Taipei. CKLTMHC, II.47 (as anon. Sung).

Vimalakīrti, Nat. Pal. Mus., Taipei. 300 M., 141.

Thousand-armed Kuanyin, Nat. Pal. Mus., Taipei. CAT, 65.

A Bodhisattva, Chang Pe-chin collection. Tien Yin Tang, I.7.

Figure Compositions and Portraits

Scholars occupied at their writing-desks on a garden terrace, Nat. Pal. Mus., Taipei, (AL). CKLTMHC, II.34; KKMH, IV.32.

Portrait of Lu Chih (754-805), Nat. Pal. Mus., Taipei, (AL). KKMH, IV.37.

A lady accompanied by three servants "washing the moon", Nat. Pal. Mus., Taipei, (AL). CH mei-shu, I; CKLTMHC, I.14; CKLTSHH; KKMH, I.23* (all as anon. Five Dyn.).

Seven small children picking dates, Nat. Pal. Mus., Taipei, (AL).
CKLTMHC, II.26.

Breaking the balustrade, Nat. Pal. Mus., Taipei, (AL). 300 M.,
134*; CAT, 44; CCAT, pl. 104; CKLTMHC, II.31; KKMH, IV.
39; WW, 1955.7.19 (41).

Refusing the seat, Nat. Pal. Mus., Taipei, (AL). 300 M., 135; CH
mei-shu, I; CKLTMHC, II.32; CKLTSHH; KKMH, III.42.

Palace musicians, Nat. Pal. Mus., Taipei, (AL; also listed as Palace ladies seated around a table making music under anon. before Sung). 300 M., 204* (as anon. Yüan); CAT, 10 (as anon.
Five Dyn.); CCAT, pl. 12 (as anon. Five Dyn.); CKLTMHC, II.15
(as anon. Sung); KKMH, I.22 (as anon. Five Dyn.); WW, 1955.7.
8 (40) (as anon. Sung).

Four pictures representing the Eighteen Scholars of the T'ang Dynasty,
Nat. Pal. Mus., Taipei, (AL). CKLTMHC, II.63, 64, 65, 66.

Two children playing with a cat in a garden, Nat. Pal. Mus., Taipei,
(AL). CKLTMHC, II.27.

Ts'ai Wen-chi returning to China, fan, (AL). WW. 1959.5.3.

Wen-chi's captivity in Mongolia and her return to China, Museum of
Fine Arts, Boston, (AL). WW, 1959.6.35 (street scene).

Study of classics, album leaf, Nat. Pal. Mus., Taipei, (AL, Chan
Tzu-ch'ien). 300 M., 34 (as anon. T'ang in style of Chan Tzu-
ch'ien); CKLTMHC, II.71 (as anon. Sung).

Two ladies seated on the ground in the act of writing a poem, album
leaf, Nat. Pal. Mus., Taipei, (AL, Chou Fang). CKLTMHC,
II.70 (as anon. Sung).

Two ladies playing double-sixes, handscroll, Freer Gallery of Art,
Washington, D.C., (39.37), (AL, Chou Fang). TWSY ming-chi,
9 (as anon. N. Sung).

Copy of Ku K'ai-chih's Nymph of the Lo River, handscroll, Palace
Museum, Peking, (AL, Ku K'ai-chih). CK ku-tai, 5 (two sections,
as Ku K'ai-chih); Ku K'ai-chih, 25-26 (two sections, as Ku K'ai-
chih); KK-c tzu-liao, 10-26 (as an anon. copy); KK-c yen-chiu,
1 (as Ku K'ai-chih); Li-tai jen-wu, 2 (two sections, as Ku K'ai-
chih); WW, 1958.6.21 (section, as anon. Sung copy).

Copy of Ku K'ai-chih's Nymph of the Lo River, handscroll, Liao-ning
Provincial Museum. KK-c tzu-liao, 27-29 (three sections, as an
anon. copy); KK-c yen-chiu, 2 (five sections, as Ku K'ai-chih);
Liao-ning, I.1-12 (as Ku K'ai-chih in caption, anon. Sung copy
in notes); WW, 1961.6. cover (section, as anon. Sung copy).

Copy of Ku K'ai-chih's Admonitions of the Instructress to the Ladies
of the Palace, handscroll, Palace Museum, Peking. KK-c yen-
chiu, 5 (seven sections, as Ku K'ai-chih); WW, 1961.6.8-9
(three sections, as anon. Sung copy).

Copy of Ku K'ai-chih's <u>Lieh-nü t'u</u>, four groups of famous women, handscroll, Palace Museum, Peking, (AL, Ku K'ai-chih). Ku K'ai-chih, 11-24 (as anon. Sung copy); KK-c tzu-liao, 35-37 (three sections, as anon. Sung copy); KK-c yen-chiu, 6 (six sections, as Ku K'ai-chih); Li-tai jen-wu, 3 (as Ku K'ai-chih); WW, 1958. 6. 22-24 (sections, as anon. Sung copy).

Copy of Ku K'ai-chih's making a <u>ch'in</u>, handscroll, Palace Museum, Peking. KK-c tzu-liao, 38 (one section, as anon. Sung copy).

A literary meeting, Nat. Pal. Mus. , Taipei, (AL, Ch'iu Wen-po). 300 M. , 56 (as Ch'iu Wen-po); CKLTMHC, II. 35 (as anon. Sung); KKMH, II. 18 (as Ch'iu Wen-po).

Three women washing children in tubs, fan, Freer Gallery of Art, Washington, D. C. (35. 8), (AL, Chou Wen-chü). TWSY ming-chi, 91 (as anon. S. Sung).

A fairy riding on a flying feng-bird, fan, Palace Museum, Peking (AL, Chou Wen-chü). PM, 23* (as anon. Sung); Sung hua shih fu, 4* (as anon. Sung); Sung-jen hua-ts'e, A. 1* (att. to Chou Wen-chü); B. I. 1* (as anon. Sung).

A Khitan soldier in front of his horse, album leaf, Nat. Pal. Mus. , Taipei, (AL, Li Tsan-hua). 300 M. , 36 (as Li Tsan-hua); CKLTMHC, II. 96 (as anon. Sung).

A fairy riding on a dragon, Nat. Pal. Mus. , Taipei, (AL, Chao Po-chü). CKLTMHC, II. 38 (as anon. Sung).

Illustrations to <u>Chiu ko</u>, Songs of the Nine Spirits, by Ch'ü Yüan, handscroll, signed Li Kung-lin, (AL, Li Kung-lin). Li Kung-lin, 1-3 (sections); WW, 1964. 3. 7 (last section, as anon. Sung).

A scholar listening to a lady playing a <u>p'i-p'a</u>, Nat. Pal. Mus. , Taipei, (AL, Li Sung). CKLTMHC, II. 50 (as anon. Sung); KKMH, III. 15* (as Li Sung).

The Lantern Festival, Nat. Pal. Mus.,Taipei, (AL,Li Sung). CKLTMHC, II. 51 (as anon. Sung); KKMH, IV. 10 (as Li Sung).

The village doctor, Nat. Pal. Mus. , Taipei, (AL, Li T'ang). 300 M. , 99 (as Li T'ang); CH mei-shu, I (as Li T'ang); CKLTMHC, II. 33 (as anon. Sung); CKLTSHH (as Li T'ang); KKMH, III. 3 (as Li T'ang).

A celestial girl offering flowers to a Bodhisattva and some monks, album leaf, Nat. Pal. Mus. , Taipei, (AL, Liu Sung-nien). 300 M., 110 (as Liu Sung-nien); CKLTMHC, II. 95 (as anon. Sung); NPM Bulletin, I. 4. 4 (as Liu Sung-nien).

Five scholars on a garden terrace examining books and writings, Nat. Pal. Mus. , Taipei, (AL, Liu Sung-nien). CH mei-shu, I (as Liu Sung-nien); CKLTMHC, II. 5 (as anon. Sung); CKLTSHH (as Liu Sung-nien); KKMH, III. 14 (as Liu Sung-nien).

Three men discussing the Tao under pine-trees, fan, Palace Museum, Peking, (AL, Liu Sung-nien). Sung-jen hua-ts'e, A. 89* (as anon. Sung); B. VII. 4* (as anon. Sung).

The hundred children enjoying spring, fan, signed Han-ch'en, Palace Museum, Peking, (AL, Su Han-ch'en). Sung-jen hua-ts'e, A. 85* (as anon. Sung); B. I. 7* (as anon. Sung).

A warrior returning from the hunt, album leaf, Palace Museum, Peking. Sung-jen hua-ts'e, A. 19* (att. to Chao Po-su); B. V. 1* (as anon. Sung).

Three children playing in a courtyard, fan, Palace Museum, Peking. Sung-jen hua-ts'e, A. 66* (att. to Ch'en Tsung-hsün); B. VIII. 5* (as anon. Sung).

Children playing, one chasing butterflies, one holding a fan, album leaf, signed Su Han-ch'en, Tientsin Art Museum. I-yüan chi-chin, 2* (as anon. Sung); Liang Sung, 7* (as Su Han-ch'en); Sung-jen hua-ts'e, B. XVI* (as anon. Sung).

Two ladies standing by a stone and flowering plants, album leaf, attributed to Ch'ien Hsüan, Nat. Pal. Mus., Taipei. CKLTMHC, II. 97 (as anon. Sung).

A noble scholar under a willow, Nat. Pal. Mus., Taipei. CAT, 26 (as anon. Sung); CKLTMHC, III. 87 (as anon. Yüan); KKMH, III. 40 (as anon. Sung).

Mongol camp scene, album leaf, Nat. Pal. Mus., Taipei. CKLTMHC, II. 88 (as anon. Sung); KKMH, VI. 48 (as anon. Yüan).

A literary gathering, fan, Nat. Pal. Mus., Taipei. KKMH, III. 41.

A fairy offering birthday congratulations, album leaf, Nat. Pal. Mus., Taipei. KKMH, III. 44.

Five men dancing to music played by a man in a pavilion, Nat. Pal. Mus., Taipei. CKLTMHC, II. 19; KKMH, III. 43.

A gentleman and his portrait, album leaf, Nat. Pal. Mus., Taipei. CAT, 64; KKMH, IV. 38*; NPM Bulletin, I. 2. 3.

Collating the texts, Nat. Pal. Mus., Taipei. KKMH, IV. 40.

Illustrations of events in the reign of Chen-tsung, handscroll, Nat. Pal. Mus., Taipei. CH mei-shu, I.

An illustration to the Book of Poetry, silk manufacture, album leaf, Nat. Pal. Mus., Taipei. CKLTMHC, II. 98.

An immortal flying on a lotus petal, fan, illegible signature, Palace Museum, Peking. Sung-jen hua-ts'e, A. 11*; B. IX. 3*.

Mid-summer rest under a locust tree, album leaf, Palace Museum, Peking. Sung-jen hua-ts'e, A. 14*; B. II. 3*.

The shepherd Huang Ch'u-p'ing, fan, Palace Museum, Peking. Sung-jen hua-ts'e, A. 42*; B. IV. 3*.

Children at play, fan, Palace Museum, Peking. Sung-jen hua-ts'e, A. 67*; B. X. 4*.

Four children playing in a small courtyard, album leaf, Palace Museum, Peking. Sung-jen hua-ts'e, A.68*; B.III.6*.

Playing the yüan in a bamboo grove, fan, Palace Museum, Peking. Sung-jen hua-ts'e, A.88*; B.IX.8*; STSS*.

The Three Laughers of Hu Stream, fan, Palace Museum, Peking. Sung-jen hua-ts'e, B.XI*.

Two entertainers, illustration of an opera scene, album leaf, Palace Museum, Peking. Liang Sung, 59*; Sung-jen hua-ts'e, B.XI*; WWCH, I, p. 31*.

Illustration to the play "The Eye-Medicine Vendor", album leaf, Palace Museum, Peking. Liang Sung, 58*; Sung-jen hua-ts'e, B.XII*; WWCH, I, p. 29*.

Scholars and ladies clustered around a table in front of a lotus pool, album leaf, Palace Museum, Peking. Sung-jen hua-ts'e, XV*.

Fifteen children playing around a garden rock and plantain trees, fan, Palace Museum, Peking. Liang Sung, 4*; Sung-jen hua-ts'e, B.XIX*.

Chao-chün on her way to Mongolia, handscroll, signed Chang___, composition identical to the scroll by Kung Su-jan, Kirin Provincial Museum. WW, 1964.3.1-2.

The Four Greybeards of Mt. Shang, handscroll, Liao-ning Provincial Museum. Liao-ning, I.67-70.

The Nine Ancients of Hui-ch'ang, handscroll, Liao-ning Provincial Museum. Liao-ning, I.71-74; NPM Bulletin, I.2.5 (detail).

Portraits of Chu Hsi, short handscroll, Liao-ning Provincial Museum. Liao-ning, I.75.

A Taoist resting beneath a pine, album leaf, Shanghai Museum. Liang Sung, 34*; Sung-jen hua-ts'e, XVII*.

Greeting the emperor at the village, Shanghai Museum. CK hua, I.15; TSYMC hua-hsüan, 13; Wang-hsien ying-chia*.

Spending a summer day looking at paintings, album leaf, Suchou Museum. Liang Sung, 60*; Su-chou, 2.

Portrait of a standing official. CK ku-tai, 53.

Historical subject, officials with retainers greeting each other, handscroll. TSYMC hua-hsüan, 12.

Palaces and Buildings

The Emperor Yüan-tsung of the Southern T'ang Dynasty with his court ladies assembled in a pavilion where a Taoist is boiling snow, Nat. Pal. Mus., Taipei, (AL). CKLTMHC, II.36.

A lady in a pavilion contemplating the moon, Nat. Pal. Mus., Taipei, (AL). CKLTMHC, II.61.

Pavilions of the Shang-lin Park in snow, fan, Nat. Pal. Mus., Taipei, (AL). CKLTMHC, II. 78.

High pavilions along a mountain river, Nat. Pal. Mus., Taipei, (AL). CKLTMHC, II. 55; KKMH, IV. 52.

Palace pavilions and tall trees at the foot of a snow-covered slope, Nat. Pal. Mus., Taipei, (AL). CKLTMHC, II. 43; KKMH, IV. 29.

The Yellow Crane Tower, album leaf, (AL, The Yellow Stork Tower?). WW, 1957. 11. 49.

The Pavilion of Prince T'eng, album leaf, Li Pa-k'o collection, (AL). WW, 1957. 11. 50.

A dragon-boat race, fan, Palace Museum, Peking, (AL, Li Chao-tao). Sung-jen hua-ts'e, A. 100* (as anon. Sung); B. VI. 3* (as anon. Sung).

The A-fang Palace, Nat. Pal. Mus., Taipei, (AL, Chao Po-chü). CKLTMHC, II. 4 (as anon. Sung); CH mei-shu, I (as Chao Po-chü).

Boat race on the Chin-ming Lake, album leaf, signed Chang Tse-tuan, Tientsin Art Museum. I-yüan chi-chin, 1* (as anon. Sung); Liang Sung, 16* (att. to Chang Tse-tuan); Sung-jen hua-ts'e, B. XVI* (as anon. Sung); WW, 1960. 7. 5 (as anon. Sung).

Elaborate palace complex and courtyard, album leaf, Nat. Pal. Mus., Taipei. CKLTMHC, II. 94.

Pavilions by the river, fan, Palace Museum, Peking. Sung-jen hua-ts'e, A. 41*; B. II. 2*; STSS*.

Avoiding the heat in the Chiu-ch'eng Palace, fan, Palace Museum, Peking. Sung-jen hua-ts'e, B. XV*.

Palace and gardens by a river, fan, Palace Museum, Peking. Sung-jen hua-ts'e, B. XV*.

Pavilions of the Immortals, Immortal on a phoenix, fan, Liao-ning Provincial Museum. Liang Sung, 43*; Liao-ning, I. 77; Sung-jen hua-ts'e, B. XIX*; Sung Yüan shan-shui, 8*.

A palace by a river, Shanghai Museum. Shang-hai, 5*.

Elaborate palace, ladies in corridors and halls, fan, Shanghai Museum. Sung-jen hua-ts'e, B. XIV*; STSS*.

Landscapes

Mountain landscape with a temple in a gully, Nat. Pal. Mus., Taipei, (AL). 300 M., 47 (as Chü-jan); CKLTMHC, II. 69 (as anon. Sung); KKMH, I. 16 (as Chü-jan).

Pine-trees and rocks by a waterfall, Nat. Pal. Mus., Taipei, (AL). 300 M., 144; CKLTMHC, II. 23; KKMH, IV. 27.

Deeply creviced mountains in autumn, Nat. Pal. Mus., Taipei, (AL). CKLTMHC, II. 6; KKMH, IV. 30; NPM Bulletin, II. 6, p. 1.

Snow-covered mountains by a river, Nat. Pal. Mus., Taipei, (AL). 300 M., 143; CAT, 43; CKLTMHC, II. 57; KKMH, IV. 28.

Sailing boats returning to a harbour at the foot of verdant mountains,
handscroll, Nat. Pal. Mus., Taipei, (AL). CAT, 21; CH mei-
shu, I; CKLTMHC, II. 12; KKMH, IV. 31.

The Min Mountains after snowfall, Nat. Pal. Mus., Taipei, (AL).
CAT, 47; CKLTMHC, II. 58; KKMH, III. 32; NPM Bulletin, II. 6,
fig. 6; NPM Quarterly, I. 2, pls. XXII*; XXIII. B.

River valley with buildings at the foot of deeply creviced mountains,
Nat. Pal. Mus., Taipei, (AL). CKLTMHC, II. 7; KKMH, III. 34;
NPM Bulletin, II. 6. inside cover.

The poet under the pine-trees looking at the moon, Nat. Pal. Mus.,
Taipei, (AL). CKLTMHC, II. 41.

Numberless peaks and valleys, Nat. Pal. Mus., Taipei, (AL).
CKLTMHC, III. 97 (as anon. Yüan); KKMH, III. 30 (as anon. Sung).

Fishing boats on the river at the foot of high mountains, Nat. Pal. Mus.,
Taipei, (AL). CKLTMHC, II. 40.

A man in a snow-covered pavilion looking at plum-blossoms, Nat. Pal.
Mus., Taipei, (AL). CH mei-shu, I; CKLTSHH.

Fishermen in two boats on the river, Nat. Pal. Mus., Taipei, (AL).
CKLTMHC, II. 17.

Creviced mountains with old trees in snow, Nat. Pal. Mus., Taipei,
(AL). CH mei-shu, I.

A road-side inn and travelling carts in snow-bound mountains, Nat.
Pal. Mus., Taipei, (AL). CKLTMHC, II. 29; KKMH, III. 35.

A clump of knotty old trees on a river-bank, Nat. Pal. Mus., Taipei,
(AL). CKLTMHC, II. 67.

A mighty old tree in the cold, Nat. Pal. Mus., Taipei, (AL).
CKLTMHC, II. 8; KKMH, III. 33.

Landscape in snow, attributed to Chü-jan by Tung Ch'i-ch'ang, Nat.
Pal. Mus., Taipei, (AL, Chü-jan). 300 M., 133 (as anon. Sung);
CH mei-shu, I (as Chü-jan); CKLTMHC, I. 19 (as Chü-jan); KKMH,
II. 13 (as Chü-jan).

Mountain stream between wooded shores, Nat. Pal. Mus., Taipei,
(AL, Chü-jan). 300 M., 48 (as Chü-jan); CKLTMHC, II. 25 (as
anon. Sung); KKMH, II. 12 (as Chü-jan).

The western mountains at sunset, fan, Palace Museum, Peking, (AL,
Kuan T'ung). Sung-jen hua-ts'e, B. XV* (as anon. Sung).

A hostel in the mountains, travellers with bullock carts approaching
and leaving, fan, Palace Museum, Peking, (AL, Kuo Chung-shu).
Sung-jen hua-ts'e, A. 82* (as anon. Sung); B. VII. 6* (as anon.
Sung); STSS* (as anon. Sung).

Pavilions on the Mountain of the Immortals, Nat. Pal. Mus., Taipei,
(AL, Tung Yüan). 300 M., 43* (as Tung Yüan); CAT, 14 (as Tung
Yüan); CH mei-shu, I (as Tung Yüan); CKLTMHC, II. 18 (as anon.
Sung); CKLTSHH (as Tung Yüan); KKMH, II. 10 (as Tung Yüan).

A village by the water in mist, fan, Palace Museum, Peking, (AL, Chao Ling-jang). Sung-jen hua-ts'e, A. 78* (as anon. Sung); B. VI. 2* (as anon. Sung).

Mountains in spring, Nat. Pal. Mus., Taipei, (AL, Chao Po-chü). CKLTMHC, II. 39 (as anon. Sung).

Immortals on the P'eng-lai Island, Nat. Pal. Mus., Taipei, (AL, Chao Ta-heng). CKLTMHC, II. 54 (as anon. Sung).

Illustration to Su Tung-p'o's fu-poem The Red Cliff, handscroll, formerly att. to Chu Jui, now given to Wu Yüan-chih, Nat. Pal. Mus., Taipei, (AL, Chu Jui). 300 M., 132 (as Wu Yüan-chih); CAT, 46 (sections, att. to Wu Yüan-chih); CKLTMHC, II. 2 (as anon. Sung).

Temples in a mountain, fan, Palace Museum, Peking, (AL, Hsia Kuei). Liang Sung, 30* (as anon. Sung); Sung-jen hua-ts'e, B. XI* (as Hsia Kuei).

Misty mountains, fan, Palace Museum, Peking, (AL, Hsia Kuei). Sung-jen hua-ts'e, A. 51* (as Hsia Kuei); B. VII. 1* (as anon. Sung).

Old leafless trees on bare cliffs, Nat. Pal. Mus., Taipei, (AL, Hsü Tao-ning). CKLTMHC, II. 11 (as anon. Sung).

A returning boat in storm, fan, Palace Museum, Peking, (AL, Hsü Tao-ning). Sung-jen hua-ts'e, A. 94* (as anon. Sung); B. III. 8* (as anon. Sung); STSS* (as anon. Sung).

Blue mountains and white clouds, fan, Palace Museum, Peking, (AL, Hsü Tao-ning). Sung-jen hua-ts'e, A. 95* (as anon. Sung); B. III. 1* (as anon. Sung).

River landscape with a fishing-boat, fan, poem by emperor Kao-tsung, Palace Museum, Peking, (AL, Emperor Kao-tsung). Sung-jen hua-ts'e, A. 16* (as anon. Sung); B. II. 8* (as anon. Sung).

Fishing boats at the shore, two others approaching, fan, Palace Museum, Peking, (AL, Kuo Hsi). Sung-jen hua-ts'e, A. 43* (as anon. Sung); B. II. 6* (as anon. Sung).

Old pine-trees on snowy rocks, a fisherman in a boat, Nat. Pal. Mus., Taipei, (AL, Li Ch'eng). CAT, 17 (att. to Li Ch'eng); CKLTMHC, II. 9 (as anon. Sung).

Old cedar trees by a swirling stream, Nat. Pal. Mus., Taipei, (AL, Li Ch'eng). 300 M., 61 (as Li Ch'eng); CKLTMHC, II. 10 (as anon. Sung); KKMH, II. 21 (as Li Ch'eng).

Men conversing in a hall, album leaf, Palace Museum, Peking, (AL, Li T'ang). Sung-jen hua-ts'e, A. 90* (as anon. Sung); B. X. 1* (as anon. Sung).

Landscape with high pavilions, fan, Palace Museum, Peking, (AL, Ma Shih-jung). Sung-jen hua-ts'e, A. 32* (att. to Ma Shih-jung); B. X. 5* (as anon. Sung).

Two men under pine-trees on a terrace overlooking a misty valley, Nat. Pal. Mus., Taipei, (AL, Ma Yüan). CKLTMHC, II. 42 (as anon. Sung).

Mountains and tall pine-trees by a cottage in snow, signed Ma Yüan,
Nat. Pal. Mus., Taipei, (AL, Ma Yüan). CKLTMHC, II.44 (as
anon. Sung).

A feast of lanterns, now attributed to Ma Yüan, Nat. Pal. Mus., Taipei, (AL, Ma Yüan). CAT, 56 (as anon. Sung); KKMH, III.18 (as
Ma Yüan); NPM Bulletin, II.2.inside cover (as Ma Yüan).

Ladies looking at the moon under wu-t'ung trees, fan, Palace Museum,
Peking, (AL, Su Han-ch'en). Sung-jen hua-ts'e, A.76* (as anon.
Sung); B.VIII.6* (as anon. Sung).

Boating on a lotus lake, fan, Palace Museum, Peking (AL, Wang Shen).
Sung-jen hua-ts'e, B.XV* (as anon. Sung).

A homestead on a rocky shore among large pine-trees, fan, signed
Yen Tz'u-p'ing, Nat. Pal. Mus., Taipei, (AL, Yen Tz'u-p'ing).
CKLTMHC, II.77 (as anon. Sung); KKMH, III.11 (as Yen Tz'u-p'ing).

Mountain landscape with travellers, known as Emperor Ming-huang's
journey to Shu, Nat. Pal. Mus., Taipei, (AL, anon. before Sung).
300 M., 35* (as anon. T'ang); CAT, 2* (section, as anon. T'ang);
CKLTMHC, II.1 (as anon. Sung); KKMH, I.7 (as anon. T'ang);
NPM Quarterly, I.2, pl. XVIII (as anon. T'ang); WW, 1961.6.15
(as anon. T'ang).

Fishing boat in a spring landscape, fan, Palace Museum, Peking. Sung-
jen hua-ts'e, A.31* (att. to Chang Hsün-li); B.IX.2* (as anon.
Sung); STSS* (as anon. Sung).

Temple by the cliff pass, album leaf, signed Chia Shih-ku, Nat. Pal.
Mus., Taipei. CAT, 38 (as Chia Shih-ku); CKLTMHC, II.53 (as
anon. Sung); KKMH, IV.4 (as Chia Shih-ku).

A man in a pavilion by a river, fan, Liao-ning Provincial Museum.
Liang Sung, 36* (as anon. Sung); Liao-ning, I.40 (as Chu Kuang-
p'u); Sung-jen hua-ts'e, B.XVIII* (as anon. Sung); Sung Yüan
shan-shui, 3* (as Chu Kuang-p'u).

Visitors arriving at a country estate, fan, signed Ho Ch'üan, dated
hsin-mao, Palace Museum, Peking. Liang Sung, 45* (as Ho
Ch'üan); Sung-jen hua-ts'e, B.XI* (as anon. Sung).

Man seated on a terrace under pines looking at clouds, album leaf, att.
to Hsia Kuei, Nat. Pal. Mus., Taipei. CKLTMHC, II.86 (as
anon. Sung).

Scholar's study by a pond, album leaf, signed Hsia Kuei, Palace Museum, Peking. Sung-jen hua-ts'e, A.48* (as Hsia Kuei); B.VIII.
1* (as anon. Sung).

A ch'in player by a stream, fan, Palace Museum, Peking. Sung-jen
hua-ts'e, A.49* (att. to Hsia Kuei); B.IX.1* (as anon. Sung).

Distant peaks, two scholars and servant looking across a misty valley,
album leaf, Palace Museum, Peking. PM, 2* (att. to Hsia Kuei);

Sung-jen hua-ts'e, A. 50* (att. to Hsia Kuei); B. IX. 6* (as anon. Sung).

Red trees in autumn mountains, fan, Liao-ning Provincial Museum. HC Ch'iu-shan*; Liang Sung, 20* (as anon. Sung); Liao-ning, I. 39 (as Hsiao Chao); Sung-jen hua-ts'e, B. XVIII* (as anon. Sung); Sung Yüan shan-shui, 4* (as Hsiao Chao).

Sandy beach and misty trees, album leaf, Liao-ning Provincial Museum. H-c Sha-t'ing*; Liang Sung, 10* (as anon. Sung); Liao-ning, I. 23 (as Hui-ch'ung); Sung-jen hua-ts'e, B. XVIII* (as anon. Sung); Sung Yüan shan-shui, 1* (as Hui-ch'ung).

Village market on pine-covered cliff, fan, attributed to Kao K'o-ming, Nat. Pal. Mus., Taipei. CKLTMHC, II. 76 (as anon. Sung).

Boating by plum trees and cliffs, fan, signed Li Sung, Nat. Pal. Mus., Taipei. CKLTMHC, II. 89 (as anon. Sung).

Three scholars in a pavilion over water under a misty mountain cliff, fan, signed Li Sung, Palace Museum, Peking. Sung-jen hua-ts'e, B. XV* (as anon. Sung).

Island peak with temples, album leaf, attributed to Li T'ang, Nat. Pal. Mus., Taipei. CKLTMHC, II. 105 (as anon. Sung).

Fishing under a pine-covered cliff, fan, once attributed to Li T'ang, Liao-ning Provincial Museum. Liang Sung, 41* (as anon. Sung); Liao-ning, I. 79 (as anon. Sung); Sung-jen hua-ts'e, B. XIX* (as anon. Sung); Sung Yüan shan-shui, 11* (as anon. Sung); LT Sung-hu*.

A fisherman selling fish to a woman in a pavilion along a snowy river, fan, signed Li Tung, Palace Museum, Peking. LT Hsüeh-chiang*; PM, 4* (as anon. Sung); Sung-jen hua-ts'e, A. 63* (as Li Tung); B. VII. 9* (as Li Tung).

Ladies enjoying the moonlight on a terrace, fan, Palace Museum, Peking. Sung-jen hua-ts'e, A. 10* (att. to Liu Tsung-ku); B. VIII. 8* (as anon. Sung).

Scholar with a staff and a servant in a landscape, fan, signed Ma Lin, Shanghai Museum. Liang Sung, 23* (as Ma Lin); Sung-jen hua-ts'e, B. XIII* (as anon. Sung).

Man in pavilion in snow, servant walking along riverside under plum tree, album leaf, attributed to Ma Yüan, Nat. Pal. Mus., Taipei. CKLTMHC, II. 85 (as anon. Sung).

Burning incense by a mountain brook, fan, Palace Museum, Peking. CK shu-hua, I. cover* (as Ma Yüan); Sung-jen hua-ts'e, A. 46* (att. to Ma Yüan); B. VII. 10* (as anon. Sung).

Garden and two-storied pavilion, two ladies on the balcony, album leaf, attributed to Wang Shen, Nat. Pal. Mus., Taipei. CKLTMHC, II. 90 (as anon. Sung).

A man in a pavilion on a river bank, misty mountains, fan, once attributed to Wang Shen, Liao-ning Provincial Museum. Liang Sung,
17* (as anon. Sung); Liao-ning, I. 76 (as anon. Sung); Sung-jen
hua-ts'e, B. XVIII* (as anon. Sung); Sung Yüan shan-shui, 6* (as
anon. Sung); WS Yü-lou*.

Peasants at work, fan, Palace Museum, Peking. Sung-jen hua-ts'e,
A. 9* (att. to Yang Wei); B. VI. 1* (as anon. Sung).

Pine cliffs and pavilions, Nat. Pal. Mus., Taipei. KKMH, III. 31.

Courtyard with shady pines, fan, Nat. Pal. Mus., Taipei. KKMH, III. 36.

Fishing on a willow bank, album leaf, Nat. Pal. Mus., Taipei. KKMH,
III. 37.

Waiting for the ferry by an autumn river, album leaf, Nat. Pal. Mus.,
Taipei. KKMH, III. 38.

Travellers in snowy mountains, fan, Nat. Pal. Mus., Taipei. KKMH,
III. 39.

Whiling away the summer in a lotus pavilion, album leaf, Nat. Pal.
Mus., Taipei. KKMH, IV. 33; NPM Bulletin, I. 4. cover*.

Travelling amid streams and mountains, album leaf, Nat. Pal. Mus.,
Taipei. KKMH, IV. 34.

Travelling on muleback in the autumn woods, album leaf, Nat. Pal.
Mus., Taipei. KKMH, IV. 35.

Fishing in the moonlight, album leaf, Nat. Pal. Mus., Taipei. KKMH,
IV. 36.

Two scholars conversing in a bamboo grove, Nat. Pal. Mus., Taipei.
CKLTMHC, II. 46.

Scholar walking on a path toward a pavilion on a river cliff, album
leaf, Nat. Pal. Mus., Taipei. CKLTMHC, II. 75.

Watching the tide bore at sunrise, fan, Nat. Pal. Mus., Taipei.
CKLTMHC, II. 81.

Watching the tide bore, album leaf, Nat. Pal. Mus., Taipei.
CKLTMHC, II. 82.

Clearing after snow on a lake, a pavilion and bare trees on shore,
fan, Nat. Pal. Mus., Taipei. CKLTMHC, II. 83.

Watching geese by the lake, fan, Nat. Pal. Mus., Taipei. CKLTMHC,
II. 84.

A flock of magpies over a snowy river, album leaf, Nat. Pal. Mus.,
Taipei. CKLTMHC, II. 104.

Resting under a willow, album leaf, Palace Museum, Peking. Sung-
jen hua-ts'e, A. 13*; B. III. 3*.

A boat returning in an autumn evening, fan, inscribed by Emperor
Kao-tsung, Palace Museum, Peking. Sung-jen hua-ts'e, A. 17*;
B. II. 7*; STSS*.

Snow-covered mountain pass, fan, Palace Museum, Peking. Sung-
jen hua-ts'e, A. 28*; B. III. 5*; STSS*.

A long bridge across a river, fan, Palace Museum, Peking. Sung
   hua shih fu, 5*; Sung-jen hua-ts'e, A. 35*; B. IV. 5*; STSS*.
Pavilion in a willow grove, junks on the river, fan, Palace Museum,
   Peking. Sung-jen hua-ts'e, A. 36*; B. I. 10*.
Riding through snowy mountains, album leaf, Palace Museum, Peking.
   Sung-jen hua-ts'e, A. 37*; B. II. 1*.
Returning from a spring outing, fan, Palace Museum, Peking. Sung-
   jen hua-ts'e, A. 71*; B. V. 6*; STSS*.
Playing the ch'in in a secluded mountain dwelling, fan, Palace Museum,
   Peking. CK shu-hua, I. 19; Sung-jen hua-ts'e, A. 72*; B. VIII. 10*;
   STSS*.
A study by the river, fan, Palace Museum, Peking. Sung-jen hua-ts'e,
   A. 73*; B. VIII. 7*; STSS*.
Fishing boat on the river in spring, fan, Palace Museum, Peking.
   Sung hua shih fu, 10*; Sung-jen hua-ts'e, A. 79*; B. V. 4*.
Autumn reeds along the lake, fan, Palace Museum, Peking. Sung-
   jen hua-ts'e, A. 81*; B. III. 7*.
Preparations for dawn departure, fan, Palace Museum, Peking.
   Sung-jen hua-ts'e, A. 87*; B. V. 10*.
A water wheel under willow trees, album leaf, Palace Museum, Pe-
   king. Sung-jen hua-ts'e, A. 93*; B. VII. 5*.
Willows by the stream in spring, fan, Palace Museum, Peking. Sung-
   jen hua-ts'e, A. 96*; B. X. 10*; STSS*.
Gentleman and three servants in a boat on a lotus pond enjoying the
   moon, fan, Palace Museum, Peking. Liang Sung, 52*; Sung-jen
   hua-ts'e, B. XI*.
Boating on West Lake, fan, Palace Museum, Peking. Liang Sung, 55*;
   Sung-jen hua-ts'e, B. XI*; STSS*.
Two ducks, flight of cranes in river scenery, album leaf, Palace Mu-
   seum, Peking. Liang Sung, 51*; Sung-jen hua-ts'e, B. XI*; STHN*.
Sharp peaks and river view, fan, Palace Museum, Peking. Liang
   Sung, 49*; Sung-jen hua-ts'e, B. XI*; STSS*.
Sunrise behind clouds and high waves, fan, Palace Museum, Peking.
   Liang Sung, 35*; Sung-jen hua-ts'e, B. XII*.
Two men playing chess in a hut on a promontory, fan, Palace Museum,
   Peking. Liang Sung, 31*; Sung-jen hua-ts'e, B. XII*.
Boating under blossoming plum, fan, Palace Museum, Peking. Sung-
   jen hua-ts'e, B. XII*.
Fishermen in boats under pines, fan, Palace Museum, Peking. Sung-
   jen hua-ts'e, B. XII*.
Ladies on a pavilion terrace by a tree-lined river in spring, album
   leaf, Palace Museum, Peking. Sung-jen hua-ts'e, B. XII*.
Scholar and two servants picking chrysanthemums, fan, Palace Mu-
   seum, Peking. Sung-jen hua-ts'e, B. XV*.

Scholar in a boat gazing at misty peaks, fan, Palace Museum, Peking.
Sung-jen hua-ts'e, B. XV*.

A servant sweeping the courtyard of a pavilion on a promontory, fan,
Palace Museum, Peking. Liang Sung, 29*; Sung-jen hua-ts'e,
B. XIX*.

Travellers in streams and mountains, album leaf, Liao-ning Provincial Museum. Liang Sung, 18*; Liao-ning, I. 78; Sung-jen hua-
ts'e, B. XVIII*; Sung Yüan shan-shui, 7*.

Ranges of mountains, streams and bridges, album leaf, Liao-ning
Provincial Museum. Liao-ning, I. 80; Sung-jen hua-ts'e, B. XVIII*;
Sung Yüan shan-shui, 12*.

Travellers in snowy mountains, water mills and pagodas, Shanghai
Museum. Shang-hai, 6*.

Paying New Year's visits, guests in and arriving at a pavilion, Shanghai Museum. Shang-hai, 7*.

A phoenix flying over pavilions in a misty valley, two scholars and a
servant on a bridge, Shanghai Museum. Shang-hai, 8*.

Two scholars, servant with ch'in walking toward a pavilion hidden
behind pines and rocks, album leaf, Shanghai Museum. Liang
Sung, 12*; Sung-jen hua-ts'e, B. XIII*.

Enjoying music by a lotus pool, album leaf, Shanghai Museum. Liang
Sung, 32*; Sung-jen hua-ts'e, B. XIV*.

Travellers approaching a bridge, folding fan, Shanghai Museum. Liang
Sung, 27*; Sung-jen hua-hsüan, 4*; Sung-jen hua-ts'e, B. XIV*.

A tipsy scholar on a donkey returning home, fan, Shanghai Museum.
Liang Sung, 48*; Sung-jen hua-ts'e, B. XIV*; STSS*.

Two boats at anchor and a hut in snowy mountains, fan, Shanghai
Museum. Liang Sung, 44*; Sung-jen hua-hsüan, 7*; Sung-jen
hua-ts'e, B. XV*.

Oxcarts crossing the river, album leaf, signed Chu___, Shanghai
Museum. Liang Sung, 9*; Sung-jen hua-ts'e, B. XVI*.

Wind and rain in mountains and streams, fan, Shanghai Museum.
Liang Sung, 42*; Sung-jen hua-ts'e, B. XVII*.

Three boats on a river, sharp peaks and low distant hills, fan, Shanghai Museum. Liang Sung, 50*; Sung-jen hua-ts'e, B. XVII*.

Figures on a path between steep cliffs and vine-filled trees, fan,
Shanghai Museum. Sung-jen hua-ts'e, B. XVII*.

A man with a staff on a bridge in the mountains, a river view on the
left, fan, Shanghai Museum. Sung-jen hua-ts'e, B. XVII*.

Halls and pavilions in cloudy mountains, fan, Shanghai Museum. Sung-
jen hua-ts'e, B. XVII*.

A house under pines, servant at the gate, river view, fan, Shanghai
Museum. Sung-jen hua-ts'e, B. XIX*.

A man sleeping in a pavilion over a lotus pool, fan, Shanghai Museum.
Sung-jen hua-ts'e, B. XIX*.

Scholar and a servant on a path going toward a pavilion in a pine grove
high in the mountains, fan, Shanghai WWPKWYH. Sung-jen hua-
ts'e, B. XIV*.

A fisherman by a willow bank, fan, Shanghai WWPKWYH. Sung-jen
hua-ts'e, B. XIV*; STSS*.

Scholar on a donkey in a wintry grove, fan, Shanghai WWPKWYH.
Sung-jen hua-hsüan, 9*; Sung-jen hua-ts'e, B. XIV*.

Autumn tide bore on the Ch'ien-t'ang River, fan, signed Hsia ___,
Suchou Museum. Liang Sung, 39*; Su-chou, 1; Sung-jen hua-
ts'e, B. XIX*.

Drinking on a hilltop in the moonlight, album leaf, poem inscribed
by Empress Yang, Tientsin Art Museum. I-yüan chi-chin, 3*;
Liang Sung, 25*; Sung-jen hua-ts'e, B. XVI*; T'ien-ching, II. 7, 8.

A sailboat going toward a rocky shore with pines, fan, crude signature
of Liu Sung-nien, Tientsin Art Museum. I-yüan chi-chin, 4*;
Sung-jen hua-ts'e, B. XVI*.

A snow landscape, a servant bringing an umbrella to a man on a horse,
Tientsin Art Museum. I-yüan chi-chin, 5.

A man sitting alone by a willow tree, Chang Pe-chin collection. Tien
Yin Tang, I. 3.

Admiring plum blossoms on a moonlit night, Chang Pe-chin collection.
Tien Yin Tang, I. 4.

Travellers returning on a snowy day, fan, Chang Pe-chin collection.
Tien Yin Tang, II. 10.

Mountains and woods, temple on a cliff, water-side pavilion, sailing
boats, fan, Chang Pe-chin collection. Tien Yin Tang, II. 11.

Three people reading in a pavilion in a bamboo grove, fan, Chang
Pe-chin collection. Tien Yin Tang, II. 13.

Two men under a pine viewing sharp cliffs and a waterfall, fan, Chang
Pe-chin collection. Tien Yin Tang, II. 14.

Fisherman under pines returning home, fan, Chang Pe-chin collection.
Tien Yin Tang, II. 16.

Four people gathered in a pavilion under pines, a servant entering the
gate, fan, Chang Pe-chin collection. Tien Yin Tang, II. 18.

Misty mountain landscape, winding verandah by the riverside, J. D.
Ch'en collection, Hong Kong. TWSY ming-chi, 8.

Snowy mountains, S. M. Siu collection, Hong Kong. CK ku-hua, B. 33.

Boat being poled toward shore on which two scholars converse beneath trees, album leaf. Sung-jen hua-ts'e, B. XIII*.

Scholar in a pavilion built over a lotus pond, album leaf. Sung-jen
hua-hsüan, 2*; Sung-jen hua-ts'e, B. XIII*.

Two men, one on a bank, one in a boat, conversing under a pine tree,
   fan. Sung-jen hua-ts'e, B. XIII*; Sung-jen hua-hsüan, 5*.
A lady and two servants on a terrace under blossoming trees enjoying
   the moon, album leaf. Sung-jen hua-hsüan, 8*.
Returning fisherman crossing a rustic bridge, fan. Sung-jen hua-
   hsüan, 10*.

Animals

A black rabbit, Nat. Pal. Mus., Taipei, (AL). 300 M., 142; KKMH,
   IV. 43.
A herd-boy leading home two buffaloes, Nat. Pal. Mus., Taipei, (AL).
   CKLTMHC, II. 59.
Two monkeys in a loquat tree, Nat. Pal. Mus., Taipei, (AL). 300 M.,
   138; CAT, 24; CH mei-shu, I; CKLTMHC, II. 14; CKLTSHH;
   KKMH, III. 45.
A cat under some mu-tan plants, Nat. Pal. Mus., Taipei, (AL).
   CKLTMHC, II. 28; KKMH, III. 46.
A buffalo with its calf, Nat. Pal. Mus., Taipei, (AL). 300 M., 140;
   CKLTMHC, II. 45; KKMH, IV. 41.
Water buffaloes and herd boys by a river, handscroll, Nat. Pal. Mus.,
   Taipei, (AL). CKLTMHC, II. 52.
Four Mongols on horseback holding falcons, album leaf, Nat. Pal.
   Mus., Taipei, (AL, Hu Kuei). CAT, 8 (as Hu Kuei); CKLTMHC,
   II. 80 (as anon. Sung); KKMH, II. 7 (as Hu Kuei).
Tending horses by the willow stream, fan, Palace Museum, Peking,
   (AL, Ch'en Chü-chung). Sung-jen hua-ts'e, A. 27* (att. to Ch'en
   Chü-chung); B. I. 8* (as anon. Sung).
Tending buffaloes, fan, Palace Museum, Peking, (AL, Li T'ang).
   Sung-jen hua-ts'e, A. 80* (as anon. Sung); B. III. 4* (as anon. Sung).
Deer hunting on the plain, album leaf, (att. to Ch'en Chü-chung), Nat.
   Pal. Mus., Taipei. CKLTMHC, II. 72 (as anon. Sung).
Monkey reaching for a spider, fan, Palace Museum, Peking. Sung
   hua shih fu, 6* (as anon. Sung); Sung-jen hua-ts'e, A. 7* (att. to
   I Yüan-chi); B. III. 2* (as anon. Sung).
A kitten, album leaf, Nat. Pal. Mus., Taipei. KKMH, IV. 42; NPM
   Bulletin, II. 1. cover*.
Herding sheep, fan, Nat. Pal. Mus., Taipei. NPM Bulletin, II. 2,
   cover*.
A monkey swinging on a tall pine, fan, Nat. Pal. Mus., Taipei.
   CKLTMHC, II. 87.
A herdboy on a buffalo, a buffalo calf, album leaf, Nat. Pal. Mus.,
   Taipei. CKLTMHC, II. 99.

A herd boy riding a water buffalo, fan, Nat. Pal. Mus., Taipei. CKLTMHC, II. 100.

A water buffalo and herd boy in an autumn landscape, fan, Palace Museum, Peking. Sung-jen hua-ts'e, A. 29*; B. IV. 6*; STSS*.

Monkeys picking fruit, fan, Palace Museum, Peking. Sung-jen hua-ts'e, A. 83*; B. II. 5*.

A dog and butterflies in a garden, fan, Liao-ning Provincial Museum. Liang Sung, 11*; Liao-ning, I. 81; Sung-jen hua-ts'e, B. XIX*.

Water buffalo and calf under a willow, a farmer in a paddy, fan, Shanghai Museum. Liang Sung, 56*; Sung-jen hua-ts'e, B. XVII*.

A monkey at the base of a pine tree holding a crane chick, adult crane above, fan, Shanghai Museum. Liang Sung, 53*; Sung-jen hua-ts'e, B. XIII*.

Three puppies and a bitch by stones and flowers, fan, Shanghai WWPKWYH. Sung-jen hua-hsüan, 3*; Sung-jen hua-ts'e, B. XIV*.

Herding water buffaloes under willows, S. M. Siu collection, Hong Kong. CK ku-hua, B. 34.

Flowers and Birds

A wild goose standing by some lotus plants, Nat. Pal. Mus., Taipei, (AL). CKLTMHC, II. 60; KKMH, III. 49.

A branch of camellia flowers, Nat. Pal. Mus., Taipei, (AL). KKMH, IV. 51*.

Three melons. handscroll, Nat. Pal. Mus., Taipei, (AL). CH mei-shu, I; CKLTMHC, II. 62; KKMH, III. 53.

Four quails by a tuft of millet, Nat. Pal. Mus., Taipei, (AL). KKMH, III. 47.

Four magpies and other birds in a flowering tree, Nat. Pal. Mus., Taipei, (AL). KKMH, IV. 50.

Two wild geese standing by some reeds in winter, Nat. Pal. Mus., Taipei, (AL). CKLTMHC, II. 20; KKMH, III. 52.

Doves descending on a hillock grown with shrubs and bamboo, Nat. Pal. Mus., Taipei, (AL). CKLTMHC, II. 56; KKMH, IV. 49.

Two pheasants and mynah-birds among bamboos in winter, Nat. Pal. Mus., Taipei, (AL). 300 M., 137; CCAT, pl. 105; CKLTMHC, II. 16; KKMH, III. 48; WW, 1955. 7. 10 (44).

A white hen and five chickens, Nat. Pal. Mus., Taipei, (AL). 300 M., 139; KKMH, IV. 44.

Small birds in a blossoming plum-tree and a tuft of bamboo, Nat. Pal. Mus., Taipei, (AL). 300 M., 136; CAT, 33; CKLTMHC, II. 13; KKMH, IV. 45.

Ten doves on a large branch, album leaf, Nat. Pal. Mus. , Taipei, (AL, Huang Chü-ts'ai). CKLTMHC, II. 74 (as anon. Sung).

Sparrows fighting among reeds, fan, Palace Museum, Peking, (AL, Huang Chü-ts'ai). Sung-jen hua-ts'e, A. 39* (as anon. Sung); B. III. 9* (as anon. Sung).

Four crows in a bare willow and two ducks on the water in snow, album leaf, Nat. Pal. Mus. , Taipei, (AL,Huang Ch'üan). CKLTMHC, II. 79 (as anon. Sung); KKMH, II. 17* (as Huang Ch'üan).

Ducks among reeds, album leaf, Palace Museum, Peking, (AL, Huang Ch'üan). Sung-jen hua-ts'e, A. 3* (att. to Huang Ch'üan); B. II. 4* (as anon. Sung).

A branch of white jasmine, fan, once attributed to Chao Ch'ang, Sugahara collection, Kamakura, (AL, Chao Ch'ang). NPM Quarterly, I. 2, pl. XII. B.

Two mandarin ducks on a beach in autumn, album leaf, Nat. Pal. Mus. , Taipei (AL, Hui-ch'ung). 300 M. , 69* (as Hui-ch'ung); CAT, 22 (att. to Hui-ch'ung); CH mei-shu, I (as Hui-ch'ung); CKLTMHC, II. 101 (as anon. Sung); CKLTSHH (as Hui-ch'ung); KKMH, I. 29 (as Hui-ch'ung).

A white goose resting on a shore and a red polygonum plant, seal of Emperor Hui-tsung, Nat. Pal. Mus. , Taipei, (AL, Hui-tsung). 300 M. , 90* (as Hui-tsung); CH mei-shu, I (as Hui-tsung); CKLTMHC, II. 3 (as anon. Sung); CKLTSHH (as Hui-tsung); KKMH, I. 42 (as Hui-tsung).

Two quails among chrysanthemums and thorny shrubs, album leaf, Nat. Pal. Mus. , Taipei, (AL, Li An-chung). CKLTMHC, II. 102 (as anon. Sung).

A pair of peacocks, fan, Nat. Pal. Mus. , Taipei, (AL, Lin Ch'un). CKLTMHC, II. 92 (as anon. Sung).

Fishes playing among aquatic plants, fan, Palace Museum, Peking, (AL, Liu Ts'ai). Sung-jen hua-ts'e, A. 6* (att. to Liu Ts'ai); B. I. 4* (as anon. Sung).

A small bird on the stalk of lotus plant and a dragonfly, album leaf, Palace Museum, Peking, (AL, Ma Hsing-tsu). Sung-jen hua-ts'e, A. 18* (att. to Ma Hsing-tsu); B. IV. 2* (as anon. Sung); STHN* (as anon. Sung).

An orchid plant, fan, Palace Museum, Peking, (AL, Ma Lin). Sung-jen hua-ts'e, A. 84* (as anon. Sung); B. VII. 7* (as anon. Sung).

Ducks on the water below a blossoming tree, album leaf, signed Ma Yüan, Palace Museum, Peking, (AL, Ma Yüan). Sung-jen hua-ts'e, A. 44* (as Ma Yüan); B. IV. 7* (as anon. Sung).

A goose and some reeds on a low shore, signed Ts'ui Po, Nat. Pal. Mus. , Taipei, (AL, Ts'ui Po). 300 M. , 80* (as Ts'ui Po); CKLTMHC, II. 22 (as anon. Sung).

A wild goose resting on a rushy beach, Nat. Pal. Mus., Taipei, (AL, Ts'ui Po). CKLTMHC, II.21 (as anon. Sung); KKMH, I.37* (as Ts'ui Po).

Insects and butterflies on grasses, album leaf, attributed to Wu Ping, Nat. Pal. Mus., Taipei, (AL, Wu Ping, Butterflies among tall grass?). CKLTMHC, II.103 (as anon. Sung).

Fish swimming in spring stream, album leaf, Palace Museum, Peking. Sung-jen hua-ts'e, A.65* (att. to Ch'en K'o-chiu); B.III.10* (as anon. Sung).

Butterflies among chrysanthemums, fan, signed Chu ___, Palace Museum, Peking. Sung-jen hua-ts'e, A.69* (att. to Chu Shao-tsung); B.V.8* (as anon. Sung).

Bird on smartweed, fan, Palace Museum, Peking. KKPWY hua-niao, 4* (as anon. Sung); Sung-jen hua-ts'e, A.5* (att. to Hsü Ch'ung-chü); B.I.2* (as anon. Sung); SYHN* (as anon. Sung).

Long-tailed bird on a branch of loquat tree, fan, attributed to Hsü Ch'ung-ssu, Nat. Pal. Mus., Taipei. CKLTMHC, II.73 (as anon. Sung).

Dragonfly and bean flower, fan, Palace Museum, Peking. Sung-jen hua-ts'e, A.2* (att. to Hsü Hsi); B.VI.8* (as anon. Sung).

Bamboo and rocks in snow. TSYMC hua-hsüan, 11 (as anon. Sung); TWSY ming-chi, 3 (as Hsü Hsi).

Crab and fading lotus, fan, Palace Museum, Peking. Sung hua shih fu, 9* (as anon. Sung); Sung-jen hua-ts'e, A.4* (att. to Huang Chü-ts'ai); B.I.5* (as anon. Sung).

Ducks on a snowy bank under bamboo and plum, album leaf, attributed to Huang Ch'üan, Nat. Pal. Mus., Taipei. CKLTMHC, II.24 (as anon. Sung).

Butterflies, fan, Palace Museum, Peking. Sung-jen hua-ts'e, A.21* (att. to Li An-chung); B.VI.4* (as anon. Sung); STHN* (as anon. Sung).

Grapes and insects, fan, signed Lin Ch'un, Palace Museum, Peking. KKPWY hua-niao, 6* (as Lin Ch'un); Sung-jen hua-ts'e, A.22* (as Lin Ch'un); B.VIII.4* (as anon. Sung); STHN* (as Lin Ch'un).

Summer flowers, fan, Palace Museum, Peking. Sung-jen hua-ts'e, A.64* (att. to Lu Tsung-kuei); B.X.9* (as anon. Sung); STHN* (as anon. Sung).

Bamboo and plum blossoms reflected in a stream, album leaf, Nat. Pal. Mus., Taipei. CCAT, pl. 102 (as Ma Lin); CH mei-shu, I (as Ma Lin); CKLTMHC, II.93 (as anon. Sung); KKMH, IV.21* (as Ma Lin).

Peacocks and red plum blossoms, album leaf, signed Ma ___, Palace Museum, Peking. KKPWY hua-niao, 5* (as anon. Sung); Sung-jen hua-ts'e, A.53* (att. to Ma Lin); B.IX.7* (as anon. Sung).

Lotus blossom on the water, fan, Palace Museum, Peking. KKPWY
hua-niao, 13* (as anon. Sung); PM, 36* (as anon. Sung); Sung-jen
hua-ts'e, A. 20* (att. to Wu Ping); B. I. 9* (as anon. Sung); STHN*
(as anon. Sung).

Chrysanthemums in a vase, fan, poem by Emperor Ning-tsung, Palace Museum, Peking. Sung-jen hua-ts'e, A. 54* (att. to Yao Yüeh-
hua); B. IX. 10* (as anon. Sung).

Egrets, bamboo and rock, album leaf, Nat. Pal. Mus., Taipei. KKMH,
III. 50.

Two sparrows on a branch of plum blossom, album leaf, Nat. Pal.
Mus., Taipei. KKMH, III. 51.

Camellias, album leaf, Nat. Pal. Mus., Taipei. KKMH, III. 54.

A bird on a branch of wu-t'ung tree, Nat. Pal. Mus., Taipei. KKMH,
IV. 46.

Geese by an autumn pond, fan, Nat. Pal. Mus., Taipei. KKMH, IV. 47.

A duckling, album leaf, Nat. Pal. Mus., Taipei. KKMH, IV. 48; NPM
Bulletin, I. 5. cover*.

Peach blossoms, album leaf, Nat. Pal. Mus., Taipei. NPM Bulletin,
II. 2, fig. 4.

Peonies, Nat. Pal. Mus., Taipei. CKLTMHC, II. 30.

A branch of oranges, album leaf, Nat. Pal. Mus., Taipei. CKLTMHC,
II. 91.

Mynah on a withering tree, fan, Palace Museum, Peking. KKPWY
hua-niao, 19*; Sung-jen hua-ts'e, A. 12*; B. V. 5*.

Crab apple blossoms and butterflies, album leaf, Palace Museum,
Peking. Sung hua shih fu, 7*; Sung-jen hua-ts'e, A. 15*; B. I. 6*;
STHN*.

Loquats and a white-eye, album leaf, Palace Museum, Peking. Sung-
jen hua-ts'e, A. 24*; B. VII. 3*; STHN*.

Five sparrows on a dry autumn branch, album leaf, Palace Museum,
Peking. Sung-jen hua-ts'e, A. 25*; B. VIII. 3*; STHN*.

White camellias, fan, Palace Museum, Peking. Sung-jen hua-ts'e,
A. 33*; B. V. 9*; STHN*.

Peach blossoms, fan, Palace Museum, Peking. KKPWY hua-niao,
15*; Sung hua shih fu, 3*; Sung-jen hua-ts'e, A. 34*; B. V. 3*;
STHN*.

Insects and wild grasses, album leaf, Palace Museum, Peking. Sung-
jen hua-ts'e, A. 38*; B. X. 6*.

A white-head on bamboo, fan, Palace Museum, Peking. KKPWY hua-
niao, 16*; Sung-jen hua-ts'e, A. 40*; B. VI. 7*.

Branch of weeping willow, album leaf, inscription and seal of Empress
Yang, Palace Museum, Peking. Sung-jen hua-ts'e, A. 55*; B. VI. 5*.

Bamboo, plum blossoms and two birds, album leaf, Palace Museum,
Peking. Sung hua shih fu, 8*; Sung-jen hua-ts'e, A. 70*; B. VII. 8*;

STHN*.

Birds and pine trees in a narrow gorge, album leaf, Palace Museum, Peking. Sung-jen hua-ts'e, A. 74*; B. VI. 6*.

Golden oriole on a pomegranate tree, album leaf, Palace Museum, Peking. Sung-jen hua-ts'e, A. 75*; B. V. 7*; STHN *.

Prometheus moth and maple bough, fan, Palace Museum, Peking. Sung-jen hua-ts'e, A. 77*; B. V. 2*; STHN*.

Two ducks on a pond, plum blossoms, narcissi and camellias, album leaf, Palace Museum, Peking. Sung-jen hua-ts'e, A. 86*; B. IX. 9*.

Bamboo and five sparrows, album leaf, Palace Museum, Peking. Sung-jen hua-ts'e, A. 91*; B. VIII. 2*; STHN*.

A wagtail on a fading lotus leaf, album leaf, Palace Museum, Peking. KKPWY hua-niao, 17*; Sung-jen hua-ts'e, A. 92*; B. IV. 1*.

Narcissi, fan, Palace Museum, Peking. Sung-jen hua-ts'e, A. 97*; B. VIII. 9*.

Two birds in a tallow tree above a snowy stream, album leaf, Palace Museum, Peking. Sung-jen hua-ts'e, A. 98*; B. X. 7*.

Two birds on bare branches in a frost-covered gorge, album leaf, Palace Museum, Peking. Sung-jen hua-ts'e, A. 99*; B. X. 8*.

Pied wagtail on a rock, album leaf, Palace Museum, Peking. Sung-jen hua-ts'e, B. XI*.

Four ducks on a wintry spit of land, fan, Palace Museum, Peking. Liang Sung, 13*; Sung-jen hua-ts'e, B. XII*.

A large bird perched on the edge of a bowl, album leaf, Palace Museum, Peking. Sung-jen hua-ts'e, B. XII*.

Cluster of chrysanthemums, fan, Palace Museum, Peking. Sung-jen hua-ts'e, B. XII*.

A hawk with a captured duck on the ground, another duck flying away, Palace Museum, Peking. KKPWY hua-niao, 20*.

Hundred flowers, a long handscroll of flowers, fruits and insects, Palace Museum, Peking. Sung-jen Pai-hua t'u; WW, 1959. 2. inside back cover (sections).

Magpies on a wintry bank, handscroll, colophons by Chao Meng-fu and others, Liao-ning Provincial Museum. Liao-ning, I. 64-66.

Pied wagtail eying an insect from a lotus stalk, Shanghai Museum. Liang Sung, 37*; Sung-jen hua-ts'e, B. XIII*.

A quail on a grassy bank, album leaf, Shanghai Museum. Liang Sung, 3*; Sung-jen hua-hsüan, 6*; Sung-jen hua-ts'e, B. XV*.

Butterfly and camellia, fan, Shanghai Museum. Liang Sung, 19*; Sung-jen hua-ts'e, B. XVI*.

Pink lotus, fan, Shanghai Museum. Liang Sung, 33*; Sung-jen hua-ts'e, B. XVI*.

Flower basket, fan, Shanghai Museum. Sung-jen hua-ts'e, B. XVII*.

White flowers, fan, Szechuan Provincial Museum. Liang Sung, 24*;
Sung-jen hua-ts'e, B. XVI*.
Three ducks swimming in a lotus pond, album leaf, Szechuan Provin-
cial Museum. Liang Sung, 26*; Sung-jen hua-ts'e, B. XVI*.
Ducks and lotus flowers, Chang Pe-chin collection. Tien Yin Tang, I. 5.
Lotus, cassia and three egrets, Chang Pe-chin collection. Tien Yin
Tang, I. 6.
Rice plant and bird, fan, Chang Pe-chin collection. Tien Yin Tang,
II. 12.
Plum blossoms and reflection of the moon, fan, Chang Pe-chin collec-
tion. Tien Yin Tang, II. 15.
Two birds flying toward a bank, four birds on a cliff under pines, fan,
Chang Pe-chin collection. Tien Yin Tang, II. 17.
Pink hollyhocks, fan. Sung-jen hua-ts'e, B. XIII*.

Painters of the Yüan Dynasty

Chang Chung		Ch'en Hsüan	
Chang Hsün		Ch'en Li-shan	
Chang Shen		Ch'en Lin	
Chang Shou-chung		Cheng Hsi	
Chang Shun-tzu		Chieh-hsi Ssu	
Chang Wu		Ch'ien Hsüan	
Chang Yü		Chu Shu-chung	
Chao Ch'i		Chu Te-jun	
Chao Chung		Chuang Lin	
Chao Hsi-yüan		Fang Ts'ung-i	
Chao Lin		Fang-yai	
Chao Meng-fu		Hsia Shu-wen	
Chao Yung		Hsia Yung	
Chao Yüan		Hsieh Po-ch'eng	
Ch'en Chen		Hsieh T'ing-chih	
Ch'en Chih		Hsüeh-chieh	
Ch'en Chung-jen		Hu T'ing-hui	

Huang Chin
Huang Kung-wang
Jen Jen-fa
K'ang-li Nao
Kao K'o-kung
K'o Chiu-ssu
Ku An
Ku Te-hui
Kuan Tao-sheng
Kuo Pi
Leng Ch'ien
Li Jung-chin
Li K'an
Li K'ang
Li Sheng
Li Shih-hsing
Lin Chüan-a
Liu Kuan-tao
Lu Kuang
Ma Yüan
Ni Tsan
Pien Wu
Po-yen Pu-hua
P'u-ming

Sa Tu-la
Shang Ch'i
Sheng Ch'ang-nien
Sheng Hung
Sheng Mou
Shih Chiang
Su Ta-nien
Sun Chün-tse
Tai Shun
T'ang Ti
T'ao Fu-ch'u
Ts'ao Chih-po
Wang Chen-p'eng
Wang I
Wang Meng
Wang Mien
Wang Yüan
Wei Chiu-ting
Wu Chen
Wu Kuan
Wu T'ing-hui
Yang Wei-chen
Yao T'ing-mei
Yen Hui

CHANG CHUNG 張中 , see Chang Shou-chung.

CHANG HSÜN 張遜 , t. Chung-min 仲敏 , h. Ch'i-yün 溪雲
From Suchou; studied bamboo with Li K'an; also painted landscapes after Chü-jan. (CP, VII, AL, 99.)
    Outline bamboo by a rock, signed, dated 1301, S. M. Siu collection,

Hong Kong. CK ku-hua, A.21; B.52.

Bamboo, rocks and pines, handscroll, inscribed, signed, dated 1349, done for Wang Yü, Palace Museum, Peking. CH Shuang-kou.

CHANG SHEN 張紳 , t. Shih-hsing 士行 and Chung-shen 仲紳 , h. Yün-men shan-ch'iao 雲門山樵 . From Chi-nan; served as Governor of Chekiang in the Hung-wu period (1368–1398), painted bamboos. (CP, VII, AL, 99.)

An old tree and bamboos by a rock, painted together with Ni Tsan and Ku An, poem by Ni Tsan dated 1373, Nat. Pal. Mus., Taipei, (AL). CH mei-shu, II; CKLTMHC, III.74; KKMH, VI.38.

Bamboo hanging from a rock, inscribed, signed, dated 1375, S.M. Siu collection, Hong Kong. CK ku-hua, B.140.

CHANG SHOU-CHUNG 張守中 , or 張守忠 ; also named Chang Chung 張中 , t. Tzu-cheng 子政 or 正 and Yü-cheng 于政 . From Sung-chiang, Kiangsu; active in the middle of the 14th century, painted landscapes, flowers and birds. (CP, VII, AL, 99–100.)

Bird on an apricot branch, signed, dated 1350, five colophons, S.M. Siu collection, Hong Kong. CK ku-hua, A.40; B.90.

Two ducks swimming under a camellia shrub, inscribed, signed, dated 1353. TSYMC hua-hsüan, 28.

A bird on the branch of a blossoming peach-tree, signed, several poems by contemporaries, Nat. Pal. Mus., Taipei, (AL). CKLTMHC, III.33; KKMH, VI.4.

A pair of mandarin ducks among rushes, signed, Nat. Pal. Mus., Taipei, (AL). 300 M., 182; CKLTMHC, III.32.

CHANG SHUN-TZU 張舜咨 , also named Chang I-shang 張義上 or Chang Hsi-shang 張義上 , t. Shih-k'uei 師夔 , h. Li-li-tzu 櫟里子 . From Hangchou; active c. 1330–1350, painted land-scapes. (CP, VII, AL, 100.)

Old trees and rocks by a stream, signed, dated 1347, poem by Yang I, Nat. Pal. Mus., Taipei, (AL). 300 M., 170; CKLTMHC, III.69; KKMH, V.37.

A bare tree by a rockery, signed, dated 1349, Nat. Pal. Mus., Taipei, (AL). CH mei-shu, II; CKLTMHC, III.68.

Cypress trees and rocks, signed, dated 1351, S.M. Siu collection, Hong Kong. CK ku-hua, A.41; B.95.

An eagle in a juniper tree, signed, done with Hsüeh-chieh, Huang Chou collection. CK hua, XIII.20.

CHANG WU 張渥 , t. Shu-hou 叔厚 , h. Chen-hsien-sheng 真閒生 and Chen-ch'i-sheng 貞期生 . From Hangchou; active c. 1360, figures, followed Li Kung-lin. (CP, VII, AL, 100.)

Peach Festival at the Lake of Gems, signed, dated 1341, Nat. Pal. Mus., Taipei. 300 M., 183.

River landscape: visiting Tai K'uei on a snowy night, signed, dated 1344, S.M. Siu collection, Hong Kong. CK ku-hua, A.32; B.78.

Wang Hui-chih on his way to Tai K'uei on a snowy night, signed, poem by Ch'ien-lung, Shanghai Museum, (AL). Che-chiang, 41; Li-tai jen-wu, 38; Shang-hai, 25*.

Illustrations to Ch'ü Yüan's Nine Songs, text by Ku Han, Cleveland Museum of Art, (AL). CK ku-tai, 63 (section).

A grass hut across the river from a bamboo grove, handscroll, artist's seal, poem by Yang Yü, colophons by Yang Wei-chen, Chang Yü and others, Liao-ning Provincial Museum. Liao-ning, I.87.

CHANG YÜ 張雨 , also named Chang T'ien-yü 張天雨 , t. Po-yü 伯雨 , h. Chü-ch'ü wai-shih 句曲外史 . B. 1277, d. 1348; from Ch'ien-t'ang, Chekiang, a Taoist monk, painted landscapes. (CP, VII, AL, 100.)

Fungus, bamboo and rock, signed, dated 1336, colophons by K'o Chiu-ssu and Wang Tzu-fang, Chang Pe-chin collection. Tien Ying Tang, I.9.

CHAO CH'I 趙淇 , t. Yüan-te 元德 , h. P'ing-yüan 平遠 , T'ai-ch'u tao-jen 太初道人 , P'ing-ch'u 平初 , Ching-hua-weng 靜華翁 . From Ch'ang-sha, Hunan, held an office in Hunan; painted bamboo. (H.5; I.53; M. p. 615.)

Bamboo, signed, dated 1281, S.M. Siu collection, Hong Kong. CK ku-hua, B.39.

CHAO CHUNG 趙束 , t. Yüan-ch'u 原初 , h. Tung-wu yeh-jen 東吳野人 . From Wu-chiang; active in the Yüan period as a doctor and calligrapher, painted figures in pai-miao. (CP, VII, AL, 101.)

Three flower studies: lily, narcissus, peony, handscroll, inscribed, Cleveland Museum of Art. TWSY ming-chi, 107.

CHAO HSI-YÜAN 趙希遠 . A contemporary of Wang Meng, painted landscapes. (CP, VII, AL, 101.)

Landscape, signed, dated 1348, S.M. Siu collection, Hong Kong. CK ku-hua, B.134.

Steep wooded mountains divided by deep gullies, signed, dated 1349, poem by Wen Chia, Nat. Pal. Mus., Taipei, (AL). KKMH, VI.23.

CHAO LIN 趙麟 , t. Yen-cheng 彥徵 . Son of Chao Yung; active second half of the 14th century, painted figures and horses. (CP,

VII, AL, 101.)

A horse and a groom, handscroll, inscribed, signed, dated 1359, mounted with two other paintings of horses and grooms by Chao Meng-fu and Chao Yung, John M. Crawford collection, New York. CK shu-hua, I. 20; Li-tai jen-wu, 36; TWSY ming-chi, 97.

Dressing a horse by a stream, after Li Kung-lin, signed, dated 1365, Fujii Yūrinkan, Kyōto, (AL). Che-chiang, 38.

A man in a red coat seated at the foot of a tree in front of a horse which is ready to lie down, signed, Nat. Pal. Mus., Taipei, (AL). KKMH, V. 16.

CHAO MENG-FU 趙孟頫 , t. Tzu-ang 子昂 , h. Sung-hsüeh 松雪 and Ou-po 鷗波 . B. 1254, d. 1322; also called Chao Wu-hsing after his native place in Chekiang, calligrapher, painted horses, figures, landscapes, bamboo. (CP, VII, AL, 102-104.)

The Ch'iao and Hua Mountains in autumn, handscroll, signed, dated 1296, painted for Chou Kung-chin, Nat. Pal. Mus., Taipei, (AL). 300 M., 146*; CAT, 69* (section); CKLTMHC, III. 7; KKMH, V. 2*; NPM Quarterly, I. 2, pl. XV. A (section).

An official on horseback, short handscroll, inscribed, signed, dated 1296, eighteen colophons, Palace Museum, Peking. CM-f Jen-chi*.

A horse and a groom, handscroll, inscribed, signed, dated 1296, mounted with two other paintings of horses and grooms by Chao Yung and Chao Lin, John M. Crawford collection, New York. CK shu-hua, I. 20; Li-tai jen-wu, 34; TWSY ming-chi, 95.

Withering trees and young bamboo, signed, dated 1298, three colophons, S. M. Siu collection, Hong Kong. CK ku-hua, A. 17; B. 42.

Leafless trees by a rock, signed, dated 1299, poems by Ch'en Lin and K'o Chiu-ssu, Nat. Pal. Mus., Taipei, (AL). CH mei-shu, II; CKLTSHH.

A spray of bamboo, signed, dated 1299, S. M. Siu collection, Hong Kong. CK ku-hua, A. 18; B. 44.

Two horses and old trees, handscroll, signed, dated 1300, Nat. Pal. Mus., Taipei. KKMH, V. 4.

Water village, handscroll, signed, dated 1302, Palace Museum, Peking. CK hua, XII. 16.

Winding waters, deep bays and high cliffs, handscroll divided into sections, signed, dated 1303, Nat. Pal. Mus., Taipei (AL). 300 M., 145; CH mei-shu, II; CKLTMHC, III. 6.

A red-robed foreign monk seated under a tree, handscroll, signed, dated 1304, colophons by Tung Ch'i-ch'ang and Ch'en Chi-ju, Liao-ning Provincial Museum. Liao-ning, I. 82-3; Li-tai jen-wu, 33.

Bamboo in wind, signed, dated 1305, S. M. Siu collection, Hong Kong.
CK ku-hua, B. 43.

Watering horses in the autumn fields, handscroll, signed, dated 1312,
Palace Museum, Peking, (AL). Che-chiang, 20; CK hua, IX. 10-
11; CK ku-tai, 57; WW, 1958. 6. 1*.

Liu Ling and a copy of his Chiu-te Sung, handscroll, inscribed, signed,
dated 1316, S. M. Siu collection, Hong Kong. CK ku-hua, B. 41.

An old tree, bamboo and rocks, short handscroll, signed; part of col-
lected scroll of Yüan works called Yüan-jen chi-chin, Nat. Pal.
Mus. , Taipei, (AL). (CAT, 90a); CH mei-shu, II; CKLTMHC,
III. 11; KKMH, V. 5.

A dry old tree and some bamboos by a rock, signed, inscription by
Ni Tsan dated 1365, Nat. Pal. Mus. , Taipei, (AL). 300 M. ,
147; CCAT, pl. 106; CKLTMHC, III. 10.

A woodpecker on a bamboo branch, short handscroll, signed, Palace
Museum, Peking, (AL). KKPWY hua-niao, 23*.

Bamboos by a rock, album leaf, seals of the painter, Nat. Pal. Mus. ,
Taipei, (AL). CKLTMHC, III. 8.

A bird on a withering lotus leaf, after Huang Ch'üan, Nat. Pal. Mus. ,
Taipei, (AL). 300 M. , 148; CH mei-shu, II; KKMH, V. 1.

A groom leading a horse in the wind, album leaf, signed, Nat. Pal.
Mus. , Taipei, (AL). KKMH, V. 6.

Bamboos and orchids growing from a rock, handscroll, signed, done
for Shan-fu, Cleveland Museum of Art, (AL). TWSY ming-chi, 94.

Kuan-yin with a fishing creel, artist's seal, Nat. Pal. Mus. , Taipei.
300 M. , 149.

Bodhidharma seated on a rock, Nat. Pal. Mus. , Taipei. CKLTMHC,
III. 9.

Tuan-mu Tz'u (Tzu-kung) visiting Yüan Hsien, handscroll, inscribed,
signed, Nat. Pal. Mus. , Taipei. KKMH, V. 3.

Washing horses, seven horses and eight grooms under willow trees,
handscroll, signed (? reproduction too faint to read), Palace
Museum, Peking. WW, 1966. 4. 40.

T'ung-t'ing tung-shan t'u. A small boat on a river between a promontory and mountain, inscribed, signed, poem, Shanghai Museum.
Shang-hai, 10*.

Landscapes, three album leaves. TSYMC hua-hsüan, 15, 16, 17.

A gentleman seated in a pavilion under wu -t'ung trees, a servant
bringing a ch'in, handscroll, signed. Che-chiang, 21; TSYMC
hua-hsüan, 14*; TWSY ming-chi, 93.

Wen-chi returning to China. WW, 1959. 6. 32.

Three friends of winter, fan. WW, 1962. 12. 3.

CHAO YUNG 趙 雍 , t. Chung-mu 仲 穆 . B. 1289; son of Chao
Meng-fu, painted landscapes, figures, horses, bamboo, rocks. (CP,
VII, AL, 104-105.)

Gathering water-chestnuts, signed, dated 1342, Nat. Pal. Mus., Taipei, (AL). CH mei-shu, II; CKLTMHC, III. 25.

A mountain inlet, signed, dated 1345, colophons, S. M. Siu collection,
Hong Kong. CK ku-hua, A. 36; B. 91.

A Mongol in a red coat leading a black-and-white horse, handscroll,
after Li Kung-lin, signed, dated 1347, Freer Gallery of Art,
Washington, D. C. (45. 32), (AL). Che-chiang, 30.

Horses on pasture in a wood, signed, dated 1352, poems by Liu Jung
and Wang Kuo-ch'i, Nat. Pal. Mus., Taipei, (AL). 300 M., 157;
CH mei-shu, II; CKLTMHC, III. 26; KKMH, V. 15.

A horse and a groom, handscroll, signed, dated 1359, mounted with
two other paintings of horses and grooms by Chao Meng-fu and
Chao Lin, John M. Crawford collection, New York. CK shu-hua,
I. 20; Li-tai jen-wu, 35; TWSY ming-chi, 96.

A gentleman boating on the river, travellers on a bridge, village in
the mountains, attributed, Nat. Pal. Mus., Taipei. KKMH, V. 14*.

Tree-covered rocky shore, distant mountains, four flying birds, fan,
artist's seal, Palace Museum, Peking. Yüan-jen hua-ts'e, II*.

A man in a boat under a winter moon, fan, signed, Liao-ning Provincial Museum. Liao-ning, I. 84; Sung Yüan shan-shui, 14*.

Bamboo, handscroll, inscribed, signed, Liao-ning Provincial Museum.
Liao-ning, I. 85-86.

A long procession of baggage mules, oxen, camels and men in various
garb on horseback, handscroll, signed, Liao-ning Provincial Museum. Liao-ning, I. 99-110 (as anon. Yüan).

Epidendrum and bamboo by a rock, signed, Shanghai Museum. Shanghai, 16*; TSYMC hua-hsüan, 23.

Three horses and groom under a tree, signed. CK hua, VI. 14.

CHAO YÜAN 趙 原 or 趙 元 , t. Shan-ch'ang 善 長 , h. Tan-lin
丹 林 . From Suchou; active c. 1370, painted landscapes. (CP, VII,
AL, 105-106.)

River landscape with a fisherman in a boat and a scholar in a pavilion
among trees on the low shore, signed, dated 1363, Shanghai Museum, (AL). Shang-hai, 29*.

Pavilion by a stream at the foot of mountains, signed, dated 1377,
S. M. Siu collection, Hong Kong. CK ku-hua, B. 143.

A thatched hut in the mountains, signed, dated 1378, two colophons,
S. M. Siu collection, Hong Kong. CK ku-hua, A. 55; B. 141.

Pavilion by a stream at the foot of a rocky mountain, signed, poems
by Yeh Meng-hsien, Wang Ming-chi, Chang Chien and two others,

Nat. Pal. Mus., Taipei, (AL). CKLTMHC, III. 76; KKMH, VI. 34.

Lu Yü preparing tea, handscroll, signed, part of collected scroll of
Yüan works called <u>Yüan-jen chi-chin</u>, Nat. Pal. Mus., Taipei,
(AL). 300 M., 200; CAT, 9 0f (section); CH mei-shu, II; CKLTMHC,
III. 77; KKMH, VI. 35.

Fisherman by the shore, inscribed, signed, S. M. Siu collection, Hong
Kong. CK ku-hua, B. 142.

CH'EN CHEN 陳　植, t. Li-yüan 履　元 . From Ch'ien-t'ang, Chekiang; active c. 1350, painted landscapes. (CP, VII, AL, 106.)

The study in the white cloud mountains, signed, dated 1351, Nat. Pal.
Mus., Taipei, (AL). KKMH, VI. 28.

Landscape, scholar's study in the mountains, signed, dated 1361,
S. M. Siu collection, Hong Kong. CK ku-hua, A. 46; B. 106.

CH'EN CHIH 陳　植 , t. Shu-fang 叔　方 , h. Shen-tu 慎　獨 .
B. 1293, d. 1362; from Suchou, painted landscapes. (CP, VII, AL, 106.)

Cloudy mountains, signed, dated 1355, S. M. Siu collection, Hong Kong.
CK ku-hua, B. 109.

CH'EN CHUNG-JEN 陳　仲　仁 . From Kiangsi; active at the beginning
of the 14th century, painted flowers, birds, figures and landscapes. (CP,
VII, AL, 106.)

The hundred sheep, signed, Nat. Pal. Mus., Taipei, (AL). CKLTMHC,
III. 15.

Two birds on a camellia shrub, signed, dated (illegible), S. M. Siu
collection, Hong Kong. CK ku-hua, B. 60.

Two pheasants on a rock under peach blossoms and bamboo, S. M. Siu
collection, Hong Kong. CK ku-hua, B. 57.

A pair of ducks under a mallow shrub, S. M. Siu collection, Hong Kong.
CK ku-hua, B. 58.

Two ducks under hibiscus, S. M. Siu collection, Hong Kong. CK ku-
hua, B. 59.

CH'EN HSÜAN 陳選 . Unidentified.

Mountain landscape, inscribed, signed, dated 1357, six colophons,
Tientsin Art Museum. T'ien-ching, I. 6.

CH'EN LI-SHAN 陳立善 . From Hai-yen, Chekiang; served in the
Chih-cheng period (1341-1367) as a Censor in Chekiang, painted plum blossoms. (CP, VII, AL, 106-107.)

Slender branches of a plum-tree in bloom, signed, dated 1351, Nat.
Pal. Mus., Taipei, (AL). CH mei-shu, II; KKMH, VI. 21.

Plum blossoms and narcissus, signed, dated 1353, S. M. Siu collection, Hong Kong. CK ku-hua, A. 42; B. 105.

CH'EN LIN 陳 琳 , t. Chung-mei 仲美 . From Hangchou; lived
c. 1260-1320; friend of Chao Meng-fu, painted landscapes, figures, flowers
and birds. (CP, VII, AL, 107.)

A duck standing on a river shore, dated 1301, colophons by Chao Meng-
fu, Ch'iu Yüan and K'o Chiu-ssu, Nat. Pal. Mus. , Taipei, (AL).
300 M. , 156; CAT, 72; Che-chiang, 26; CH mei-shu, II; CKLTMHC,
III. 13; KKMH, V. 13.

River landscape with old trees on the rocky shore, handscroll, Nat.
Pal. Mus. , Taipei, (AL). CKLTMHC, III. 12.

A duck under hibiscus, signed, S. M. Siu collection, Hong Kong. CK
ku-hua, B. 54.

A pheasant, signed, S. M. Siu collection, Hong Kong. CK ku-hua,
A. 22; B. 55.

Two birds on a leafy tree branch, signed, S. M. Siu collection, Hong
Kong. CK ku-hua, B. 56.

CHENG HSI 鄭 禧 , t. Hsi-chih 熙之 or 禧之 . From Suchou;
active c. 1350, painted landscapes, bamboo and birds. (CP, VII, AL, 107.)

Pavilion among trees at the bay shore, handscroll, signed, dated 1353,
Nat. Pal. Mus. , Taipei, (AL). KKMH, V. 43.

CHIEH-HSI SSU 揭傒斯 , t. Man-shih 曼碩 . B. 1274, d.
1344; from Lung-hsing, Kiangsi, painted landscapes. (CP, VII, AL, 108.)

An old cypress, signed, dated 1322, S. M. Siu collection, Hong Kong.
CK ku-hua, A. 24; B. 53.

CH'IEN HSÜAN 錢 選 , t. Shun-chü 舜舉 , h. Yü-t'an 玉潭 .
From Wu-hsing, Chekiang, c. 1235-1300 , painted figures, landscapes,
flowers, and birds; one of the "Eight Talents of Wu-hsing". (CP, VII,
AL, 108-110.)

Radish, cabbage and bamboo shoots, signed, dated 1299, S. M. Siu
collection, Hong Kong. CK ku-hua, A. 14; B. 40.

Lu T'ung preparing tea on a garden terrace, artist's seal, Nat. Pal.
Mus. , Taipei, (AL). 300 M. , 127*; KKMH, III. 28.

The trunk of a tall lichee-tree, signed, Nat. Pal. Mus. , Taipei, (AL).
300 M. , 129.

Egg-plants, melons, turnips, goosefoot and cabbage, handscroll, Nat.
Pal. Mus. , Taipei, (AL). CH mei-shu, II.

A melon plant with fruits and flowers, signed, poem, Nat. Pal. Mus. ,
Taipei, (AL). 300 M. , 128; CKLTMHC, III. 2.

A squirrel on the branch of a peach-tree, handscroll, artist's seals,
Nat. Pal. Mus., Taipei, (AL). CAT, 68; Che-chiang, 19; CH
mei-shu, II; CKLTMHC, III.1; CKLTSHH; KKMH, IV.26*.

Flowers and leaves of two mutan plants, in the style of Hsü Hsi, handscroll, signed, poem by Ch'ien-lung, Nat. Pal. Mus., Taipei,
(AL). 300 M., 130 (section); KKMH, III.29*.

T'ao Yüan-ming walking along followed by a servant who carries a
wine-jar, handscroll, inscribed, signed, (AL). Li-tai jen-wu,32.

House on a mountain island, people on a bridge, handscroll, inscribed,
signed, (AL, Dwelling in the mountains?). CK ku-tai, 58.

Awaiting a ferry by a misty river, inscribed, signed, Nat. Pal. Mus.,
Taipei. KKMH, IV. 25.

Two ladies standing by a stone and flowering plants, album leaf, attributed, Nat. Pal. Mus., Taipei. CKLTMHC, II.97 (as anon.
Sung).

Wang Hsi-chih viewing geese, handscroll, attributed, same composition
as scroll in the C. C. Wang collection, Nat. Pal. Mus., Taipei.
CCAT, pl. 103 (section).

Bamboo shoots, album leaf, signed, S. M Siu collection, Hong Kong.
CK ku-hua, B.145.1.

Lin Pu gazing at plum branch in a vase, servant and crane at left,
handscroll, inscribed, signed. TWSY ming-chi, 92.

CHU SHU-CHUNG 朱叔重 . From Lou-tung, Kiangsu; active c. 1365,
poet, painted landscapes. (CP, VII, AL, 110.)

Landscape, signed, dated 1364, S. M. Siu collection, Hong Kong.
CK ku-hua, B.86.

A wooded mountain ridge rising through the mist, signed, dated 1365,
Nat. Pal. Mus., Taipei, (AL). 300 M., 178; CAT, 87; CKLTMHC,
III.41; KKMH, V.47.

Willows by a stream in spring, signed, Nat. Pal. Mus., Taipei, (AL).
300 M., 177.

CHU TE-JUN 朱德潤 , t. Tse-min 澤民 . B. 1294, d. 1365;
from Sui-yang, Honan, lived in K'un-shan, Kiangsu, painted landscapes
in imitation of Kuo Hsi. (CP, VII, AL, 110-111.)

The Cold Spring Pavilion, handscroll, signed, dated 1352, S. M. Siu
collection, Hong Kong. CK ku-hua, B.69.

Returning late under the pines, signed, dated 1360, S. M. Siu collection, Hong Kong. CK ku-hua, B.70.

Hsiu-yeh hsüan. The Pavilion of Flowering Fields, handscroll, long
inscription, signed, dated 1364, Palace Museum, Peking, (AL).
CK hua, XV. 12-13; CK ku-tai, 62 (section); WW, 1956.1.

Mountains and water in autumn mist, attributed by Tung Ch'i-ch'ang,
    Nat. Pal. Mus. , Taipei, (AL). CKLTMHC, III. 100 (as anon. Yüan).
River landscape in haze, three men seated under pine-trees, signed,
    poem by Wang Feng, Nat. Pal. Mus. , Taipei, (AL). 300 M. ,
    169; CAT, 82; CH mei-shu, II; CKLTMHC, III. 27; KKMH, V. 35.
Three men seated under pines by a stream, one playing a ch'in, fan,
    poem by artist, signed, Nat. Pal. Mus. , Taipei. KKMH, V. 36.

CHUANG LIN 莊麟 , t. Wen-chao 文昭 . Native of Chiang-tung;
lived in Peking; active at the end of the Yüan period. (CP, VII, AL, 111.)
    A scholar crossing a bridge toward a house, handscroll, signed, colo-
        phon by Tung Ch'i-ch'ang, part of collected scroll of Yüan works
        called Yüan-jen chi-chin, Nat. Pal. Mus. , Taipei, (AL). 300 M. ,
        202; CAT, 90h (section); CH mei-shu, II; CKLTMHC, III. 85;
        KKMH, VI. 37.

FANG TS'UNG-I 方從義 , t. Wu-yü 無隅 , h. Fang-hu 方壺 .
From Kuei-ch'i, Kiangsi; active c. 1340-1380; Taoist monk in the Shang-
ch'ing Temple in Kiangsi, painted landscapes, followed Mi Fei and Kao
K'o-kung. (CP, VII, AL, 112.)
    A sacred mountain and wonderful trees, signed, dated 1365, Nat. Pal.
        Mus. , Taipei, (AL). 300 M. , 196*; CAT, 89; CKLTMHC, III. 81;
        KKMH, VI. 24.
    Clouds and snow on the Shan-yin Mountains, after Kao K'o-kung, signed,
        Nat. Pal. Mus. , Taipei, (AL). CH mei-shu, II; CKLTMHC, III. 82.
    Pavilion on a steep terrace, signed, colophon by the artist, Nat. Pal.
        Mus. , Taipei, (AL). CH mei-shu, II; CKLTMHC, III. 83; CKLTSHH.
    A thatched hut in a mountain valley, album leaf, attributed, Nat. Pal.
        Mus. , Taipei. KKMH, VI. 25.
    Alone looking at a lofty hill, fan, signed, Nat. Pal. Mus. , Taipei.
        KKMH, VI. 26.
    Pavilions of the Immortals in the mountains, signed, colophon, S. M.
        Siu collection, Hong Kong. CK ku-hua, A. 33; B. 79.
    A hermit in the cloudy mountains, inscribed, signed, S. M. Siu collec-
        tion, Hong Kong. CK ku-hua, B. 80.
    Bamboo, inscribed, signed, S. M. Siu collection, Hong Kong. CK
        ku-hua, B. 81.
    A man in a pavilion looking at misty mountains, handscroll, signed.
        TSYMC hua-hsüan, 30.

FANG-YAI 方崖 . Lived at the end of the Yüan period in Su-chou;
ordained as a priest, close friend of Ni Tsan, painted trees, bamboos
and stones. (CP, VII, AL, 112.)

Slender bamboos by a rockery, artist's seal, poem and colophon by
Ma Chih dated 1382, Nat. Pal. Mus., Taipei, (AL). 300 M.,
197; CCAT, pl. 111. B; CH mei-shu, II; CKLTMHC, III. 75; KKCP,
I. 4; KKMH, VI. 29; NPM Quarterly, I. 4, pl. 10.

HSIA SHU-WEN 夏叔文 . Unrecorded in standard biographies, name
and native place (Feng-ch'eng) mentioned in Lu Hsin-yüan, Jang-li kuan
Kuo-yen lu, V. 11a.
 Various birds on a willow bank, artist's seal, Liao-ning Provincial
 Museum. Liao-ning, I. 96.

HSIA YUNG 夏永 , t. Ming-yüan 明遠 . 14th century? (CP, VII,
AL, 113.)
 The Yo-yang Palace, fan, inscribed, signed, dated 1347, Palace Mu-
 seum, Peking. Yüan-jen hua-ts'e, II*.
 The Palace of Prince T'eng, album leaf, inscribed, Freer Gallery of
 Art, Washington, D. C. (15. 36h). TWSY ming-chi, 101.
 The Yo-yang Palace (The Yellow Crane Tower), album leaf, inscribed,
 artist's seal, Freer Gallery of Art, Washington, D. C. (15. 36i).
 CK ku-tai, 61; TWSY ming-chi, 102.

HSIEH PO-CH'ENG 謝伯誠 . From Jen-yang; friend of Yang Wei-
chen (1296-1370), painted landscapes. (CP, VII, AL, 113.)
 A man in a pavilion looking at a waterfall, signed, dated 1355, S. M.
 Siu collection, Hong Kong. CK ku-hua, B. 96.

HSIEH T'ING-CHIH 謝廷芝 , t. Chung-ho 仲和 , h. Yün-ts'un
雲村 . From K'un-shan, Kiangsu, poet, painted bamboo, stones,
landscapes. (H. 5; I. 53; M. p. 703.)
 Bamboo and rocks, signed, dated 1345, Palace Museum, Peking.
 KKPWY hua-niao, 27*.

HSÜEH-CHIEH 雪界 . Unidentified.
 An eagle in a juniper tree, signed, done with Chang Shun-tzu, Huang
 Chou collection. CK hua, XIII. 20.

HU T'ING-HUI 胡庭暉 . From Wu-hsing, Chekiang; active c. 1300,
painted landscapes. (CP, VII, AL, 114.)
 Dragon boat race, attributed, Nat. Pal. Mus., Taipei. CKLTMHC,
 III. 16.

HUANG CHIN 黄溍 , t. Chin-ch'ing 晉卿 . B. 1277, d. 1357;
from I-wu, Chekiang, Han-lin scholar, official and a lecturer in the classics to the emperor, followed Huang Kung-wang and Wang Meng. (CP,

VII, AL, 114.)

    Reading in a mountain study, signed, dated 1345, S. M. Siu collection, Hong Kong. CK ku-hua, A. 37; B. 85.

HUANG KUNG-WANG 黄公望 , t. Tzu-chiu 子久 , h. I-feng 一峰 , Ta-ch'ih 大癡 , Ching-hsi tao-jen 井西道人 . B. 1269, d. 1354; from Ch'ang-shu, Kiangsu, painted landscapes, one of the "Four Great Masters" of the Yüan period. (CP, VII, AL, 114-115.)

    Autumn colors on the mountain peaks, a gully extending into the mountains, signed, dated 1301, one colophon, S. M. Siu collection, Hong Kong. CK ku-hua, B. 113.

    A man in a pavilion by a stream, album leaf, signed, dated 1332, S. M. Siu collection, Hong Kong. CK ku-hua, B. 145. 3.

    Hsien-shan t'u. Sloping hills with rows of trees, signed, dated 1338, painted for Cheng Yu, colophon by Ni Tsan dated 1359, Shanghai Museum, (AL). HK-w/WM, 10; Shang-hai, 12*.

    River landscape, inscribed, signed, dated 1338, S. M. Siu collection, Hong Kong. CK ku-hua, B. 112.

    The heavenly lake in the mountains, done when 73 (1341), colophon by Liu Kuan dated 1342, (same composition as painting by the same title listed by Sirén). TWSY ming-chi, 99.

    Mountain inlet, signed, dated 1342, S. M. Siu collection, Hong Kong. CK ku-hua, A. 29; B. 111.

    The Nine Peaks after snowfall, signed, dated 1349, Palace Museum, Peking, (AL). CK hua, I. 16; CK ku-tại, 64; HK-w/WM, 11; WW, 1956. 1.

    A house in a mountain valley, signed, done when age 81 (1349). TSYMC hua-hsüan, 19.

    Fu-ch'un shan-chü t'u. Dwelling in the Fu-ch'un Mountain, long handscroll, inscription by the artist stating that the painting was begun in 1347 and finished in 1350, Nat. Pal. Mus., Taipei (AL). 300 M., 161; CAT, 74 (section); Che-chiang, 23-25; CKLTMHC, III. 19; HK-w/WM, 1-8; NPM Quarterly, I. 2, pl. XX (section); WW, 1958. 6. 2 (section); 1964. 3. 20 (two sections from the two versions).

    A Taoist temple in the misty mountains, album leaf, signed, poem by the artist, Nat. Pal. Mus., Taipei, (AL). KKMH, V. 20.

    Clearing after snowfall on the river, handscroll, Palace Museum, Peking, (AL). WW, 1956. 1.

    Peaks of the Fu-ch'un Mountain and the winding road along the river, inscribed, signed, (AL). HK-w/WM, 9.

    The Nine Pearl Peaks, attributed, three colophons, Nat. Pal. Mus., Taipei. CCAT, pl. 109; KKMH, V. 19.

JEN JEN-FA 任 仁 發 , t. Tzu-ming 子 明 , h. Yüeh-shan 月 山 .
B. 1254, d. 1327; from Sung-chiang, Kiangsu; Vice-president of the River
Conservation Bureau, painted horses and landscapes. (CP, VII, AL,
115-116; for dates see Tsung Tien, "Yüan Jen Jen-fa mu-chih-ti fa-hsien",
WW, 1959. 11. 25-26.)

> The Taoist sorcerer Chang Kuo-lao before the Emperor Hsüan-tsung
> of T'ang, creating a small horse that speeds through the air,
> handscroll, signed, Palace Museum, Peking, (AL). JJ-f Chang
> Kuo*.
>
> Two horses, one strong and fat, another lean and tired, handscroll,
> Palace Museum, Peking, (AL). CK hua, II. 10; PM, 31*.
>
> A ch'in player seated on a cliff by a mountain stream, poem by the
> artist, seal, Nat. Pal. Mus., Taipei, (AL). 300 M., 172; KKMH,
> V. 41*.
>
> Two ducks, one pecking its wing, the other swimming in the water,
> four small birds in a hai-t'ang tree above, artist's seals, Shang-
> hai Museum, (AL). Shang-hai, 11*; TSYMC hua-hsüan, 18.
>
> Two grooms and a horse, handscroll, inscription by Ch'ien-lung. CK
> ku-tai, 59 (section).

K'ANG-LI NAO 康 里 巎 or K'ang-li Nao-nao 康 里 巎 巎 t.,
Tzu-shan 子 山 , h. Cheng-chai shu-sou 正 齋 恕 叟 , Shu-sou
恕 叟 , P'eng-lei-sou 蓬 累 叟 . B, 1295, d. 1345; a
Mongol; calligrapher. (I. 37.)

> Landscape, pavilion in the mountains, signed, dated 1342, S. M. Siu
> collection, Hong Kong. CK ku-hua, B. 73.

KAO K'O-KUNG 高 克 恭 , original name Shih-an 士 安 , t. Yen-
ching 彥 敬 , h. Fang-shan 房 山 . B. 1248, d. 1310; from
Ta-t'ung, Shansi; appointed by Kublai Khan to an official position and
made President of the Board of Justice, painted landscapes, followed Mi
Fei and Mi Yu-jen. (CP, VII, AL, 117.)

> Cloudy mountains, signed, dated 1299, S. M. Siu collection, Hong Kong.
> CK ku-hua, A. 16; B. 50.
>
> Clearing after a spring rain over the mountains, colophon by Li K'an
> dated 1299, Nat. Pal. Mus., Taipei, (AL). CK ku-tai, 55;
> CKLTMHC, III. 3.
>
> Cloud-encircled, luxuriant mountains, inscription by Li K'an dated
> 1309, Nat. Pal. Mus., Taipei, (AL). 300 M., 152*; CAT, 70;
> CCAT, pl. 107; CKLTMHC, III. 4; KKMH, V. 9*.
>
> Mountains in rain, signed, poem by Ch'ien-lung, Nat. Pal. Mus.,
> Taipei, (AL). 300 M., 153.
>
> Clouded hills and a waterfall, signed, Nat. Pal. Mus., Taipei. 300
> M., 154.

Bamboo and rock, signed, colophon by Chao Meng-fu, Palace Museum, Peking. KKPWY hua-niao, 22*.

Rainy spring mountains, attributed, Shanghai Museum. Shang-hai, 9*.

Misty mountains and cloudy trees, handscroll, signed, S. M. Siu collection, Hong Kong. CK ku-hua, B. 48.

A temple in cloudy mountains, signed, S. M. Siu collection, Hong Kong. CK ku-hua, B. 49.

K'O CHIU-SSU 柯九思 , t. Ching-chung 敬仲 , h. Tan-ch'iu 丹丘 . B. 1290, d. 1343, from T'ai-chou, Chekiang; connoisseur, painted bamboo and old trees. (CP, VII, AL, 118; for dates see Tsung Tien, K'o Chiu-ssu shih-liao, Shanghai, 1963, pp. 181-200.)

Bamboos by a garden rock, dated 1338, Palace Museum, Peking, (AL). KC-s shih-liao, between pp. 44-45.

Bamboo and thorn by a rock, signed, dated 1342, S. M. Siu collection, Hong Kong. CK ku-hua, A. 31; B. 76.

A branch of bamboo, signed, dated 1343, after Wen T'ung, C. C. Wang collection, New York, (AL). KC-s shih-liao, between pp. 44-45.

River landscape, signed, colophon by Yo Yü dated 1344, Nat. Pal. Mus., Taipei, (AL). KC-s shih-liao, between pp. 46-47.

A tall bamboo and a chrysanthemum plant by a rock, signed, colophon by Yü Chi, poem by Ch'ien-lung, Nat. Pal. Mus., Taipei, (AL). 300 M., 180; CAT, 79; CH mei-shu, II; CKLTSHH; KC-s shih-liao, before p. 41; KKCP, I.2; KKMH, V.48; NPM Quarterly, I.4, pl. 9.

Bamboos by a stone, signed, Nat. Pal. Mus., Taipei, (AL). KC-s shih-liao, between pp. 44-45.

Branches of a blossoming plum-tree, signed, (AL). KC-s shih-liao, after p. 46.

A pavilion built over a stream at the foot of high mountains, signed, Nat. Pal. Mus., Taipei, (AL). KC-s shih-liao, opposite p. 47.

Bamboos growing from a rock, fan, signed, Nat. Pal. Mus., Taipei, (AL). CKLTMHC, III.35; KC-s shih-liao, before p. 45.

A branch of bamboo, inscription by the painter and by Ch'ien-lung, Abe collection, Ōsaka Museum, (AL). KC-s shih-liao, between pp. 44-45.

An old knotted tree, bamboos and epidendrums by a rock, signed, (AL). KC-s shih-liao, between pp. 46-47.

Two bamboos, signed, Shanghai Museum (AL). Che-chiang, 35; KC-s shih-liao, after p. 44; Shang-hai, 26*.

Bamboo studies, six album leaves. KC-s shih-liao, pp. 40-41.

Morning colors in an autumn grove, signed. KC-s shih-liao, opposite p. 58.

A small pavilion in an autumn grove. KC-s shih-liao, opposite p. 151.

KU AN 顧安 , t. Ting-chih 定之 . From Yangchou, Kiangsu;
served as a judge in Ch'üan-chou in the Yüan-t'ung era (1333-1334),
painted bamboos. (CP, VII, AL, 118.)

Bamboo in wind, signed, dated 1348, S. M. Siu collection, Hong Kong.
CK ku-hua, A. 38; B. 87.

Bamboos on a rock in wind, signed, dated 1350, Nat. Pal. Mus.,
Taipei, (AL). CH mei-shu, II; CKLTMHC, III. 71; CKLTSHH;
KKMH, V. 40.

Bamboo and rock, signed, dated 1359, Nat. Pal. Mus., Taipei.
CKLTMHC, III. 72.

Bamboo and rock, signed, dated 1364, S. M. Siu collection, Hong Kong.
CK ku-hua, B. 88.

Ch'üan-shih hsin-huang t'u. Rocks and fresh bamboo-sprouts, album
leaf, signed, dated 1365, colophons by Mo Chin-kung and Ch'ien-
lung, Nat. Pal. Mus., Taipei, (AL, listed also as Fresh and slender bamboos on a rock). CKLTMHC, III.73; KKMH, V.39.

Bamboo, signed, dated 1365, S. M. Siu collection, Hong Kong. CK
ku-hua, B. 89.

An old tree and bamboos by a rock, painted in co-operation with Ni
Tsan and Chang Shen, poem by Ni Tsan dated 1373, Nat. Pal. Mus.,
Taipei, (AL). CH mei-shu, II; CKLTMHC, III.74; KKCP, I.3;
KKMH, VI.38.

Bamboos in wind, artist's seals, Nat. Pal. Mus., Taipei, (AL).
300 M., 173; CH mei-shu, II; CKLTMHC, III.70.

Bamboo and garden stone, signature partly effaced, one colophon,
also partly effaced, Hsü Shih-hsüeh collection. CK hua, I.17;
TWSY ming-chi, 103.

KU TE-HUI 顧德輝 or Ku Ying 顧瑛 , t. Chung-ying 仲瑛 ,
h. Chin-su tao-jen 金粟道人 . B. 1310, d. 1369; from K'un-shan,
Kiangsu, poet and connoisseur. (CP, VII, AL, 119.)

Butterflies and vegetables, signed, dated 1352, S. M. Siu collection,
Hong Kong. CK ku-hua, B.92.

KUAN TAO-SHENG 管道昇 , t. Chung-chi 仲姬 . B. 1262,
d. 1319; from Wu-hsing, Chekiang; wife of Chao Meng-fu, calligrapher,
painted bamboo, plum blossoms, epidendrums and landscapes. (CP, VII,
AL, 119.)

Branch of apricot blossoms, signed, dated 1303, S. M. Siu collection,
Hong Kong. CK ku-hua, A.20; B.46.

Bamboo grove along a river-bank, handscroll, signed, dated 1308,
part of collected scroll of Yüan works called Yüan-jen chi-chin,
Nat. Pal. Mus., Taipei, (AL). 300 M., 150; CAT, 90b (section);
CH mei-shu, II; KKMH, V.8.

Slender bamboos by a rock, artist's seal, Nat. Pal. Mus., Taipei,
(AL). 300 M., 151; Che-chiang, 22; KKMH, V.7.

Two full stalks of bamboo and a short clump of bamboo by a rock,
signed, three colophons, S.M. Siu collection, Hong Kong. CK
ku-hua, A.19; B.45.

A stalk of bamboo, inscribed, signed, S.M. Siu collection, Hong Kong.
CK ku-hua, B.47.

KUO PI 郭畀 , t. T'ien-hsi 天錫 and Yu-chih 祐之 , h. Pei-
shan 北山 . B. 1301, d. 1355; from Ching-k'ou, Kiangsu, painted
landscapes after Mi Fei. (CP, VII, AL, 120.)

Mountains in mist, signed, dated 1339, illustration to two lines of a
poem by Kao Shih, Nat. Pal. Mus., Taipei, (AL). 300 M., 174;
CH mei-shu, II; KKMH, V.42.

Cloud sea, signed, dated 1342, colophon by Ch'ien-lung, S.M. Siu
collection, Hong Kong. CK ku-hua, A.30; B.75.

A bamboo grove in snow, handscroll, signed, Nat. Pal. Mus., Taipei,
(AL). CAT, 78.

LENG CH'IEN 冷謙 , t. Ch'i-ching 啟敬 , h. Lung-yang-tzu
龍陽子 . A legendary Taoist from Wu-ling, Hunan; in the Chih-yüan
period (1335-1340) he is said to have been 100 years old, became a Court
Musician in the Hung-wu period (1368-1398), landscapes in the style of
Li Ssu-hsün. (CP, VII, AL, 120-121.)

A study under the plum trees, signed, S.M. Siu collection, Hong Kong.
CK ku-hua, B.110.

LI JUNG-CHIN 李容瑾 , t. Kung-yen 公琰 . First half of the 14th
century, specialized in boundary painting, followed Wang Chen-p'eng.
(CP, VII, AL, 121.)

Imperial palaces of the Han period, signed, Nat. Pal. Mus., Taipei,
(AL). 300 M., 175; CKLTMHC, III.30; KKMH, V.44.

LI K'AN 李衎 , t. Chung-pin 仲賓 , h. Hsi-chai tao-jen 息齋道人 .
B. 1245, d. 1320; from Chi-ch'iu, near Peking; President of the Board
of Officials, painted trees and bamboo, author of the Chu-p'u.
(CP, VII, AL, 121.)

Outline bamboo, signed, dated 1300, Chang Pe-chin collection. Tien
Yin Tang, I. 8.

Two large tufts of bamboo with widely spreading branches, handscroll,
signed, painted for Hsüan-ch'ing, colophon by Chao Meng-fu
dated 1308, colophon by Yüan Ming-shan dated 1309, Nelson Gallery of Art, Kansas City, (AL). NPM Quarterly, I.4, pls. 4-5
(sections).

A pair of tall pine-trees and some jujube shrubs, artist's seal, Nat.
　　Pal. Mus., Taipei, (AL). 300 M., 155; CKLTMHC, III. 5; KKMH,
　　V. 10.
Four bamboos by a stone, signed, Nat. Pal. Mus., Taipei. CCAT,
　　pl. 106.
Four bamboo stalks and smaller clusters by a rock, bare tree branches,
　　artist's seal, Palace Museum, Peking. CK ku-tai, 60; KKPWY
　　hua-niao, 21*.
Withering trees and bamboo, signed, two colophons, S. M. Siu collec-
　　tion, Hong Kong. CK ku-hua, A. 15; B. 51.
Bamboo grove and rock. TWSY ming-chi, 98.
Bamboo and trees, handscroll. WW, 1956. 1 (section).

LI K'ANG 李康 , t. Ning-chih 甯之 . Native of T'ung-lu, Che-
kiang; active c. 1340-1360. (CP, VII, AL, 122.)
　　Fu-hsi seated on rock holding brush and paper, attributed, (AL).
　　Che-chiang, 42.

LI SHENG 李升 , t. Tzu-yün 子雲 , h. Tzu-yün-sheng 紫篔生 .
From Hao-liang; active at the end of the Yüan dynasty, painted bamboo,
rocks and landscapes. (CP, VII, AL, 122.)
　　Mountain landscape with small buildings on hillocks among pine-trees,
　　handscroll, inscribed, dated 1346, Shanghai Museum, (AL). CK
　　hua, I. 18-19.

LI SHIH-HSING 李士行 , t. Tsun-tao 遵道 . B. 1282, d. 1328;
son of Li K'an, painted landscapes, bamboo and stones. (CP, VII, AL,
122.)
　　Bamboo in the wind, signed dated 1324, S. M. Siu collection, Hong
　　Kong. CK ku-hua, A. 25; B. 93.
　　A knotted old pine-tree and bamboos, signed, Nat. Pal. Mus., Taipei,
　　(AL). CH mei-shu, II; CKLTMHC, III. 24; CKLTSHH; KKMH, V. 11.
　　Two intertwined old trees and slender bamboos, signed, colophon by
　　the Monk Chih-yüan, Shanghai Museum, (AL). Shang-hai, 15*.
　　River landscape in late autumn, handscroll, artist's seal, Nat. Pal.
　　Mus., Taipei, (AL). CH mei-shu, II; CKLTMHC, III. 23; KKMH,
　　V. 12.
　　Bamboo and stones, signed, Liao-ning Provincial Museum. Liao-
　　ning, I. 88.
　　A dwarf pine in a tray, signed, colophon by Ch'ien-lung, S. M. Siu
　　collection, Hong Kong. CK ku-hua, A. 26; B. 94.

LIN CHÜAN-A 林卷阿 , t. Tzu-huan 子奐 , h. Yu-yu-sheng

優遊生.. Landscapes, followed Kuo Hsi. (CP, VII, AL, 122.)
  A broad river-view with a fishing-boat, handscroll, signed, dated
    1373, part of a collected scroll of Yüan works called <u>Yüan-jen chi-</u>
    <u>chin,</u> Nat. Pal. Mus., Taipei, (AL). 300 M., 201; (CAT, 90g);
    CH mei-shu, II; CKLTMHC, III. 84.

LIU KUAN-TAO 劉貫道 , t. Chung-hsien 仲賢 . From Chung-
shan, Hopei; active c. 1270-1300, painted Buddhist and Taoist figures,
portraits and landscapes. (CP, VII, AL, 123.)
  Emperor Kublai Khan with a party of men on horseback hunting, signed,
    dated 1280, Nat. Pal. Mus., Taipei, (AL). 300 M., 158; CCAT,
    pl. 108; CKLTMHC, III. 14; KKMH, V. 17.
  Snowy mountains, signed, dated 1349, S. M. Siu collection, Hong Kong.
    CK ku-hua, B. 77.
  A man resting on a couch in the open, according to an inscription by
    Wu Fu-han, the picture is signed Kuan-tao, Nelson Gallery of
    Art, Kansas City, (AL). Li-tai jen-wu, 29 (section).
  Seven Sages, handscroll, signed Liu Chung-hsien, dated 1437, Nat.
    Pal. Mus., Taipei. CCAT, pl. 113 (section).

LU KUANG 陸廣 , t. Chi-hung 季弘 , h. T'ien-yu 天遊 . From
Suchou; active during the second quarter of the 14th century, painted land-
scapes. (CP, VII, AL, 124.)
  Towers and pavilions on the Mountains of the Immortals, inscribed,
    signed, dated T'ien-li 4 (1332?), Nat. Pal. Mus., Taipei, (AL).
    KKMH, VI. 22.
  A man in an open pavilion by a river, attributed by Wu K'uan, Shang-
    hai Museum, (AL). Shang-hai, 24*.
  Villas in the mountains, inscribed, signed, S. M. Siu collection, Hong
    Kong. CK ku-hua, A. 54; B. 99.
  A deep retreat in the autumn mountains, inscribed, signed, S. M. Siu
    collection, Hong Kong. CK ku-hua, B. 100.
  Old trees and bamboo, inscribed, signed, one colophon, S. M. Siu
    collection, Hong Kong. CK ku-hua, B. 101.

MA YÜAN 馬琬 , t. Wen-pi 文璧 , h. Lu-ch'un 魯純 or Lu-
tun 魯鈍 . From Nanking; active c. 1325-1365; Governor of Wu-
chou in the Hung-wu period, painted landscapes, followed Tung Yüan and
Mi Fei. (CP, VII, AL, 124-125.)
  High terraced and deeply crevassed mountains in snow, signed, dated
    1349, Nat. Pal. Mus., Taipei, (AL). CKLTMHC, III. 78; KKMH,
    VI. 31.
  <u>Mu-yün shih-i t'u.</u> The evening clouds conveying poetic ideas, signed,
    dated 1349, Shanghai Museum, (AL). Shang-hai, 30*.

Wintry trees and rocks, signed, dated 1360, S. M. Siu collection,
Hong Kong. CK ku-hua, B. 136.

Clearing over spring mountains, handscroll, signed, dated 1366, part
of collected scroll of Yüan works called Yüan-jen chi-chin, Nat.
Pal. Mus. , Taipei, (AL). 300 M. , 198; (CAT, 90e); CH mei-
shu, III; CKLTMHC, III. 80; KKMH, VI. 30.

An angler in a boat by the shore in autumn, signed, Nat. Pal. Mus. ,
Taipei, (AL). CH mei-shu, III; KKMH, VI. 33.

Mountains in autumn with travellers, attributed by Tung Ch'i-ch'ang,
Nat. Pal. Mus. , Taipei, (AL). CKLTMHC, III. 79; KKMH, VI. 32.

Snowy river valley, handscroll, signed, S. M. Siu collection, Hong
Kong. CK ku-hua, B. 135.

NI TSAN 倪 瓚 , t. Yüan-chen 元鎮 , h. Yün-lin 雲林 , Yü
迂 , Ching-ming chü-shih 凈名居士 . B. 1301, d. 1374; from
Wu-hsi, Kiangsu; poet, calligrapher and painter of landscapes, one of the
"Four Great Masters" of the Yüan period. (CP, VII, AL, 125-128.)

An old man in an open pavilion under autumn trees by a stream, two
inscriptions by the artist, the first dated 1339, John M. Crawford collection, New York, (AL). NPM Quarterly, I. 3, pls. 1, 2.

Six trees on a rocky islet, colophon by the artist dated 1345; poems
by Huang Kung-wang and three others, (AL). Ni Tsan, 1; Ni Yün-
lin, 1; NPM Quarterly, I. 3, pl. 3.

Bamboo, handscroll, poem by the artist, dated 1350, S. M. Siu collection, Hong Kong. CK ku-hua, B. 126.

Two leafless trees and slender bamboos growing by some stones, inscription by the artist dated 1353, colophons by Wen Cheng-ming
and Chang Ta-ch'ien, C. C. Wang collection, New York, (AL).
NPM Quarterly, I. 3, pl. 4.

A pavilion under tall trees by a river, poem by the artist dated 1354,
colophon by Tung Ch'i-ch'ang, Nat. Pal. Mus. , Taipei, (AL).
CKLTMHC, III. 61; Ni Tsan, 2; Ni Yün-lin, 2; NPM Quarterly,
I. 3, pl. 5.

Bamboo, stone and tree, poem, signed, dated 1357, Shanghai Museum.
Shang-hai, 21*.

Bamboos and bare trees by some strange cliffs, poem and colophon
by the artist dated 1360, Shanghai WWPKWYH, (AL). CK hua,
I. 20; Ni Tsan, 5.

A pavilion under five trees, poem by the artist, signed, dated 1360,
S. M. Siu collection, Hong Kong. CK ku-hua, B. 122.

Landscape, artist's inscription and poem, signed, dated 1360, done
with Wang Meng, inscription by Wang Meng, S. M. Siu collection,
Hong Kong. CK ku-hua, B. 124.

Looking at the waterfall, according to the inscription, painted with
Wang Meng, dated 1361, Nat. Pal. Mus. , Taipei, (AL). KKMH,
VI. 39.

River landscape: mountain ridge on the farther shore; spare trees
and low pavilion in front, handscroll, signed, dated 1362, (AL).
Ni Yün-lin, 3.

River view: two steep mountains rising out of the water, poem by
the artist dated 1363, Nat. Pal. Mus. , Taipei, (AL). 300 M. ,
185; CAT, 84; CH mei-shu, II; CKLTMHC, III. 52; CKLTSHH;
KKMH, VI. 9; NPM Quarterly, I. 2, pl. XXXI; I. 3, pl. 7. A.

Fresh bamboo and dry trees at a stone, poem and inscription by the
artist, signed, dated 1363, Nat. Pal. Mus. , Taipei, (AL).
CKLTMHC, III. 55; KKMH, VI. 11; NPM Quarterly, I. 3, pl. 6.

Portrait of Yang Chu-hsi in a landscape, handscroll, inscribed, signed,
dated 1363, figure by Wang I, landscape by Ni Tsan, Palace Museum, Peking, (AL). CK hua, XVIII. 16; Li-tai jen-wu, 40; TSYMC
hua-hsüan, 27.

Landscape: saying farewell at Nan-ch'ih, handscroll, poem, inscription, signed, dated 1364, S. M. Siu collection, Hong Kong. CK
ku-hua, B. 125.

Landscape done for Chou Po-ang, poem, signed, dated 1364, a second
poem and inscription by the artist, two additional colophons.
TSYMC hua-hsüan, 26.

Riverside pavilion under trees, hills in the background, signed, dated
1365, ex-Wu Hu-fan collection. Ni Tsan, 3; Ni Yün-lin, 4; NPM
Quarterly, I. 3, pl. 8.

The Western Garden, low pavilion on foreground bank, mountain with
waterfall in background, poem by artist, signed, dated 1365.
NPM Quarterly, I. 3, pl. 7. B.

Pavilion on a promontory, inscribed, signed, dated 1366, Nat. Pal.
Mus. , Taipei. NPM Quarterly, I. 3, pl. 9.

River landscape with three trees and a pavilion in a bamboo grove,
signed, dated 1366, two colophons, S. M. Siu collection, Hong
Kong. CK ku-hua, A. 51; B. 120.

Yü-hou k'ung-lin t'u: scattered trees on a rocky shore after rain,
inscription, signed, dated 1368, colophons by four contemporaries,
painted in colors, Nat. Pal. Mus. , Taipei, (AL). 300 M. , 184*;
CH mei-shu, II; CKLTMHC, III. 53; KKMH, V. 6*; NPM Quarterly,
I. 3, pl. 11*.

Low straw-covered pavilion and five thin trees on a rocky ledge, poem,
signed, dated 1368, painted for Shu-kuei, C. C. Wang collection,
New York, (AL). Ni Tsan, 11; NPM Quarterly, I. 3, pl. 10.

Bamboo by a rock, poem, signed, dated 1368, S. M. Siu collection,
Hong Kong. CK ku-hua, B. 123.

A low pavilion on a promontory, album leaf, poem, signed, dated
1369, S. M. Siu collection, Hong Kong. CK ku-hua, B. 145. 5.

High mountains by a river, signed, dated 1371, poems by Wang Ju-
yü and Ch'ien-lung, colophon by Tung Ch'i-ch'ang, Nat. Pal.
Mus. , Taipei, (AL). CKLTMHC, III. 54.

Leafless trees and young bamboos by a strange stone, album leaf,
signed, dated 1371, Nat. Pal. Mus. , Taipei, (AL). CKLTMHC,
III. 57; NPM Quarterly, I. 3, pl. 12.

The top-section of a bamboo plant, poem, signed, dated 1371, eight
inscriptions, Nat. Pal. Mus. , Taipei, (AL). CKLTMHC, III. 56;
NPM Quarterly, I. 3, pl. 15.

Mountains and valleys of the Yü Mountains, signed, dated 1371, colophon by Ch'ien-lung, C. C. Wang collection, New York. Ni Tsan,
6; NPM Quarterly, I. 3, pl. 14.

Rocky river shore, path leading over bridge to houses by tall cliffs,
signed, dated 1371, Yen Sheng-p'o collection, Hong Kong. NPM
Quarterly, I. 3, pl. 13.

The Jung-ch'i Studio. Spare trees and a low pavilion on the shore,
poem and colophon by the artist, dated 1372, Nat. Pal. Mus. ,
Taipei, (AL). 300 M. , 186; CH mei-shu, II; CKLTMHC, III. 58;
KKMH, VI. 7; NPM Quarterly, I. 3, pl. 16.

A place for fishing after rain in autumn, poem, signed, dated 1372,
Shanghai Museum, (AL). Ni Tsan, 4; Shang-hai, 20*.

Mountain scenery with river lodge, inscribed, signed, dated 1372,
Nat. Pal. Mus. , Taipei. CAT, 85; CCAT, pl. 111; KKMH, VI. 10;
NPM Quarterly, I. 3, pl. 18.

Low pavilion under trees next to barren strip of rocks, compact hills
in background, long inscription, signed, dated 1372, two colophons
by Tung Ch'i-ch'ang. NPM Quarterly, I. 3, pl. 17.

Views from the Shih-tzu-lin (garden), handscroll, inscribed, signed,
dated 1373, (AL). Ni Yün-lin, 5-7.

An old tree trunk and some bamboos by a rock, poem by Ni Tsan
dated 1373, painted together with Chang Shen and Ku An, Nat.
Pal. Mus. , Taipei, (AL). CH mei-shu, II; CKLTMHC, III. 74;
KKCP, I. 3; KKMH, VI. 38.

A slender bamboo branch, long inscription dated 1374, colophons by
Chang Shen, Wang Ju-yü and Miao-sheng, Nat. Pal. Mus. , Tai-
pei, (AL). 300 M. , 187; CKLTMHC, III. 59; KKMH, VI. 8; NPM
Quarterly, I. 3, pl. 19.

Spring river scene with low pavilion and five thin trees, signed, dated
1374, poem by the artist, S. M. Siu collection, Hong Kong. CK
ku-hua, A. 52; B. 119.

The Pavilion of the Purple Fungus on the river, poem, signed, Nat.
Pal. Mus. , Taipei, (AL). CKLTMHC, III. 60; Ni Tsan, 7; Ni

Yün-lin, 8; NPM Quarterly, I. 3, pl. 21.

The An-ch'u Study, handscroll, poem, signed, part of collected scroll of Yüan works called <u>Yüan-jen chi-chin</u>, Nat. Pal. Mus. , Taipei, (AL). (CAT, 90c); CH mei-shu, II; CKLTMHC, III. 51; KKMH, VI. 12.

A few bamboos and a tall <u>wu-t'ung</u> tree by a garden rock, inscribed, signed, Palace Museum, Peking, (AL). CK ku-tai, 66; Ni Tsan, 8; Ni Yün-lin, 10; WW, 1961. 6. 4.

Pavilion and spare trees in autumn on a river shore; mountains in the distance, inscription by the artist and a poem to a friend, Palace Museum, Peking, (AL). PM, 8*.

A slender branch of bamboo, handscroll, inscription by the painter, Palace Museum, Peking, (AL). CK hua, II. 8; Ni Tsan, 9; Ni Yün-lin, 11.

The Ch'an study in the western grove, handscroll, signed, (AL). Ni Yün-lin, 9.

Two leafless trees and slender bamboos by a rock, inscribed, signed, dedicated to Lü-shui-yüan, dated: sixth month, fifth day (no year), C. C. Wang collection, New York, (AL). NPM Quarterly, I. 3, pl. 23.

Two trees, a high stone and some bamboos around a house on the shore; mountain silhouettes on the opposite shore, poem, signed, C. C. Wang collection, New York, (AL). NPM Quarterly, I. 3, pl. 20.

River view. Five trees on the shore, large rocks on the farther shore; a narrow stretch of water, inscription by the painter, C. C. Wang collection, New York, (AL). NPM Quarterly, I. 3, pl. 22.

A river winding between cliffs, trees and a pavilion in the foreground, inscribed, signed, Palace Museum, Peking, (AL, under 1372, <u>I-shu ts'ung-pien</u>, 9). Ni Tsan, 10; Ni Yün-lin, 12.

Bamboo, stone and dry tree, signed, Nat. Pal. Mus. , Taipei. NPM Quarterly, I. 3, pl. 24.

Bamboo, album leaf, signed, Freer Gallery of Art, Washington, D. C. NPM Quarterly, I. 3, pl. 25; I. 4, pl. 16.

Trees and bamboo in a landscape, inscribed, signed, S. M. Siu collection, Hong Kong. CK ku-hua, B. 121.

PIEN WU 邊武 , t. Po-ching 伯京 . From Peking; active first half of the 14th century, a calligrapher, painted flowers, birds, bamboo and stones. (CP, VII, AL, 128.)

Ink play: bird on a vine-covered tree, signed, dated 1337?, S. M. Siu collection, Hong Kong. CK ku-hua, B. 61.

PO-YEN PU-HUA 伯顏不花 , t. Ts'ang-yen 蒼岩 . D. 1359; a

Mongol nobleman, distinguished military commander, painted dragons and landscapes. (CP, VII, AL, 129.)

Cloudy ravine, signed, dated 1357, S. M. Siu collection, Hong Kong. CK ku-hua, A. 44; B. 74.

P'U-MING 普明 . Family name Ts'ao 曹 , h. Hsüeh-ch'uang 雪窓 . From Sung-chiang, Kiangsu; a priest of the Ch'eng-t'ien Temple in Suchou; active c. 1340-1350, specialized in epidendrums. (CP, VII, AL, 129.)

Bamboo and orchids in wind, signed, Cleveland Museum of Art, (AL). NPM Quarterly, I. 4, pl. 17.

SA TU-LA 薩都拉 , t. T'ien-hsi 天錫 , h. Chih-chai 直齋 . B. 1308, d. c. 1340; a Mongol, family lived at Yen-men, Shansi, poet and calligrapher. (CP, VII, AL, 130.)

A rock, signed, dated 1334, S. M. Siu collection, Hong Kong. CK ku-hua, B. 72.

A man under old pines looking at a distant waterfall, inscribed, signed, dated 1337, S. M. Siu collection, Hong Kong. CK ku-hua, A. 28; B. 71.

SHANG CH'I 商琦 , t. Te-fu 德符 . From Ts'ao-chou, Shantung; employed as a teacher at the court of the Emperor Ch'eng-tsung (1295-1307), painted landscapes and bamboo. (CP, VII, AL, 130.)

A bird on a reed, signed, dated 1296, colophon by Wang Yün, S. M. Siu collection, Hong Kong. CK ku-hua, B. 63.

Visiting the recluse in the mountains, signed, S. M. Siu collection, Hong Kong. CK ku-hua, B. 64.

SHENG CH'ANG-NIEN 盛昌年 . Unrecorded, according to the painting, his t. was Yüan-ling 元齡 and he was from Wu-iin, Chekiang.

Two swallows and a willow tree, inscribed, signed, dated 1353, Palace Museum, Peking. KKPWY hua-niao, 28*.

SHENG HUNG 盛洪 or Sheng Hung-fu 盛洪甫 , t. Wen-yü 文裕 . From Hangchou, lived in Chia-hsing, Chekiang; father of Sheng Mou, painted landscapes, figures and birds. (CP, VII, AL, 130.)

Landscape, fisherman in a boat, signed, dated 1342, S. M. Siu collection, Hong Kong. CK ku-hua, B. 68.

Narcissi, signed, dated 1354, two colophons, S. M. Siu collection, Hong Kong. CK ku-hua, A. 43; B. 67.

SHENG MOU 盛懋 , t. Tzu-chao 子昭 . From Chia-hsing, Chekiang; active c. 1310-1360, painted landscapes, figures and birds, followed Tung Yüan and Chü-jan and later Sung masters. (CP, VII, AL, 130-131.)

Landscape, signed, dated 1343, S. M. Siu collection, Hong Kong. CK ku-hua, B. 102.

A man in a boat under five trees, album leaf, inscribed, signed, dated 1344, Nat. Pal. Mus., Taipei. KKMH, VI. 3.

Waiting for the ferry-boat on a river-bank in autumn, signed, dated 1351, Freer Gallery of Art, Washington, D. C. (54. 12), (AL). TWSY ming-chi, 100.

A man playing the flute on a river bank under curving trees, signed, dated 1351. Li-tai jen-wu, 37.

A rocky slope with old pine-trees, handscroll, signed, eight inscriptions by contemporaries, the last one by Wei Chiu-ting dated 1361, Nat. Pal. Mus., Taipei, (AL). CAT, 80 (section).

A hermit seated under autumn trees, high mountains rising through thick clouds, signed, Nat. Pal. Mus., Taipei, (AL). 300 M., 181; CAT, 81; CH mei-shu, II; CKLTMHC, III. 40; KKMH, VI. 1*.

A summer-day in the mountains; river valley with numerous figures and pavilions, Nat. Pal. Mus., Taipei, (AL). CKLTMHC, III. 36.

A mountain stream, two men in a small boat; leafy trees on the shore, signed, Nat. Pal. Mus., Taipei, (AL). CKLTMHC, III. 38.

A man angling in a boat on a quiet lake, fan, artist's seal, Nat. Pal. Mus., Taipei, (AL). CKLTMHC, III. 37.

Autumn scene: a man in a boat on the river, attributed, Shanghai Museum, (AL). Che-chiang, 29; Shang-hai, 17*.

Pavilions under pine-trees by a mountain stream, Nat. Pal. Mus., Taipei, (AL, Chü-jan). 300 M., 49 (as Chü-jan); CKLTMHC, III. 39 (as Sheng Mou).

Landscape, a man riding a donkey on a bridge, fan, attributed, Nat. Pal. Mus., Taipei. KKMH, VI. 2.

Fishing from a boat in a clear stream, fan, artist's seals, Palace Museum, Peking. Yüan-jen hua-ts'e, I*.

Fishing by an autumn grove, album leaf, signed, Palace Museum, Peking. Yüan-jen hua-ts'e, I*.

A man holding a ju-i seated on a promontory watching two flying geese, misty mountains, fan, artist's seal, Palace Museum, Peking. Yüan-jen hua-ts'e, II*.

Boat at the shore, album leaf, signed, S. M. Siu collection, Hong Kong. CK ku-hua, B. 145. 7.

A man seated on a river bank, enframing tree trunks and branches, attributed. TSYMC hua-hsüan, 22.

SHIH CHIANG (KANG) 史杠 , t. Jou-ming 柔明 , h. Chü-chai tao-jen 橘齋道人 . From Yung-ch'ing, Hopei; first half of the 14th century, painted figures, landscapes, flowers and birds. (CP, VII, AL, 131-132.)

Flowers and birds, signed, dated 1315, colophon by Ch'ien-lung, S. M. Siu Collection, Hong Kong. CK ku-hua, B. 66.

SU TA-NIEN 蘇大年 , t. Ch'ang-ling 昌齡 , h. Hsi-chien 西澗 , Hsi-chien lao-ch'iao 西澗老樵 , Hsi-p'o 西陂 , Lin-wu tung chu 林屋洞主 . B. 1296, d. 1364; from Chen-ting, Kiangsu, lived in Yangchou; poet, calligrapher, painted bamboo, stones and trees after Wen T'ung and Su Shih. (H. 5; I. 54; M. p. 731.)

Pine tree and bamboo, inscribed, signed, dated 1342, S. M. Siu collection, Hong Kong. CK ku-hua, B. 82.

SUN CHÜN-TSE 孫君澤 . From Hang-chou; active at the beginning of the 14th century, painted landscapes with figures and boundary paintings. (CP, VII, AL, 132.)

A man on a terrace in front of a pavilion under a twisted pine, signed, (AL). Che-chiang, 40.

TAI SHUN 戴淳 , t. Hou-fu 厚夫 . From Ch'ien-t'ang, Chekiang; active c. 1317, landscapes. (CP, VII, AL, 133.)

A hermit's lodge in the mountains, signed, dated 1317, colophon by Ch'ien-lung, S. M. Siu collection, Hong Kong. CK ku-hua, A. 23; B. 62.

The K'uang-lu Mountain, signed, dated 1318, Nat. Pal. Mus., Taipei, (AL). KKMH, V. 45.

T'ANG TI 唐棣 , t. Tzu-hua 子華 . B. 1296, d. 1364; from Wu-hsing, Chekiang; pupil of Chao Meng-fu, also followed Kuo Hsi. (CP, VII, AL, 133-134.)

Gentlemen picnicking on a river bank, signed, dated 1334. CK hua, V. 15; TSYMC hua-hsüan, 20.

The returning woodcutter, signed, dated 1334, S. M. Siu collection, Hong Kong. CK ku-hua, A. 27; B. 83.

Fishermen walking under tall trees along a river-bank, signed, dated 1338, Nat. Pal. Mus., Taipei, (AL). 300 M., 171; CAT, 83; Che-chiang, 43; CH mei-shu, II; CKLTMHC, III. 29; KKMH, V. 38.

A monk under pine trees, signed, dated 1348, S. M. Siu collection, Hong Kong. CK ku-hua, B. 84.

Fishing in a snowy mountain harbour, signed, dated 1352, Shanghai Museum. CK hua, X. 13; Shang-hai, 18*.

A boat on a misty stream, signed, Nat. Pal. Mus., Taipei, (AL). CKLTMHC, III. 28.

T'AO FU-CH'U 陶復初 , t. Ming-pen 明本 , h. Chieh-hsüan lao-jen 介軒老人 . From T'ien-t'ai, Chekiang; first half of the 14th century, calligrapher, followed Li K'an in bamboo painting. (CP, VII, AL, 134.)

> A hermit in an autumn grove, inscribed, signed, Nat. Pal. Mus., Taipei. KKMH, VI. 5.

TS'AO CHIH-PO 曹知白 , t. Yu-yüan 又元 and Chen-su 貞素 , h. Yün-hsi 雲西 . B. 1272, d. 1355, from Hua-t'ing, Kiangsu, landscapes, followed Li Ch'eng and Kuo Hsi. (CP, VII, AL, 134-135.)

> Crows and old trees, signed, dated 1316, S. M. Siu collection, Hong Kong. CK ku-hua, B. 65.
> A grove of wintry trees, album leaf, inscribed, signed, dated 1325, Palace Museum, Peking. Yüan-jen hua-ts'e, I*.
> Two pine-trees and some shrubs, signed, dated 1329, Nat. Pal. Mus., Taipei, (AL). CH mei-shu, II; CKLTMHC, III. 20; KKMH, V. 33.
> A man on a path, a flock of birds, album leaf, signed, dated 1342, S. M. Siu collection, Hong Kong. CK ku-hua, B. 145. 2.
> A pavilion among sparse trees, signed, dated 1344, Nat. Pal. Mus., Taipei, (AL). KKMH, V. 32.
> Snow-covered hills by a river, signed, done in 1350, inscription by Huang Kung-wang, Nat. Pal. Mus., Taipei, (AL). 300 M., 168; CAT, 75; CH mei-shu, II; CKLTMHC, III. 21; CKLTSHH; KKMH, V. 31.
> Landscape with two pine-trees, signed, dated 1351, Palace Museum, Peking, (AL). PM, 6*; WW, 1956. 1.
> A hermitage among pine-trees by a river; misty mountains in the background, album leaf, signed, six poems, one by Wang Mien, Nat. Pal. Mus., Taipei, (AL). CKLTMHC, III. 22; KKMH, V. 34.
> Landscape with two fishermen in boats on a lake, signed, colophon by Ni Tsan dated 1362, Shanghai Museum, (AL). CK shu-hua, I. 22; Shang-hai, 13*.

WANG CHEN-P'ENG 王振鵬 , t. P'eng-mei 朋梅 , h. Ku-yün ch'u-shih 孤雲處士 . From Yung-chia, Chekiang, early 14th century, prominent as a boundary painter, also did landscapes and figures. (CP, VII, AL, 135-136.)

> A toy-peddler and a man and a woman with their child, signed, dated 1310, (AL). TSYMC hua-hsüan, 29 (as anon. Yüan).
> The Dragon-boat Festival on the Chin-ming Lake, handscroll, inscribed, signed, dated 1323, Nat. Pal. Mus., Taipei, (AL). 300 M., 160; CAT, 73 (sections); CH mei-shu, II; CKLTMHC, III. 18.
> The night revels of Han Hsi-tsai, handscroll. Che-chiang, 36 (section).

WANG I 王繹 , t. Ssu-shan 思 善 , h. Ch'ih-chüeh 癡絶 .
Lived in Hangchou; active c. 1360, painted portraits and landscapes.
(CP, VII, AL, 136.)

> Portrait of Yang Chu-hsi in a landscape, handscroll, dated 1363; fig-
> ure by Wang I, landscape by Ni Tsan, Palace Museum, Peking,
> (AL). CK hua, XVIII.16; Li-tai jen-wu, 40; TSYMC hua-hsüan, 27.

WANG MENG 王蒙 , t. Shu-ming 叔 明 , h. Huang-hao shan-
ch'iao 黄鶴山樵 . B. 1308, d. 1385; from Wu-hsing, Chekiang;
nephew of Chao Meng-fu, landscapes, followed mainly Tung Yüan and Chü-
jan, one of the "Four Great Masters" of the Yüan period. (CP, VII, AL,
137-139.)

> Tung Shan homestead at the foot of high mountains by the water, signed,
> dated 1343, Nat. Pal. Mus., Taipei, (AL). KKMH, VI.17.
> A pine cliff and a waterfall, signed, dated 1344, Nat. Pal. Mus., Tai-
> pei. 300 M., 192.
> A deep gully between wooded cliffs; two men on the bridge in the fore-
> ground, signed, dated 1344, Nat. Pal. Mus., Taipei, (AL). 300
> M., 190; KKMH, VI.16.
> River scene in wind and rain, signed, dated 1346. Che-chiang, 33;
> HK-w/WM, 14.
> The summer retreat in the mountains: view over a broad stream with
> a large mountain-cone rising in the centre, signed, dated 1354,
> Freer Gallery of Art, Washington, D.C., (59.17), (AL). TWSY
> ming-chi, 104.
> A man on a bridge in front of mountains, album leaf, signed, dated
> 1355, S.M. Siu collection, Hong Kong. CK ku-hua, B.145.4.
> Landscape, signed, done with Ni Tsan, Ni's inscription dated 1360,
> S.M. Siu collection, Hong Kong. CK ku-hua, B.124.
> A man by a mountain stream looking at the waterfall, painted together
> with Ni Tsan, poems and colophons by both painters, Ni's dated
> 1361, Nat. Pal. Mus., Taipei, (AL). KKMH, VI.39.
> Ch'iu-shan hsiao-ssu t'u. A mountain ridge is rising steep, tall pine-
> trees below, signed, dated 1362, done for Tsou Fu-lei, Nat. Pal.
> Mus., Taipei, (AL). 300 M., 195; CH mei-shu, II.
> Bamboo and rock, poem, signed, dated 1364, Suchou Museum. Su-
> chou, 3.
> A hermit's lodge in the mountains, signed, dated 1364, S.M. Siu collec-
> tion, Hong Kong. CK ku-hua, A.47; B.114.
> A hermit's abode in the Ch'ing-pien Mountains, signed, dated 1366,
> Shanghai Museum, (AL). CK hua, I.20; KH-w/WM, 12; Shang-hai,
> 22*; TSYMC hua-hsüan, 25.
> Staying in the mountains on a summer day, signed, dated 1368, painted for
> Tung Hsüan, Palace Museum, Peking, (AL). Che-chiang, 32; PM, 7*.

A scholar's study in summer mountains, signed, dated 1369, S. M.
  Siu collection, Hong Kong. CK ku-hua, A. 48; B. 116.

Ko Hung moving his residence, signed, (AL). CK ku-tai, 69; CK shu-
  hua, I. 23; HK-w/WM, 18.

Ch'iu-shan ts'ao-t'ang t'u. The autumn mountains form a ridge around
  the bay, inscribed, signed, poem by Ch'ien-lung, Nat. Pal. Mus.,
  Taipei, (AL). 300 M., 193*; CAT, 88; CCAT, pl. 110; CKLTMHC,
  III. 65; KKMH, VI. 19*.

Chu-shih liu-ch'üan t'u. A bamboo grove, poems by the painter and
  Yao Kung-hsiao, Nat. Pal. Mus., Taipei, (AL). NPM Bulletin,
  II. 5, p. 8.

Hua-ch'i yü-yin t'u. A fisherman in a boat at the lower edge; a large
  bay between curving mountains, poem, signed, inscription by
  Shen Meng-lin dated 1393, Nat. Pal. Mus., Taipei, (AL).
  CKLTMHC, III. 66; NPM Quarterly, I. 1. 2 (two other versions of
  the same composition given to Wang Meng in NPM Quarterly I. 1,
  pls. 1, 3).

Scenic dwellings at Chü-ch'ü, signed, Nat. Pal. Mus., Taipei, (AL,
  Fantastically hollowed and split mountains?). 300 M., 191; KKMH,
  VI. 20; NPM Quarterly, I. 2, pls. 7, 9 B.

Tilling the soil in a mountain valley, poem, signed, Nat. Pal. Mus.,
  Taipei, (AL). 300 M., 188; CH mei-shu, II; CKLTMHC, III. 67;
  KKMH, VI. 14.

A scholar's pavilion by a mountain stream under leafy trees, signed,
  Nat. Pal. Mus., Taipei, (AL). 300 M., 189; CH mei-shu, II;
  CKLTSHH; KKMH, VI. 15.

A scholar's study in the spring mountains, two poems by the artist,
  signed, Shanghai Museum, (AL). HK-w/WM, 13; Shang-hai, 23*.

A temple in a mountain-gorge, signed, poem by Ch'ien-lung, (AL).
  HK-w/WM, 15.

Woods and mountains in autumn, signed, poem by Ch'ien-lung, Nat.
  Pal. Mus., Taipei. 300 M., 194; KKMH, VI. 18.

The T'ai-po Mountain, handscroll, artist's seal, colophon by Ch'ien-
  lung, Liao-ning Provincial Museum. Liao-ning, I. 92-95.

A study under trees by a stream, inscribed, signed, S. M. Siu collection, Hong Kong. CK ku-hua, B. 115.

Landscape, playing chess in a pavilion over the water, signed, poem
  by Ch'ien-lung, S. M. Siu collection, Hong Kong. CK ku-hua,
  A. 49; B. 117.

Bamboo by a spring, signed, S. M. Siu collection, Hong Kong. CK
  ku-hua, A. 50; B. 118.

A gentleman on a promontory watching a high waterfall, album leaf.
  HK-w/WM, 16.

A man on a bridge watching rapids, a pagoda in the background, album
leaf. HK-w/WM, 17.

Tan-shan p'eng-hai t'u. Seascape, bridge leading to a mountain promontory, handscroll, signed. TSYMC hua-hsüan, 24.

Fisherman by a riverside cliff, large inlet with rounded hills, handscroll, signed, poem by Ch'ien-lung. TWSY ming-chi, 105-106.

WANG MIEN 王 冕 , t. Yüan-chang 元 章 , h. Lao-ts'un 老 村 ,
Chu-shih shan-nung 煮 石 山 農 . B. 1335, d. 1407; from K'uai-chi,
Chekiang, specialized in plum-blossoms. (CP, VII, AL, 139-140.)

Three bamboos in outline, inscription, signed, dated 1349, Palace
Museum, Peking, (AL). CK hua, IX.12; Wang Mien, 3.

Plum-blossoms, poem, signed, dated 1353, Nat. Pal. Mus., Taipei,
(AL). CH mei-shu, II.

A branch of plum-tree over the water, signed, colophon and poem dated
1355 (or 1415?), inscription at top describing a legendary account
of plum trees, ex-Shao Fu-ying collection, (AL). Wang Mien, 6.

Widely spreading branches of a blossoming plum-tree, handscroll,
signed, dated 1355, (AL). Che-chiang, 44.

Nan-chih ch'un-tsao t'u. A long branch of blossoming plum-tree,
hanging down in a double curve, poem, signed, dated 1357, Nat.
Pal. Mus., Taipei, (AL). 300 M., 199; CKLTMHC, III.86.

Plum blossoms, signed, dated 1379, S.M. Siu collection, Hong Kong.
CK ku-hua, B.144.

Branch of a blossoming plum-tree, handscroll, poem, signed, Palace
Museum, Peking, (AL). CK hua, II.9; CK ku-tai, 68; KKPWY
hua-niao, 26*; PM, 37*; Wang Mien, 1.

Ink plum blossoms, two poems by the artist, one signed, three other
inscriptions, Shanghai Museum. Shang-hai, 33*; Wang Mien, 5.

A hanging curved branch of plum blossom, poem, signed. Wang Mien, 2.

An upward branch of plum blossoms, poem, signed. Wang Mien, 4.

WANG YÜAN 王 淵 , t. Jo-shui 若 水 , h. Tan-hsüan 澹 軒 .
From Hangchou; active c. 1310-1350; pupil of Chao Meng-fu, painted flowers, birds and landscapes. (CP, VII, AL, 140-141.)

A traveller in autumnal mountains, signed, dated 1299, poem by Ch'ien-
lung, Nat. Pal. Mus., Taipei. 300 M., 159; KKMH, V.18.

Two turkeys on a rockery, signed, dated 1344, Shanghai Museum,
(AL). Che-chiang, 34; CK hua, V.14; Shang-hai, 19*; WW, 1957.
8.74; 1964.3.17.

A bird on a young peach-tree and some bamboos; ducks sleeping below, signed, dated 1346, Nat. Pal. Mus., Taipei, (AL).
CKLTMHC, III.31.

Two ducks on an autumn bank, signed, dated 1346, S. M. Siu collection, Hong Kong. CK ku-hua, B.98.

Birds in bamboo, signed, dated 1349, after Huang Ch'üan, S. M. Siu collection, Hong Kong. CK ku-hua, A.39; B.97.

Pheasant on a rock, peach blossoms, signed, dated 1349, Palace Museum, Peking. KKPWY hua-niao, 25*.

A hawk chasing a thrush, signed, Nat. Pal. Mus., Taipei, (AL). CCAT, pl. 108; CH ming-hua*.

A large pheasant on a rock; blossoming magnolia, bamboos and other plants, signed (?), Palace Museum, Peking, (AL). KKPWY hua-niao, 24*.

Sparrows gathering at a tuft of bamboo, two quails on the ground, signed, after Huang Ch'üan, Abe collection, Ōsaka Museum, (AL). CK ku-tai, 67.

WEI CHIU-TING 衛九鼎 , t. Ming-hsüan 明鉉 . From T'ien-t'ai, Chekiang; active c. 1350-1370, landscapes and boundary paintings. (CP, VII, AL, 141.)

Clearing after snow, returning home, signed, dated 1352, S. M. Siu collection, Hong Kong. CK ku-hua, B.103.

The Nymph of the Lo River walking on the waves, poem by Ni Tsan dated 1368, Nat. Pal. Mus., Taipei, (AL). 300 M., 176; Che-chiang, 37; CKLTMHC, III.62; KKMH, V.46.

WU CHEN 吳鎮 , t. Chung-kuei 仲圭 , h. Mei-hua tao-jen 梅花道人 . B. 1280, d. 1354; from Chia-hsing, Chekiang, poet and calligrapher, painted landscapes after Chü-jan, bamboo after Wen T'ung, one of the "Four Great Masters" of the Yüan period. (CP, VII, AL, 141-143.)

Two old pine-trees on a stony beach, signed, dated 1328, Nat. Pal. Mus., Taipei, (AL). 300 M., 166; CH mei-shu, II; CKLTMHC, III.42; KKMH, V.25; Wu Chen, 1.

Fishermen in a boat, river landscape, hills in the background, signed, dated 1336, Palace Museum, Peking, (AL, River landscape with fishermen in a boat?). CK hua, XIV.14; CK ku-tai, 65; PM, 5*.

A landscape with rounded mountain peaks, handscroll, signed, dated 1336, part of a collected scroll of Yüan works called Yüan-jen chi-chin, Nat. Pal. Mus., Taipei, (AL). CAT, 90d (section); CH mei-shu, II; CKLTMHC, III.47; KKMH, V.29.

Pine tree by a flowing stream, signed, dated 1338, poem by the artist. Wu Chen, 2.

A lonely fisherman on the Tung-t'ing Lake, poem, signed, dated 1341, Nat. Pal. Mus., Taipei, (AL). 300 M., 163; CH mei-shu, II; KKMH, V.22; Wu Chen, 4.

View over a broad river between low hills; two men in a fishing-boat, poem, signed, dated 1342, Nat. Pal. Mus., Taipei, (AL). 300 M., 165; CAT, 76; CKLTMHC, III. 43; KKMH, V. 24; Wu Chen, 3.

Returning in a boat on a mountain stream, album leaf, signed, dated 1342, in the manner of Chü-jan, Nat. Pal. Mus., Taipei, (AL, also listed as Returning boat on a stream, grassy mountain slopes). KKMH, V. 28.

The fishermen's pleasure, handscroll, inscribed, done in 1342, Freer Gallery of Art, Washington, D. C., (AL). Wu Chen, 8-9 (2 sections).

A bamboo stem and a bamboo shoot, signed, dated 1343, (AL). Wu Chen, 5.

Eight views from the Chia-ho district, handscroll, signed, dated 1344, Lo Chia-lun collection, Taipei, (AL). Che-chiang, 27 (section); Wu Chen, 6 (section).

Fishermen at leisure in a cove, signed, dated 1345, S. M. Siu collection, Hong Kong. CK ku-hua, A. 34; B. 129.

A hermit in a boat, a flock of birds, signed, dated 1346, S. M. Siu collection, Hong Kong. CK ku-hua, B. 128.

Thatched pavilion in a landscape, handscroll, signed, dated 1347, Cleveland Museum of Art. CK shu-hua, I. 21.

Two slender bamboos by a stone, inscribed, dated 1347, Nat. Pal. Mus., Taipei, (AL). 300 M., 167; CH mei-shu, II; CKLTMHC, III. 49; KKMH, V. 27; NPM Quarterly, I. 4, pl. 6; Wu Chen, 7.

Ink plum blossoms, handscroll, signed, dated 1348, Liao-ning Provincial Museum. Liao-ning, I. 89-90.

A slender branch of bamboo in wind, inscribed, signed, dated 1350, Freer Gallery of Art, Washington, D. C., (AL). NPM Quarterly, I. 4, pl. 7.

Twenty studies of bamboo, album, signed, dated 1350, Nat. Pal. Mus., Taipei, (AL). CAT, 77 (leaf 8); Che-chiang, 28 (leaf 3); CKLTMHC, III. 50 (entire album); NPM Quarterly, I. 4, pl. 8 (leaf 3).

A slender branch of bamboo, poem, signed, dated 1350, Nat. Pal. Mus., Taipei, (AL). CKLTMHC, III. 44; KKMH, V. 26.

Album of twelve landscapes, each signed, inscription by the artist dated 1351, twelve poems by Ch'ien-lung, S. Siu collection, Hong Kong. WC Shan-shui.

A lonely fisherman on an autumn river below a steep cliff, poem, signed, Nat. Pal. Mus., Taipei, (AL). 300 M., 164; CKLTMHC, III. 45; KKMH, V. 23.

Ch'ing-chiang ch'un-hsiao t'u. The clear river on a spring morning, signed, Nat. Pal. Mus., Taipei, (AL). 300 M., 162; CH mei-shu, II; CKLTMHC, III. 48; CKLTSHH; KKMH, V. 21.

Mountains after rain, large trees and a cottage, inscribed, signed, (AL). Wu Chen, 13.

Two dragon-pines with intertwined stems, poem by the painter, (AL).
Wu Chen, 12.

Mountain landscape after rain, poem by the artist, signed, (AL). Wu
Chen, 14.

River landscape in autumn, Nat. Pal. Mus., Taipei, (AL, Chü-jan).
300 M., 45 (as Chü-jan); CKLTMHC, III.46 (as Wu Chen); KKMH,
II.11 (as Chü-jan).

Pine and rock, inscribed and signed, Shanghai Museum. Shang-hai,
14*; TSYMC hua-hsüan, 21.

Bamboo, rock and tree branch, inscribed, signed, Tientsin Art Museum. T'ien-ching, II.9.

Bamboo in wind by rock, signed, S.M. Siu collection, Hong Kong.
CK ku-hua, A.35; B.127.

Bamboo and trees, handscroll, inscribed, signed, S.M. Siu collection,
Hong Kong. CK ku-hua, B.130.

Bamboo, handscroll, divided into four sections, inscriptions on each,
signed, possibly dated (reproduction too dark to read), S.M. Siu
collection, Hong Kong. CK ku-hua, B.131.

Four bamboo studies, handscroll, signed, S.M. Siu collection, Hong
Kong. CK ku-hua, B.132.

A man in a boat on a river, album leaf, attributed, S.M. Siu collection,
Hong Kong. CK ku-hua, B.145.6.

Bamboo, handscroll, seven sections, each section signed. Wu Chen,
10-11 (2 sections).

WU KUAN 吳 瓘 , t. Ying-chih 瑩 之 . From Chia-hsing, Che-
kiang; active c. 1348; connoisseur and collector, painted ink plum blossoms,
studied Yang Pu-chih. (H.5; M. p. 160.)

Plum blossoms and bamboo, handscroll, signed, dated 1348, colophons
by Ch'ien-lung and others, Liao-ning Provincial Museum. Liao-
ning, I.91.

WU T'ING-HUI 吳廷暉 . From Wu-hsing, Chekiang; 14th century,
painted landscapes in blue and green, flowers and birds. (CP, VII, AL,
143.)

A dragon-boat race on a river below a misty temple hill, attributed,
Nat. Pal. Mus., Taipei, (AL). KKMH, VI.27.

YANG WEI-CHEN 楊維楨 , t. Lien-fu 廉夫 , h. T'ieh-ya
鐵崖 . B. 1296, d. 1370; from Chu-chi, Chekiang, calligrapher.
(CP, VII, AL, 143.)

Spring rain on bamboo-covered banks, inscribed, signed, dated 1355,
S.M. Siu collection, Hong Kong. CK ku-hua, B.104.

An old pine tree branch, album leaf, signed, dated 1361, S. M. Siu
collection, Hong Kong. CK ku-hua, B. 145. 8.

A knotted old pine, poems by the painter and two of his pupils, Nat.
Pal. Mus. , Taipei, (AL). Che-chiang, 31; CKLTMHC, III. 34.

YAO T'ING-MEI 姚廷美 . From Wu-hsing, Chekiang, active around
the middle of the 14th century. (CP, VII, AL, 144.)

The river under snow, handscroll, Palace Museum, Peking. PM,
9*; WW, 1956. 1.

YEN HUI 顏輝 , t. Ch'iu-yüeh 秋月 . From Chiang-shan, Chekiang; 14th century, painted Buddhist and Taoist figures, landscapes.
(CP, VII, AL, 144.)

Winter landscape, Yüan An lying in the snow; the mayor approaching
in an ox-cart, attributed, Nat. Pal. Mus. , Taipei, (AL).
CKLTMHC, III. 109 (as anon. Yüan).

Two monkeys on the branch of a p'i-pa tree, signature incomplete,
Nat. Pal. Mus. , Taipei, (AL). 300 M. , 179; CH mei-shu, II;
CKLTMHC, III. 17; KKMH, V. 30.

Li T'ieh-kuai watching his anima mounting on high, artist's seal,
Chion-in, Kyōto, (AL). Li-tai jen-wu, 31.

Liu Hai-chan with the three-legged toad, Chion-in, Kyōto, (AL).
Che-chiang, 39.

White-robed Kuan-yin seated on a rock by a waterfall, Nelson Gallery
of Art, Kansas City, (AL). Li-tai jen-wu, 30.

Two Immortals, attributed, Chang Pe-chin collection. Tien Yin Tang,
I. 10.

Chung K'uei on a donkey. CK ku-tai, 56 (section).

Anonymous paintings of the Yüan Period

Taoist and Buddhist

An Indian monk seated on a rock explaining a Sutra, Nat. Pal. Mus. ,
Taipei (AL). CKLTMHC, III. 94; KKMH, VI. 51*.

The three Taoist patriarchs (San Ch'ing) seated under trees and some
devotees, Nat. Pal. Mus. , Taipei, (AL). CKLTMHC, III. 93.

Five hundred arhats at a Hua-yen meeting, Nat. Pal. Mus. , Taipei.
CKLTMHC, III. 89.

Nine arhats with two servants, Nat. Pal. Mus. , Taipei. CKLTMHC,
III. 92.

Figure Compositions and Portraits

Shooting wild geese, huntsmen on horseback passing through a mountain defile in snow, Nat. Pal. Mus., Taipei, (AL). CKLTMHC, III. 88; KKMH, VI. 40.

A toy-peddler and a man and a woman with their child, signed Wang Chen-p'eng, dated 1310, (AL, Wang Chen-p'eng). TSYMC hua-hsüan, 29 (as anon. Yüan).

Palace ladies seated around a table making music, Nat. Pal. Mus., Taipei, (AL, anon. before Sung; also listed as Palace musicians under anon. Sung). 300 M., 204* (as anon. Yüan); CAT, 10 (as anon. Five Dyn.); CCAT, pl. 12 (as anon. Five Dyn.); CKLTMHC, II. 15 (as anon. Sung); KKMH, I. 22 (as anon. Five Dyn.); WW, 1955. 7. 8 (40) (as anon. Sung).

A noble scholar under a willow, Nat. Pal. Mus., Taipei. CAT, 26 (as anon. Sung); CKLTMHC, III. 87 (as anon. Yüan); KKMH, III. 40 (as anon. Sung).

Portrait of Ni Tsan, handscroll, inscription by Chang Yü (1277-1348), Nat. Pal. Mus., Taipei. 300 M., 205; CAT, 86; CH mei-shu, II; CKLTMHC, III. 110; KKMH, VI. 13*.

Mongol camp scene, album leaf, Nat. Pal. Mus., Taipei. CKLTMHC, II. 88 (as anon. Sung); KKMH, VI. 48 (as anon. Yüan).

A man seated on a garden terrace surrounded by six ladies, fan, Palace Museum, Peking. Yüan-jen hua-ts'e, I*.

A gentleman and two servants in front of a laden table on a garden terrace, fan, Palace Museum, Peking. Yüan-jen hua-ts'e, I*.

A gentleman on horseback with his retinue in a courtyard watching a cockfight, fan, Palace Museum, Peking. Yüan-jen hua-ts'e, I*.

Burning incense on a terrace, fan, Palace Museum, Peking. Yüan-jen hua-ts'e, I*.

A gentleman seated on a chair on a garden terrace surrounded by seven ladies and servants, fan, Palace Museum, Peking. Yüan-jen hua-ts'e, II*.

Dancers performing for a king seated beneath a canopy, handscroll, Tientsin Art Museum. T'ien-ching, II. 10.

Elegant Gathering in the Western Garden, handscroll. Li-tai jen-wu, 39.

Palaces and Buildings

A portion of the Emperor Han Wu-ti's gorgeous palace compound, the Chien-chang Palace, handscroll, Nat. Pal. Mus., Taipei, (AL). CKLTMHC, III. 108.

The Palace of Prince T'eng, Nat. Pal. Mus. , Taipei, (AL). KKMH, VI. 50.

A two-storied pavilion by a broad river, Nat. Pal. Mus. , Taipei, (AL). CKLTMHC, III. 102.

A water mill in the mountains, Liao-ning Provincial Museum. Liao-ning, I. 111.

Ladies in pavilions, open river scenery in background, album leaf, Liao-ning Provincial Museum. Liao-ning, I. 113.

The Kuang-han Palace, Shanghai Museum. Shang-hai, 27*.

Landscapes

Two fishermen in boats, their homes on the promontory, Nat. Pal. Mus. , Taipei, (AL). KKMH, VI. 42.

Cloudy mountains, after Mi Fei, Nat. Pal. Mus. , Taipei, (AL). 300 M. , 203; CAT, 71; CKLTMHC, III. 107; KKMH, VI. 52.

Blue mountains and white clouds, handscroll, Nat. Pal. Mus. , Taipei, (AL). CKLTMHC, III. 98.

Leafless trees on the rocky shore of a river, Nat. Pal. Mus. , Taipei, (AL). KKMH, VI. 49.

Mountain in spring, a temple at the bottom of a gorge, poem by Yang Wei-chen, Nat. Pal. Mus. , Taipei, (AL). CKLTMHC, III. 99.

A richly wooded mountain in autumn, a homestead by a river, now attributed to Chiang Ts'an, Nat. Pal. Mus. , Taipei, (AL). CKLTMHC, I. 43 (as Chiang Ts'an); NPM Bulletin, I. 3, figs. 2, 4, 6, 7 (as Chiang Ts'an); KKMH, VI. 41 (as anon. Yüan).

Buildings with figures by a river, large mountains covered by snow, Nat. Pal. Mus. , Taipei, (AL). KKMH, VI. 43.

Numberless peaks and valleys, Nat. Pal. Mus. , Taipei, (AL, anon. Sung). CKLTMHC, III. 97 (as anon. Yüan); KKMH, III. 30 (as anon. Sung).

Mountains and water in autumn mist, attributed to Chu Te-jun by Tung Ch'i-ch'ang, Nat. Pal. Mus. , Taipei, (AL, Chu Te-jun). CKLTMHC, III. 100 (as anon. Yüan).

Winter landscape, Yüan An lying in the snow; the mayor approaching in an ox-cart, Nat. Pal. Mus. , Taipei, (AL, Yen Hui). CKLTMHC, III. 109 (as anon. Yüan).

A man fishing from a boat near a wooded shore, album leaf, signed Sheng Chu, Nat. Pal. Mus. , Taipei. CKLTMHC, III. 105 (as anon. Yüan).

Figures on a flower terrace enjoying the view of a pavilion in the valley, fan, Nat. Pal. Mus. , Taipei. KKMH, VI. 44.

A ferry boat under a cliff, album leaf, Nat. Pal. Mus. , Taipei.
KKMH, VI. 45.

A boat anchored at the riverside in autumn, album leaf, Nat. Pal.
Mus. , Taipei. KKMH, VI. 47.

Cloudy mountains, in the style of Mi Fei, Nat. Pal. Mus. , Taipei.
KKMH, VI. 53.

Playing the ch'in and enjoying the view, fan, Nat. Pal. Mus. , Taipei.
CKLTMHC, III. 103.

Landscape with five people in a dragon boat, fan, Nat. Pal. Mus. ,
Taipei. CKLTMHC, III. 104.

Boat approaching a pavilion on a wooded shore, album leaf, Nat. Pal.
Mus. , Taipei. CKLTMHC, III. 106.

A fisherman selling fish from a boat at a pavilion, snowscape, fan,
Palace Museum, Peking. Yüan-jen hua-ts'e, I*.

A man and a servant with a fan in a waterside pavilion under willows,
fan, Palace Museum, Peking. Yüan-jen hua-ts'e, I*.

A man walking with a staff, a servant with a ch'in, fan, Palace Museum, Peking. Yüan-jen hua-ts'e, II*.

Buildings along the banks of a mountain stream, fan, Palace Museum,
Peking. Yüan-jen hua-ts'e, II*.

Fisherman poling a boat toward a cove, another fisherman in the cove,
fan, Palace Museum, Peking. Yüan-jen hua-ts'e, II*.

A scholar seated by a river inlet under red trees, album leaf, Palace
Museum, Peking. Yüan-jen hua-ts'e, II*.

People in an extensive mountain villa, travellers, snow scene, fan,
Palace Museum, Peking. Yüan-jen hua-ts'e, II*.

A pavilion on a lofty cliff in winter, album leaf, Palace Museum, Peking. Yüan-jen hua-ts'e, II*.

Admiring plum blossoms at night: lady leaning on a tree, the moon
reflected in a stream, fan, Liao-ning Provincial Museum. Liao-
ning, I. 98.

Scholar leaning on a pine-tree, album leaf, Liao-ning Provincial Museum. Liao-ning, I. 112; Sung Yüan shan-shui, 13*.

Traffic on the bridge, Museum of History, Peking. WW, 1962.10.10.

Travellers in mountains and on rivers, Tientsin Art Museum. I-yüan
chi-chin, 6.

Fishermen returning along a snowy bay, Chang Pe-chin collection.
Tien Yin Tang, I. 12.

Animals

A Taoist fairy with a basket of fungi seated between a lion and a tiger, Nat. Pal. Mus., Taipei, (AL). CKLTMHC, III.91.

A Tartar on horseback by a river, Nat. Pal. Mus., Taipei, (AL). CKLTMHC, III.90.

Two buffaloes and cowherd under autumn trees, fan, Nat. Pal. Mus., Taipei. KKMH, VI.46.

A groom holding a horse drinking at a stream, album leaf, Liao-ning Provincial Museum. Liao-ning, I.97.

A long procession of baggage mules, oxen, camels and men in various garb on horseback, handscroll, signed Chung-mu (Chao Yung), Liao-ning Provincial Museum. Liao-ning, I.99-110 (as anon. Yüan).

Flowers and Birds

Ten crows in an old tree, Nat. Pal. Mus., Taipei, (AL). CKLTMHC, III.95.

A tuft of giant rice, Nat. Pal. Mus., Taipei, (AL). CKLTMHC, III.96.

Six quails by a rock and small birds on stalks of millet, Nat. Pal. Mus., Taipei, (AL). CKLTMHC, III.101.

Hundred sparrows on plum and bamboo, Nat. Pal. Mus., Taipei. CH ming-hua*.

Two peaches on a branch, album leaf, Palace Museum, Peking. Yüan-jen hua-ts'e, I*.

Ducks and birds among flowering plants, Liao-ning Provincial Museum. Liao-ning, I.114.

Ducks under blossoming apricot tree, Shanghai Museum. Shang-hai, 28*.

Three birds in blossoming plum tree, bamboo and rock, Chang Pe-chin collection. Tien Yin Tang, I.11.

Painters of the Ming Dynasty

Chan Ho	詹	和	Chang Ling	張	靈
Chang Ch'ung	張	沖	Chang Lu	張	路
Chang Ho	張	翮	Chang Yü	張	羽
Chang Hung	張	宏	Chang Yüan-shih	張 元	士
Chang Jui-t'u	張 瑞	圖	Ch'ang-ying	常	瑩

Chao Pei	趙備	英	Ch'iu Ying	仇	英
Chao Shun-fu	趙夫	臣	Chou Ch'en	周	臣
Chao Tso	趙左	之	Chou Chih-mien	周	冕
Ch'en Chi	陳繼	天	Chou Ch'üan	周	全
Ch'en Chi-ju	陳儒	文	Chou Fan	周	蕃
Ch'en Chia-yen	陳言	之	Chou T'ien-ch'iu	周	位
Ch'en Huan	陳煥	南	Chou Wei	周	靖
Ch'en Hung-shou	陳綬	戀	Chou Wen-ching	周	蕃
Ch'en Ju-yen	陳言	孝	Chu Chih-fan	朱	節
Ch'en Jui	陳瑞	戀	Chu Fei	朱	鷺
Ch'en Kua	陳括		Chu Lu	朱	端
Ch'en Kuan	陳裸	煒	Chu Nan-yung	朱	完
Ch'en Lu	陳錄	繼	Chu Tuan	朱	時
Ch'en Shun	陳淳	嘉	Chu Wan	朱	學
Ch'en Ts'an	陳粲	洪	Chü Mou-shih	居	孺
Ch'en Tsun	陳遵	汝	Chung Hsüeh	鍾	清
Cheng Chung	鄭重		Fang Hsiao-ju	方	鎮
Cheng Shih	鄭石		Fu Ch'ing	傅	功
Cheng Yüan-hsün	鄭勳	元	Ho Chen	賀	昶
Ch'eng Chia-sui	程燧	嘉	Hou Mou-kung	侯	芷
Ch'eng Nan-yün	程雲	南	Hsia Ch'ang	夏	昜
Chiang Ch'ien	蔣乾		Hsia Chih	夏	謨
Chiang Sung	蔣嵩		Hsia Ping	夏	汴
Chiang Yin	姜隱	聖	Hsiang Sheng-mo	項	環
Ch'ien Ku	錢穀	元	Hsiang Yüan-pien	項	臣
Ch'ien Kung	錢貢	時	Hsieh Huan	謝	靜
Chin Shih	金湜	慈	Hsieh Shih-ch'en	謝	霖
Ch'in I	欽揖		Hsing Tz'u-ching	刑	
Ch'iu Shih	仇氏		Hsü Lin	徐	

Hsü Pen	徐賁		Liu Chüeh	劉玨
Hsü Wei	徐渭		Liu Chung-hsien	劉仲賢
Hsü Yüan	徐垣		Liu Mai	劉邁
Hsüan-tsung, of Ming	明宣宗		Liu Shih-ju	劉世儒
Hsüeh Shih-heng	薛始亨		Liu Yüan-ch'i	劉原起
Hsüeh Su-su or Hsüeh Wu	薛素素		Lu Ch'ao-yang	盧朝陽
Huang Chüan	黃筌		Lu Chih	陸治
Huang Tao-chou	黃道周		Lu Fu	陸復
Ku Cheng-i	顧正誼		Lu Shih-tao	陸師道
Ku Chung	顧仲		Lü Chi	呂紀
Ku Fu	顧復		Lü T'ang	呂棠
Ku Lu	顧祿		Lü Tuan-chün	呂端俊
Ku Ning-yüan	顧凝遠		Ma Shih	馬軾
Kuan Ssu	關思		Ma Shou-chen	馬守貞
Kuei Ch'ang-shih	歸昌世		Mi Wan-chung	米萬鍾
Kuei Chuang	歸莊		Miu Fu	繆輔
Kuo Hsü	郭詡		Ni Tuan	倪端
Lan Ying	藍瑛		Ni Ying	倪瑛
Li Chao-heng	李肇亨		Ni Yüan-lu	倪元璐
Li Chen	李在		Pien Wen-chin	邊文進
Li Jih-hua	李日華		Shang Hsi	商喜
Li Liu-fang	李流芳		Shang Tsu	商祚
Li Shao-ch'i	李紹箕		Shao Mi	邵彌
Li Shih-ta	李士達		Shen Chen	沈貞
Li Sui-ch'iu	李遂球		Shen Chou	沈周
Li Tsai	李在		Shen Shih	沈仕
Li Tsung-mo	李宗謨		Shen Shih-ch'ung	沈士充
Lin Liang	林良		Shen Shih-keng	沈士鯁
Liu Chi	劉基		Sheng Chu	盛著

Sheng Lin	盛琳		Wang Ch'ien	王謙
Sheng Mao-hua	盛茂燁		Wang Ch'ien	王乾
Sheng Shao-hsien	盛紹先		Wang Chung-li	王中立
Sheng Ying	盛穎		Wang Chung-yü	王仲玉
Shih Chung	史忠		Wang Ch'ung	王寵
Shih K'o-fa	史可法		Wang E	王諤
Sun Ai	孫艾		Wang Fu	王紱
Sun Chao-lin	孫兆麟		Wang Ku-hsiang	王穀祥
Sun Chih	孫枝		Wang Li	王履
Sun K'o-hung	孫克弘		Wang Shao-ch'uan	汪少川
Sun Lung	孫龍		Wang Shih-ch'ang	王世昌
Sung Chüeh	宋珏		Wang Shun-kuo	王舜國
Sung Hsü	宋旭		Wang To	王鐸
Sung Mou-chin	宋懋晉		Wang Wei-lieh	王維烈
Tai Chin	戴進		Wang Wen	王問
T'an Chih-i	談志伊		Wei Chih-huang	魏之璜
T'ang Chih-yin	唐志尹		Wen Cheng-ming	文徵明
T'ang Yin	唐寅		Wen Chia	文嘉
T'ao Ch'eng	陶成		Wen Po-jen	文伯仁
Ting Yün-p'eng	丁雲鵬		Wen Shu	文淑
Tseng Ch'ing	曾鯨		Wen Ts'ung-chien	文從簡
Tsou Chih-lin	鄒之麟		Wen Yüan-shan	文元善
Ts'ui Tzu-chung	崔子忠		Wu Ling	吳令
Tu Chin	杜堇		Wu Pin	吳彬
Tu Ch'iung	杜瓊		Wu Wei	吳偉
Tu Ta-ch'eng	杜大成		Yang Pu	楊補
Tung Ch'i-ch'ang	董其昌		Yang Ta-lin	楊大臨
Wang Chao	汪肇		Yang Wen-ts'ung	楊文驄
Wang Ch'i	王篆		Yao Kuang-hsiao	姚廣孝

Yao Shou	姚綬	Yü Shun-ch'en	俞舜臣
Yeh Kuang	葉廣	Yüan Shang-t'ung	袁尚統
Yen Ling	嚴令	Yün Hsiang	惲向
Yu Ch'iu	尤求		

CHAN HO 詹和 , or Chan Chung-ho 詹仲和 , t. Hsi-ho 僖和 , h. T'ieh-kuan tao-jen 鐵冠道人 . From Ssu-ming, Chekiang; active c. 1500, painted ink bamboo in the style of Wu Chen, also did figures. (CP, VII, AL, 152.)

A branch of bamboo, signed, colophon dated 1513, Hongan-ji, Kyōto, (AL). NPM Quarterly, I.4, pl. 18.

CHANG CH'UNG 張翀 , t. Tzu-yü 子羽 , h. T'u-nan 圖南 . From Nanking; active c. 1570-1610, painted figures and landscapes. (CP, VII, AL, 153.)

A man in a pavilion in a bamboo grove near a stream, folding fan, signed, dated 1631, Shanghai WWPKWYH. Shan-mien-hua, 31*.

CHANG HO 張翮 , t. Feng-i 鳳翼 . From Suchou; active c. 1630, painted landscapes and figures. (CP, VII, AL, 153-154.)

Chung K'uei in a forest, signed, dated 1622, Tientsin Art Museum. T'ien-ching, II.51.

A fisherman crossing a bridge in a mountain landscape, folding fan, poem, signed, dated 1633, Hui Hsiao-t'ung collection. Shan-mien chi-chin, 6*.

Two gentlemen on horseback travelling in spring mountains, folding fan, signed, dated 1635, Hui Hsiao-t'ung collection. Shan-mien chi-chin, 7*.

CHANG HUNG 張宏 , t. Chün-tu 君度 , h. Hao-chien 鶴澗 . B. 1580, d. after 1660; from Suchou, painted landscapes, figures, flowers and buffaloes. (CP, VII, AL, 154-155.)

The Shih-hsieh Mountain, signed, dated 1613, Nat. Pal. Mus., Taipei, (AL). CKLTMHC, IV.124.

Mountain stream after snow, signed, dated 1626, Nat. Pal. Mus., Taipei, (AL). CKLTMHC, IV.125.

Camellia and narcissus, signed, dated 1626, after Lu Chih, Nat. Pal. Mus., Taipei, (AL). CKLTMHC, IV.126.

Landscape with a small pavilion, signed, dated 1629, Nat. Pal. Mus., Taipei, (AL). CKLTMHC, IV.127.

Two boys leading buffaloes across a river, inscribed, signed, date

partly effaced (possibly 1639), Cheng Te-k'un collection, Cambridge, (AL). Mu-fei, opposite p. 16.

Portrait of Wang Hsin-i, handscroll, signed, done with Shu K'u-ch'ing,
Shu's signature dated 1641, three colophons, Tientsin Art Museum.
T'ien-ching, II. 70.

Two scholars and servant listening to the rapids, inscribed, signed,
dated 1649, Tso Hai collection. CK hua, XII. 17.

A man in a boat on a mountain stream, signed, Tientsin Art Museum.
T'ien-ching, I. 34.

CHANG JUI-T'U 張瑞圖 , t. Ch'ang-kung 長 公 , h. Erh-shui
二水 , Kuo-t'ing 果亭 and other names. From Ch'üan-chou, Fukien; chin-shih in 1607, painted landscapes. (CP, VII, AL, 155-156.)

A scholar reading in a pavilion over a stream, high mountains with
empty pavilion on a terrace, signed, dated 1626, Cheng Te-k'un
collection, Cambridge. Mu-fei, before p. 13.

CHANG LING 張靈 , t. Meng-chin 夢晉 . From Suchou; neigh-
bour and friend of T'ang Yin, painted figures, landscapes, flowers and
birds. (CP, VII, AL, 156.)

Figures and calligraphy, 12 leaf album, signed, dated 1508, S. M.
Siu collection, Hong Kong. CK ku-hua, B. 192.

CHANG LU 張路 , t. T'ien-ch'ih 天馳 , h. P'ing-shan 平山 .
B. 1464, d. 1538; from K'aifeng, painted figures after Wu Wei, landscapes
in the style of Tai Chin. (CP, VII, AL, 156-157.)

Lao-tzu riding a buffalo, signed, Nat. Pal. Mus., Taipei, (AL).
CKLTMHC, IV. 37.

People engaged in various activities, handscroll, attributed, Tientsin
Art Museum. T'ien-ching, I. 11-12.

Winter landscape, a man in a pavilion, a crane in the courtyard, signed,
Tientsin Art Museum. T'ien-ching, I. 13.

Travellers in windy mountains, signed, Tientsin Art Museum. I-yüan
chi-chin, 10.

Fishing on the river, signed, Chang Pe-chin collection. Tien Yin Tang,
I. 17.

A man holding a leafy branch, walking with a tiger, signed, Hui Hsiao-
t'ung collection. CK hua, IX. 12.

A man fishing from a riverbank, around him are dishes and antiques,
a servant with a staff, signed. Li-tai jen-wu, 46; TSYMC hua-
hsüan, 43.

CHANG YÜ 張羽 , originally named Fu-feng 附鳳 , t. Lai-i 來儀 ,
h. Ching-chü 靜居 . B. 1333, d. 1385; from Hsinyang, Kiangsi;

painted landscapes in the style of Mi Fei. (I. 55; N. 1; O. 2; M. p. 465.)
    Cloudy mountain ravine and temple, signed, dated 1367, S. M. Siu
        collection, Hong Kong. CK ku-hua, A. 53; B. 133.

CHANG YÜAN-SHIH 張元士 , t. Shu-shang 叔上 , h. Chih-feng
文峯 . Active c. 1570, painted landscapes and flowers. (CP, VII,
AL, 158.)
    Narcissi, signed, colophon dated 1572, Nat. Pal. Mus., Taipei, (AL).
        CKLTMHC, IV. 95.

CH'ANG-YING 常瑩 , the priest-name of Li Chao-heng 李肇亨 ,
t. Hui-chia 會嘉 , h. K'o-hsüeh 珂雪 and Tsui-ou 醉鷗 . From
Chia-hsing, Chekiang; active c. 1630-1647; son of Li Jih-hua, painted
landscapes and grapevines. (CP, VII, AL, 158.)
    Fisherman in a boat under pines, signed, Tientsin Art Museum.
        T'ien-ching, II. 62.
    Small buildings under tall trees by a river, poem, signed Li Chao-
        heng, Tientsin Art Museum. T'ien-ching, II. 63.

CHAO PEI 趙備 , t. Hsiang-nan 湘南 or Hsiang-lan 湘蘭 . B.
1536, d. after 1613; from Ssu-ming, Chekiang, painted ink bamboos. (CP,
VII, AL, 159.)
    Bamboo and rocks along a stream, handscroll, signed, dated 1610,
        done when 75 years old, Suchou Museum. Su-chou, 19-22.

CHAO SHUN-FU 趙焞夫 , t. Yü-tzu 裕子 . B. 1578; from Fan-
yü, Kuangtung, became a recluse at the fall of the Ming dynasty; friend
of Li Sui-ch'iu, painted landscapes and flowers, especially peonies.
(W. I. 2.)
    Ink peonies, album leaf, signed, dated 1659. Kuang-tung hua-chia, 12*.
    Flowers, folding fan, signed, Chang Ku-ch'u collection. Kuang-tung
        shu-hua, 13.
    Farewell party for General Yüan, friends on a bank, three boats,
        handscroll, signed, Ho Hsien collection. Kuang-tung shu-hua,
        12.

CHAO TSO 趙左 , t. Wen-tu 文度 . From Hua-t'ing (Sung-chiang),
Kiangsu; active c. 1610-1630; pupil of Sung Hsü, painted landscapes in the
styles of Tung Yüan, Mi Fei and the Yüan masters, founder of the Su-sung
School.
    Autumn mountains and red trees, after Yang Sheng, signed, dated 1611,
        Nat. Pal. Mus., Taipei, (AL). CKLTMHC, IV. 106.
    Buildings in a grove of pine, bamboo and other trees, folding fan,
        signed, dated 1611, Shanghai WWPKWYH. Shan-mien-hua, 28*.

Landscape, signed, a line of poetry, dated 1615, Nat. Pal. Mus.,
Taipei, (AL). CKLTMHC, IV. 107.
Autumn landscape, signed, dated 1622, poem by Ch'en Chi-ju, Chang
Pe-chin collection. Tien Yin Tang, I. 51.
Precipitous rocks rising over a bay, trees below, signed, Nat. Pal.
Mus., Taipei, (AL). CKLTMHC, IV. 108.
Mountain landscape, double album leaf, signed, Cheng Te-k'un collec-
tion, Cambridge, (AL). Mu-fei, opposite p. 12.
A scholar in a pavilion at the foot of mountains watching a waterfall,
inscribed, signed, Tientsin Art Museum. T'ien-ching, II. 58.
Marshy landscape with trees and buildings, distant boats, signed,
Tientsin Art Museum. I-yüan chi-chin, 20.

CH'EN CHI 陳 繼 , t. Ssu-ch'u 嗣 初 . B. 1370, d. 1434; from
Ch'ing-chiang, Kiangsi; son of Ch'en Ju-yen; painted bamboo. (I. 55; O. 7;
M. p. 431.)
Bamboo in wind, inscribed, signed, dated 1408, S. M. Siu collection,
Hong Kong. CK ku-hua, B. 155.

CH'EN CHI-JU 陳 繼 儒 , t. Chung-shun 仲 醇 , h. Mi-kung
麋公 , Mei-kung 眉 公 , Hsüeh-t'ang 雪 堂 , Po-shih-ch'iao 白
石 樵 and other names. B. 1558, d. 1639; from Hua-t'ing, Kiangsu;
writer and poet, painted landscapes, plum blossoms and bamboo; author
of numerous books on painting and calligraphy. (CP, VII, AL, 160-161.)
Ink plum blossoms, leaves two and four of an album, inscribed, signed,
Liao-ning Provincial Museum. Liao-ning, II. 53, 54.
Plum blossom branch, folding fan, signed, Shanghai WWPKWYH. Shan-
mien-hua, 36*.
Ink plum blossoms, handscroll, inscribed, signed, S. M. Siu collection,
Hong Kong. CK ku-hua, B. 198.

CH'EN CHIA-YEN 陳 嘉 言 , t. K'ung-chang 孔 彰 . B. 1539, d.
after 1625; from Chia-hsing, Chekiang, flowers. (CP, VII, AL, 161.)
Turtle dove on a branch of plum blossoms, signed, dated 1573, Palace
Museum, Peking. KKPWY hua-niao, 58*.
An album of flowers and animals, twelve leaves, the last dated 1577,
Chang Pe-chin collection. Tien Yin Tang, I. 36-47.
Four mynahs, magnolias, peonies and plum blossoms and a rock,
signed, dated 1587, Chang Wan-li collection. CK hua, XV. 14.
Bamboo and chrysanthemum, album leaf, signed, dated 1598, Liao-
ning Provincial Museum. Liao-ning, II. 73.
A garden stone and some spring flowers, signed, dated 1604, Nat. Pal.
Mus., Taipei, (AL). CKLTMHC, IV. 116.

Three birds in a flowering plum-tree and bamboos, signed, dated
  1607, Tientsin Art Museum, (AL). T'ien-ching, I. 37.
Bamboo, narcissus and plum blossoms, signed, dated 1607, Cheng
  Te-k'un collection, Cambridge. Mu-fei, opposite p. 14.
Butterfly, dragonfly and cicada on autumn flowers, folding fan, signed,
  dated 1616, Shanghai WWPKWYH. Shan-mien-hua, 29*.
Bird on wintry bamboo and plum, inscribed, signed, dated 1619, Tien-
  tsin Art Museum. I-yüan chi-chin, 15.
Plum, pine, cypress and narcissi by a stream, done with Liu Yüan-
  ch'i, Sheng Mao-hua, Wang Tzu-yüan and Wang Chung-li, Ch'en
  Chia-yen did the plum blosssoms, dated 1625, Tientsin Art Mu-
  seum. T'ien-ching II. 61.
Two birds and hibiscus, folding fan, inscribed, signed, dated (effaced),
  Hui Hsiao-t'ung collection. Shan-mien chi-chin, 11*.

CH'EN HUAN 陳煥 , t. Tzu-wen 子文 , h. Yao-feng 堯峯 . From
Suchou; active c. 1600, painted landscapes after Shen Chou. (CP, VII, AL,
162.)
Guests arriving at a pavilion under pines, signed, dated 1595, Tientsin Art Museum. T'ien-ching, II. 42.
The Tsui-weng Pavilion, handscroll, signed, dated 1613, Chang Pe-
  chin collection. Tien Yin Tang, I. 53.
A scholar in a pavilion watching a waterfall, a man crossing a bridge,
  signed, dated 1615, Suchou Museum. Su-chou, 28.

CH'EN HUNG-SHOU 陳洪綬 , t. Chang-hou 章侯 , h. Lao-lien
老蓮 , Fu-ch'ih 弗遲 , Yün-men-seng 雲門僧, and other names.
B. 1599, d. 1652; from Chu-chi, Chekiang, painted figures, flowers,
birds and landscapes. (CP, VII, AL, 163-164.)
Camellias growing from a rock, signed, dated 1626, Nat. Pal. Mus.,
  Taipei, (AL). 300 M. , 250; CH mei-shu, III; CKLTMHC, IV. 148.
Two of ten studies of figures, flowers and birds, album, one leaf
  dated 1645, Nat. Pal. Mus., Taipei, (AL). Che-chiang, 65 (1
  leaf: Plum blossoms); CKLTMHC, IV. 146 (2 leaves: Plum blos-
  soms; Landscape, dated 1645).
A man standing under pines by a riverbank, mountain and village in
  background, inscribed, signed, dated 1648, Tientsin Art Museum.
  I-yüan chi-chin, 21.
The four joys of Po Hsiang-shan (Po Chü-i), handscroll, signed, dated
  1649, (AL). Ch'en Hung-shou, 11 (section).
Two figures, one carrying a staff and a branch of plum, the other a
  ch'in, folding fan, signed, dated 1649, Shanghai WWPKWYH.
  Shan-mien-hua, 51*.

Illustration to T'ao Yüan-ming's poem Kuei-ch'ü-lai, handscroll, signed, dated 1650, Honolulu Academy of Art, (AL). Che-chiang,
64(section); Ch'en Hung-shou, 12 (section).

Sixteen illustrations to the life of a hermit, album, dated 1651, Nat.
Pal. Mus., Taipei, (AL). CAT, 105 (two leaves); CKLTMHC,
IV. 145 (two leaves).

A sparrow on a bamboo branch, handscroll, signed, dated 1651, (AL).
Ch'en Hung-shou, 17 (section).

An old man with a staff, poem, signed, Nat. Pal. Mus., Taipei, (AL,
also listed as Leaning on a staff and singing). CH mei-shu, III;
CKLTMHC, IV. 149; CKLTSHH.

A plum-tree by a rock, signed, Palace Museum, Peking, (AL). WW,
1966. 4. 43.

A lotus plant rising above a big stone, and two mandarin ducks, inscribed, signed, Palace Museum, Peking. (AL). KKPWY hua-
niao, 66*.

Lotuses and a rock, poem, signed, Shanghai Museum, (AL). Ch'en
Hung-shou, 16; CK shu-hua, I. 27; Shang-hai, 64*.

A scholar admiring a vase of chrysanthemums, inscribed, signed,
Nat. Pal. Mus., Taipei. CCAT, pl. 15*.

Two birds on a dry tree, signed, Nat. Pal. Mus., Taipei. CKLTMHC,
IV. 147.

An album of eight leaves, landscapes, figures, flowers, each leaf in-
scribed and signed, some after old masters, Palace Museum,
Peking. CH-s Hua-ts'e, B*; KKPWY hua-niao, 65* (leaf one:
Magnolia and strange stone).

An album of twelve leaves, flowers, birds, figures, landscapes,
Nanking Museum. CH-s Hua-ts'e, A.

Gentlemen gathered to worship a Buddhist image, handscroll, signed,
name inscribed next to each figure, Shanghai WWPKWYH. CK
hua, XI. 16; Li-tai jen-wu, 57; TSYMC hua-hsüan, 61.

A gentleman reading in the shade of banana and other trees, folding
fan, signed, Shanghai WWPKWYH. Shan-mien-hua, 48*.

A man seated on a stone, a female genii emerging from a gourd-
shaped jar, a Taoist (?) on the right, folding fan, signed, Shanghai WWPKWYH. Shan-mien-hua, 49*.

Two figures, one holding a book, folding fan, inscribed, signed, Shanghai WWPKWYH. Shan-mien-hua, 50*.

A gentleman and a lady seated in a garden listening to a flautist, handscroll, done with Yen Chan and Li Wan-sheng; made for Ho T'ien-
chang, Suchou Museum. Su-chou, 32.

Reading and walking with a staff, signed, Tientsin Art Museum. T'ien-
ching, I. 50.

Two stalks of bamboo, handscroll, inscribed, signed, Tientsin Art
Museum. T'ien-ching, I. 51.
A man holding a branch of plum blossoms, a servant with a vase,
signed, Tientsin Art Museum. T'ien-ching, II. 81.
A Confucian and a Buddhist discussing the <u>Tao</u>, signed, Chang Pe-
chin collection. Tien Yin Tang, I. 68.
Four children worshipping a Buddhist image, signed, Cheng Te-k'un
collection, Cambridge. Mu-fei, between pp. 24-25.
Peach blossom and rock, poem, signed, S. M. Siu collection, Hong
Kong. CK ku-hua, B. 216.
Five children flying a kite, inscribed, signed. Ch'en Hung-shou, 10.
Landscape, a man playing a <u>yüan</u> in a boat under a tree, album leaf,
signed. Ch'en Hung-shou, 13.
A lady seated on banana leaves holding a fan. Ch'en Hung-shou, 14
(detail).
Figures on a river terrace under a huge pine tree, inscribed, signed.
Ch'en Hung-shou, 15.
Two fairies carrying emblems of longevity standing next to a rock,
inscribed, signed. CK ku-tai, 89.
Oak, bamboo and bird on plum branch by a rock, signed. TSYMC
hua-hsüan, 62.

CH'EN JU-YEN 陳汝言 , t. Wei-yün 惟允 , h. Ch'iu-shui
秋水 . From Suchou; active 1340-1380; Provincial Secretary in Chi-
nan, Shantung, executed by order of emperor Hung-wu, painted landscapes
in the style of Chao Meng-fu, figures after Ma Ho-chih. (CP, VII, AL, 165.)
Mountain landscape, houses in a valley, signed, dated 1358, S. M. Siu
collection, Hong Kong. CK ku-hua, A. 45; B. 107.
Landscape with a waterfall, signed, dated 1360, Nat. Pal. Mus., Taipei, (AL). CH mei-shu, III; CKLTMHC, III. 64.
A scholar approaching a hut in a mountain valley, signed, dated 1363,
S. M. Siu collection, Hong Kong. CK ku-hua, B. 108.
A view of the Chin River, poems and colophons by Wang Meng, Ni Tsan
and others, Nat. Pal. Mus., Taipei, (AL). CH mei-shu, III;
CKLTMHC, III. 63.

CH'EN JUI 陳瑞 , t. Te-chen 德貞 . From Hsin-hui, Kuang-
tung, a contemporary of Lin Liang. (I. 56; W. I. 1; M. p. 432.)
Banana plant and stone, album leaf, inscribed, signed. Kuang-tung
hua-chia, 6*.

CH'EN KUA 陳括 , t. Tzu-cheng 子正 , h. T'o-chiang 沱江 .
From Suchou; active c. 1550-1554; son of Ch'en Shun, painted flowers in

the style of Hsü Ch'ung-ssu, landscapes after Huang Kung-wang. (CP, VII, AL, 165.)

    Chrysanthemum and stone, signed, Tientsin Art Museum. T'ien-ching, II.38.

CH'EN KUAN 陳　裸 , originally called Ch'en Tsan 陳瓚 and t. Shu-kuan 叔　裸 . Later used Ch'eng-chiang 誠將 as his tzu and Po-shih 白　室 as his hao. From Suchou; active c. 1610-1640, painted landscapes in the styles of Chao Po-chü, Chao Meng-fu and Wen Cheng-ming. (CP, VII, AL, 165-166 as Ch'en Lo.)

    Landscape, poem, colophon, signed, dated 1614, Nat. Pal. Mus., Taipei, (AL). CKLTMHC, IV.128.

    Walking with a staff in an autumn mountain, fisherman in boat, rustic buildings, folding fan, signed, dated 1638, Hui Hsiao-t'ung collection. Shan-mien chi-chin, 8*.

CH'EN LU 陳錄 , t. Hsien-chang 憲章 , h. Ju-yin chü-shih 如隱 居士 . From K'uai-chi, Chekiang; active c. 1440, painted pine trees, bamboo, orchids and particularly plum blossoms. (CP, VII, AL, 166.)

    Plum blossoms, signed, dated 1437, Nat. Pal. Mus., Taipei, (AL). Che-chiang, 48; CKLTMHC, IV.17.

    Curving branch of plum blossoms, signed, dated 1437, Nat. Pal. Mus., Taipei. 300 M., 216; CH mei-shu, III; CKLTMHC, IV.18.

    A branch of plum blossoms by moonlight, signed, Palace Museum, Peking, (AL). KKPWY hua-niao, 35*.

    A spreading branch of blossoming plum tree, inscribed, signed, Palace Museum, Peking. CK hua, X.14; PM, 38*.

    Snowy plum blossoms in moonlight, inscribed, signed, Tientsin Art Museum. T'ien-ching, II.11.

CH'EN SHUN 陳淳 , t. Tao-fu 道復 , h. Po-yang 白陽 ;later took Tao-fu as his name and Fu-fu 復甫 as his tzu. B. 1483, d. 1544; from Suchou; pupil of Wen Cheng-ming, painted flowers. (CP, VII, AL, 166-167.)

    An angler in a boat under a tree near a city gate, poem, signed, dated 1522, Cheng Te-k'un collection, Cambridge, (AL). Mu-fei, opposite p. 6.

    Eight flower studies, handscroll, signed, dated 1540, two colophons, one by Wang Ku-hsiang, Tientsin Art Museum. T'ien-ching, II.29-37.

    Flowers, long handscroll, signed, poems, Nat. Pal. Mus., Taipei, (AL). CH mei-shu, III.

    Grass and flowering plants at the foot of a garden stone, inscribed,

signed, Palace Museum, Peking, (AL). CK ku-tai, 83; KKPWY
hua-niao, 53*.

Camellia flowers and narcissi, inscribed, signed, Shanghai Museum,
(AL). Shang-hai, 56*.

Village roofs seen through cloudy trees and mountains, folding fan,
inscribed, Shanghai WWPKWYH. Shan-mien-hua, 13*.

White clouds on the Hsiao and Hsiang, handscroll, signed, Chang Pe-
chin collection. Tien Yin Tang, I.29.

An album of eight leaves of flowers and fruits, last leaf signed, S. M.
Siu collection, Hong Kong. CK ku-hua, B.193.

Wu-t'ung tree and garden rock, inscribed and signed. TSYMC hua-
hsüan, 52.

CH'EN TS'AN 陳粲 , t. Lan-ku 蘭谷 or Tao-kuang 道光 , h.
Hsüeh-an 雪庵 or Yün-ku-tzu 雪谷子 . From Ch'ang-chou; late 16th-
early 17th century; painted birds and flowers. (O.6; M. p. 436.)

Peach and crab apple blossoms, swimming ducks and flying swallows,
signed, Liao-ning Provincial Museum. Liao-ning, II.45.

CH'EN TSUN 陳遵 . From Chia-hsing, Chekiang; lived in Suchou,
painted flowers and birds. (CP, VII, AL, 168.)

Two pheasants by a blossoming plum-tree and red camellia in snow,
signed, Palace Museum, Peking, (AL). KKPWY hua-niao, 60*.

A rabbit under cassia and rock, signed, Tientsin Art Museum. T'ien-
ching, II.49.

CHENG CHUNG 鄭重 , t. Ch'ien-li 千里 . From Hsieh-hsien, Anhui; lived in Nanking; active c. 1565-1630, painted Buddhist figures and
landscapes. (CP, VII, AL, 169.)

Ko Hung moving his residence, after Wang Meng, signed, dated 1612,
Nat. Pal. Mus., Taipei, (AL). CKLTMHC, IV.111.

CHENG SHIH 鄭石 . Officer in the Imperial Guard in the Ming period.
(CP, VII, AL, 169.)

Herons and hibiscus by a willow on the riverbank, signed, Nat. Pal.
Mus., Taipei, (AL). CKLTMHC, IV.32.

CHENG YÜAN-HSÜN 鄭元勳 , t. Ch'ao-tsung 超宗 . B. 1598,
d. 1645; lived in Yang-chou, painted landscapes. (N.7; O.5; M. p. 642.)

Landscape, after Shen Chou, a homestead by a river, inscribed,
signed, dated 1631, Suchou Museum. Su-chou, 29.

CH'ENG CHIA-SUI 程嘉燧 , t. Meng-yang 孟陽 , h. Sung-yüan
lao-jen 松園老人 . B. 1565, d. 1643; from Hsiu-ning, Anhui; lived

in Chia-ting, Kiangsu, poet, painted landscapes in Yüan styles, one of the "Nine Friends of Painting". (CP, VII, AL, 169-170.)

> Walking with a staff in the autumn woods, signed, dated 1617, two colophons. TSYMC hua-hsüan, 60.
>
> The evening tidal bore, folding fan, poem, signed, dated 1625, Shang-hai WWPKWYH. Shan-mien-hua, 37*.
>
> A study in a banana tree grove, signed, dated 1626, S. M. Siu collection, Hong Kong. CK ku-hua, B. 206.
>
> Two horsemen riding on a willow bank, signed, dated 1639, Tientsin Art Museum. T'ien-ching, II. 64.

CH'ENG NAN-YÜN 程南雲 , t. Ch'ing-hsien 青軒 or 清軒 , Yüan-chai 遠齋 . From Nan-ch'eng, Kiangsi, lived c. 1403-1436, painted plum blossoms and bamboo. (H. 6; I. 56; N. 1; O. 6; M. p. 533.)

> Bamboo in snow, signed, dated 1421, S. M. Siu collection, Hong Kong. CK ku-hua, B. 151.

CHIANG CH'IEN 蔣乾 , t. Tzu-chien 子健 , h. Hung-ch'iao 虹橋 . From Nanking; lived in Suchou; son of Chiang Sung; active c. 1540-1560, landscapes. (CP, VII, AL, 170-171.)

> Fishing in the autumn stream, signed, Tientsin Art Museum. T'ien-ching, II. 50.

CHIANG SUNG 蔣嵩 , t. San-sung 三松 . From Nanking; active c. 1500, painted landscapes and figures, followed Wu Wei and Chang Lu. (CP, VII, AL, 171.)

> Two men fishing from a boat, signed, Tientsin Art Museum. T'ien-ching, I. 23.

CHIANG YIN 姜隱 , t. Chou-tso 周佐 . From Huang-hsien, Shan-tung; 16th century, painted figures, flowers and fruits. (CP, VII, AL, 171.)

> A banana plant by a stone, signed, Nat. Pal. Mus., Taipei. CKLTMHC, IV. 89.

CH'IEN KU 錢穀 , t. Shu-pao 叔寶 , h. Ch'ing-shih 磬室 . B. 1508, d. 1572; from Suchou; pupil of Wen Cheng-ming, painted landscapes, orchids and bamboo. (CP, VII, AL, 172-173.)

> A man seated in a thatched hut in a grove by a wall, folding fan, sign-ed, dated 1563, poem by P'eng Nien, Shanghai WWPKWYH. Shan-mien-hua, 20*.
>
> Preparing tea on Hui Shan, signed, dated 1570, Nat. Pal. Mus., Taipei, (AL, also listed as Six men and two servants round a well). CKLTMHC, IV. 77.

A view of Tiger Hill, signed, dated 1572, Tientsin Art Museum. T'ien-ching, I. 27.

A gentleman fishing in front of his rustic mountain home, inscribed, signed, dated 1573. Shanghai Museum. Shang-hai, 60*.

Epidendrum, bamboo, narcissi and prunus, handscroll, signed, dated 1576, Liao-ning Provincial Museum. Liao-ning, II. 34.

CH'IEN KUNG 錢貢 , t. Yü-fang 禹方 , h. Ts'ang-chou 滄洲 . From Wu-hsien; active in the Wan-li period (1573-1620), painted landscapes and figures. (CP, VII, AL, 173.)

Temples and villas south of the city wall, handscroll, signed, dated 1588, Tientsin Art Museum. T'ien-ching, I. 28-29.

Three ladies and servants on a hill looking at the moon, folding fan, signed, Shanghai WWPKWYH. Shan-mien-hua, 27*.

CHIN SHIH 金湜 , t. Pen-ch'ing 本清 , h. T'ai-shou-sheng 太瘦生 and Hsiu-mu chü-shih 朽木居士 . From Ning-po, Chekiang; chü-jen in 1441, painted rocks and bamboo in outlines; calligrapher. (CP, VII, AL, 173.)

Bamboo by a rock, inscribed, signed, Palace Museum, Peking. KKPWY hua-niao, 33*.

CH'IN I 欽揖 or 楫 , t. Yüan-yu 遠猶 , h. Wu-chuang 兀莊 . From Wu-hsien, Kiangsu, 17th century; landscapes. (M. p. 501.)

Myriad peaks and valleys, inscribed, signed, Nat. Pal. Mus., Taipei. CKLTMHC, IV. 133.

CH'IU SHIH 仇氏 (Miss Ch'iu) or Ch'iu Chu 仇珠 , h. Tu-ling nei-shih 杜陵內史 . From Suchou; active c. 1550; daughter of Ch'iu Ying, figures. (CP, VII, AL, 173.)

A lady in a garden, illustration to a T'ang poem, signed, Nat. Pal. Mus., Taipei, (AL). CKLTMHC, IV. 112.

CH'IU YING 仇英 , t. Shih-fu 實父 , h. Shih-chou 十洲 . From T'ai-ts'ang, Kiangsu; lived in Suchou; first half of the 16th century. Figures, landscapes, architectural scenery. (CP, VII, AL, 174-177.)

Portrait of Ni Tsan, epitaph copied by Wen P'eng dated 1542, (AL). Li-tai jen-wu, 52.

Six album-leaves representing landscapes after Sung and Yüan masters, colophon by Hsiang Yüan-pien dated 1547, Nat. Pal. Mus., Taipei, (AL). CH mei-shu, III.

The Fairy Mountain, signed, a rhymed prose by Lu Shih-tao dated 1548, Nat. Pal. Mus., Taipei, (AL). 300 M., 243.

A boat moored among reeds, country villa, distant village, folding
  fan, signed, dated 1548, Shanghai WWPKWYH. Shan-mien-hua,
  10*.
Playing the ch'in and the p'i-p'a in the shade of banana-trees, signed,
  Nat. Pal. Mus., Taipei, (AL). CKLTMHC, IV. 85.
Waiting for the ferry-boat; a broad riverview, artist's seals, Nat. Pal.
  Mus., Taipei, (AL). 300 M., 241*; CAT, 102; CCAT, pl. 116;
  CH mei-shu, III; CKLTMHC, IV. 87.
The gathering of poets at Lan-t'ing, artist's seals, Nat. Pal. Mus.,
  Taipei, (AL). CKLTMHC, IV. 83.
A scholar in a fishing-boat on the willow-stream, signed, inscription
  by Wen Chia, Nat. Pal. Mus., Taipei, (AL). CKLTMHC, IV. 84.
Two men under a wu-t'ung tree, signed, Nat. Pal. Mus., Taipei, (AL).
  300 M., 242; CAT, 103; CH mei-shu, III; CKLTMHC, IV. 86;
  CKLTSHH.
Travellers riding through the Chien-ko Pass in winter, inscribed,
  signed, Shanghai Museum, (AL). Shang-hai, 59*.
Trying the spring water, signed, Nat. Pal. Mus., Taipei. 300 M.,
  244.
Realms of the Immortals, Nat. Pal. Mus., Taipei. CH mei-shu, III;
  CH ming-hua*.
The Jade Grotto and the Immortals' Spring, a man in a landscape hold-
  ing a ch'in, four servants, signed, Palace Museum, Peking. PM,
  28* (section); WW, 1966. 4. 43.
Palace scene with figures, handscroll, Museum of History, Peking.
  WW, 1962. 10. 12, 25.
The Red Cliff, three men and two servants in a boat in front of the cliff,
  handscroll, signed, inscriptions by P'eng Nien, Wen P'eng, Wen
  Chia and Chou T'ien-ch'iu, Liao-ning Provincial Museum. Liao-
  ning, II. 32-33.
Making tea under the pines, folding fan, signed, Shanghai WWPKWYH.
  Shan-mien-hua, 11*.
Ladies in boats gathering lotuses, folding fan, signed, Shanghai
  WWPKWYH. Shan-mien-hua, 12*.
A gentleman seated under pine trees on the bank of a stream, folding
  fan, seal, Tientsin Art Museum. T'ien-ching, I. 22.
Recluses, handscroll, signed, Tientsin Art Museum. T'ien-ching,
  II. 24-25.
Elegant Gathering in the Western Garden, signed, inscription by Wen
  Chen-ming, Chang Pe-chin collection. Tien Yin Tang, I. 30.
A scholar in a pine grove, pavilion among peach trees, signed, Hsü
  Shih-hsüeh collection. CK hua, I. 24*.
A scholar resting in a bamboo grove, handscroll, signed, S. M. Siu
  collection, Hong Kong. CK ku-hua, B. 188.

Floating in the sea, signed, colophon by Wen P'eng, S. M. Siu collection, Hong Kong. CK ku-hua, B. 189.

Garden and pavilions, handscroll, signed, S. M. Siu collection, Hong Kong. CK ku-hua, B. 190.

Album of nine leaves depicting ladies at various diversions, signed, S. M. Siu collection, Hong Kong. CK ku-hua, B. 191.

Man and servant outside a riverside homestead, rice paddies, inscribed, signed. CK ku-tai, 72.

Gentleman leaning on a rock near a river. Li-tai jen-wu, 51.

Hunting party, signed. TSYMC hua-hsüan, 50*.

Virtuous women, handscroll, signed. TSYMC hua-hsüan, 51.

Two men in a pavilion looking at rapids, album leaf, signed. WW, 1956. 1, cover*.

Man on a horse and his servant by the lakeside, steep cliffs, album leaf, signed. CY Shan-shui*.

CHOU CH'EN 周臣 , t. Shun-ch'ing 舜卿 , h. Tung-ts'un 東邨 .
From Suchou; active c. 1500-1535; landscapes and figures. (CP, VII, AL, 177-178.)

Landscape, after Tai Chin, signed, dated 1534, Nat. Pal. Mus., Taipei, (AL). CKLTMHC, IV. 42.

Ning Ch'i feeding a buffalo, signed, Nat. Pal. Mus., Taipei, (AL). CKLTMHC, IV. 43.

A man bidding farewell, ready to step into a boat at the shore, signed, (AL). Li-tai jen-wu, 49; TSYMC hua-hsüan, 42.

Receiving guests in a mountain studio, signed, Shanghai Museum. Shang-hai, 51*.

Gentlemen conversing under the pines, folding fan, signed, Shanghai WWPKWYH. Shan-mien-hua, 3*.

A man in a pavilion in a gully, distant mountains, folding fan, signed, Shanghai WWPKWYH. Shan-mien-hua, 4*.

Nine gentlemen playing chess, reading, walking in garden landscape, signed, Tientsin Art Museum. T'ien-ching, I. 14.

CHOU CHIH-MIEN 周之冕 , t. Fu-ch'ing 服卿 , h. Shao-ku 少谷 .
From Suchou; active c. 1580-1610; flowers and birds. (CP, VII, AL, 178-179.)

Bamboo, rocks and flowers, signed, dated 1594 (?), S. M. Siu collection, Hong Kong. CK ku-hua, B. 204.

Flower studies, handscroll, signed, dated 1598, Tientsin Art Museum. T'ien-ching, II. 45-48.

Lilies, flowers and cat by a stone, signed, dated 1600. TSYMC hua-hsüan, 57.

A cock by a cliff and some bamboos, signed, dated 1602, Palace Museum, Peking (AL). KKPWY hua-niao, 59*.

A grasshopper on a peavine, folding fan, signed, poem by Kuo Ping-chan dated 1619, Shanghai WWPKWYH. Shan-mien-hua, 26*.

Grapevine and squirrels, signed, Nat. Pal. Mus., Taipei, (AL, also listed as Climbing vine and squirrels). CKLTMHC, IV.91.

Ducks and birds along a flowery bank with stone, willow, banana and <u>wu-t'ung</u> trees, folding fan, signed, Shanghai WWPKWYH. Shan-mien-hua, 25*.

Album of ten leaves depicting birds and flowers, each leaf signed, S. M. Siu collection, Hong Kong. CK ku-hua, B.205 (four leaves).

CHOU CH'ÜAN 周全 . 15th century; officer of the Imperial Guard; horses. (CP, VII, AL, 179.)

A Mongol chief on a white horse shooting pheasants, signed, Nat. Pal. Mus., Taipei, (AL). CKLTMHC, IV.33.

CHOU FAN 周蕃 , t. Tzu-ken 自根 , h. Huang-t'ou 黄頭 . From Suchou; active c. 1570-1590; flowers and birds. (CP, VII, AL, 179.)

Hollyhock and two cocks, signed, dated 1594, Nat. Pal. Mus., Taipei, (AL). CKLTMHC, V.3.

CHOU T'IEN-CH'IU 周天球 , t. Kung-hsia 公瑕 , h. Huan-hai 幻海 , Yu-hai 幼海 , Liu-chih-sheng 六止生 , and other names. B. 1514, d. 1595; from Suchou; landscapes and orchids. (CP, VII, AL, 180.)

Narcissus and bamboo, inscribed, signed, dated 1554, handscroll, Liao-ning Provincial Museum. Liao-ning, II.37-40.

CHOU WEI 周位 , t. Yüan-su 元素 . From Chen-yang, Kiangsu; active during the Hung-wu period (1368-1398); landscapes. (CP, VII, AL, 181.)

T'ao Yüan-ming returning home drunk, album leaf, signed, Nat. Pal. Mus., Taipei, (AL). CH mei-shu, III.

CHOU WEN-CHING 周文靖 , h. San-shan 三山 . From P'u-t'ien, Fukien; active c. 1430-1460; court painter; landscapes, figures, flowers, birds, buildings. (CP, VII, AL, 181.)

Wang Hui-chih visiting Tai K'uei on a snowy night, signed, Nat. Pal. Mus., Taipei, (AL). CKLTMHC, IV.34.

Crows flying and roosting in an old tree, signed, Shanghai Museum. Shang-hai, 41*.

CHU CHIH-FAN 朱之蕃 , t. Yüan-chieh 元介 or Yüan-sheng 元升 ,
h. Lan-yü 蘭嵎 . From Chin-ling (Nanking); chin-shih in 1619; landscapes, bamboos. (CP, VII, AL, 181.)

    Withered trees, bamboo and rock, inscribed, signed, dated 1623,
      S. M. Siu collection, Hong Kong. CK ku-hua, B. 213.

CHU FEI 朱苇 , t. Meng-pien 孟辨 , h. Ts'ang-chou-sheng 滄洲
    生 . From Sung-chiang, Kiangsu, active during the Hung-wu period
(1368-1398); wild geese, landscapes, figures. (CP, VII, AL, 182.)
    Wild ducks by a stream, inscribed, signed, dated 1371, S. M. Siu
      collection, Hong Kong. CK ku-hua, B. 150.
    Geese flocking on the shore among reeds, signed, dated 1374, Nat.
      Pal. Mus., Taipei, (AL). 300 M., 207; CH mei-shu, III;
      CKLTSHH.

CHU LU 朱鷺 , original name Chia-tung 家棟 , t. Po-min 伯民 ,
h. Hsi-k'ung lao-jen 西空老人 and other names. B. 1553, d. 1632;
from Suchou; bamboo. (CP, VII, AL, 182.)
    Bamboo in the wind, signed, dated 1624, S. M. Siu collection, Hong
      Kong. CK ku-hua, B. 207.

CHU NAN-YUNG 朱南雍 , t. Yüeh-ching 越崝 . From Shan-
yin, Chekiang; chin-shih in 1568; landscapes, rocks. (CP, VII, AL, 183.)
    River-views; hills and leafy trees, handscroll, signed, colophon by
      Yeh Kung-cho, Cheng Te-k'un collection, Cambridge, (AL).
      Mu-fei, opposite p. 10.

CHU TUAN 朱端 , t. K'o-cheng 克正 , h. I-ch'iao 一樵 . From
Hai-yen, Chekiang; court-painter in the Cheng-te period (1506-1521); landscapes, figures, flowers, birds, bamboo. (CP, VII, AL, 183.)
    Looking for plum-blossoms on a snowy day, signed, Nat. Pal. Mus.,
      Taipei, (AL). CKLTMHC, IV. 44.
    A solitary angler on a snowy river, signed, National Museum, Tokyo,
      (AL). Che-chiang, 52.
    A guest and a servant approaching a pavilion gate, signed, Tientsin
      Art Museum. T'ien-ching, I. 15.
    Two scholars looking at a waterfall, signed, S. M. Siu collection,
      Hong Kong. CK ku-hua, B. 168.

CHU WAN 朱完 , t. Hsiu-mei 秀美 , h. Po-yüeh shan-jen 白岳山人 .
B. 1529, d. 1617; from Nan-hai, Kuangtung; ink bamboo. (O. 7; W. I. 1;
M. p. 99.)
    Bamboos by a rock, signed, dated 1593. Kuang-tung hua-chia, 8*.

CHÜ MOU-SHIH 居懋時 . From Suchou; active c. 1600; son of Chü Chieh. (CP, VII, AL, 184.)
>   Reading on an autumn day, signed, Nat. Pal. Mus., Taipei, (AL). CKLTMHC, IV. 113.

CHUNG HSÜEH 鍾學 , t. Hsüeh-fang 雪舫 . From Nan-hai, Kuangtung; active during the T'ien-shun era (1457-1464). (W.I.1.)
>   A tiger lily by a rock, artist's seals. Kuang-tung hua-chia, 7*.

FANG HSIAO-JU 方孝孺 , t. Hsi-chih 希直 and Hsi-ku 希古 ; called Master Cheng-hsüeh 正學先生 . B. 1357, d. 1402; from Ning-hai, Chekiang. (CP, VII, AL, 185.)
>   Pine and bamboo, signed, dated 1393, S. M. Siu collection, Hong Kong. CK ku-hua, B.147.

FU CH'ING 傅清 , t. Chung-su 仲素 or Ju-ch'ing 汝清 Kung-su 功素 . From Hua-t'ing, Kiangsu; lived during the T'ien-ch'i period (1621-28); flowers, birds. (O.6; M. p. 512.)
>   A black bird on a plum branch, folding fan, signed, dated 1629, Shang-hai WWPKWYH. Shan-mien-hua, 34*.

HO CHEN 賀鎮 . Unidentified.
>   Riverside pavilions and buildings, two boats, folding fan, inscribed, signed, after Chang Shih-heng, Hui Hsiao-t'ung collection. Shan-mien chi-chin, 9*.

HOU MOU-KUNG 侯懋功 , t. Yen-shang 延賞 , h. I-men 夷門 . From Suchou, active at the end of the 16th century; landscapes. (CP, VII, AL, 186.)
>   Peaks and bluffs along the river, handscroll, signed, dated 1577, Cheng Te-k'un collection, Cambridge. Mu-fei, between pp. 10-11.
>   Mountains and bower in autumn, fisherman and pavilion, signed, dated 1604, after Wang Meng, Chang Pe-chin collection, (AL, A tall mountain landscape?). Tien Yin Tang, I.33.
>   Mountain landscape after a Yüan master, signed, Nat. Pal. Mus., Taipei, (AL). CKLTMHC, IV.90.

HSIA CH'ANG 夏昶 , t. Chung-chao 仲昭 , h. Tzu-tsai chü-shih 自在居士 and Yü-feng 玉峯 . B. 1388, d. 1470; from K'un-shan, Kiangsu; calligrapher, bamboo-painter. (CP, VII, AL, 186-187.)
>   Bamboo by a rock, signed, dated 1440, S. M. Siu collection, Hong Kong. CK ku-hua, B.157.
>   Kuanyin seated under a few swaying bamboos, signed, dated 1446, Nat. Pal. Mus., Taipei, (AL). CKLTMHC, IV.6.

Bamboos in wind, signed, dated 1450, Nat. Pal. Mus., Taipei, (AL).
CKLTMHC, IV. 8; KKCP, I. 7.

Tall bamboos among strange rocks, signed, Nat. Pal. Mus., Taipei,
(AL). 300 M., 210; CKLTMHC, IV. 9; NPM Quarterly, I. 4,
pl. 14.

A branch of bamboo, signed, Nat. Pal. Mus., Taipei, (AL). CH mei-
shu, III; CKLTMHC, IV. 7; CKLTSHH.

Two large stalks of bamboo, inscribed, signed, made for Wang Meng,
Shanghai Museum. CK hua, VIII. 17; Shang-hai, 35*.

Branch of bamboo, signed, Suchou Museum. Su-chou, 5.

Bamboo in wind by rock, signed, Chang Pe-chin collection. Tien Yin
Tang, I. 13.

Bamboo, signed, S. M. Siu collection, Hong Kong. CK ku-hua, A. 56;
B. 156.

Hanging branch of bamboo, signed, S. M. Siu collection, Hong Kong.
CK ku-hua, B. 158.

Bamboo, handscroll. CK ku-tai, 74 (sections).

Bamboo and rock, signed. TSYMC hua-hsüan, 31.

HSIA CHIH 夏芷 , t. T'ing-fang 廷芳 . From Ch'ien-t'ang, Chekiang, 15th century; landscapes. (CP, VII, AL, 187.)

A scholar on the bank of a river gazing at a waterfall, signed, (AL).
Che-chiang, 47.

One illustration to T'ao Ch'ien's "The Return", handscroll, artist's
seal, remaining six illustrations by Ma Shih and Li Tsai, Li
Tsai's painting dated 1424, Liao-ning Provincial Museum. Liao-
ning, II. 14.

HSIA PING 夏昺 , t. Meng-yang 孟暘 . From K'un-shan, Kiangsu;
active c. 1450; elder brother of Hsia Ch'ang; calligrapher, painted landscapes, bamboos, stones. (CP, VII, AL, 187.)

Bamboos and stones, signed, dated 1459, Nat. Pal. Mus., Taipei,
(AL). KKCP, I. 6.

HSIANG SHENG-MO 項聖謨 , t. K'ung-chang 孔彰 , h. I-an 易菴
and Hsü-shan-ch'iao 胥山樵 . B. 1597, d. 1658; from Chia-hsing,
Chekiang; landscapes, bamboos, flowers. (CP, VII, AL, 188-189.)

Album of twelve leaves, landscapes, epidendrum, bamboo, inscribed,
signed, dated 1620, Suchou Museum. Su-chou, 30, 31 (two
leaves: Bamboo in snow; landscape).

Two fishermen in boats near a spring shore, folding fan, signed,
dated 1627, Shanghai WWPKWYH. Shan-mien-hua, 46*.

A scholar's study, surrounded by a wall, among trees, signed, dated

1632, Cheng Te-k'un collection, Cambridge, (AL). Mu-fei, before p. 23.

A creek of a river, with trees in snow, signed, dated, 1641, Palace Museum, Peking, (AL). CK ku-tai, 90; WW, 1966.4.44.

Peaches on a branch, signed, dated 1642, S.M. Siu collection, Hong Kong. CK ku-hua, B.211.

A scholar gazing at an autumn grove, album leaf, inscribed, signed, dated 1646. CK shu-hua, I.25.

Two birds and crab on rice stalks, poem, signed, dated 1651, Tientsin Art Museum. T'ien-ching, II.80.

Yellow and white chrysanthemums, signed, dated 1654, Palace Museum, Peking. KKPWY hua-niao, 63*.

A branch of peach-blossoms, poem, signed, Nat. Pal. Mus., Taipei, (AL). CKLTMHC, IV.153.

Wild geese on the reedy shore, poem, signed, Nat. Pal. Mus., Taipei, (AL). CKLTMHC, IV.152.

A butterfly on the calamus, inscribed, signed, Palace Museum, Peking, (AL). PM, 39*.

Friends arriving in boats, section of handscroll, Nat. Pal. Mus., Taipei, (AL). Che-chiang, 63.

A man walking with a staff along a river-bank, album leaf, inscribed, signed, Nat. Pal. Mus., Taipei, (AL). CH mei-shu, III.

Plum blossoms, album leaf, poem, signed, Palace Museum, Peking. KKPWY hua-niao, 64*.

Landscape with a pavilion in a grove and fenced-in cottages, handscroll, inscribed, signed, Tientsin Art Museum. T'ien-ching, I.40-44.

Bare tree in front of leafy tree, rock, bamboo and stream, inscribed, signed. TSYMC hua-hsüan, 63.

HSIANG YÜAN-PIEN 項元汴 , t. Tzu-ching 子京 , h. Mo-lin 墨林 . B. 1525, d. 1590; from Chia-hsing, Chekiang; collector and connoisseur; landscapes, plum-blossoms, orchids, bamboos and stones. (CP, VII, AL, 189-190.)

Bamboo and orchids, signed, dated 1582, S.M. Siu collection, Hong Kong. CK ku-hua, B.210.

Bamboos, epidendrum and stones, poem, signed, Nat. Pal. Mus., Taipei, (AL). CKLTMHC, IV.100; KKCP, I.9.

Lotus plants, poem, signed, (AL). Che-chiang, 59.

HSIEH HUAN 謝環 , t. T'ing-hsün庭循 ; later adopted this as his name. From Yung-chia, Chekiang; active c. 1368-1435, painted landscapes. (CP, VII, AL, 191.)

The Elegant Gathering in the Apricot Garden, handscroll, a colophon by

Yang Shih-ch'i naming Hsieh as the artist, another colophon by
Yang Jung giving the date of 1437. WW, 1963.4.3-4.

HSIEH SHIH-CH'EN 謝 時 臣 , t. Ssu-chung 思 忠 , h. Ch'u-hsien
樗仙 . B. 1487, d. after 1567; from Suchou; landscpaes, seascapes.
(CP, VII, AL, 191-192.)

    Landscape, handscroll, signed, dated 1551, poem by Wen P'eng, Nat.
        Pal. Mus., Taipei, (AL). CKLTMHC, IV.68.

    Three gentlemen and servant in a pavilion on a river bank, two boats
        on the river, inscribed, signed, dated 1553, Tientsin Art Museum.
        T'ien-ching, II.26.

    Traveller at the door of a hut in snowy mountains, temple in the dis-
        tance, inscribed, signed, dated 1560, Tientsin Art Museum. I-
        yüan chi-chin, 12.

    Green pine-trees and white clouds, poem, signed, Nat. Pal. Mus.,
        Taipei (AL). CKLTMHC, IV.63.

    The Four Hermits of Shang Shan, signed, Nat. Pal. Mus., Taipei, (AL).
        CKLTMHC, IV.66.

    A homeward boat on a river in snow, signed, Nat. Pal. Mus., Taipei,
        (AL). CKLTMHC, IV.67.

    Autumn landscape, signed, Nat. Pal. Mus., Taipei, (AL). CKLTMHC,
        IV.64.

    An illustration to one of the Odes of Pin, Nat. Pal. Mus., Taipei.
        CKLTMHC, IV.65.

    Two gentlemen approaching a bridge in springtime mountains, in-
        scribed, signed, Huang Pao-hsi collection, Hong Kong. Lo-tsai
        hsüan, I.7*.

    Two boats coming down river rapids, inscribed, signed. TSYMC hua-
        hsüan, 53.

HSING TZ'U-CHING 邢 慈 静 . From Chi-nan, Shantung; younger sister of Hsing T'ung (chin-shih in 1574); flowers, Kuanyin. (CP, VII, AL,
193.)

    Kuanyin, inscribed, signed, painted in gold, Nat. Pal. Mus., Taipei,
        (AL). CKLTMHC, IV.156.

HSÜ LIN 徐霖 , t. Tzu-jen 子仁 , h. Chiu-feng 九峯 and K'uai-yüan-
sou 快 園 叟 , also known as Jan-weng 髯 翁 . From Suchou; lived
in Nanking; active c. 1510-1550; landscapes, flowers. (CP, VII, AL, 193.)

    Hare, chrysanthemum, bamboo and rock, poem, signed, Palace Mu-
        seum, Peking, (AL, Chrysanthemums and a hare?). KKPWY
        hua-niao, 50*.

HSÜ PEN or Hsü Fen 徐賁 , t. Yu-wen 幼文 , h. Pei-kuo-sheng
北郭生 . D. 1403; from Szechuan, lived in Suchou, poet, calligrapher; landscapes. (CP, VII, AL, 193-194.)

> A mountain in Szechuan, poem, inscribed, signed, colophon by Sung
> K'o dated 1371, Nat. Pal. Mus., Taipei, (AL). 300 M., 206;
> CH mei-shu, III; CKLTMHC, IV.1; CKLTSHH.
>
> Travellers in a mountain pass, signed, dated 1395, S.M. Siu collection, Hong Kong. CK ku-hua, B.138.
>
> Clearing after snowfall on a river, handscroll, Palace Museum, Peking, (AL). WW, 1956.1.
>
> Scholar in a thatched hut in a grove by a river below a tall mountain
> peak, poem, signed, colophon by Ch'en Hsün, Shanghai Museum.
> Shang-hai, 31*.
>
> Fishing houseboat at the foot of cliffs, inscribed, signed, S.M. Siu
> collection, Hong Kong. CK ku-hua, B.137.
>
> Bamboo, inscribed, signed, S.M. Siu collection, Hong Kong. CK
> ku-hua, B.139.

HSÜ WEI 徐渭 , t. Wen-ch'ing 文清 and Wen-ch'ang 文長 , h.
T'ien-ch'ih 天池 and Ch'ing-t'eng 青藤 . B. 1521, d. 1593; from Shanyin, Chekiang; writer, poet, calligrapher; landscapes, figures, flowers, bamboos, stones. (CP, VII, AL, 194-195.)

> Figures, handscroll, inscribed, signed, dated 1568, S.M. Siu collection, Hong Kong. CK ku-hua, B.197.
>
> The Study of the Green Creeper, inscribed, signed, (AL). Che-chiang, 54.
>
> The Study of the Green Creeper, two lines of poetry, signed, Cheng
> Te-k'un collection, Cambridge, (AL). Mu-fei, opposite p. 8.
>
> A pomegranate fruit, two lines of poetry, signed, Nat. Pal. Mus.,
> Taipei, (AL). 300 M., 245; CKLTMHC, IV.88; Hsü Wei, 12.
>
> Lotus leaves and a crab, inscribed, signed, Palace Museum, Peking,
> (AL). KKPWY hua-niao, 56; WW, 1961.6.6.
>
> A lotus plant, poem, (AL). Hsü Wei, 3.
>
> A banana-plant by a rock, two poems by the artist, (AL). Hsü Wei, 2.
>
> A donkey-rider, poems, signed, (AL). Hsü Wei, 1.
>
> An album of thirty-six leaves once owned by Sung Lo and Wu Li, inscribed, Kikuchi collection, Tokyo, (AL). Hsü Wei, 4 (A man
> with a ch'in seated on the ground under pine-trees, AL); 5 (Peony);
> 6 (Two cats); 7 (Bamboo and moon); 8 (Two fish).
>
> Ink grapevines, poem, signed, Palace Museum, Peking. CK ku-tai,
> 82; KKPWY hua-niao, 55*; WW, 1961.6.33.
>
> Flowers, handscroll of sixteen sections, poem, Palace Museum, Peking. WW, 1961.6.31.

Flowers, fruits, banana-tree, handscroll, signed, Nanking Museum.
Hsü Wei, 10-11 (sections).

Peony, banana and rock, inscribed, signed, Shanghai Museum. Shanghai, 61*.

Ten scholars gathered for a feast, album leaf, seal, Huang Pin-hung
Memorial Hall, Hangchou. Che-chiang, 55; Hsü Wei, 9.

Ink flowers, handscroll. TSYMC hua-hsüan, 56 (two sections: Bird
on a lily, inscribed; Banana leaves, inscribed.).

HSÜ YÜAN 徐潚   or Hsü Ta-yüan 徐大淵 , t. Tzu-hsü 子胥 .
From Lung-ch'i, Fukien; active c. 1600, painted flowers and birds. (CP,
VII, AL, 195.)

Hibiscus and lotus by a riverside rock, signed, dated 1587, Chang Pe-
chin collection. Tien Yin Tang, I. 50.

HSÜAN-TSUNG, EMPEROR HSÜAN-TE OF MING 明宣宗 (r. 1426-
1435). B. 1398, d. 1435; poet, calligrapher; landscapes, figures, animals.
(CP, VII, AL, 195-196.)

Monkeys, signed, dated 1427, Nat. Pal. Mus., Taipei, (AL). 300 M.,
214; CKLTMHC, IV. 15.

A squirrel on a stone watching fruits hanging from a tree, handscroll,
signed, dated 1427, Palace Museum, Peking, (AL). KKPWY hua-
niao, 32*.

Ten-thousand year pine, handscroll, signed, dated 1431, Liao-ning
Provincial Museum. Liao-ning, II. 6-7.

Two chickens with chicks, signed, Nat. Pal. Mus., Taipei. CH ming-
hua*.

HSÜEH SHIH-HENG 薛始亨 , t. Kang-sheng 剛生 , h. Chien-
kung 劍公 , Chien-tao-jen 劍道人 , Erh-ch'iao shan-jen 二樵山人 .
B. 1617, d. 1686; from Shun-te, Kuangtung; poet. (W.I.1.)

A rock, long inscription, signed, Ho Man-an collection. Kuang-tung
shu-hua, 17.

HSÜEH SU-SU 薛素素 (also called Wu 五), t. Jun-ch'ing 潤卿 or
Su-ch'ing 素卿 , h. Jun-niang 潤娘 . Born in Suchou c. 1564; lived
in Nanking, died c. 1637; a woman, painted bamboo, epidendrum, Buddhist
figures. (CP, VII, AL, 196.)

Bamboo and rock, folding fan, inscribed, dated 1599, Shanghai WWP
KWYH. Shan-mien-hua, 52*.

HUANG CHÜAN 黃卷 , t. Sheng-mo 聖模 . From P'u-t'ien, Fu-
kien; active during the Wan-li and T'ien-ch'i periods (1573-1627); landscapes, figures. (CP, VII, AL, 197.)

Five ladies on a plum-blossom-viewing excursion, folding fan, signed, dated 1570, Shanghai WWPKWYH. Shan-mien-hua, 32*.

HUANG TAO-CHOU 黃道周 , t. Yu-yüan 幼元 and Ch'ih-jo 螭若 , h. Shih-chai 石齋 . B. 1585, d. 1646; from Chang-p'u, Fukien; landscapes. (CP, VII, AL, 198.)
 Landscape, empty pavilion on a shore, angular cliffs in background, poem, signed, dated 1642, Cheng Te-k'un collection, Cambridge. Mu-fei, before p. 17.
 Fantastic landscape with sharp peaks, inscribed, signed, dated (illegible in reproduction), Tientsin Art Museum. T'ien-ching, II. 75.

KU CHENG-I 顧正誼 , t. Chung-fang 仲方 , h. T'ing-lin 亭林 . From Hua-t'ing, Kiangsu; active c. 1580; poet and writer; landscapes, founder of the Hua-t'ing School. (CP, VII, AL, 200.)
 Trees and stones, after Ni Tsan, signed, poems by the artist and his contemporaries, Nat. Pal. Mus., Taipei, (AL). CKLTMHC, IV. 101.

KU CHUNG 顧重 . Unrecorded. According to information on the painting, t. Chuang-shan 庄山 .
 A literary gathering, signed, dated chi-mao, Tientsin Art Museum. I-yüan chi-chin, 14.

KU FU 顧復 . From Ching-chiang, active in the Ch'eng-hua era (1465-1487). (CP, VII, AL, 200.)
 Landscape, after Ni Tsan's An-ch'u chai, inscribed, dated 1488, Nat. Pal. Mus., Taipei, (AL). CH mei-shu, III.

KU LU 顧祿 , t. Chin-chung 謹中 . From Hua-t'ing (Sung-chiang), Kiangsu; active during the Hung-wu period (1368-1398); poet; landscapes, flowers, bamboo and stones. (I. 55; O. 2; M. p. 737.)
 Bamboo and rock, inscribed, signed, dated (illegible in reproduction), S. M. Siu collection, Hong Kong. CK ku-hua, B. 149.

KU NING-YÜAN 顧凝遠 , t. Ch'ing-hsia 青霞 . From Suchou; active c. 1636; landscapes; author of Hua-yin. (CP, VII, AL, 201.)
 Landscape after Chao Meng-fu, signed, Nat. Pal. Mus., Taipei, (AL). CKLTMHC, IV. 157.

KUAN SSU 關思 , t. Ho-ssu 何思 , h. Hsü-po 虛伯 . Also used the name Chiu-ssu 九思 , t. Chung-t'ung 仲通 . From Wu-ch'eng, Chekiang; active c. 1590-1630; landscapes. (CP, VII, AL, 201-202.)
 Landscape, signed, dated 1600, Nat. Pal. Mus., Taipei, (AL). CKLTMHC, IV. 130.

A large river landscape, with strolling scholars, inscribed, signed,
dated 1625, Nat. Pal. Mus., Taipei, (AL). CKLTMHC, IV.131.

High mountains forming terraces; a boat on the river below, after
Wang Meng, inscribed, signed, dated 1627, Nat. Pal. Mus., Taipei, (AL). CKLTMHC, IV.132.

Pavilions built on a mountain river bank, high mountain peaks, signed,
dated 1627. Che-chiang, 58.

KUEI CH'ANG-SHIH 歸昌世 , t. Hsiu-wen 休文 or Wen-hsiu 文休 ,
h. Chia-an 假庵 . B. 1574, d. 1645; from K'un-shan, Kiangsu; landscapes, bamboo. (CP, VII, AL, 202.)

Bamboo and rock, signed, Suchou Museum. Su-chou, 26.

Ink bamboo and rocks, handscroll, signed, Cheng Te-k'un collection,
Cambridge. Mu-fei, between pp. 14-15.

KUEI CHUANG 歸莊 , also called Kuei Tsu-ming 歸祚明 , t. Yüan-
kung 元恭 , h. Heng-hsüan 恒軒 , and other names. B. 1613, d.
1673; son of Kuei Ch'ang-shih; friend of Ku Yen-wu; bamboos. (CP, VII,
AL, 202.)

Bamboo and rock, inscribed, signed, dated 1666, Tientsin Art Museum. T'ien-ching, I.61.

Bamboo and stone, signed, dated 1667, colophon by Chu I-ts'un, S.M.
Siu collection, Hong Kong. CK ku-hua, B.219.

KUO HSÜ 郭詡 , t. Jen-hung 仁宏 , h. Ch'ing-k'uang 清狂 .
B. 1456, d. after 1526; from T'ai-ho, Kiangsi; friend of Wu Wei, Shen
Chou; landscapes, figures. (CP, VII, AL, 203.)

Lady and servant with a ch'in, signed, dated 1520, S.M. Siu collection,
Hong Kong. CK ku-hua, B.170.

Hsieh An with his concubines, poem dated 1526 (at 71), Nat. Pal. Mus.,
Taipei, (AL). CCAT, pl. 114; CKLTMHC, IV.41; Li-tai jen-wu,
48.

A boy on a water buffalo playing a flute, signed, Shanghai Museum.
Shang-hai, 45*.

An album of eight leaves depicting landscapes, figures, birds and
flowers, each leaf inscribed and/or signed, Shanghai Museum.
KH Hua-ts'e; Shang-hai, 46* (one leaf: A frog on a lotus leaf).

LAN YING 藍瑛 , t. T'ien-shu 田叔 , h. Tieh-sou 蝶叟 and
Shih-t'ou-t'o 石頭蛇 . B. 1585, d. after 1664; from Ch'ien-t'ang,
Chekiang; landscapes. (CP, VII, AL, 203-205.)

River and temples in pine-covered mountains, signed, dated 1622,
Tientsin Art Museum. I-yüan chi-chin, 18*.

Men in a pavilion built over rapids, two inscriptions by the artist, one dated 1622, in the style of Li Ch'eng, Liao-ning Provincial Museum. Liao-ning, II. 46.

Landscape after snow, signed, dated 1623, Nat. Pal. Mus., Taipei. 300 M., 252.

Two ladies seated on a carpet under plum trees, folding fan, inscribed, signed, dated 1636, after Chao Meng-fu, Shanghai WWPKWYH. Shan-mien-hua, 43*.

A jay on a red-leafed tree branch, folding fan, inscribed, signed, dated 1637, Shanghai WWPKWYH, (AL, Bird on the branch of a maple-tree?). Shan-mien-hua, 42*.

Angling from a boat on the autumn river, folding fan, signed, dated 1637, Hui Hsiao-t'ung collection. Shan-mien chi-chin, 2*.

Cloudy landscape, in the manner of Kao K'o-kung, signed, dated 1639, (AL). TSYMC hua-hsüan, 64.

Fishermen on a wintry river, handscroll, inscribed, signed, dated 1648, Tientsin Art Museum. T'ien-ching, I. 36.

Autumn on Hua Shan, in the manner of Kuan T'ung, signed, dated 1652, Shanghai Museum (AL). Shang-hai, 62*.

People in pavilions and in a boat listening to rapids, album leaf, inscribed, signed, dated 1655, after Hsü Tao-ning, Palace Museum, Peking. PM, 13*; LY T'ing-ch'üan*.

Autumn trees and crows at evening, album leaf, inscribed, signed, in the style of Chiang Ts'an, possibly part of same album as preceding painting, Palace Museum, Peking. PM, 12*.

Man seated on a river bank watching a waterfall, folding fan, inscribed, signed, dated 1656, Hui Hsiao-t'ung collection. Shan-mien chi-chin, 1*.

Men in a pavilion at the foot of mountains, inscribed, signed, dated 1656, Chinese Painting Hall, Peking. CK hua, X. 15.

Portrait of Shao Mi, figure by Hsü T'ai, painted when Lan Ying was 73 (1657), Palace Museum, Peking. CK hua, XVIII. 19; PM, 29*.

A lady washing an ink-stone by a garden rock under a banana-plant, inscribed, signed, dated 1659, done with Hsü T'ai, Tientsin Art Museum, (AL). I-yüan chi-chin, 17; T'ien-ching, II. 71.

Epidendrum, chrysanthemums, bird on a willow, signed, dated 1659, Chang Pe-chin collection. Tien Yin Tang, I. 66.

Two men in an autumn grove on a terrace, folding fan, signed, dated 1659, Hui Hsiao-t'ung collection. Shan-mien chi-chin, 3*.

A bird on a branch of wu-t'ung tree, inscribed, signed, Nat. Pal. Mus., Taipei, (AL). CKLTMHC, IV. 140.

Landscape, album leaf, signed, Nat. Pal. Mus., Taipei. CKLTMHC, IV. 139.

Snow scene, man on a bridge, after Wang Wei, folding fan, signed,
  Shanghai WWPKWYH. Shan-mien-hua, 41*.

Autumn landscape, a man with a staff on a path, in the manner of
  Kuan T'ung, inscribed, signed, Huang Pao-hsi collection, Hong
  Kong. Lo-tsai hsüan, I. 11*.

Scholar and servant on path in the woods at the foot of a high mountain
  peak, inscribed, signed, after Ching Hao. Che-chiang, 60.

Man on a bridge among white clouds and red trees, inscribed, signed,
  dated (?). WW, 1966. 4. 44.

Scholar on a path going toward a mountain temple, album leaf, inscribed, signed. LY Hsia-ching*.

LI CHAO-HENG, see Ch'ang-ying.

LI CHEN 李辰 or 宸 , t. K'uei-nan 李南 . B. 1570, d. after
1640; from Yin-hsien, Chekiang; painted birds. (I. 58; O. 8; M. p. 201.)

  Two birds on snowy willow branches, signed, Palace Museum, Peking.
  KKPWY hua-niao, 61*.

LI JIH-HUA 李日華 , t. Chün-shih 君實 , h. Chiu-i 九疑 and
Chu-lan 竹嬾 . B. 1565, d. 1635; From Chia-hsing, Chekiang;
connoisseur, critic; landscapes. (CP, VII, AL, 206.)

  Ink bamboo, signed, dated 1625, S. M. Siu collection, Hong Kong. CK
  ku-hua, B. 209.

LI LIU-FANG 李流芳 , t. Ch'ang-heng 長衡 , h. T'an-yüan 檀園
and other names. B. 1575, d. 1629; from Hsieh-hsien, Anhui;
lived in Chia-ting, Kiangsu; scholar, poet; landscapes, flowers and birds,
one of the "Nine Friends in Painting. " (CP, VII, AL, 207-208.)

  Mists and rain over West Lake, handscroll, inscribed, signed, dated
  1609, Tientsin Art Museum. T'ien-ching, II. 67-78.

  Vacant pavilion on rocky river shore, signed, dated 1618, Tientsin
  Art Museum. T'ien-ching, I. 33.

  Autumn mountains, low hills by a river, folding fan, inscribed, signed,
  dated 1625, after Huang Kung-wang, Shanghai WWPKWYH. Shan-
  mien-hua, 38*.

  Album of twelve leaves depicting landscapes and flowers, last leaf
  signed, dated 1625, Chang Pe-chin collection. Tien Yin Tang,
  I. 54-65.

  Scholar on a terrace under trees, distant mountains, inscribed, signed, dated 1626. TSYMC hua-hsüan, 59.

  Landscape after Wu Chen, one leaf of an eight leaf album of landscapes
  after old masters, Suchou Museum. Su-chou, 27.

LI SHAO-CH'I 李紹箕 , t. Mou-ch'eng 懋承 . From Hua-t'ing, Kiangsu; active during the Wan-li period (1573-1619); son-in-law of Ku Cheng-i; landscapes. (CP, VII, AL, 208.)

    Landscape, signed, dated 1589, Nat. Pal. Mus., Taipei, (AL). CKLTMHC, IV. 158.

LI SHIH-TA 李士達 , t. Yang-huai 仰槐 . From Suchou; chin-shih in 1574; landscapes, figures. (CP, VII, AL, 208-209.)

    Chung K'uei and the demons, signed, dated 1614, Nat. Pal. Mus., Taipei, (AL). CKLTMHC, IV. 117.

    Listening to the sounds of the pine-trees, signed, dated 1616, Nat. Pal. Mus., Taipei, (AL). CKLTMHC, IV. 118.

    The Elegant Gathering in the Western Garden, handscroll, signed, Su-chou Museum. Su-chou, 23-25.

LI SUI-CH'IU 黎遂球 , t. Mei-chou 美周 . B. 1602, d. 1646; from Fan-yü, Kuangtung; high official in the Bureau of War; governor of Kiangsi at the fall of the Ming Dynasty; poet and calligrapher, painted landscapes. (Q. I. fu-lu; W. I. 2; M. p. 630.)

    Bare trees by a river, inscribed, signed, dated 1641. Kuang-tung hua-chia, 9*.

LI TSAI 李在 , t. I-cheng 以政 . From P'u-t'ien, Fukien; lived for some time in Yünnan; served in the court together with Tai Chin in the Hsüan-te era (1426-1435); landscapes. (CP, VII, AL, 209.)

    Three illustrations to T'ao Ch'ien's poem "The Return", handscroll, inscribed, signed, dated 1424, remaining illustrations done by Ma Shih and Hsia Chih, Liao-ning Provincial Museum. Liao-ning, II. 11-13.

    Ch'in Kao riding on a carp, signed, Shanghai Museum, (AL). Shang-hai, 40*.

LI TSUNG-MO 李宗謨 , h. Hsiao-ch'iao 小樵 . From Yung-an, Fukien; active during the Wan-li period (1573-1619); figures, landscapes. (CP, VII, AL, 209.)

    The Lan-t'ing Meeting, handscroll, signed, Nat. Pal. Mus., Taipei, (AL). CCAT, pl. 118 (two sections).

LIN LIANG 林良 , t. I-shan 以善 . From Nan-hai, Kuangtung; served in the palace during the Hung-chih period (1488-1505); flowers and birds, trees in ink. (CP, VII, AL, 210.)

    An eagle and a crow, signed, Nat. Pal. Mus., Taipei, (AL). 300 M., 215; CK ku-tai, 78; CKLTMHC, IV. 26.

Two magpies on bamboo, signed, Nat. Pal. Mus., Taipei. CCAT,
pl. 112.

Birds among rushes, handscroll, signed, Palace Museum, Peking.
WW, 1966.4.40.

Two wild geese flying over water and grasses, signed, Palace Museum, Peking. KKPWY hua-niao, 36*; Kuang-tung hua-chia, 1*.

A pair of white-winged pheasants and a pair of black-and-white birds
in mountain vegetation, signed, Shanghai Museum. Kuang-tung
hua-chia, 3*; Shang-hai, 48*; TSYMC hua-hsüan, 37.

Two eagles on snowy rocks, signed, Liang collection. Kuang-tung
hua-chia, 2*; Kuang-tung shu-hua, 3.

Six birds on a hanging branch, signed. Kuang-tung hua-chia, 4*.

Mynah and sparrows on autumn trees, signed. Kuang-tung hua-chia, 5*.

A pair of eagles on a branch, signed. TSYMC hua-hsüan, 36.

LIU CHI 劉基 , t. Po-wen 伯溫 , h. Yu-li-tzu 有離子 , Li-
mei-kung 犁眉公 . B. 1311, d. 1375; from Ch'ien-t'ang, Chekiang;
painted landscapes. (N. 6; O. 2; M. p. 660.)

Village in a valley, signed, dated 1354, S. M. Siu collection, Hong
Kong. CK ku-hua, B. 146.

LIU CHÜEH 劉珏 , t. T'ing-mei 廷美 , h. Wan-an 完菴 .
B. 1410, d. 1472; from Suchou; poet, calligrapher, official; landscapes.
(CP, VII, AL, 211-212,)

The Ch'ing-po Pavilion, poem and inscription, signed, dated 1458,
Nat. Pal. Mus., Taipei, (AL). CKLTMHC, IV. 19.

Pavilion on a river bank, distant mountains, poem, signed, Suchou
Museum. Su-chou, 7.

Six gentlemen on a mountain path, handscroll, inscribed, signed,
Tientsin Art Museum. T'ien-ching, I. 8.

Dwellings in the mountains, handscroll, signed, dated (? indistinct
in reproduction), S. M. Siu collection, Hong Kong. CK ku-hua,
B. 171.

LIU CHUNG-HSIEN 劉仲賢 . Unidentified; probably Liu Kuan-tao
is intended.

Seven Sages, handscroll, signed, dated 1437, Nat. Pal. Mus., Taipei. CCAT, pl. 113 (section).

LIU MAI 劉邁 , t. Chung-te 種德 . From Nanking; 17th century; flowers. (M. p. 661.)

Two swallows on a blossoming branch, signed, dated 1621, Nat. Pal.
Mus., Taipei. CKLTMHC, IV. 134.

LIU SHIH-JU 劉世儒 , t. Chi-hsiang 繼相 , h. Hsüeh-hu 雪湖 . From Shan-yin, Chekiang; first half of the 16th century; plum blossoms; author of <u>Mei-p'u.</u> (CP, VII, AL, 212.)

>Branch of plum blossoms, poem, signed, one colophon, Palace Museum, Peking. CK hua, XIV. 16; KKPWY hua-niao, 51*.

>Two rabbits under plum blossoms in snow, inscribed, signed, Tientsin Art Museum. T'ien-ching, II. 27.

LIU YÜAN-CH'I 劉原起 ; originally called Liu Tsu 劉祚 , t. Tzu-cheng 子正 , h. Chen-chih 振之 . From Suchou; active c. 1620-1633; pupil of Ch'ien Ku; poet; landscapes. (CP, VII, AL, 213.)

>Village by a river in snow, signed, dated 1612, Nat. Pal. Mus., Taipei. CKLTMHC, IV. 122.

>Plum, pine, cypress and narcissus by a stream, signed, dated 1625, done with Sheng Mao-hua, Ch'en Chia-yen, Wang Tzu-yüan and Wang Chung-li; Liu did the pine, Tientsin Art Museum. T'ien-ching, II. 61.

>New Year's Day, landscape with figures, signed, dated 1632, Nat. Pal. Mus., Taipei, (AL). CKLTMHC, IV. 123.

>Man seated under tall pine-trees, signed, Nat. Pal. Mus., Taipei, (AL). CKLTMHC, IV. 121.

LU CH'AO-YANG 盧朝陽 . From Sha-hsien, Fukien; 16th century; birds. (CP, VII, AL, 213.)

>Eagles and sparrows, signed, Shanghai Museum, (AL). WW, 1963. 10. 19.

LU CHIH 陸治 , t. Shu-p'ing 叔平 , h. Pao-shan 包山 . B. 1496, d. 1576; from Suchou; pupil of Wen Cheng-ming and Chu Yün-ming; flowers, landscapes. (CP, VII, AL, 213-215.)

>T'ao Yüan-ming, album leaf, poem, colophon dated 1572, fifty years after the painting was done (1523), Nat. Pal. Mus., Taipei, (AL). CKLTMHC, IV. 70.

>Bird on a plum branch, handscroll, inscribed, signed, dated 1542, Shanghai Museum. WW, 1963. 10. 21.

>Butterfly and bee among white flowers, folding fan, signed, dated 1543, after Huang Ch'üan, Shanghai WWPKWYH. Shan-mien-hua, 15*.

><u>T'ien-ch'ih shih-pi.</u> Steep over-hanging rocks by a river, poem, signed, dated 1550, Nat. Pal. Mus., Taipei, (AL). CKLTMHC, IV. 71.

>Mountain landscape with a man seated in meditation in a cave, poem, signed, dated 1552, Shanghai Museum, (AL). Shang-hai, 57*; TSYMC hua-hsüan, 54.

Landscape, boats on the river, temples in the mountains, handscroll, inscribed, signed, dated 1558, Tientsin Art Museum. T'ien-ching, I. 24-26.

Pavilion on a high cliff by a river, inscribed, signed, dated 1568, Nat. Pal. Mus., Taipei. CKLTMHC, IV. 72.

Lily and pomegranate, signed, dated 1570, Nat. Pal. Mus., Taipei, (AL). CKLTMHC, IV. 73.

White clouds and red leaves, folding fan, poem, signed, dated 1571, Shanghai WWPKWYH. Shan-mien-hua, 16*.

Magnolia and bamboo, poem, signed, Nat. Pal. Mus., Taipei, (AL). CH mei-shu, III; CKLTMHC, IV. 76; CKLTSHH.

A branch of flowering pear, poem, signed, Nat. Pal. Mus., Taipei, (AL). CKLTMHC, IV. 75.

Various flowers growing beside an ornamental rock, inscribed, signed, Nat. Pal. Mus., Taipei, (AL). CKLTMHC, IV. 74.

Crab apple blossoms, album leaf, seal of artist, Palace Museum, Peking. KKPWY hua-niao, 54*.

Two men on a mountain path, folding fan, poem, signed, Shanghai WWPKWYH. Shan-mien-hua, 14*.

Peony plant, inscribed, signed, Tientsin Art Museum. T'ien-ching, II. 28.

Plum blossoms, inscribed, signed, Honolulu Academy of Art. CK shu-hua, I. 26.

LU FU 陸復 , t. Ming-pen 明本 , h. Mei-hua chu-jen 梅花主人 . From Wu-chiang, Kiangsu; 15th century; plum blossoms. (CP, VII, AL, 215.)

Plum-blossoms in snow, signed, two lines of poetry, Nat. Pal. Mus., Taipei, (AL). CKLTMHC, IV. 38.

LU SHIH-TAO 陸師道 , t. Tzu-ch'uan 子傳 , h. Yüan-chou 元洲 , Wu-hu 五湖 . From Suchou; lived c. 1510-1570; chin-shih in 1538; pupil of Wen Cheng-ming; poet, calligrapher; landscapes. (CP, VII, AL, 216.)

Mist over a mountain river, poem, signed, dated 1544, Nat. Pal. Mus., Taipei, (AL). CKLTMHC, IV. 82.

A man watching wheeling crows, signed, dated 1552, S. M. Siu collection, Hong Kong. CK ku-hua, B. 195.

LÜ CHI 呂紀 , t. T'ing-chen 廷振 , h. Lo-yü 樂愚 or 樂漁 . From Chin-hsien, Chekiang; active c. 1500; summoned to the palace in the Hung-chih period; appointed an officer in the Imperial Guard; flowers and birds. (CP, VII, AL, 216-217.)

Wild geese in the moonlight, signed, Nat. Pal. Mus., Taipei, (AL).
  CAT, 93; CH mei-shu, III.

Birds in snow, signed, Nat. Pal. Mus., Taipei, (AL, Ku-kung, X).
  CH mei-shu, III; CKLTMHC, IV.28.

A pheasant in snow, signed, Nat. Pal. Mus., Taipei, (AL). CH mei-
  shu, III; CKLTSHH.

Herons among lotus plants in autumn, signed, Nat. Pal. Mus., Taipei, (AL, also listed as Three egrets, one standing and two flying,
  among hibiscus and lotus-plants). CKLTMHC, IV.30.

Peacock and apricot-blossoms, signed, Nat. Pal. Mus., Taipei, (AL).
  CKLTMHC, IV.27.

Tall reeds, grass and pair of pheasants, signed, poem by Shen Chou,
  poem and colophon by Ch'ien-lung, Nat. Pal. Mus., Taipei, (AL,
  also listed as A pair of pheasants among reeds by the shore).
  300 M., 217*.

Birds in snow, signed, Nat. Pal. Mus., Taipei, (AL, K-k shu-hua
  chi, XIX). CKLTMHC, IV.29.

A mynah and other large birds; rocks and chrysanthemums, signed,
  Palace Museum, Peking, (AL). KKPWY hua-niao, 46*; WW,
  1966.4.41.

An eagle on a cliff, a magpie below, signed, Palace Museum, Peking,
  (AL). KKPWY hua-niao, 45*.

Three white herons and flowering lilies under a willow by a winding
  stream, attributed, (AL). Che-chiang, 50.

Three birds on a bank by rapids, attributed, Nat. Pal. Mus., Taipei,
  300 M., 218.

A hawk chasing a crane and smaller birds among reeds and lotus,
  signed, Palace Museum, Peking. CK ku-tai, 76; KKPWY hua-
  niao, 44*.

Four swimming ducks, a mynah on a rock, a cliff with flowering plants,
  signed, Shanghai Museum. Shang-hai, 50*.

Three cranes under peonies and hibiscus, signed, Tientsin Art Museum. I-yüan chi-chin, 11*.

Three doves on snowy plum branch, signed, Ch'in Chung-wen collection. CK hua, XI.15.

Two pheasants under bamboo, signed, Huang Pao-hsi collection, Hong
  Kong. Lo-tsai hsüan, I.6*.

Two cranes by a stream, large bluff with drooping trees, signed,
  colophon by Ch'ien-lung, S. M. Siu collection, Hong Kong. CK
  ku-hua, A.57; B.160.

A pair of orioles and a pair of ducks on bamboo shore, signed. TSYMC
  hua-hsüan, 38.

LÜ T'ANG 呂棠 , t. Hsiao-ts'ung 小村 , h. Te-fang 德芳 .
From Chin-hsien, Chekiang; nephew of Lü Chi; birds. (M. p. 124.)
> Two ducks under a rock, artist's seals, Palace Museum, Peking.
> KKPWY hua-niao, 47*.

LÜ TUAN-CHÜN 呂端俊 . From Yao-chiang; Ming dynasty; bamboo. (CP, VII, AL, 217.)
> Bamboos in wind by a garden rock, signed, Nat. Pal. Mus., Taipei,
> (AL). CKLTMHC, IV.40.

MA SHIH 馬軾 , t. Ching-chan 景瞻 . From Chia-ting, Kiangsu;
served in the Imperial Observatory in the Hsüan-te period (1426-1435);
landscapes. (CP, VII, AL, 218.)
> Three illustrations to T'ao Ch'ien's poem "The Return", handscroll,
> artist's seal; remaining paintings done by Li Tsai and Hsia Chih,
> Li's painting dated 1424, Liao-ning Provincial Museum. Liao-
> ning, II.8-10; NPM Bulletin, I.2.6 (detail).

MA SHOU-CHEN 馬守貞 , h. Hsiang-lan 湘蘭 , Yüeh-chiao
月嬌. Woman; from Nanking; active c. 1592-1628; poetess; orchids,
bamboo. (CP, VII, AL, 218-219.)
> Epidendrum and bamboo, folding fan, signed, dated 1589, Shanghai
> WWPKWYH. Shan-mien-hua, 30*.

MI WAN-CHUNG 米萬鍾 , t. Chung-chao 仲詔 , h. Yu-shih
友石 . D. 1628; from Shensi, lived in Peking; chin-shih in 1595;
calligrapher; landscapes. (CP, VII, AL, 219.)
> A temple in the autumn mountains, signed, dated 1617 (?), Tientsin
> Art Museum. T'ien-ching, II.60.
> Scholars on mountain paths, signed, dated 1624, Liao-ning Provin-
> cial Museum. Liao-ning, II.47.
> Cloudy mountains, inscribed, signed, in the style of Mi Fei, Chang
> Pe-chin collection. Tien Yin Tang, I.35.

MIU FU 繆輔 . Unrecorded; according to information on the painting,
he was from Suchou and worked in the court.
> Fish and aquatic weeds, signed, Palace Museum, Peking. KKPWY
> hua-niao, 41*.

NI TUAN 倪端 , t. Chung-cheng 仲正 . From Hang-chou, Chekiang; summoned to the palace in the Hsüan-te period (1426-1435); Buddhist and Taoist figures, landscapes. (CP, VII, AL, 220.)
> Fisherman drawing his net, signed, Nat. Pal. Mus., Taipei, (AL).
> CKLTMHC, IV.14.

NI YING 倪瑛 , or Ni Shih-ying 倪世瑛 , t. Po-yüan 伯遠 .
From K'un-shan, Kiangsu; copied old masters. (M. p. 316.)

    Scholar in a riverside pavilion looking at river and mist-filled pine
        grove, handscroll, signed, dated 1624, several colophons, Liao-
        ning Provincial Museum. Liao-ning, II.48-50.

NI YÜAN-LU 倪元璐 , t. Yü-ju 玉汝 or 玉如 , h. Hung-pao
鴻寶 . B. 1593, d. 1644; from Shang-yü, Chekiang; high official,
hanged himself at the fall of the Ming dynasty; poet, calligrapher; landscapes, bamboos, orchids. (CP, VII, AL, 220.)

    Studies of rocks and trees, handscroll, inscribed, signed, dated 1632,
        Tientsin Art Museum. T'ien-ching, II.76-79.
    Fruits and flowers of various seasons, handscroll, signed, dated 1634,
        Cheng Te-k'un collection, Cambridge, (AL). Mu-fei, opposite
        p. 18.
    A gnarled pine and stones, poem by the artist, (AL). Che-chiang, 61.
    Cottages in a grove, trees and mountains in mist, folding fan, inscri-
        bed, signed, in Mi style, Shanghai WWPKWYH. Shan-mien-hua,
        44*.

PIEN WEN-CHIN 邊文進 , t. Ching-chao 景昭 . From Sha-
hsien, Fukien; summoned to palace and appointed tai-chao in the Yung-
lo period; served through the Hsüan-te period (1426-1435); flowers and
birds. (CP, VII, AL, 221.)

    Hundred birds, bamboos, pines and plum-trees, signed, dated 1413,
        Nat. Pal. Mus., Taipei, (AL). CKLTMHC, IV.5.
    Magpie and chestnut tree, signed, Nat. Pal. Mus., Taipei, (AL).
        300 M., 211.
    Cranes and bamboos, signed, the bamboo by Wang Fu, Palace Mu-
        seum, Peking, (AL). KKPWY hua-niao, 30*; Wang Fu, 4.
    Four magpies and four small birds among branches of blossoming
        trees and rocks, signed, Shanghai Museum. Shang-hai, 37*.
    Crane, pheasant and smaller birds in a flower garden, signed, colo-
        phon by Wu I, Cheng Te-k'un collection, Cambridge. Mu-fei,
        opposite p. 4.
    Two mynahs on plum blossoms and bamboo, signed, S. M. Siu collec-
        tion, Hong Kong. CK ku-hua, B.159.

SHANG HSI 商喜 , t. Wei-chi 惟吉 . From P'u-yang, Honan;
court-painter c. 1430-1440; officer in the Imperial Guard; tigers, landscapes, figures, flowers and birds. (CP, VII, AL, 221.)

    Plum, bamboo and rock in snow, signed, dated 1445, poem by Ch'ien-
        lung, S. M. Siu collection, Hong Kong. CK ku-hua, B.165.

The emperor Hsüan-tsung's hunting party, (AL). CK ku-tai, 73; Li-tai jen-wu, 41.

SHANG TSU 商祚 , t. T'ien-chüeh 天爵 . From P'u-yang, Honan; grandson of Shang Hsi; tigers, flowers. (CP, VII, AL, 222.)
    Autumn hollyhocks, signed, Nat. Pal. Mus., Taipei, (AL). CKLTMHC, IV. 31.

SHAO MI 邵彌 , t. Seng-mi 僧彌 , h. Kua-ch'ou 瓜疇 , Kuan-yüan-sou 灌園叟 , and other names. From Suchou; active c. 1620-1660; one of the "Nine Friends of Painting"; landscapes. (CP, VII, AL, 222-223.)
    Kuanyin, signed, dated 1626, Nat. Pal. Mus., Taipei, (AL). CKLTMHC, IV. 150.
    A seated goose, inscribed, signed, Shanghai Museum. Shang-hai, 63*.
    Two men on a plateau admiring a distant view, folding fan, signed, Shanghai WWPKWYH. Shan-mien-hua, 39*.
    Landscapes, album leaves, Tientsin Art Museum. T'ien-ching, II. 65 (after Chü-jan); 66 (inscribed).

SHEN CHEN 沈貞 , t. Chen-chi 貞吉 , h. Nan-chai 南齋 , T'ao-jan tao-jen 陶然道人 . B. 1400, d. after 1480; from Suchou; uncle of Shen Chou; landscapes. (CP, VII, AL, 223.)
    Two scholars standing on a bridge looking at a high waterfall, poem, signed, dated 1425, Suchou Museum. Su-chou, 6.

SHEN CHOU 沈周 , t. Ch'i-nan 啟南 , h. Shih-t'ien 石田 , Po-shih weng 白石翁 , Yü-t'ien weng 玉田翁 . B. 1427, d. 1509; from Suchou; poet, calligrapher; landscapes, flowers, birds. (CP, VII, AL, 223-229.)
    The lofty Lu Mountain, inscribed, signed, dated 1467, in the style of Wang Meng, Nat. Pal. Mus., Taipei, (AL). 300 M., 219*; CAT, 94; CH mei-shu, III; CKLTMHC, IV. 23; CKLTSHH; NPM Quarterly, I. 2, pls. VIII, IX. A; Shen Shih-t'ien, 1; SS-t hua-chi, 57.
    The lofty Lu Mountain, inscribed, signed, dated 1467, Chang Pe-chin collection, (AL). Tien Yin Tang, I. 15.
    Hollyhocks, poem, signed, dated 1475, Nelson Gallery of Art, Kansas City (AL). Shen Shih-t'ien, 2.
    An album of six leaves of fruits and flowers, one leaf dated 1477, S. M. Siu collection, Hong Kong. CK ku-hua, B. 178. B.
    A man reading in the shade of a large banana-plant, poem, dated 1482, (AL). Shen Shih-t'ien, 3.
    Scenes from Wu-chiang, handscroll, inscription and two poems by the artist, dated 1483, (AL). SS-t hua-chi, 48-49 (sections).

Three old scholars standing and conversing under tall pine-trees by
    a brook, inscribed, poem, dated 1484, (AL). SS-t hua-chi, 54.
Young geese and a peach-tree, inscribed, signed, dated 1484, Ting
    Teng-ju collection, (AL). Shen Shih-t'ien, 4.
Mountain landscape with rushing streams and pavilions, signed, dated
    1491, in the style of Wang Meng, Freer Gallery of Art, Wash-
    ington, D.C. (56.28), (AL). SS-t hua-chi, 56.
Two bamboo plants by a rock, signed, dated 1491, S.M. Siu collection,
    Hong Kong. CK ku-hua, B.174.
A scholar's hermitage at the foot of pointed mountains, inscribed,
    dated 1492, Nat. Pal. Mus., Taipei, (AL). 300 M., 220; CH
    mei-shu, III.
River scene with fishing boats, village in a mountain valley, travel-
    lers on a bridge, inscribed, signed, dated 1494, after Huang
    Kung-wang, Shanghai Museum. Shang-hai, 43*.
Large album of sixteen leaves; flowers, vegetables, birds, fishes
    and animals, signed, dated 1494, Nat. Pal. Mus., Taipei, (AL,
    separate leaves also listed as: Two double album leaves, one a
    curled-up cat, the other a walking donkey and: A donkey; a frog
    on a lotus-leaf). 300 M., 221-228 (eight leaves); CAT, 96 (Lo-
    tus; Cat); CKLTMHC, IV.25 (Lotus; Cock).
Eggplant and rock, signed, dated 1495, S.M. Siu collection, Hong
    Kong. CK ku-hua, A.58; B.173.
Landscape, poem, signed, dated 1501, poems by Liu Chüeh, Wu K'uan,
    Wen Lin, etc., Nat. Pal. Mus., Taipei, (AL, Li-tai, III). CH
    mei-shu, III.
Landscape; a man standing on a terrace under pine-trees, poem,
    signed, dated 1501, (AL). Shen Shih-t'ien, 6.
A boat anchored by the shore, signed, dated 1501, S.M. Siu collection,
    Hong Kong. CK ku-hua, B.172.
Two swallows on a willow branch, inscribed, signed, dated 1503, S.M.
    Siu collection, Hong Kong. CK ku-hua, B.176.
White crane and snowy banana-plant, poem, inscribed, dated 1504.
    Shen Shih-t'ien, 11; TSYMC hua-hsüan, 34.
Self-portrait, two inscriptions by the artist dated 1506 and 1507, Pal-
    ace Museum, Peking. CK hua, XVIII.17 (as anon. Ming); PM,
    25* (as Shen Chou).
Landscape illustration to Yen-chiang tieh-chang. Misty river and
    layered mountains, handscroll, signed, dated 1507, Liao-ning
    Provincial Museum. Liao-ning, II.22-24; Yen-chiang tieh-chang.
Landscape in the manner of Ni Tsan: a man with a long staff among
    the spare trees on the shore, poem, Nat. Pal. Mus., Taipei,
    (AL). CAT, 95; CCAT, pl. 114; CKLTMHC, IV.24; SS-t hua-
    chi, 55.

Sketchy landscape, long inscription, signed, Nat. Pal. Mus. , Taipei,
(AL). CKLTMHC, IV. 22.

A bird on a branch, poem, signed, Nat. Pal. Mus. , Taipei, (AL,
also listed as A wild pigeon on a dry branch). CH mei-shu, III.

The three cypresses, handscroll in three sections, Nanking Museum,
(AL). Shen Shih-t'ien, 5 (section).

Two birds perched on a branch in winter, poem, signed, (AL). Shen
Shih-t'ien, 10; TSYMC hua-hsüan, 35.

Views of T'ai-hu, handscrolls, signed, (AL). SS-t hua-chi, 50-51.

Waterside pavilion under peach-tree, poem, signed, (AL, Misty Landscape?). SS-t hua-chi, 53.

Lily, stones and magpie, poem, signed, (AL). SS-t hua-chi, 52.

Listening to the cicada's song, poem, Piacentini collection, Tokyo,
(AL). Shen Shih-t'ien, 7.

Reading by the river in the mountains, poem, signed, in Yüan style,
(AL). Shen Shih-t'ien, 8.

Album with eight double-leaves: landscape studies with grassy mountains, streams and cottages; the last one with a man seated under
bamboos by a river, each leaf signed, Museum of Fine Arts, Boston, (AL). SS-t hua-chi, 27-34.

Album of twelve leaves: sketchy studies of mountains, streams, cliffs
and buildings, in the broad manner of Wu Chen; the last one with
an old man holding a staff and standing under a cliff; some leaves
with artist's seal, (AL). SS-t hua-chi, 1-12.

Album of fourteen leaves called Wo-yu. Studies of landscapes, flowers,
fruits, animals and insects, all with a poem by the artist, last
leaf a long inscription by the artist, Palace Museum, Peking, (AL).
KKPWY hua-niao, 38* (Loquats); PM, 11* (Scholar reading in autumn); SS-t hua-chi, 13-26; Shen Shih-t'ien, 13 (Water buffalo);
WW, 1964. 3. 7 (Water buffalo).

Album of thirteen leaves called Sui-hsing. Landscapes from nature,
some with figures; branches of blossoming trees, first and last
leaf with poem and inscription, (AL). SS-t hua-chi, 35-47.

A branch of apricot blossoms, inscribed, signed, Palace Museum,
Peking. KKPWY hua-niao, 37*.

Scenery of Ts'ang-chou, handscroll, inscribed, signed, Palace Museum, Peking. Ts'ang-chou.

Landscape in the style of Tung Yüan, a scholar in a thatched hut in
a bamboo grove by the river, handscroll, inscribed, signed, Palace Museum, Peking. PM, 10*.

Album of twenty-one leaves depicting scenes of Tung-chuang, originally twenty-four scenes, Nanking Museum. SC Tung-chuang.

Flowers, handscroll, Shanghai Museum. WW, 1963. 10. 18 (section:
Lotus).

Floating on the lake at night, folding fan, poem, signed, three other
inscriptions, Shanghai WWPKWYH. Shan-mien-hua, 1*.

Two men on a promontory looking at a steep cliff across the river,
folding fan, inscribed, signed, Shanghai WWPKWYH. Shan-mien-
hua, 2*.

Album of ten leaves depicting flowers and a duck, artist's seal on each
leaf, title by Wen Cheng-ming, Suchou Museum. SC Hua-ts'e*;
Su-chou, 8 (Peonies); 9 (Flowering plant by a rock); 10 (Hollyhock
by a rock); 11 (Plum blossoms).

Admiring the moon, handscroll, inscription, signed, Tientsin Art Museum. T'ien-ching, II. 13-18.

Four album leaves, Tientsin Art Museum. T'ien-ching, I. 16 (Two
men seated on a river bank, heating wine, after Chao Meng-fu);
17 (Two men on a bank, roofs in mist, seal); 18 (Playing chess
under pines, after Ch'ien Hsüan); 19 (Playing chess on a ledge,
after Wang Wei); Shen Shih-t'ien, 12 (Playing chess under pines).

Two album leaves, possibly part of preceding album, Tientsin Art
Museum. I-yüan chi-chin, 7 (Man poling a boat toward shore,
man in a thatched hut, inscribed); 8 (Watching cranes, inscribed,
after Chao Ling-jang).

A man with a staff in front of a mountain retreat, inscribed, signed,
Chou Huai-min collection. CK hua, IX. 14.

A duck in a lotus pond, signed, Huang Pao-hsi collection, Hong Kong.
Lo-tsai hsüan, I. 2*.

Loquats, inscribed, signed, S. M. Siu collection, Hong Kong. CK
ku-hua, B. 175.

A cock by a bare branch, inscribed, signed, S. M. Siu collection,
Hong Kong. CK ku-hua, B. 177.

Album of six leaves of fruits and flowers, last leaf inscribed and signed, S. M. Siu collection, Hong Kong. CK ku-hua, B. 178. A.

Landscape after Tung Yüan and Chü-jan, inscribed, signed. CK ku-
tai, 79.

A man fishing in a canal in front of a small hut between wu-t'ung trees,
album leaf. CK shu-hua, I. 25.

A man walking in an autumn grove, poem, signed. Shen Shih-t'ien, 9.

Liang Chiang ming-sheng, scenic spots in the Chiang and Che area,
album of ten leaves, each leaf with artist's seal. SC Liang Chiang*;
Shen Shih-t'ien, 14 (one leaf).

Mountain landscape, a man standing by an empty pavilion over a stream,
poem, signed, one colophon. TSYMC hua-hsüan, 33.

SHEN SHIH 沈 仕 , t. Mou-hsüeh 懋 學 and Tzu-teng 子 登 ,
h. Ch'ing-men shan-jen 青 門 山 人 . From Hangchou; 16th century;
collector; landscapes, flowers, birds. (CP, VII, AL, 230.)

Flowers, handscroll, several inscriptions by the artist, dated 1550
or 1610. Che-chiang, 53 (section).

SHEN SHIH-CH'UNG 沈士充 , t. Tzu-chü 子居 . From Hua-
t'ing, Kiangsu; active c. 1611-1640; pupil of Sung Mou-chin and Chao Tso;
landscapes. (CP, VII, AL, 230.)
>   Landscape after Huang Kung-wang, signed, dated 1607, Tientsin Art
>   Museum. T'ien-ching, I.33.
>   Travellers in snowy mountains, signed, dated 1624, Tientsin Art Mu-
>   seum. T'ien-ching, II.59.

SHEN SHIH-KENG 沈士鯁 . Active c. 1620-1640; landscapes, figures. (CP, VII, AL, 230.)
>   A woman picking mulberries, signed, dated 1642, Tientsin Art Mu-
>   seum. I-yüan chi-chin, 19.

SHENG CHU 盛著 , t. Shu-chang 叔彰 . From Hangchou, Chekiang, active during the Hung-wu era (1368-1398); nephew of Sheng Mou;
landscapes, figures, flowers, birds. (I.55; O.2; M. p. 389.)
>   A man fishing from a boat near a wooded shore, album leaf, signed,
>   Nat. Pal. Mus., Taipei. CKLTMHC, III.105 (as anon. Yüan).

SHENG LIN 盛琳 , h. Wu-lin 五林 . From Chiang-ning, Kiangsu,
17th century; landscapes. (M. p. 390.)
>   An old temple in the autumn mountains, signed, dated 1635, Liao-
>   ning Provincial Museum. Liao-ning, II.57.

SHENG MAO-HUA 盛茂燁 or Mao-yeh 茂曄 , h. Yen-an 研菴.
From Suchou; active c. 1625-1640; landscapes, flowers.   (CP,
VII, AL, 230-231.)
>   Plum, pine, cypress and narcissus by a stream, done with Liu Yüan-
>   ch'i, Ch'en Chia-yen, Wang Tzu-yüan and Wang Chung-li, dated
>   1625, Tientsin Art Museum. T'ien-ching, II.61.
>   A man in a boat near a reedy shore, folding fan, signed, dated 1629,
>   in the style of Wu Chen, Shanghai WWPKWYH. Shan-mien-hua,
>   47*.

SHENG SHAO-HSIEN 盛紹先 , t. K'o-chen 克振 . From Yang-
chou, Kiangsu; active c. 1600; landscapes. (CP, VII, AL, 231.)
>   Landscape after Kao K'o-kung, poem, signed, Chang Pe-chin collec-
>   tion, (AL). Tien Yin Tang, I.52.

SHENG YING 盛穎 . Possibly Sheng Mao-ying 盛茂穎 , Sheng
Mao-hua's younger brother; landscapes. (M. p. 390.)

A temple in mist and rain, handscroll, signed, dated 1633?, Liao-ning
Provincial Museum. Liao-ning, II. 55.

SHIH CHUNG 史忠 , originally called Hsü Tuan-pen 徐端本 ,
t. T'ing-chih 廷直 , h. Ch'ih-weng 癡翁 . B. 1437, d. c. 1517;
from Nanking; friend of Shen Chou; landscapes. (CP, VII, AL, 231-232.)
Landscape after Huang Kung-wang, poem, inscription, signed, dated
1504, Nat. Pal. Mus., Taipei, (AL). CKLTMHC, IV. 39.
Album of twenty leaves of landscapes, figures, flowers, some inscribed and signed, Shanghai Museum. HT-p Hua-ts'e; Shang-hai,
47* (A fisherman watching a flock of birds).
A man on a donkey, a servant following, album leaf. Li-tai jen-wu,
42; TSYMC hua-hsüan, 39.

SHIH K'O-FA 史可法 , t. Hsien-chih 憲之 , h. Tao-lin 道
鄰 . B. 1601, d. 1645; from Ta-hsing, Hopei; calligrapher. (Ming
Shih, 274.)
Peony, inscribed. WW, 1964.3.13.

SUN AI 孫艾 , t. Shih-chieh 世節 , h. Hsi-ch'uan-weng 西川翁
From Ch'ang-shu, Kiangsu; late 15th-early 16th century; pupil of Shen
Chou; landscapes. (CP, VII, AL, 232.)
A branch of flowering shrub, inscription by Shen Chou, Palace Mu-
seum, Peking, (AL). KKPWY hua-niao, 39*.
Mulberry and silkworms, inscribed, signed, poem by Shen Chou,
Palace Museum, Peking. KKPWY hua-niao, 40*.

SUN CHAO-LIN 孫兆麟 , t. K'ai-su 開素 . From Hua-t'ing
(Sung-chiang), Kiangsu; portraits, landscapes, birds, flowers. (M. p. 348.)
Portrait of Shui-chai ch'an-shih, signed, dated jen-shen, poem by
Tung Ch'i-ch'ang, Tientsin Art Museum. T'ien-ching, I. 32.

SUN CHIH 孫枝 , t. Shu-ta 叔達 , h. Hua-lin chü-shih 華林居士
From Suchou; active c. 1550-1580; landscapes, figures, flowers. (CP,
VII, AL, 233.)
Plum blossoms and narcissi, signed, dated 1559, Nat. Pal. Mus.,
Taipei, (AL). CKLTMHC, IV.93.
Travellers in snowy mountains, signed, dated 1595, Suchou Museum.
Su-chou, 17.
The Jade Cave and the Peach-tree Forest, signed, Nat. Pal. Mus.,
Taipei, (AL). CKLTMHC, IV.92.

SUN K'O-HUNG 孫克弘 , t. Yün-chih 允執 , h. Hsüeh-
chü 雪居 . B. 1532, d. 1610; from Hua-t'ing, Kiangsu; flowers,

landscapes, Buddhist and Taoist figures. (CP, VII, AL, 233.)

> Flowers of the four seasons, handscroll, inscribed, signed, dated 1577, Liao-ning Provincial Museum. Liao-ning, II. 41-44.
>
> Red bamboo by a rock, signed, dated 1600, S. M. Siu collection, Hong Kong. CK ku-hua, B. 200.
>
> Banana tree, bamboo and rock, inscribed, signed, Tientsin Art Museum. T'ien-ching, II. 43.

SUN LUNG 孫龍 , t. Ts'ung-chi 從吉 , h. Tu-ch'ih 都癡 . From P'i-ling (Wu-chin), Kiangsu; active in the mid-15th century. (CP, VII, AL, 234.)

> An album of twelve leaves: vegetables, flowers, birds and insects, attributed, Shanghai Museum, (AL). Shang-hai, 49* (one leaf: Pink autumn flower); WW, 1963. 10. 25 (one leaf: Cicada on a plant).
>
> A goose under flowers and rocks, artist's seals, Palace Museum, Peking. KKPWY hua-niao, 42*.

SUNG CHÜEH 宋珏 or Sung Ku 宋穀 , t. Pi-yü 比玉 , h. Li-chih-hsien 荔枝仙 . B. 1576, d. 1632; from P'u-t'ien, Fukien; lived in Nanking; poet, calligrapher; landscapes. (CP, VII, AL, 234.)

> A man being poled in a boat past a willow-lined shore, poem, signed, Cheng Te-k'un collection, Cambridge. Mu-fei, before p. 15.

SUNG HSÜ 宋旭 , t. Ch'u-yang 初暘 , Shih-men 石門 . B. 1525, d. after 1605; from Chia-hsing, Chekiang; became a monk, called Tsu-hsüan 祖玄 ; landscapes. (CP, VII, AL, 234.)

> Cloudy peaks and waterfall in autumn, signed, dated 1583, Nat. Pal. Mus., Taipei, (AL). CKLTMHC, IV. 105.
>
> The rainbow over the T'ien-mu Mountain, signed, dated 1589, (AL). Che-chiang, 57.
>
> Snow-covered mountains and waterfall, signed, dated 1589, Chang Pe-chin collection. Tien Yin Tang, I. 32.
>
> A large pavilion among misty mountains, folding fan, inscribed, signed, Shanghai WWPKWYH. Shan-mien-hua, 21*.

SUNG MOU-CHIN 宋懋晉 , t. Ming-chih 明之 . From Sung-chiang, Kiangsu; late 16th century; pupil of Sung Hsü. (CP, VII, AL, 234-235.)

> The Han Palace on a spring morning, folding fan, inscribed, signed, dated 1616?, Shanghai WWPKWYH. Shan-mien-hua, 33*.

TAI CHIN 戴 進 , t. Wen-chin 文 進 , h. Ching-an 靜 菴 .
B. 1388, d. 1462; from Ch'ien-t'ang, Chekiang; landscapes, figures,
flowers and birds; principal master of the Che school. (CP, VII, AL,
235-236.)

> Old pine-trees on a slope; a scholar followed by his servant, signed,
> dated 1449, Shanghai Museum, (AL). Shang-hai, 38*.
>
> Rainstorm over a river; two men in a boat, others passing over a
> bridge, signed, Nat. Pal. Mus. , Taipei, (AL). Che-chiang, 45;
> CK ku-tai, 75; CKLTMHC, IV. 13.
>
> An arhat with a tiger seated in front of a cave, signed, Nat. Pal. Mus.
> Taipei, (AL). CKLTMHC, IV. 10.
>
> Five deer in a pine forest, poem by Wen Cheng-ming, Nat. Pal. Mus.,
> Taipei, (AL). 300 M. , 212.
>
> Wen-wang of the Chou Dynasty visiting T'ai-kung Wang on the river-
> bank, Nat. Pal. Mus. , Taipei, (AL). CKLTMHC, IV. 11.
>
> Returning home on a spring evening, Nat. Pal. Mus. , Taipei, (AL).
> CAT, 92; CKLTMHC, IV. 12.
>
> Butterflies and hollyhock, signed, poems by four contemporaries,
> Palace Museum, Peking, (AL). KKPWY hua-niao, 31*.
>
> Peasants happily returning on a mountain path, signed, after Ma Yüan,
> (AL). Che-chiang, 46.
>
> Chiang-shan ta-kuan. Views along a broad river, handscroll, signed,
> Cheng Te-k'un collection, Cambridge, (AL). Mu-fei, before p. 7
> (section).
>
> The Six Patriarchs of the Ch'an Sect, handscroll, signed, colophons
> by T'ang Yin and three others, Liao-ning Provincial Museum.
> Liao-ning, II. 15-19.
>
> Chung K'uei on an excursion on a snowy night, signed, School of Art,
> Peking. CK hua, I. 21.
>
> Landscape, guests arriving and being greeted by two gentlemen, hand-
> scroll, Suchou Museum. Su-chou, 4.
>
> Winter landscape, travellers on bridges, signed, poem by Wei Kuang-
> wei, Tientsin Art Museum. T'ien-ching, I. 9.
>
> A houseboat on the river, signed, S. M. Siu collection, Hong Kong.
> CK ku-hua, B. 161.
>
> Fisherman on a snowy river, signed, S. M. Siu collection, Hong Kong.
> CK ku-hua, B. 162.
>
> Village in the mountains, mule train on a bridge, signed. TSYMC
> hua-hsüan, 32.

T'AN CHIH-I 談 志 伊 , t. Kung-wang 公 望 and Ssu-chung
思 重 or 思 仲 , h. Hsüeh-shan 學 山 . From Wu-hsi,
Kiangsu; active late 16th-early 17th century, poet; birds, flowers. (N. 7;
U. II. 1; M. p. 628.)

A bird on a pine branch, signed, dated 1586 or 1646, Nat. Pal. Mus.,
Taipei. CKLTMHC, IV. 109.

T'ANG CHIH-YIN 唐志尹　　t. P'ing-san 聘三　　. From Hai-
ling, Kiangsu; active in the late 16th century; younger brother of T'ang
Chih-ch'i; they were called the "Two T'angs"; flowers, birds. (CP, VII,
AL, 236.)

 Hoopoe on a branch, album leaf, signed, Palace Museum, Peking.
  KKPWY hua-niao, 62*.

T'ANG YIN 唐寅　, t. Po-hu 伯虎　　and Tzu-wei 子畏　, h.
Liu-ju chü-shih 六如居士　, T'ao-hua an-chu 桃花庵主
and other names. B. 1470, d. 1523; from Suchou; landscapes, figures,
flowers. (CP, VII, AL, 237-241.)

 Two gentlemen on a bank near a clump of trees, rocky shore opposite,
  handscroll, signed, colophon by Chu Yün-ming dated 1500, colo-
  phons by Shen Chou and others, Tientsin Art Museum. T'ien-
  ching, II. 20-23.
 Ink plum blossoms, handscroll, inscribed, signed, dated 1513, S. M.
  Siu collection, Hong Kong. CK ku-hua, B. 186.
 A man seated on the bank of a stream; spare trees, handscroll, signed,
  dated 1513, (AL). TL-j hua-chi, 33-35.
 Chrysanthemums and other plants, inscribed, signed, dated 1519,
  S. M. Siu collection, Hong Kong. CK ku-hua, B. 183.
 A day lily, signed, dated 1519, S. M. Siu collection, Hong Kong. CK
  ku-hua, A. 59; B. 181.
 A branch of plum-blossoms, poem, signed, dated 1520, (AL). TL-j
  hua-chi, 36.
 Gathering lotus seeds, handscroll, signed, dated 1520, Nat. Pal. Mus.,
  Taipei, (AL). 300 M., 234; CH mei-shu, III; CKLTMHC, IV. 45.
 Pavilions along a river, misty pines, folding fan, signed, dated 1520,
  Shanghai WWPKWYH. Shan-mien-hua, 7*.
 A man looking at bare trees, two servants, signed, dated 1521, colo-
  phon by Tung Ch'i-ch'ang, Suchou Museum. Su-chou, 14.
 A young lady and two maids by a garden rock, poem, signed, (AL).
  TL-j hua-chi, 26.
 Straw-covered huts and two men on a river-bank at the foot of a moun-
  tain, poem, signed, (AL). TL-j hua-chi, 11.
 A lady with a fan, poem, signed, Shanghai Museum, (AL). Shang-hai,
  53*; TL-j hua-chi, 6.
 Listening to the pine-trees, poem, signed, Nat. Pal. Mus., Taipei,
  (AL). 300 M., 229; CAT, 100; CH mei-shu, III; CK ku-tai, 80;
  CKLTMHC, IV. 49; TL-j hua-chi, 1.

The Han-ku Pass in snow, poem, signed, Nat. Pal. Mus., Taipei, (AL, also listed as Han-kuan hsüeh-chi t'u). CCAT, pl. 115; CH mei-shu, III.

Hibiscus flowers at the waterside, signed, Nat. Pal. Mus., Taipei, (AL, also listed as The fu-yung flower bending over a stone in the water). CKLTMHC, IV. 50.

The painter speaking of old times with his friend Hsi-chou, poem, inscription, signed, Nat. Pal. Mus., Taipei, (AL). 300 M., 231; CH mei-shu, III; CKLTSHH; NPM Bulletin, I. 2, p. 8; TL-j hua-chi, 9.

Farmsteads in Chiang-nan, poem, signed, Nat. Pal. Mus., Taipei, (AL). CH mei-shu, III; CKLTMHC, IV. 47.

Mu-ch'un lin-ho t'u. Rocky mountain and trees in late spring, poem, signed, Nat. Pal. Mus., Taipei, (AL). 300 M., 230; TL-j hua-chi, 16.

Ch'i-shan yü-yin t'u. A fisherman among mountains and streams, handscroll, poem, signed, Nat. Pal. Mus., Taipei, (AL). CAT, 101* (section).

Spring view in a garden, inscribed, signed, Nat. Pal. Mus., Taipei, (AL). 300 M., 233*; CAT, 99; CKLTMHC, IV. 51.

A weeping man seated between two old trees which are shaken by the storm, handscroll, signed, Palace Museum, Peking, (AL). PM, 26*.

Old trees and bamboo by a stream, inscribed, signed, (AL). TL-j hua-chi, 29.

T'ao Ku in his garden, listening to a young girl playing the p'i-p'a, poem, signed, Nat. Pal. Mus., Taipei, (AL). 300 M., 232; CKLTMHC, IV. 46; TL-j hua-chi, 20.

Portrait of Tung-fang So, an old man holding a peach, inscribed, signed, (AL). TL-j hua-chi, 15.

A scholar in a pavilion by the river beneath an overhanging cliff, poem, dedicated to a Mr. Te-fu, (AL). CK hua, VIII. 16; TL-j hua-chi, 7.

Meditating in a water pavilion, poem, signed, (AL). TL-j hua-chi, 17.

A crow on a dry branch, two lines of poetry, signed, Shanghai Museum, (AL). CK hua, I. 23; Shang-hai, 54*; TL-j hua-chi, 28; TSYMC hua-hsüan, 46.

Four court ladies in the Shu country, poem, inscription, signed, Palace Museum, Peking, (AL). Li-tai jen-wu, 50; PM, 27*; TL-j hua-chi, 5.

Ladies, poem, signed, (AL). TL-j hua-chi, 27.

A boat coming to a bamboo-covered cove, inscribed, signed, Nat. Pal. Mus., Taipei. CH mei-shu, III; CKLTMHC, IV. 48.

Wild flower and rock, album leaf, inscribed, signed, Nat. Pal. Mus.,
Taipei. NPM Bulletin, I. 1. 7.

A branch of plum blossoms, poem, signed, Palace Museum, Peking.
KKPWY hua-niao, 52*.

Two friends seated on the bank of a mountain stream, poem, signed,
Shanghai Museum. Shang-hai, 52*; TL-j hua-chi, 3.

A fisherman in a boat under leafless willow, folding fan, signed, Shanghai WWPKWYH. Shan-mien-hua, 5*.

Two gentlemen in a pavilion under trees surrounded by mountain boul-
ders and cliffs, folding fan, inscribed, signed, Shanghai WWPKWYH.
Shan-mien-hua, 6*; TL-j hua-chi, 37.

Gentleman standing below a pine next to a stormy sea, folding fan, inscribed, Tientsin Art Museum. T'ien-ching, I. 21.

A recluse in a mountain abode, poem, signed, Chang Pe-chin collection. Tien Yin Tang, I. 18.

Night rain over the Hsiao and Hsiang, inscribed, signed, Huang Pao-
hsi collection, Hong Kong. Lo-tsai hsüan, I. 5*.

Fisherman in a boat in a bamboo grove, inscribed, signed, S. M. Siu
collection, Hong Kong. CK ku-hua, B. 182.

Thatched huts at the foot of mountains, poem, signed, S. M. Siu collection, Hong Kong. CK ku-hua, B. 184.

A scholar admiring leafy trees, inscribed, signed, S. M. Siu collection, Hong Kong. CK ku-hua, B. 185.

Bamboo and plum blossoms, handscroll, inscribed, signed, S. M. Siu
collection, Hong Kong. CK ku-hua, B. 187.

A woodgatherer crossing a bridge, poem, signed, colophon by Chu
Yao-tz'u. TL-j hua-chi, 2; TSYMC hua-hsüan, 44.

A gentleman on a path, a servant with a ch'in approaching a bridge,
a village in the background, poem, signed. TL-j hua-chi, 4.

Two men seated, watching a waterfall, poem, signed. TL-j hua-chi, 8.

Scholar and crane by a waterfall in rugged mountain area, poem, signed, colophon by a group of scholars dated 1527. TL-j hua-chi, 10.

Two men reminiscing in a thatched hut, poem, signed. TL-j hua-chi,
12.

Travelling through the pine forest in the mountains, poem, signed.
TL-j hua-chi, 13.

A gentleman seated in front of a landscape screen, four ladies in at-
tendance, poem, signed. TL-j hua-chi, 14; TSYMC hua-hsüan,
45.

Vine-covered tree over a bamboo bank, poem, signed. TL-j hua-chi, 18.

Playing the ch'in in snowy mountains, poem, signed. TL-j hua-chi, 19.

A man in loose clothing holding a bow, poem, signed. TL-j hua-chi, 21.

Spring travellers in the Nü-chi Mountain, poem, signed. TL-j hua-
chi, 22.

Meeting in a thatched hut, poem, signed. TL-j hua-chi, 23.

Lofty mountains and strange trees, poem, signed. TL-j hua-chi, 24.

Travellers in snowy mountains, poem, signed. TL-j hua-chi, 25.

A man with a staff standing on flat land between two groups of rocks
and trees, handscroll, inscribed, signed. TL-j hua-chi, 30.

A man in a pavilion under pine on a low bank, a visitor approaching
over a bridge, handscroll, poem, signed, poem by Ch'ien-lung.
TL-j hua-chi, 31.

Gentleman looking at plum blossoms, handscroll, poem, signed, made
for Wang Ching-hsi. TL-j hua-chi, 32.

Bamboo in rain, folding fan, poem, signed. TL-j hua-chi, 38.

A man watching a waterfall, folding fan, signed. TL-j hua-chi, 39.

A man on a cliff watching a waterfall, folding fan, signed, three poems
by later men. TL-j hua-chi, 40.

T'AO CH'ENG 陶 成 , t. Meng-hsüeh 孟 學 or Mou-hsüeh
懋 學 , h. Yün-hu hsien-jen 雲 湖 仙 人 . From Pao-ying,
Kiangsu; active c. 1480-1532; landscapes, figures, flowers. (CP, VII,
AL, 241.)

Rabbit on a grassy knoll under bamboo in moonlight, signed, dated
1495, Palace Museum, Peking. KKPWY hua-niao, 43*.

Bird on plum blossom branch, signed, dated 1532, S. M. Siu collection, Hong Kong. CK ku-hua, B. 169.

TING YÜN-P'ENG 丁 雲 鵬 , t. Nan-yü 南 羽 , h. Sheng-hua
chü-shih 聖 華 居 士 . From Hsiu-ning, Anhui; active c. 1584-
1638; friend of Tung Ch'i-ch'ang; Buddhist and Taoist figures, landscapes.
(CP, VII, AL, 241-243.)

Waiting for an imperial audience, signed, dated 1592, (AL). Li-tai
jen-wu, 55.

A man in a boat under pine, flock of flying egrets, folding fan, inscribed, signed, dated 1599, Shanghai WWPKWYH. Shan-mien-hua,
23*.

A lady standing in a blossoming orchard in moonlight, folding fan,
signed, dated 1601, Shanghai WWPKWYH. Shan-mien-hua, 22*.

Washing the white elephant, signed, dated 1604, Huang Pao-hsi collection, Hong Kong. Lo-tsai hsüan, I. 9*.

An arhat seated in a tree, signed, dated 1608, S. M. Siu collection,
Hong Kong. CK ku-hua, B. 203.

Lan-t'ing Meeting, folding fan, signed, dated 1611, Shanghai WWPK-
WYH. Shan-mien-hua, 24*.

River and mountain landscape, two empty pavilions, signed, dated
1615, Suchou Museum. Su-chou, 18.

The white horse carrying the first Buddhist Sutras to China, signed,
　　dated 1625, Nat. Pal. Mus., Taipei, (AL). 300 M., 346; CK
　　ku-tai, 84; CKLTMHC, IV.96.
Washing the elephant, signed, Nat. Pal. Mus., Taipei. CH ming-hua*.
Taoist figures in a mountain landscape, signed, Cheng Te-k'un collec-
　　tion, Cambridge. Mu-fei, before p. 11.

TSENG CH'ING 曾 鯨 , t. P'o-ch'en 波 臣 . B. 1568, d.
1650; from P'u-t'ien, Fukien; portraits. (CP, VII, AL, 244.)
　　Portrait of Doctor Ko Ch'eng-fu, handscroll, several inscriptions,
　　　Palace Museum, Peking, (AL). CK ku-tai, 86.
　　Portrait of Ku Yü-chih (Ku Meng-yu, 1599-1660), figure by Tseng
　　　Ch'ing, landscape by Chang Feng. Li-tai jen-wu, 54.

TSOU CHIH-LIN 鄒 之 麟 , t. Ch'en-hu 臣 虎 , h. Mei-an
昧 庵 , I-po shan-jen 衣 白 山 人 , I-lao 逸 老 . From
Wu-chin, Kiangsu; chin-shih in 1610; poet, collector; landscapes. (CP,
VII, AL, 244.)
　　Landscape of the Fu-ch'un Mountains, inscribed, signed, dated 1644,
　　　Tientsin Art Museum. T'ien-ching, II.82.

TS'UI TZU-CHUNG 崔 子 忠 , t. Tao mu 道 母 , h. Pei-hai 北
海 , Ch'ing-yin 青 蚓 . D. 1644; from Lai-yang, Shantung; lived
in Peking; figures. (CP, VII, AL, 245.)
　　An arhat, signed, dated 1633, S.M. Siu collection, Hong Kong. CK
　　　ku hua, B.217.
　　Scene from the story "The Fairy Rabbit", handscroll, inscribed, sign-
　　　ed, dated 1634, (AL). CK ku-tai, 87.
　　Su Tung-p'o and his friends enjoying antiques under wu-t'ung trees,
　　　signed, dated 1640, Nat. Pal. Mus., Taipei, (AL). CKLTMHC,
　　　IV.142.
　　Chickens and dogs among the clouds; travellers in a mountain land-
　　　scape, poem, signed, Nat. Pal. Mus., Taipei, (AL). CKLTMHC,
　　　IV.143; Li-tai jen-wu, 58.
　　Su Tung-p'o in conversation with the monk Fou-yin, signed, Nat. Pal.
　　　Mus., Taipei, (AL). 300 M., 251; CH mei-shu, III; CKLTMHC,
　　　IV.144.
　　Jade lady of the clouds, inscribed, signed, colophon by Kao Shih-
　　　ch'i, Shanghai Museum. Shang-hai, 65*.

TU CHIN 杜 堇 , t. Chü-nan 爟 南 , h. Ch'eng-chü 惺 居 ,
Ku-k'uang 古 狂 , Ch'ing-hsia t'ing-ch'ang 青 霞 亭 長 . From
Tan-t'u, Kiangsu, moved to the capital in the Ch'eng-hua period (1465-
1487); landscapes. (CP, VII, AL, 245.)

A scholar on a mountain terrace, under a plum-tree, signed, Shang-hai Museum, (AL). Shang-hai, 44*.

Illustrations to nine ancient poems, handscroll, poems inscribed by Chin Tsung, Tu is mentioned as the artist of these pictures in the colophon by Chin Tsung, Palace Museum, Peking. Ku-hsien shih-i; Li-tai jen-wu, 43-44 (two sections); WW, 1962.6.5 (one section).

TU CH'IUNG 杜 瓊 , t. Yung-chia 用 嘉 , h. Lu-kuan tao-jen 鹿 冠 道 人 , Tung-yüan hsien-sheng 東 原 先 生 . B. 1396, d. 1474; from Suchou; scholar; landscapes. (CP, VII, AL, 246.)

Two men in a mountain valley, signed, dated 1466, S.M. Siu collection, Hong Kong. CK ku-hua, B.166.

Nan-hu ts'ao-t'ang t'u. A mountain landscape in the manner of Shen Chou, long inscription by the artist, signed, dated 1468, Nat. Pal. Mus., Taipei, (AL). CH mei-shu, III; CKLTSHH.

A scholar and a servant in a banana grove, album leaf, artist's seals, Shanghai Museum. CK shu-hua, I.24; Shang-hai, 36*.

TU TA-CH'ENG 杜 大 成 , t. Yün-hsiu 允 修 , h. San-shan k'uang-sheng 三 山 狂 生 , Shan-k'uang-sheng 山 狂 生 . From Nanking, a poet and musician, painted birds, flowers and insects. (I.57; N.7; O.6; M. p.122.)

Insects on flowers and grasses, two album leaves, one signed, Liao-ning Provincial Museum. Liao-ning, II.20-21.

TUNG CH'I-CH'ANG 董 其 昌 , t. Hsüan-tsai 玄 宰 , h. Ssu-po 思 白 . B. 1555, d. 1636; from Hua-t'ing (Sung-chiang), Kiangsu; calligrapher and critic; one of the "Nine Friends in Painting"; landscapes. (CP, VII, AL, 246-249.)

Landscape, poems and colophons dated 1612 and 1625, Nat. Pal. Mus., Taipei, (AL). CKLTMHC, IV.102.

River scene, handscroll, inscribed, signed, dated 1620, Tientsin Art Museum. T'ien-ching, II.53-57.

Two huts by a river, inscribed, signed, dated 1624, S.M. Siu collection, Hong Kong. CK ku-hua, B.208.

Cliffs with trees along a river, inscribed, signed, dated 1626, done for Chia Hsüan, Palace Museum, Peking, (AL). CK ku-tai, 85.

White clouds on the Hsiao and Hsiang, handscroll, inscribed, signed, dated 1627, Liao-ning Provincial Museum. Liao-ning, II.51-52.

A straw-covered hut on the eastern hill, after Ni Tsan, signed, poem and colophon dated 1629, Nat. Pal. Mus., Taipei, (AL). CH mei-shu, III.

Landscape, inscribed, signed, dated 1633, Tientsin Art Museum.
    T'ien-ching, I.31.

Peaks and clouds, poem, signed, Nat. Pal. Mus., Taipei, (AL).
    300 M., 247; CKLTMHC, IV.104.

Pavilions for study among autumn trees, signed, after Ts'ao Chih-po,
    Nat. Pal. Mus., Taipei, (AL). 300 M., 248; CH mei-shu, III.

Trees in summer, inscribed, signed, after Tung Yüan, Nat. Pal. Mus.,
    Taipei, (AL). CAT, 104; CCAT, pl. 119; CKLTMHC, IV.103;
    NPM Quarterly, I.2, pl. XXXIII.

A frosty forest, inscribed, signed, Nat. Pal. Mus., Taipei, (AL).
    300 M., 249.

The hills and valleys of Shan-yin, after Ni Tsan, inscribed and signed,
    Nat. Pal. Mus., Taipei, (AL). CH mei-shu, III; CKLTSHH.

Summer mountains, after Huang Kung-wang, Nat. Pal. Mus., Tai-
    pei. CH ming-hua*.

Houses in trees, distant mountains, folding fan, signed, Shanghai
    WWPKWYH. Shan-mien-hua, 35*.

Clearing in the spring mountains after rain, signed, after Tung Yüan,
    Chang Pe-chin collection. Tien Yin Tang, I.34.

Nearby trees and distant village, inscribed, signed, Huang Pao-hsi
    collection, Hong Kong. Lo-tsai hsüan, I.10*.

Three trees on near river bank, land-spit with pines, distant moun-
    tain, inscribed, signed. TSYMC hua-hsüan, 58; WW, 1962.12.8.

Mists in mountain valleys, inscribed, signed. WW, 1962.12.8.

WANG CHAO 汪肇 , t. Te-ch'u 德初 , h. Hai-yün 海雲 .
From Hsiu-ning, Anhui; active c. 1500; landscapes, figures. (CP, VII,
AL, 250.)

    Three geese among rushes, one flying, signed. CK hua, VI.15.

    Two wood-gatherers seated beneath pines, signed. CK hua, VII.15.

WANG CH'I 王綦 , t. Li-jo 履若 . From Suchou; active c.
1600-1637; flowers, landscapes. (CP, VII, AL, 250.)

    Autumn trees by a bridge, signed, dated 1606, Nat. Pal. Mus., Tai-
        pei, (AL). CKLTMHC, IV.120.

    Bamboo and rock, signed, dated 1621, S.M. Siu collection, Hong Kong.
        CK ku-hua, B.199.

    Chrysanthemums by a garden stone, signed, dated 1626, Nat. Pal.
        Mus., Taipei, (AL). CKLTMHC, IV.119.

WANG CH'IEN 王謙 , t. Mu-chih 牧之 , h. Ping-hu tao-
jen 冰壺道人 . From Ch'ien-t'ang, Chekiang; active c. 1500;
plum blossoms. (CP, VII, AL, 251.)

A thick branch of plum blossoms, signed, dated 1446, Shanghai Museum. Shang-hai, 39*.

A branch of blossoming plum, inscribed, signed, three poems by other men, Palace Museum, Peking. KKPWY hua-niao, 34*.

Branch of flowering plum over rock, inscribed, signed, Tientsin Art Museum. T'ien-ching, I. 7.

WANG CH'IEN 王 乾 , t. I-ch'ing 一 清 , h. Ts'ang-ch'un 藏 春 , T'ien-feng 天 峯 . From Lin-hai, Chekiang, first half of the 16th century; birds. (CP, VII, AL, 251.)

Two eagles, signed, Palace Museum, Peking. KKPWY hua-niao, 49*.

WANG CHUNG-LI 王 中 立 , t. Chen-chih 振 之 . From Su-chou; active c. 1620; flowers, birds. (CP, VII, AL, 252.)

Swallow and roses by a rockery, signed, dated 1621, Nat. Pal. Mus., Taipei, (AL). CKLTMHC, IV. 129.

Plum, pine, cypress and narcissus by a stream, done with Ch'en Chia-yen, Liu Yüan-ch'i, Wang Tzu-yüan and Sheng Mao-hua, dated 1625, Tientsin Art Museum. T'ien-ching, II. 61.

WANG CHUNG-YÜ 王 仲玉 . Active in the Hung-wu period (1368-1398). (CP, VII, AL, 252.)

Portrait of T'ao Yüan-ming, Palace Museum, Peking, (AL). PM, 24*.

WANG CH'UNG 王 寵 , t. Li-jen 履 仁 or Li-chi 履 吉 , h. Ya-i shan-jen 雅 宜 山 人 . B. 1494, d. 1533; from Suchou; poet, calligrapher; pupil of Wen Cheng-ming; landscapes. (CP, VII, AL, 252.)

A deep gorge between pointed rocks, inscribed, signed, Suchou Museum, (AL). Su-chou, 15.

WANG E 王 諤 , t. T'ing-chih 廷 直 . From Feng-hua, Che-kiang; court painter in the Hung-chih period (1488-1505); appointed officer of the Imperial Guard in the Cheng-te period (1506-1521); landscapes, figures. (CP, VII, AL, 252.)

Landscape, signed, Nat. Pal. Mus., Taipei, (AL). CKLTMHC, IV. 35.

Shore landscape with figures, Sakugen leaving for home, signed, (AL). Che-chiang, 51.

Scholar and servant on bridge approaching a pavilion under a pine, signed, S. M. Siu collection, Hong Kong. CK ku-hua, B. 167.

WANG FU 王 紱 , t. Meng-tuan 孟 端 , h. Yu-shih 友石 , Chiu-lung shan-jen 九 龍 山 人 , Ch'ing-ch'eng shan-jen 青 城 山 人 and other names. B. 1362, d. 1416; from Wu-hsi, Kiangsu;

landscapes, bamboo. (CP, VII, AL, 252-253.)

Landscape, after Ni Tsan, poem, signed, dated 1401, poems by three contemporaries, (AL). Wang Fu, 7.

Ink bamboo, signed, dated 1401, Palace Museum, Peking. KKPWY hua-niao, 29*; Wang Fu, 2; WW, 1961.6.5.

Bamboo, inscribed, signed, dated 1401, S.M. Siu collection, Hong Kong. CK ku-hua, B.154.

Three young bamboos, signed, dated 1403, Nat. Pal. Mus., Taipei, (AL). CKLTMHC, IV.3.

A literary meeting in a mountain pavilion, signed, dated 1404, Nat. Pal. Mus., Taipei, (AL). 300 M., 208; CAT, 91; CH mei-shu, III; CKLTSHH; Wang Fu, 5.

A man in a thatched hut in a misty woods, signed, dated 1405, S.M. Siu collection, Hong Kong. CK ku-hua, B.153.

A studio on a lake shore, handscroll, signed, dated 1410, Palace Museum, Peking. Wang Fu, 11.

River scenery, handscroll, inscribed, signed, dated 1410, colophons by Wen Cheng-ming and others, Liao-ning Provincial Museum. Liao-ning, II.1-5.

Autumn thoughts on the Hsiao and Hsiang, handscroll, done "when 51" (1412), Palace Museum, Peking. Wang Fu, 1-2.

Riverscape, handscroll, signed, dated 1414, S.M. Siu collection, Hong Kong. CK ku-hua, B.152.

A farewell meeting at Feng-ch'eng, poem, signed, poems by twelve friends present at the meeting, Nat. Pal. Mus., Taipei, (AL). CH mei-shu, III; CK ku-tai, 71; CKLTMHC, IV.2; Wang Fu, 6.

Reading in a hut, signed, poems by two contemporaries, Nat. Pal. Mus., Taipei, (AL). Wang Fu, 8.

Man seated in a straw-covered pavilion by a river, poem, signed, Nat. Pal. Mus., Taipei, (AL). CCAT, pl. 112.

Bamboo spray, album leaf, signed, Fogg Art Museum, Cambridge, Mass., (AL). NPM Quarterly, I.4, pl. 13.

A hanging branch of bamboo, signed, made for Liang Ch'ien (1366-1418), Nat. Pal. Mus., Taipei. 300 M., 209; CKLTMHC, IV.4; KKCP, I.5; NPM Quarterly, I.4, pl. 11.

Two cranes in a bamboo grove, signed, bamboo by Wang Fu, cranes by Pien Wen-chin, Palace Museum, Peking. KKPWY hua-niao, 30*; Wang Fu, 4.

Eight scenes of Peking, handscroll of eight sections, seal on each section, Palace Museum, Peking. Wang Fu, 12 (section three).

Bamboo and stone, inscribed, signed, Shanghai Museum. Shang-hai, 34*.

Bamboo, handscroll, Nelson Gallery of Art, Kansas City. NPM Quarterly, I.4, pl. 12 (section).

Fishermen in mountains and streams, handscroll. Wang Fu, 9-10
(sections).

WANG KU-HSIANG 王穀祥 , t. Lu-chih 祿之 , h. Yu-shih
酉室 . B. 1501, d. 1568; from Suchou; flowers, birds. (CP, VII,
AL, 254.)
> Two ling-chih on a rock, signed, dated 1564, colophon by Chang Feng-i,
> S. M. Siu collection, Hong Kong. CK ku-hua, B. 196.
> An album of eight leaves, inscribed, signed, Liao-ning Provincial
> Museum. Liao-ning, II. 35 (one leaf: Peach blossoms); 36 (one
> leaf: Narcissi).
> Hibiscus, folding fan, signed, colophon by Chang Feng-i, Shanghai
> WWPKWYH. Shan-mien-hua, 18*.

WANG LI 王履 , t. An-tao 安道 , h. Ch'i-weng 奇翁 and
Chi-sou 畸叟 . B. 1332, d. after 1383; from K'un-shan, Kiangsu;
landscapes. (CP, VII, AL, 254.)
> Landscapes of Hua-shan, album leaf, inscribed, Shanghai Museum,
> (AL). Shang-hai, 32*.

WANG SHAO-CH'UAN 汪少川 . Unidentified.
> Portrait of a man, album leaf, given to Wang in the accompanying in-
> scription dated 1617, Liao-ning Provincial Museum. Liao-ning,
> II. 66.

WANG SHIH-CH'ANG 王世昌 , h. Li-shan 歷山 . From
Li-ch'eng, Shantung; 15th century (?); landscapes, figures. (CP, VII,
AL, 255.)
> Mountain landscapes, signed, Freer Gallery of Art, Washington, D. C.,
> (16.95), (AL). WW, 1964. 3. 19.

WANG SHUN-KUO 王舜國 or Cheng-kuo 正國 , h. Kuei-kung
桂宮 . A Taoist, lived in Suchou during the Wan-li period (1573-
1619); figures in the manner of Wu Wei. (M. p. 42.)
> An Immortal floating above misty trees, a phoenix, inscribed, after
> Chao Meng-fu. Li-tai jen-wu, 47.

WANG TO 王鐸 , t. Chio-ssu 覺斯 , h. Hsüeh-shan tao-
jen 雪山道人 , Yün-yen man-shih 雪巖漫士 and
other names. B. 1592, d. 1652; from Meng-chin, Honan; calligrapher;
landscapes. (CP, VII, AL, 255-256.)
> A central promontory with a covered walk, handscroll, inscribed,
> signed, dated 1647, Tientsin Art Museum. T'ien-ching, I. 49.

An album of six leaves depicting landscapes, each leaf signed, last
inscribed and dated 1650, Liao-ning Provincial Museum. Liao-
ning, II. 67-72.

Epidendrum and other plants, handscroll, Suchou Museum. Su-chou,
34-38.

Ink bamboo, signed, Tientsin Art Museum. T'ien-ching, I. 50.

WANG WEI-LIEH 王 維 烈　　, t. Wu-ching 無 競　. From Su-
chou; active c. 1590-1620; pupil of Chou Chih-mien; flowers and birds.
(CP, VII, AL, 256.)

A pair of magpies, signed, Nat. Pal. Mus., Taipei, (AL). CKLTMHC,
IV. 114.

A duck under hibiscus, signed, Nat. Pal. Mus., Taipei. CKLTMHC,
IV. 115.

WANG WEN 王 問　, t. Tzu-yü 子 裕　, h. Chung-shan 仲山 .
B. 1497, d. 1576; from Wu-hsi, Kiangsu; landscapes. (CP, VII, AL, 256.)

A tall mountain and stream, poem, signed, dated 1552, Nat. Pal.
Mus., Taipei, (AL). CKLTMHC, IV. 69.

Two men seated on the ground; one of them boiling tea-water, the other
writing on a scroll, handscroll, inscribed, signed, dated 1558,
Nat. Pal. Mus., Taipei, (AL). CCAT, pl. 117 (section).

WEI CHIH-HUANG 魏 之 璜　, t. K'ao-shu 孝 叔　. B. 1568,
d. after 1645; from Nanking, poet, calligrapher; landscapes, flowers,
pictures of Kuanyin. (CP, VII, AL, 256.)

Two men in a lake pavilion, steep bluffs, folding fan, signed, dated
1613, Hui Hsiao-t'ung collection. Shan-mien chi-chin, 4*.

Autumn landscape, poem, signed, dated 1635. CKTLMHC, IV. 141.

Riverside village, fisherman in boat playing a flute, folding fan, signed, date effaced, Hui Hsiao-t'ung collection. Shan-mien chi-
chin, 5*.

WEN CHENG-MING 文 徵 明　, original name Pi 璧　 and t. Cheng-
ming; later adopted Cheng-ming as his name and took the tzu Cheng-chung
徵 仲　, h. Heng-shan 衡　山 . B. 1470, d. 1559; from Suchou;
scholar, poet, calligrapher and painter; followed Shen Chou; landscapes,
flowers. (CP, VII, AL, 257-263.)

Yü-yü ch'un-shu t'u. Trees after spring rain, river landscape, poem,
signed, dated 1507, Nat. Pal. Mus., Taipei, (AL). CKLTMHC,
IV. 52.

Yen-chiang tieh-chang t'u. Misty river and layered mountains, handscroll, inscribed, signed, dated 1508, artist's colophon of twenty

years later at end of scroll, Liao-ning Provincial Museum. Liao-ning Provincial Museum. Liao-ning, II. 25-29; Yen-chiang tieh-chang.

Bare trees by the river, handscroll, signed, dated 1511, Suchou Museum. Su-chou, 12.

The Goddess of the Hsiang River with her attendant, dated 1517, colophons by Wen Chia and Wang Chih-teng, Palace Museum, Peking, (AL). Wen Cheng-ming, 1.

Two gentlemen under trees in mountains, folding fan, signed, dated 1521, Shanghai WWPKWYH. Shan-mien-hua, 8*.

Landscape with old trees, in the manner of Ni Tsan, signed, dated 1530, (AL). Wen Cheng-ming, 4.

Drinking tea, poem, inscription, signed, dated 1531, Nat. Pal. Mus., Taipei, (AL). 300 M., 237*.

Five men in a pine-wood; high mountains beyond, inscribed, signed, dated 1531, Nat. Pal. Mus., Taipei, (AL). CKLTMHC, IV. 54.

Scenery of Shih-hu, handscroll, signed, dated 1532. CK ku-tai, 81.

Chung K'uei in a cold forest, dated 1534, Nat. Pal. Mus., Taipei, (AL). 300 M., 240; CKLTMHC, IV. 58.

Red bamboos, signed, dated 1534, Nat. Pal. Mus., Taipei, (AL). CKLTMHC, IV. 55.

Tall mountain landscape after Wang Meng, signed, dated 1535, Nat. Pal. Mus., Taipei, (AL). 300 M., 238; CKLTMHC, IV. 62.

Two men seated under pine-trees by a mountain river, signed, dated 1535, Nat. Pal. Mus., Taipei, (AL). CH mei-shu, III; CH ming-hua*; CKLTSHH.

Thatched hut in the shade of trees, inscribed, signed Wen Pi, inscription dated 1535 in which he says he has looked at this painting for twenty years, possibly done in 1515, Nat. Pal. Mus., Taipei. CKLTMHC, IV. 53.

Two men in a pavilion over water, guest and servant on opposite bank, strange mountain peaks, signed, dated 1536, Suchou Museum. Su-chou, 13.

Purple bamboo by a rock, signed, dated 1545, S. M. Siu collection, Hong Kong. CK ku-hua, A. 60; B. 179.

A man lying in a boat listening to the rain, colophon, signed, dated 1545, (AL). Wen Cheng-ming, 2.

Spring in Chiang-nan, poem, signed, dated 1547, Nat. Pal. Mus., Taipei, (AL). 300 M., 235; CAT, 97; CH mei-shu, III; CKLTMHC, IV. 56.

Flower, album leaf, signed, dated 1548, Shanghai Museum. WW, 1963. 10. 20.

Waterfall and old trees, signed, dated 1549, Nat. Pal. Mus., Taipei, (AL). CAT, 98; CCAT, pl. 16*; CKLTMHC, IV. 57; NPM

Quarterly, I. 2, pl. XXXII; Wen Cheng-ming, 10.

The Chen-shang Studio, handscroll, signed, dated 1549, (AL). Wen
Cheng-ming, 8-9*.

Landscape in rain, signed, dated 1549, (AL). Wen Cheng-ming, 11.

A thatched pavilion by the T'iao River, handscroll, signed, dated 1551,
(AL). Wen Cheng-ming, 12.

Houses in a river cove, folding fan, signed, dated 1551, Shanghai
WWPKWYH. Shan-mien-hua, 9*.

Red bamboos, signed, dated 1555, Nat. Pal. Mus., Taipei, (AL).
KKCP, I. 8

Man in a pavilion at the water's edge, signed, dated 1557. TSYMC
hua-hsüan, 47.

Spring clouds over a valley, poem, signed, Nat. Pal. Mus., Taipei,
(AL). CH mei-shu, III.

Epidendrum and bamboos, poem, signed, Nat. Pal. Mus., Taipei,
(AL). 300 M., 239; CKLTMHC, IV. 61.

Two men talking in a pavilion by the stream, poem, signed, Nat. Pal.
Mus., Taipei, (AL). 300 M., 236; Wen Cheng-ming, 5.

The Study in the Green Shade, poem, signed, Nat. Pal. Mus., Taipei,
(AL). CH mei-shu, III.

Listening to the sounds of the pine-trees, poem, signed, Nat. Pal.
Mus., Taipei, (AL). CKLTMHC, IV. 59.

Landscape after rain; a man seated by a stream, listening to the water,
poem, signed, Nat. Pal. Mus., Taipei, (AL). CKLTMHC, IV. 60.

Distant mountains and a rocky hump, pine-trees and pavilions built over
the water, handscroll, signed, colophon by T'ang Yin, Shanghai
Museum, (AL). Wen Cheng-ming, 14-15.

An album of ten leaves: Landscapes, trees, bamboo, etc., seals of
the artist, (AL). Wen Cheng-ming, 6 (leaf 6: Flower); 7 (leaf 1:
Trees, bamboo and rock).

Bamboos and epidendrum, handscroll, seal of the artist, (AL). Wen
Cheng-ming, 13.

Drinking tea in Hui-shan, handscroll, Palace Museum, Peking. WW,
1966. 4. 42.

River landscape, two scholars in a pavilion, two guests arriving, buildings clustered along a river bank, handscroll, signed, title written by Wang Ku-hsiang, twelve colophons, Liao-ning Provincial
Museum. Liao-ning, II. 30-31.

Two men in front of a hut on a smooth promontory, servant with a
ch'in on other bank of the stream, mountain background, poem,
signed, Shanghai Museum. Shang-hai, 55*; Wen Cheng-ming, 3.

Pavilion and bare trees in front of river and mountain background,
poem, signed, Tientsin Art Museum. T'ien-ching, I. 20.

Mists among mountain peaks rising from the river, handscroll, in-
   scribed, made for a Mr. Chu as a parting gift, Tientsin Art Mu-
   seum. T'ien-ching, II. 19.
Album of eleven leaves: landscapes and flowers, artist's seal on
   each leaf, Chang Pe-chin collection. Tien Yin Tang, I. 19-28.
Orchids and bamboo by a rock, inscribed, signed, Huang Pao-hsi
   collection, Hong Kong. Lo-tsai hsüan, I. 4*.
Man in boat under pine trees, poem, signed, S. M. Siu collection,
   Hong Kong. CK ku-hua, B. 180.
Scholar in pavilion under gnarled pine and bamboo, poem, signed.
   TSYMC hua-hsüan, 48.
Man in pavilion over water, visitor with umbrella crossing bridge,
   poem, signed. TSYMC hua-hsüan, 49.

WEN CHIA 文 嘉 , t. Hsiu-ch'eng 休 承 , h. Wen-shui 文 水 .
B. 1501, d. 1583; second son of Wen Cheng-ming; landscapes. (CP, VII,
AL, 263-264.)
   The Island of the Immortals, poem, signed, Nat. Pal. Mus., Taipei,
      (AL). CH mei-shu, III.
   Waterfall, peaks and pine-trees, poem, signed, Nat. Pal. Mus., Tai-
      pei, (AL). CKLTMHC, IV. 78.
   Fisherman in a boat playing a flute, folding fan, signed, Shanghai
      WWPKWYH. Shan-mien-hua, 17*.
   Two thin trees and bare hills, two lines of poetry, signed, Tientsin
      Art Museum. T'ien-ching, II. 41.
   Pavilions and cloudy mountains, after Ni Tsan, inscribed, signed,
      Huang Pao-hsi collection, Hong Kong. Lo-tsai hsüan, I. 8*.

WEN PO-JEN 文 伯 仁 , t. Te-ch'eng 德 承 , h. Wu-feng
五 峯 , Pao-sheng 葆 生 , She-shan lao-nung 攝 山 老 農 .
B. 1502, d. 1575; nephew of Wen Cheng-ming; landscapes. (CP, VII, AL,
265-266.)
   Returning boat on an autumn river, signed, dated 1544, Chang Pe-
      chin collection. Tien Yin Tang, I. 31.
   Streams and mountains, gentlemen in small boats, handscroll, signed,
      dated 1546, Tientsin Art Museum. T'ien-ching, II. 39-40.
   Tall river-view, creviced rocks and leafless trees, signed, dated
      1547, Nat. Pal. Mus., Taipei, (AL). CKLTMHC, IV. 80.
   River view; fishermen in boats, travellers on a bridge, distant moun-
      tains, folding fan, poem, signed, dated 1558, Shanghai WWPKWYH.
      Shan-mien-hua, 19*.
   Mountain landscape with people saying farewell near a gate, painted
      on the occasion of Ku Hsiao-hsien's departure, seven inscriptions
      by his friends, one dated 1562, (AL). TSYMC hua-hsüan, 55.

The Fang-hu Island, signed, dated 1563, Nat. Pal. Mus., Taipei,
    (AL). CKLTMHC, IV. 79.

Landscape, done in 1564, signed, poem dated 1570, Nat. Pal. Mus.,
    Taipei, (AL). CKLTMHC, IV. 81.

Fishing on a clear stream, signed, dated 1569, Shanghai Museum.
    Shang-hai, 58*.

Landscape made for Huai-ku, inscribed, signed, dated 1569, Suchou
    Museum. Su-chou, 16.

Landscape, illustration to a poem by Tu Mu, inscribed, signed, date
    indistinct, S. M. Siu collection, Hong Kong. CK ku-hua, B. 194.

WEN SHU 文淑 , t. Tuan-jung 端容 . B. 1595, d. 1634; daughter of Wen Ts'ung-chien (great-grandson of Wen Cheng-ming); married to
Chao Ling-chün (1591-1640); flowers and insects. (CP, VII, AL, 266-267.)

Butterfly and flowers, signed, dated 1630, Nat. Pal. Mus., Taipei,
    (AL). CKLTMHC, IV. 138.

Persimmon blossoms and butterfly, folding fan, signed, dated 1631,
    Shanghai WWPKWYH. Shan-mien-hua, 45*.

Iris and butterfly, signed, dated 1632, Liao-ning Provincial Museum.
    Liao-ning, II. 56.

Album of twelve leaves depicting flowers, signed, dated 1632, S. M.
    Siu collection, Hong Kong. CK ku-hua, B. 201.

WEN TS'UNG-CHIEN 文從簡 , t. Yen-k'o 彥可 , h. Chen-
yen lao-jen 枕煙老人 . B. 1574, d. 1648; eldest son of Wen
Yüan-shan; landscapes, figures, flowers, birds. (CP, VII, AL, 267.)

A gentleman seated under two gnarled pines by a river, handscroll,
    inscribed, signed, dated 1647, done for Fang T'ui-an, Tientsin
    Art Museum. T'ien-ching, II. 72-74.

A bird among lotus plants, signed, colophon by Chao Fan-fu, Nat. Pal.
    Mus., Taipei, (AL). CKLTMHC, IV. 137.

WEN YÜAN-SHAN 文元善 , t. Tzu-ch'ang 子長 , h. Hu-ch'iu
虎丘 . B. 1554, d. 1589; son of Wen Chia; calligrapher and painter.
(CP, VII, AL, 267.)

Cypress tree and chrysanthemum, signed, dated 1585, S. M. Siu col-
    lection, Hong Kong. CK ku-hua, B. 202.

WU LING 吳令 , t. Hsin-chih 信之 , h. Hsüan-yüan 宣遠 .
From Suchou; active at the end of the Ming period; flowers, birds. (CP,
VII, AL, 268.)

Pine-tree, flowers and birds, signed, dated 1649, Nat. Pal. Mus.,
    Taipei, (AL). CKLTMHC, V. 2.

WU PIN 吴 彬 , t. Wen-chung 文 中 , h. Chih-hsien 質先 .
From P'u-t'ien, Fukien, active c. 1568-1621, lived in Nanking; landscapes,
figures. (CP, VII, AL, 269.)

> Emperor Ming-huang travelling to Szechuan, signed, dated 1603, Tien-
> tsin Art Museum. I-yüan chi-chin, 16; T'ien-ching, II. 52.
> Sharp mountain-peaks and deep gullies, forming a tall landscape, sign-
> ed, dated 1609, Nat. Pal. Mus. , Taipei, (AL). CKLTMHC, IV. 97.
> Buddhist figures, signed, Nat. Pal. Mus. , Taipei, (AL). Li-tai
> jen-wu, 56.
> Two birds on a branch of a blossoming apricot-tree, signed, Nat.
> Pal. Mus. , Taipei, (AL). CKLTMHC, IV. 99.
> Pavilions in fantastic mountains, inscribed, signed, Nat. Pal. Mus. ,
> Taipei. CKLTMHC, IV. 98.
> A stream under lofty peaks, signed, Chang Pe-chin collection. Tien
> Yin Tang, I. 48.
> Snow-capped cliffs, a man crossing a bridge, attributed, Chang Pe-
> chin collection. Tien Yin Tang, I. 49.

WU WEI 吴 偉 , t. Shih-ying 士 英 , h. Lu-fu 魯 夫 . Later
t. Tz'u-weng 次 翁 , h. Hsiao-hsien 小 仙 . B. 1459, d. 1508;
from Chiang-hsia, Hupei; figure-painter, founder of the Chiang-hsia school.
(CP, VII, AL, 269-270.)

> The Iron Flute. A gentleman seated at a stone desk, a servant with a
> flute, two ladies at right, handscroll, signed, dated 1484. CK
> ku-tai, 77 (section); TSYMC hua-hsüan, 40.
> An Immortal with a fungus, signed, Nat. Pal. Mus. , Taipei, (AL).
> CKLTMHC, IV. 36.
> An angler under a pine branch, folding fan, signed, Huang Pao-hsi
> collection, (AL). Lo-tsai hsüan, I. 3*.
> The Fairy Ma-ku, signed, Chang Ta-ch'ien collection, (AL). Li-
> tai jen-wu, 45.
> Fishing boats on the river, signed, Palace Museum, Peking. WW,
> 1966. 4. 41.
> Man and servant with ch'in beneath bare willow, signed, Tientsin Art
> Museum. I-yüan chi-chin, 9; T'ien-ching, I. 10.
> Two gentlemen seated under pine trees by a riverbank, handscroll,
> signed, Tientsin Art Museum. T'ien-ching, II. 12.
> Two gentlemen and servant on a terrace under banana plants, trees,
> rock, signed, Chang Pe-chin collection. Tien Yin Tang, I. 16.
> A man leaning on a pine tree in the wind, signed, Ch'in Chung-wen
> collection. CK hua, XI. 14.
> Seeking plum blossoms in the snow, signed, Li Chih-ch'ao collection.
> CK hua, I. 22.

Music and wine among fishermen and woodgatherers, handscroll, inscribed, signed. CK hua, VIII. 10-11.
Li T'ieh-kuai and another Immortal, signed. TSYMC hua-hsüan, 41.

YANG PU 楊補 , t. Wu-pu 無補 , Po-pu 白補 , h.
Ku-nung 古農 . B. 1598, d. 1657; from Ch'ing-chiang, Kiangsi;
lived in Suchou; after 1644 retired to the Teng-wei Mountain; poet; landscapes. (CP, VII, AL, 271.)
    Mountain landscape with tall trees, signed, dated 1648, in Yüan style,
        Nat. Pal. Mus., Taipei, (AL). CKLTMHC, IV. 155.

YANG TA-LIN 楊大臨 , t. Chih-ch'ing 治卿 or Yü-ch'un
    宇春 . From Yin-hsien, Chekiang; active c. 1550-1620; flowers,
birds, especially hawks. (O. 6; M. p. 584.)
    Hawks and autumn tree over rapids, signed, dated 1607, Palace Mu-
        seum, Peking. KKWPY hua-niao, 57*.
    Nine magpies and a tree by a stream, signed, dated 1617, Ch'in Chung-
        wen collection. CK hua, I. 25*.

YANG WEN-TS'UNG 楊文驄 , t. Lung-yu 龍友 . B. 1597,
d. 1645; from Kueichou, lived in Nanking; governor of Nanking, killed by
the Manchus; scholar, calligrapher, one of the "Nine Friends in Painting";
landscapes, orchids, bamboo. (CP, VII, AL, 271.)
    Bamboos and epidendrum, signed, dated 1638, Nat. Pal. Mus., Tai-
        pei, (AL). CKLTMHC, IV. 151.
    Scholar in a thatched villa in the mountains, signed, dated 1640, Cheng
        Te-k'un collection, Cambridge. Mu-fei, opposite p. 22.
    Pavilion on rock under trees, signed, dated 1646, Chang Pe-chin col-
        lection. Tien Yin Tang, I. 67.
    Orchids over a pool, signed, Huang Pao-hsi collection, Hong Kong.
        Lo-tsai hsüan, I. 12*.

YAO KUANG-HSIAO 姚廣孝 . Originally named T'ien-hsi
    天禧 , became a monk during the Chih-cheng era and took the
names Tao-yen 道衍 , T'ao-hsü lao-jen 逃虛老人 , Lan-
ko-weng 懶閣翁 , Tu-an lao-jen 獨庵老人 ; became
a layman again and took the name Kuang-hsiao, t. Ssu-tao 斯道 .
B. 1335, d. 1419; from Suchou; poet; painted ink bamboo. (I. 55; M. p. 287.)
    Ink bamboo, inscribed, signed, dated 1409, S. M. Siu collection, Hong
        Kong. CK ku-hua, B. 148.

YAO SHOU 姚綬 , t. Kung-shou 公綬 , h. Ku-an 穀菴 ,
Yün-tung i-shih 雲東逸史 and other names. B. 1423, d. 1495;

from Chia-shan, Chekiang; poet, calligrapher, landscapes, bamboo, birds, stones. (CP, VII, AL, 272.)

Red bamboo, inscribed, signed, dated 1474, S. M. Siu collection, Hong Kong. CK ku-hua, B. 163.

A fisherman on the river in autumn, poem, dated 1476, Palace Museum, Peking. Che-chiang, 49.

A mynah bird on a dry branch, poem, signed, Nat. Pal. Mus., Taipei, (AL). 300 M., 213; CH mei-shu, III; CKLTMHC, IV. 20.

Bamboos and a tree with a spring bird flying on their top, poem, signed, Nat. Pal. Mus., Taipei, (AL). CKLTMHC, IV. 21.

Boating on the river, a flock of flying cranes, signed, Shanghai Museum. CK shu-hua, I. 24; Shang-hai, 42*.

A man in a boat moored by a willow bank, poem, inscribed, signed, Chang Pe-chin collection. Tien Yin Tang, I. 14.

A scholar in a boat looking at a waterfall, inscribed, signed, Huang Pao-hsi collection, Hong Kong. Lo-tsai hsüan, I. 1*.

Bamboo and rock, inscribed, signed, S. M. Siu collection, Hong Kong. CK ku-hua, B. 164.

YEH KUANG 葉廣 . From Ch'ao-hsien, Anhui; 16th century; landscapes. (CP, VII, AL, 273.)

A fisherman by the river, signed, Nat. Pal. Mus., Taipei, (AL). CKLTMHC, IV. 110.

YEN LING 嚴令 . Unidentified.

Fisherman in a boat pulled up at a bank, a gentleman seated on the bank, album leaf, part of the album made for Erh-hsiao, signed, dated 1598, Liao-ning Provincial Museum. Liao-ning, II. 74.

YU CH'IU 尤求 , t. Tzu-ch'iu 子求 , h. Feng-ch'iu 鳳丘 . From Suchou; lived in T'ai-ts'ang, Kiangsu; active c. 1570-1590; followed Ch'iu Ying; figures. (CP, VII, AL, 274.)

The Elegant Gathering in the Western Garden, signed, dated 1573, Tientsin Art Museum. T'ien-ching, II. 44.

Landscape with figures, signed, Nat. Pal. Mus., Taipei, (AL). CKLTMHC, IV. 94.

Six figures in a landscape, signed, Tientsin Art Museum. T'ien-ching, I. 30.

YÜ SHUN-CH'EN 俞舜臣 , t. Yeh-fu 冶甫 h. Hai-feng-tzu 海峯子 . From Ch'ien-t'ang, Chekiang; painted landscapes, birds and flowers. (I. 56; O. 1; M. p. 282.)

Hundred flowers, handscroll, inscribed, signed, dated jen-shen, 1572 (?). Che-chiang, 56.

YÜAN SHANG-T'UNG 袁尚統 , t. Shu-ming 叔明 . B. 1570,
d. 1661 (?); from Suchou; landscapes, figures. (CP, VII, AL, 274-275.)
 In a boat looking at the crows, signed, dated 1636, Nat. Pal. Mus.,
  Taipei, (AL). CKLTMHC, IV. 135.
 Storm on the Tung-t'ing Lake, signed, dated 1652, Chu Yung-k'uei
  collection. CK hua, II. 11.
 Two crows, signed, dated 1654, Nat. Pal. Mus., Taipei, (AL).
  CKLTMHC, IV. 136.

YÜN HSIANG 惲 向 , original name Tao-sheng 道生 , t. Pen-
ch'u 本初 , h. Hsiang-shan weng 香山翁 . B. 1586, d. 1655;
from Wu-chin, Kiangsu; landscapes. (CP, VII, AL, 275.)
 Landscape after Ni Tsan, signed, dated 1654, Nat. Pal. Mus., Tai-
  pei, (AL). CKLTMHC, IV. 154.
 Landscape with lakeside buildings, album leaf, inscribed, signed,
  Nat. Pal. Mus., Taipei, (AL). CH mei-shu, III.
 Landscape after Tung Yüan, inscribed, signed, Tientsin Art Museum.
  T'ien-ching, II. 83.

Anonymous paintings of the Ming Period

Taoist and Buddhist

Figures of Immortals, handscroll. CK hua, V. 16.

Figure Compositions and Portraits

Imperial procession, handscroll, Nat. Pal. Mus., Taipei. CCAT,
 pl. 131 (section).
Scholar and servants, album leaf, Nat. Pal. Mus., Taipei. NPM
 Bulletin, I. 5, p. 9.
The Nine Ancients of Hsiang-shan, Nat. Pal. Mus., Taipei. CKLTMHC,
 IV. 161 (as The Elegant Gathering in the Western Garden).
Portrait of Shen Chou, two inscriptions by Shen Chou dated 1506 and
 1507, Palace Museum, Peking. CK hua, XVIII. 17 (as anon. Ming);
 PM, 25* (as Shen Chou).
The Loyang Septuagenarian Society, handscroll, Liao-ning Provincial
 Museum. Liao-ning, II. 58-61.
A girl with a p'i-p'a, Liao-ning Provincial Museum. Liao-ning, II. 63.
Eighteen Songs for a Foreign Flute, Lady Wen-chi's return to China,
 Nanking Museum. Hu-chia shih-pa po*; WW, 1959. 5. 1* (section
 14).

Pupil and tutor studying in the presence of an aged man, all in a land-
scape, Tientsin Art Museum. T'ien-ching, I. 45.
Wang Hsi-chih writing on a fan. CK hua, VI. 16.
Playing chess in a pavilion built over a stream. Li-tai jen-wu, 59.
Three men relaxing on a grassy bank. Li-tai jen-wu, 60.

Landscapes

A thatched hut in a mountain valley, Nat. Pal. Mus., Taipei. CKLTMHC,
IV. 159.
The Yellow Millet Dream. CK hua, IX. 16.
Copy of Kuo Chung-shu's Wang-ch'uan handscroll. WW, 1957. 7. 53
(section).

Animals

Eight horses and eight grooms in a pasture, Liao-ning Provincial Museum. Liao-ning, II. 62.
A large herd of horses bathing in a stream, handscroll, signed, Ch'en
Chü-chung, Liao-ning Provincial Museum. Liao-ning, II. 64-65
(as anon. Ming).

Flowers and Birds

Birds and ducks in trees by a river, Nat. Pal. Mus., Taipei. CKLTMHC,
IV. 160.
Two egrets and hibiscus, Palace Museum, Peking. KKPWY hua-
niao, 48*.
A pair of pheasants in a peony shrub, Tientsin Art Museum. I-yüan
chi-chin, 13.
Pheasants and other birds in snow, Li Chih-ch'ao collection. CK hua,
I. 26.

Painters of the Ch'ing Dynasty

Ai Ch'i-meng	艾 啟 蒙	
Cha Shih-piao	查 士 標	
Chan-ying	湛 營	
Chang Fang	張 昉	
Chang Feng	張 風	
Chang Hao	張 鎬	
Chang Hsia	張 洽	
Chang Hsiung	張 熊	
Chang Hsüeh-tseng	張 學 曾	
Chang Ju-chih	張 如 芝	
Chang Keng	張 庚	
Chang Mu	張 穆	
Chang P'ei-tun	張 培 敦	
Chang Shen	張 深	
Chang Sheng	章 聲	
Chang Ssu-hsiao	張 四 敎	
Chang T'ing-yen	張 廷 廖	
Chang Tsung-ts'ang	張 宗 蒼	
Chang Tz'u-ning	張 賜 寧	
Chang Wei-pang	張 為 邦	
Chang Yin	張 崟	
Chang Yü	張 敔	
Chao Chih-ch'en	趙 之 琛	
Chao Chih-ch'ien	趙 之 謙	
Chao E	趙 鶚	
Chao Ming-shan	招 銘 山	
Chao T'ing-pi	趙 廷 璧	

Ch'ao-k'uei	超 揆	
Chen-jan	真 然	
Ch'en Ch'iao-sen	陳 喬 森	
Ch'en Huai	陳 懷	
Ch'en Hung-shou	陳 鴻 壽	
Ch'en Kuang-hsiang	陳 廣 祥	
Ch'en P'u	陳 璞	
Ch'en Shih-chung	陳 士 忠	
Ch'en Shih-t'ang	陳 世 堂	
Ch'en T'ai-chan	陳 太 占	
Ch'en T'eng-kuei	陳 騰 桂	
Ch'en Tzu	陳 字	
Cheng Chi	鄭 績	
Cheng Hsieh	鄭 燮	
Cheng Min	鄭 旼	
Ch'eng Chang	程 璋	
Ch'eng Cheng-k'uei	程 正 揆	
Ch'eng I	程 義	
Ch'eng Ming	程 鳴	
Ch'eng Sui	程 邃	
Ch'i Chai-chia	祁 豸 佳	
Chiang Hung	姜 泓	
Chiang Lien	蔣 蓮	
Chiang P'u	蔣 溥	
Chiang Shih-chieh	姜 實 節	
Chiang T'ing-hsi	蔣 廷 錫	
Ch'ien Tu	錢 杜	

Ch'ien Wei-ch'eng	錢維城
Chin Chün-ming	金俊明
Chin Li-ying	金禮嬴
Chin Nung	金農
Chin T'ing-piao	金廷標
Chou Ch'üan	周荃
Chou Hao	周鎬
Chu Ch'ang	祝昌
Chu Ch'eng	朱偁
Chu Han-chih	朱翰之
Chu Lun-han	朱淪瀚
Chu Sheng	諸昇
Chu Ta	朱耷
Chü Ch'ao	居巢
Chü Ch'ing	居慶
Chü Lien	居廉
Ch'üeh Lan	闕嵐
Fa Jo-chen	法若真
Fan Ch'i	樊圻
Fan Yün	樊雲
Fang Hsün	方薰
Fang I-chih	方以智
Fang Shih-shu	方士庶
Fang Ta-yu	方大猷
Fei Tan-hsü	費丹旭
Fu Mei	傅眉
Fu Shan	傅山
Fu Wen	傅雯
Han Jung-kuang	韓榮光

Ho Ch'ing-t'ai	賀清泰
Ho Chung	何淙
Ho I	何頤
Hsi Kang	奚岡
Hsiao Ch'en	蕭晨
Hsiao Yün-ts'ung	蕭雲從
Hsieh Ch'eng	謝成
Hsieh Kuan-sheng	謝觀生
Hsieh Lan-sheng	謝蘭生
Hsieh Pin	謝彬
Hsieh P'u	謝樸
Hsieh Sui	謝遂
Hsieh Sun	謝蓀
Hsiung Ching-hsing	熊景星
Hsü Fang	徐枋
Hsü I	徐嶧
Hsü-ku	虛谷
Hsü Mei	徐玫
Hsü Pin	徐濱
Hsü T'ai	許泰
Hsü Yang	徐揚
Hsüeh Hsüan	薛宣
Hu Hsi-kuei	胡錫珪
Hu Yüan	胡遠
Hua Ling	華翎
Hua Yen	華嵒
Huang Hsiang-chien	黃向堅
Huang I	黃易
Huang Kuo-lan	黃國蘭

214

Romanization	Characters
Liang Heng	梁衡
Liang Lien	梁濂
Liang Yüan-chu	梁元柱
Lin Lan	林藍
Liu Yen-chung	劉彥沖
Liu Yin	柳隱
Liu Yü	柳遇
Lo An-hsien	羅先
Lo Mu	羅牧
Lo P'ing	羅聘
Lo Yang	羅陽
Lu Tao-huai	陸道淮
Lu Yin	陸音
Lu Yüan	陸遠
Lü Hsiang	呂翔
Lü Hsüeh	呂學
Lü Huan-ch'eng	呂煥成
Lü Ts'ai	呂材
Ma Shih-pan	馬師班
Ma Yüan-yü	馬元馭
Mao Chi-k'o	毛際可
Mao Ch'i-ling	毛奇齡
Mao Lin	毛麐
Mei Ch'ing	梅清
Mei Keng	梅庚
Ming-chung	明中
Ni Jen-chi	倪仁吉
Niu Shih-hui	牛石慧
P'an Kung-shou	潘恭壽

Romanization	Characters
Pao Chün	鮑楷
P'eng Jui-hsüan	彭睿瓘
Pien Shou-min	邊壽民
Pien Wen-yü	卞文瑜
P'u-ho	普荷
P'u Hua	蒲華
Sha Fu	沙馥
Shang-jui	上睿
Shang-kuan Ch'ing	上官清
Shen Ch'üan	沈銓
Shen Hao	沈顥
Shen Shih-chieh	沈士傑
Shen Tsung-ch'ien	沈宗騫
Shen Yüan	沈源
Sheng Tan	盛丹
Shu Ku-ch'ing	舒卿
Ssu-ma Chung	司馬鍾
Su Ch'ang-ch'un	蘇長春
Su Liu-p'eng	蘇六朋
Sung Fu	宋賦
Tai Hsi	戴熙
Tai Pen-hsiao	戴本孝
Tan Chung-kuang	笪重光
T'ang I-fen	湯貽汾
T'ang Kuang	唐光
T'ang Tai	唐岱
Tao-chi	道濟
Teng Ju-ch'iung	鄧如瓊
Ting Kao	丁皋

Ting Kuan-p'eng	丁觀鵬
Ts'ai Chia	蔡嘉
Ts'ao Yüan	曹垣
Tsou Che	鄒喆
Tsou I-kuei	鄒一桂
Tsung-ch'in	宗致
T'u Cho	屠卓
Tung Pang-ta	董邦達
Wang Ch'en	王宸
Wang Chien	王鑑
Wang Hou-lai	汪後來
Wang Hui	王翬
Wang Li	王禮
Wang Shih-min	王時敏
Wang Shih-shen	汪士慎
Wang Shu-ku	王樹穀
Wang Tzu-yüan	王子元
Wang Wu	王武
Wang Wu-t'ien	王無忝
Wang Yü	王昱
Wang Yüan-ch'i	王原祁
Wang Yüan-ch'u	王原初
Wang Yün	王雲
Wei P'ao	魏艶
Wen Tien	文點
Wen Ting	文鼎
Wen Tou	文斗
Wu Chia-yu	吳嘉獻
Wu Chih	吳芷
Wu Hsü	吳旭
Wu Hsüeh-tsao	伍學藻
Wu Hung	吳宏
Wu Jui-lung	伍瑞隆
Wu Jung-kuang	吳榮光
Wu Ku-hsiang	吳穀祥
Wu Li	吳歷
Wu Po-hou	吳博厓
Wu Tan	吳丹
Wu Wei-yeh	吳偉業
Wu Ying-chen	吳應貞
Wu Yün	吳雲
Yang Chin	楊晉
Yao Wen-han	姚文瀚
Yeh Hsin	葉欣
Yeh Yü	葉雨
Yen Chan	嚴湛
Yen Lun	嚴倫
Yen Sheng-sun	嚴繩孫
Ying Pao	瑛寶
Yu Tso-chih	游作之
Yü Chih-ting	禹之鼎
Yü Hsing	余省
Yü Lien-chou	俞蓮洲
Yü Yüan	虞沅
Yüan Chiang	袁江
Yüan Hsüeh	袁雪
Yüan Teng-tao	袁登道
Yüan Yao	袁耀

Yün Hsi	允	禧
Yün Shou-p'ing	惲	壽 平
Yung Hsing	永	瑆

AI CH'I-MENG 艾啟蒙 , or Ignatius Sichelbart. B. 1708 in Bohemia, d. 1780; Jesuit missionary, arrived in China in 1745, served at the court with Lang Shih-ning. (CP, VII, AL, 282-283.)

> Eight horses, inscribed, signed, Nanking Museum. WW, 1959.2.47, 48 (3 horses).

CHA SHIH-PIAO 查士標 , t. Erh-chan 二瞻 , h. Mei-ho 梅壑. B. 1615, d. 1698; from Haiyang, Anhui; on of the "Four Masters of Anhui"; landscapes. (CP, VII, AL, 283-285.)

> Album of ten leaves: landscapes, last leaf signed, dated 1662, Chang Pe-chin collection. Tien Yin Tang, I. 72-81.
>
> Album of landscapes after Yüan masters, last leaf dated 1666, Liaoning Provincial Museum. Liao-ning, II. 86, 87 (two leaves).
>
> A man with a staff under a bare tree, mountain background, inscribed, signed, dated 1667. TSYMC hua-hsüan, 70.
>
> Bleak landscape, three trees, a pavilion on a promontory, folding fan, signed, dated 1678, Shanghai WWPKWYH. Shan-mien-hua, 64*.
>
> Wide mountain ranges rising over misty valleys beyond a river, handscroll, inscribed, signed, dated 1680, Cheng Te-k'un collection, Cambridge, (AL). Mu-fei, opposite p. 28.
>
> Yen-chiang tieh-chang. A misty landscape in Mi style, inscribed, signed, dated 1689, Suchou Museum. Su-chou, 43.
>
> Album of ten landscape-paintings after old masters, each leaf signed, some inscribed, done when 80 years old (1694), Cheng Te-k'un collection, Cambridge, (AL). Mu-fei, between pp. 30-31 (2 leaves).
>
> Two trees, bamboo and stone, inscribed, signed, Tientsin Art Museum. T'ien-ching, II. 90.

CHAN-YING 湛瑩 , h. Wei-shan 微山 , Wei-shan shan-jen 微山山人 , Wei-tao-jen 微道人 , Wei-shan 微册 . A monk of the Hai-yün Temple in Canton; active during the Tao-kuang era (1821-1850); landscapes. (W.I.11.)

> A path between pine trees in mist, inscribed, signed, dated 1853, after Huang Kung-wang. Kuang-tung hua-chia, 81*.

CHANG FANG 張昉 , t. Shu-chao 叔昭 . From Ch'ien-t'ang, Chekiang; late 17th century; flowers. (M. p. 474.)

    Bamboo, folding fan, signed, dated <u>keng-tzu,</u> Hui Hsiao-t'ung collec-
        tion. Shan-mien chi-chin, 22*.

CHANG FENG 張風 or 飆 , Ta-feng 大風 , h. Sheng-
chou tao-shih 昇州道士 . From Nanking, active c. 1645-1674;
after 1644 devoted himself to Buddhism; landscapes, figures, flowers.
(CP, VII, AL, 286-287.)

    Chu-ko Liang, signed, dated 1654, Nat. Pal. Mus., Taipei, (AL).
        300 M., 253; CKLTMHC, V.4.
    T'ao Yüan-ming smelling a chrysanthemum-flower, poem, signed,
        dated 1660, Chang Ta-ch'ien collection, (AL). Li-tai jen-wu, 53.
    A man standing on a ledge looking at a waterfall, inscribed, signed,
        dated 1660, Shanghai Museum. Shang-hai, 73*.
    A man standing under trees, looking at a waterfall, signed, (AL).
        TSYMC hua-hsüan, 65.
    Portrait of Ku Yü-chih (Ku Meng-yu, 1599-1660), landscape by Chang,
        figure by Tseng Ch'ing. Li-tai jen-wu, 54.

CHANG HAO 張鎬 , t. Wu-ch'ien 武遷 , h. Ch'ing-shan 卿山
From Ch'ien-t'ang, Chekiang; court painter in the Ch'ien-lung period
(1736-1795); figures. (CP, VII, AL, 287.)

    New Year's Day in the palace, done with Yao Wen-han and Chang
        Tsung-ts'ang, Nat. Pal. Mus., Taipei (?). CKLTMHC, V. 64, 65.

CHANG HSIA 張洽 , t. Yüeh-ch'uan 月川 and Yü-ch'uan 玉川 ,
h. Ch'ing-jo ku-yü 青弱古漁 and other names. B. 1718, d.
1799; from Suchou, nephew of Chang Tsung-ts'ang, landscapes. (CP, VII,
AL, 287.)

    A pine tree over rapids, album leaf, signed, dated 1792, fourth leaf
        in a 12 leaf album of miscellaneous subjects, Liao-ning Provin-
        cial Museum. Liao-ning, II. 118.

CHANG HSIUNG 張熊 , t. Shou-fu 壽甫 , h. Tzu-hsiang 子祥
Yüan-hu wai-shih 鴛湖外史 and other names. B. 1803, d. 1886;
from Hsiu-shui, Chekiang; followed Chou Chih-mien and Wang Wu; flowers,
birds, landscapes, figures. (CP, VII, AL, 288.)

    Bird and flowers in autumn, signed, Palace Museum, Peking. CK
        chin-pai-nien, 28.

CHANG HSÜEH-TSENG 張學曾 , t. Erh-wei 爾唯 , h. Yo-
an 約菴 . From Shan-yin, Chekiang; active c. 1630-1650; governor

of Suchou; one of the "Nine Friends in Painting"; landscapes. (CP, VII, AL, 288.)

> A pavilion under a pine on a bank, folding fan, signed, dated 1634, Shanghai WWPKWYH. Shan-mien-hua, 59*.

CHANG JU-CHIH 張 如 之 , t. Mo-ti 墨 地 and Mo-ch'ih 墨 池 or 黙 遲 , h. Mo-tao-jen 黙 道 人 . D. 1824; from Shun-te, Kuangtung; chü-jen in 1788; landscapes after Wang Hui and early Ch'ing masters. (T.I.18; W.I.4; M. p. 487.)

> Flying snow in the mountains, inscribed, signed, dated 1807, Ch'en Fan collection. Kuang-tung shu-hua, 43.
> Landscape, inscribed, signed. Kuang-tung hua-chia, 57*.

CHANG KENG 張 庚 , original name Chang T'ao 張 燾 , t. P'u-shan 浦 山 , h. Mi-chia 彌 伽 , Kua-t'ien i-shih 瓜 田 逸 史 , Po-ch'ü-ts'un-sang-che 白 苧 村 桑 者 . B. 1685, d. 1760; from Hsiu-shui, Chekiang; author of Kuo-ch'ao hua-cheng lu and P'u-shan lun-hua, and other books; landscapes; pupil of Ch'en Shu. (CP, VII, AL, 289.)

> Summer mountains, after Tung Yüan, inscribed, signed, dated 1757, Suchou Museum. Su-chou, 85.

CHANG MU 張 穆 , t. Mu-chih 穆 之 , h. T'ieh-ch'iao 鐵 橋 B. 1607, d. after 1687; from Tung-k'uan, Kuangtung; horses, eagles, landscapes, orchids, bamboo. (CP, VII, AL, 289-290.)

> A piebald horse tethered to a tree, signed, dated 1672, Liang Pai-ju collection. Kuang-tung shu-hua, 16.
> A bird on a bare branch, signed, dated 1680, Palace Museum, Peking. KKPWY hua-niao, 67*; Kuang-tung hua-chia, 18*.
> A horse resting under a leafless tree, signed. Kuang-tung hua-chia, 17*.

CHANG P'EI-TUN 張 培 敦 , t. Yen-ch'iao 硯 樵 , h. Yen-shih shan-jen 硯 石 山 人 . B. 1772, d. after 1842; from Suchou; pupil of Chai Ta-k'un; calligrapher, landscapes, portraits. (CP, VII, AL, 290.)

> Copy of a landscape by Wen Cheng-ming, inscribed, signed, dated 1819, Suchou Museum. Su-chou, 105.
> Copy of Wen Cheng-ming's Spring in Chiang-nan, handscroll, signed, dated 1825, Suchou Museum. Su-chou, 106-107.
> Landscape, handscroll, inscribed, signed, dated 1842, Suchou Museum. Su-chou, 108.
> Landscape with a flock of birds, handscroll, inscribed, signed, dated 1842, Suchou Museum. Su-chou, 109.

CHANG SHEN 張深 , t. Shu-yüan 叔淵 , h. Ch'a-nung 茶農 ,
Lang-k'o 浪客 , Hui-tso hsüeh-jen 悔作學人 , T'ui-t'ing
chü-shih 退聽居人 . B. 1781, d. 1843; from Chen-chiang, Kiangsu; son of Chang Yin; flowers and birds, landscapes. (T.I.16; U.III.2;
M. p. 486.)

> Lin-t'un hsin-chü t'u. A garden in Suchou, handscroll, signed, Su-
> chou Museum. Su-chou, 102-103.

CHANG SHENG 章聲 , t. Tzu-hao 子鶴 . From Hangchou; sec-
ond son of Chang Ku; active c. 1690; landscapes, flowers. (CP, VII, AL,
291.)

> Three men on a river bank under slanting pine tree, album leaf, sign-
> ed, dated 1671, Tientsin Art Museum. I-yüan chi-chin, 41.
> Landscape, after Li T'ang, signed. Che-chiang, 76.

CHANG SSU-HSIAO 張四教 , t. Hsüan-ch'uan 宣傳 , h. Shih-
min 石民 . From Chiang-tu, Kiangsu, moved to Yangchou; mid-
18th century; collector, calligrapher; painted figures, flowers. (M. p. 485.)

> Portrait of Hua Yen, inscribed, signed, dated 1767, Tientsin Art Mu-
> seum. T'ien-ching, I.86.

CHANG T'ING-YEN 張廷彥 . Court-painter in the Ch'ien-lung
period (1735-1795); figures, palaces. (CP, VII, AL, 291.)

> The Mid-autumn Festival: Palace view with figures, signed, Nat. Pal.
> Mus., Taipei, (AL). CKLTMHC, V.73.

CHANG TSUNG-TS'ANG 張宗蒼 , t. Mo-ts'un 默存 or Mo-
ts'en 墨岑 , h. Huang-ts'un 篁村 , Lu-shan 鹿山 , and
other names. B. 1686, d. 1756; from Suchou; pupil of Huang Ting; served
in the palace between 1751 and 1755; landscapes. (CP, VII, AL, 292-293.)

> Cloudy peaks and rushing streams, signed, Nat. Pal. Mus., Taipei,
> (AL). CKLTMHC, V.63.
> New Year's Day in the palace, done with Yao Wen-han and Chang Hao,
> Nat. Pal. Mus., Taipei (?). CKLTMHC, V.64, 65.

CHANG TZ'U-NING 張賜甯 , t. K'un-i 坤一 , h. Kuei-yen
桂巖 . B. 1743, d. after 1817; from Ts'ang-chou, Hopei; flowers, birds, figures, landscapes. (CP, VII, AL, 293.)

> Boys herding oxen under plum blossoms, folding fan, signed, Shang-
> hai WWPKWYH. Shan-mien-hua, 98*.

CHANG WEI-PANG 張為邦 . Court artist during the Ch'ien-lung
period (1736-1795); figures, birds, animals. (S.1; M. p. 480.)

Court scene, admiring lotus, Nat. Pal. Mus., Taipei. CKLTMHC,
V. 69.

CHANG YIN 張崟 , t. Pao-yen 寶巖 , h. Hsi-an 夕庵 ,
Ch'ieh-weng 且翁 and other names. B. 1761, d. 1829; from Tan-
t'u, Kiangsu; landscapes, flowers, bamboo, Buddhist figures. (CP, VII,
AL, 294.)

 Riverside homestead, handscroll, inscribed, signed, dated 1821,
  after Li T'ang, Tientsin Art Museum. T'ien-ching, II. 140-141.
 Lin-t'un hsin-chü t'u. A Suchou garden, handscroll, inscribed, signed, dated 1825, Suchou Museum. Su-chou, 98-101.

CHANG YÜ 章欸 , t. Chih-yüan 芷園 , h. Hsüeh-hung 雪鴻
and other names. B. 1734, d. 1803; from Nanking; flowers, birds, insects, landscapes, figures. (CP, VII, AL, 294.)

 Dragonfly and hibiscus, folding fan, signed, dated 1792, Shanghai
  WWPKWYH. Shan-mien-hua, 97*.

CHAO CHIH-CH'EN 趙之琛 , t. Tz'u-hsien 次閒 . B. 1781,
d. 1860; from Ch'ien-t'ang, Chekiang; landscapes, flowers, birds. (CP,
VII, AL, 295.)

 Outline bamboo and rock, signed, dated 1843. Che-chiang, 92.

CHAO CHIH-CH'IEN 趙之謙 , t. I-fu 益甫 and Hui-shu
撝叔 , h. Pei-an 悲盦 . B. 1829, d. 1884; from K'uai-
chi, Chekiang; poet, writer, calligrapher, seal engraver; flowers. (CP,
VII, AL, 295.)

 Hibiscus and banana plant, signed, dated 1866. TSYMC hua-hsüan,
  106.
 Blossoming plum branch, handscroll, signed, dated 1867. Che-
  chiang, 98.
 Branches of fruiting peach tree, signed, Palace Museum, Peking.
  CK ku-tai, 100; KKPWY hua-niao, 97*.
 Flowers, two album leaves, inscribed, signed, Palace Museum, Pe-
  king. PM, 48*, 49*.
 Old cypress and fungus, inscribed, signed, Palace Museum, Peking,
  (AL, Nanga Taisei, V. 53). CK chin-pai-nien, 5.
 Stalk of lotus, inscribed, signed, Shanghai Artists Association, (AL,
  Nanga Taisei, V. 188). CK chin-pai-nien, 1*.
 "Pile of Books" Cliff, inscribed, signed, Shanghai Museum. Shang-
  hai, 93*.
 Cassia tree, artist's seal, Shanghai Artists Association. CK chin-
  pai-nien, 3.

Flowering vine on a rock, inscribed, signed, Shanghai Artists Association. CK chin-pai-nien, 4.
Hanging hibiscus and plum branch, signed, Kuo Wei-ch'ü collection. CK hua, I. 37; CC-c hua-chi*.
Four stalks of white lotus. CC-c hua-chi*.
Wisteria and lilies by a rock, signed. CC-c hua-chi*.
Banana plant and flowers by a rock, inscribed, signed. CC-c hua-chi*.
Chrysanthemums, cassia and red leaves, signed. CC-c hua-chi*.
Hibiscus, signed. CC-c hua-chi*.
Peonies by a rock, inscribed, signed. CC-c hua-chi*.
Peach blossoms, willow and rock, signed. CC-c hua-chi*.

CHAO E 趙鶚 . Unidentified.
A pavilion on a river bank, album leaf, inscribed, signed, done for Erh-hsiao, Liao-ning Provincial Museum. Liao-ning, II. 78.

CHAO MING-SHAN 拓銘山 , t. Tzu-yung 子庸 . B. 1793, d. 1846; from Kuangtung. (CP, VII, AL, 296.)
Crabs and reeds, signed, dated 1831. Kuang-tung hua-chia, 53*.
Stalks of bamboo, signed. Kuang-tung hua-chia, 54*.

CHAO T'ING-PI 趙廷璧 or 壁 , t. Kung-shou 公售 , Feng-shih 鳳石 and Yün-ch'eng 連城 . From Hua-t'ing, Kiangsu; 17th century; landscapes, figures. (R. 2; M. p. 617.)
A kingfisher on a branch, signed. Kuang-tung hua-chia, 32*.

CH'AO-K'UEI 超揆 . Priest name of Wen Kuo 文果 , t. Lun-an 輪菴 . From Suchou; b. c. 1620, d. c. 1700; descendant of Wen Cheng-ming, entered the priesthood c. 1680, later served in the palace; landscapes. (CP, VII, AL, 296.)
River landscape with a man on his way to a friend, handscroll, poem, signed, Nat. Pal. Mus., Taipei, (AL). CKLTMHC, V. 5.

CHEN-JAN 真然 , h. Lien-ch'i 蓮溪 , Yeh-hang 野航 , Huang-shan ch'iao-tzu 黃山樵子 . B. 1816, d. 1884; a monk, from Yangchou, painted epidendrum and bamboo, figures, especially ladies. (M. p. 306.)
A lady at a round window, signed, dated 1862, after Hua Yen, Su-chou Museum. Su-chou, 117.

CH'EN CH'IAO-SEN 陳喬森 , t. Mu-kung 木公 and I-shan 一山 . B. 1834, d. 1905; from Sui-ch'i, Kuangtung; landscapes after Tao-chi. (W. I. 9.)

Scholars relaxing in a river pavilion, inscribed, signed, possibly
dated, Ch'en Fan collection. Kuang-tung shu-hua, 47.

CH'EN HUAI 陳 懷 , t. Shih-ch'iao 石 樵 . From Shun-te,
Kuangtung; active during the Ch'ien-lung period (1736-1795); landscapes.
(W.I.4.)
Carrying a ch'in and visiting friends, inscribed, signed, dated 1754.
Kuang-tung hua-chia, 38*.

CH'EN HUNG-SHOU 陳鴻壽 , t. Tzu-kung 子恭 , h. Man-sheng
曼生 and other names. B. 1768, d. 1822, from Hangchou, painted
landscapes, flowers and bamboo. (CP, VII, AL, 297.)
Two men in a grotto, inscribed, signed. Che-chiang, 90.

CH'EN KUANG-HSIANG 陳廣祥 . Unrecorded. According to the
Kuang-tung hua-chia, t. Yün-shan 雲山 ; painted flowers.
Mynah on a catalpa tree, signed, dated 1849. Kuang-tung hua-chia,
76*.

CH'EN P'U 陳璞 , t. Tzu-yü 子瑜 , h. Ku-ch'iao 古樵 ,
Ch'ih-kang kuei-ch'iao 尺岡歸樵 . B. 1820, d. 1887; from
Canton; chü-jen in 1844; painted landscapes. (W.I.8; M. p. 452.)
Cottages under trees along a mountain stream, inscribed, signed,
Li Tsu-yu collection. Kuang-tung shu-hua, 39.

CH'EN SHIH-CHUNG 陳士忠 , t. Ping-heng 秉衡 . From
Nan-hai, Kuangtung; active c. 1640; poet; painted epidendrum and bamboo.
(W.I.2.)
Epidendrum and rock, album leaf, artist's seals. Kuang-tung hua-
chia, 16*.

CH'EN SHIH-T'ANG 陳世堂 , t. Ming-chü 明舉 . From
Fan-yü, Kuangtung, active during the K'ang-hsi period (1662-1722); mu-
sician; painted landscapes. (W.I.3.)
Pavilions in the mountains, signed, dated 1716, in the style of Wu
Chen. Kuang-tung hua-chia, 33*.

CH'EN T'AI-CHAN 陳太占 , t. Hua-nung 花農 . From Chiang-
ning, Kiangsu; painted flowers, pines and landscapes. (M. p. 441.)
Orchids and stones, handscroll, poem, signed, Cheng Te-k'un collection, Cambridge. Mu-fei, opposite p. 68.

CH'EN T'ENG-KUEI 陳騰桂 . Unidentified.

Two album leaves after old masters (album consists of four leaves
by Ch'en and four by Wang Wu-t'ien; one of Ch'en's leaves is
dated 1664), Liao-ning Provincial Museum. Liao-ning, II. 84
(after Huang Kung-wang); 85 (after Chan Tzu-ch'ien).

CH'EN TZU 陳 宇 , t. Wu-ming 無 名 , h. Hsiao-lien ⼁蓮 .
Son of Ch'en Hung-shou, active in the early Ch'ing period; figures, flowers
and birds. (CP, VII, AL, 300.)
Three religious founders, signed, Tientsin Art Museum. T'ien-ching,
I. 52.

CHENG CHI 鄭 績 , t. Chi-ch'ang 紀 常 . From Hsin-hui,
Kuangtung, active during the Tao-kuang era (1821-1850); figures, landscapes. (W. I. 10.)
Tipsy fisherman on a wintry river, inscribed, signed. Kuang-tung
hua-chia, 73*.
River view in rain and wind, album leaf, inscribed, signed. Kuang-
tung hua-chia, 74*.

CHENG HSIEH 鄭 燮 , t. K'o-jou 克柔 , h. Pan-ch'iao 板橋 .
B. 1693, d. 1765; from Yangchou, Kiangsu; poet, calligrapher, painted
orchids and bamboo. (CP, VII, AL, 300-301.)
Bamboo and stone, inscribed, signed, dated 1756, Tientsin Art Museum. T'ien-ching, II. 136.
Epidendrum, bamboo and stone, inscribed, signed, dated 1758, Tientsin Art Museum. I-yüan chi-chin, 50.
Flowers, a four-panel screen, each panel inscribed and signed, one
done at age of 70 (1762), Nanking Museum. Yang-chou pa-chia,
19 (Epidendrum and bamboo; chrysanthemums); 21 (Pine and rocks;
rocks); WW, 1960. 7. 44 (Chrysanthemums; pine and rocks).
Bamboo and epidendrum, inscribed, signed, dated 1763. TSYMC
hua-hsüan, 98.
Plum blossoms and bamboo, inscribed, signed, Palace Museum, Peking. KKPWY hua-niao, 91*.
Epidendrum by a rock, poem, signed, Liao-ning Provincial Museum.
Liao-ning, II. 116.
Epidendrum, stones and bamboo, handscroll, inscribed, signed, Nanking Museum. Yang-chou pa-chia, 13-17.
Bamboo and rock, inscribed, signed, Shanghai Museum. Shang-hai,
85*.
Bamboo and epidendrum, inscribed, signed, Chinese Artists Asso-
ciation. CK hua, XIV. 17.
Epidendrum and bamboo along the edge of a sharp rock, inscribed
and signed. CK ku-tai, 99.

Bamboo, inscribed, signed. WW, 1960.7.43.
Orchids, inscribed, signed. WW, 1960.7.46.
Chrysanthemums and stone, inscribed, signed. WW, 1964.3.21.
Bamboo, signed. WW, 1964.3.21.

CHENG MIN 鄭旼 , t. Mu-ch'ien 慕倩 . B. 1607, d. after
1682; from Hsieh-hsien, Anhui; landscapes. (CP, VII, AL, 301.)
    Pavilion on a rocky shore and sparse pines, folding fan, signed, dated
        1681, Shanghai WWPKWYH. Shan-mien-hua, 63*.

CH'ENG CHANG 程璋 , t. Ta-jen 達人 . From Chiang-ning,
Kiangsu; painted landscapes, figures, birds and flowers. (M. p. 537.)
    Fish under a flowering plant and a rock, inscribed, signed, Palace
        Museum, Peking. CK chin-pai-nien, 52.

CH'ENG CHENG-K'UEI 程正揆 , original name 正葵 , t.
Tuan-po 端伯 , Chü-ling 鞠陵 and Ch'ing-ch'i tao-jen 青溪
道人 . From Hsiao-kan, Hupei; lived in Nanking, chin-shih
in 1631; became a high official in the Ch'ing dynasty, retired in 1657;
calligrapher, poet; landscapes. (CP, VII, AL, 301-302.)
    Landscape with bare trees and a lakeside pavilion, album leaf, artist's
        seal, Nat. Pal. Mus., Taipei, (AL). CH mei-shu, III.

CH'ENG I 程義 , t. Cheng-lu 正路 , h. Ching-yang-tzu 晶陽子.
From Hsi-hsien, Anhui. (M. p. 536.)
    The Lien Pavilion, inscribed, signed. WW, 1963.6, pl. 3, no. 3.

CH'ENG MING 程鳴 , t. Yu-sheng 友聲 , h. Sung-men 松門.
From Hsieh-hsien, Anhui; active at the beginning of the Ch'ien-
lung period, followed Tao-chi. (CP, VII, AL, 302.)
    A gentleman in a pavilion listening to a lady playing the flute, inscri-
        bed, signed, Tientsin Art Museum. T'ien-ching, I.80.

CH'ENG SUI 程邃 , t. Mu-ch'ien 穆倩 , h. Chiang-tung pu-i
江東布衣 and Kou tao-jen 垢道人 . B. 1605, d. 1691;
from Hsieh-hsien, Anhui; lived in Yangchou; landscapes. (CP, VII, AL,
302-303.)
    A pavilion overlooking a river with sailboats, poem, signed, dated
        1661, Cheng Te-k'un collection, Cambridge. Mu-fei, opposite
        p. 42.
    Buildings and trees along a river, high mountains, poem, signed,
        dated 1673. TSYMC hua-hsüan, 71.
    Landscape after Wang Shih-min, inscribed, signed, Suchou Museum.
        Su-chou, 40.

CH'I CHAI-CHIA 祁豸佳 , t. Chih-hsiang 止祥 , h. Hsüeh-p'iao 雪瓢 . From Shan-yin, Chekiang; chü-jen in 1627; served as an official but retired after 1644, still active in 1682; poet, calligrapher; landscapes. (CP, VII, AL, 304.)

> A man with a staff standing on a bridge looking at a waterfall, signed, dated 1653. Che-chiang, 62.

CHIANG HUNG 姜泓 , t. Tsai-mei 在湄 . From Hangchou; painted flowers. (M. p. 274.)

> Bees and blossoming plants, album leaf, artist's seal, Palace Museum, Peking. KKPWY hua-niao, 70*.

CHIANG LIEN 蔣蓮 , t. Chün-hsien 君先 , h. Hsiang-hu 薌湖 or 香湖 . From Chung-shan, Kuangtung; active c. 1796-1850; figures, ladies, copied Ch'en Hung-shou. (W.I.6.)

> Lady seated leaning on a rock under banana and bamboo plants, inscribed, signed, dated 1834, Hsü Po-chiao collection. Kuangtung shu-hua, 38.
>
> Seated Bodhidharma leaning against a tree trunk, album leaf, inscribed, signed. Kuang-tung hua-chia, 49*.
>
> A gentleman seated on a banana leaf watching a lady and some servants wash clothes, album leaf, inscribed, signed. Kuang-tung hua-chia, 50*.

CHIANG P'U 蔣溥 , t. Chih-fu 質甫 , h. Heng-hsien 恒軒 . B. 1708, d. 1761; from Ch'ang-shu, Kiangsu; son of Chiang T'ing-hsi; flowers. (CP, VII, AL, 305-306.)

> Crickets, inscribed, signed, Nat. Pal. Mus., Taipei, (AL). CKLTMHC, V.53.

CHIANG SHIH-CHIEH 姜實節 , t. Hsüeh-tsai 學在 , h. Hao-chien 鶴澗 , Ssu-wei 思未 and other names. B. 1647, d. 1709; from Lai-yang, Shantung; lived in Suchou; landscapes. (CP, VII, AL, 306.)

> An album of six leaves depicting landscapes, each leaf with accompanying inscription, Cheng Te-k'un collection, Cambridge. Mu-fei, opposite p. 48 (two leaves).

CHIANG T'ING-HSI 蔣廷錫 , t. Yang-sun 揚孫 , h. Yu-chün 酉君 , Hsi-ku 西谷 , Nan-sha 南沙 . B. 1669, d. 1732; from Ch'ang-shu, Kiangsu; writer; painted flowers. (CP, VII, AL, 306-307.)

> Mallow blossom, poem, signed, dated 1709, S.M. Siu collection, Hong Kong. CK ku-hua, B.237.

Branch of apples, album leaf from a twelve leaf album, done in 1720, Suchou Museum. Su-chou, 76.

Birds and millets, inscribed, signed, dated 1723, Nat. Pal. Mus., Taipei, (AL). CKLTMHC, V. 45.

Bamboos, stones and narcissi, signed, dated 1725, after a Yüan master, Nat. Pal. Mus., Taipei, (AL). CKLTMHC, V. 46.

Plum blossoms and narcissi, album leaf, last of twelve leaves, signed, dated 1730, Liao-ning Provincial Museum. Liao-ning, II. 112.

Two butterflies on yellow flowers, folding fan, signed, Shanghai WWPKWYH. Shan-mien-hua, 87*.

Lotus and dragonflies, signed, Chang Pe-chin collection. Tien Yin Tang, I. 93.

Pigeons gathered around a pan of water, signed, Cheng Te-k'un collection, Cambridge. Mu-fei, before p. 51.

CH'IEN TU 錢杜 , original name Ch'ien Yü 錢榆 and t. Shu-mei 叔枚 ; later used the name Ch'ien Tu, t. Shu-mei 叔美 , h. Sung-hu 松壺 . B. 1763, d. 1844; from Ch'ien-t'ang, Chekiang; author of Sung-hu hua-i and other books on painting; painted landscapes and flowers. (CP, VII, AL, 309-310.)

Two scholars in a garden kiosk, inscribed, signed, dated 1838. Chechiang, 88.

CH'IEN WEI-CH'ENG 錢維城 , t. Tsung-p'an 宗盤 , h. Ch'a-shan 茶山 , Jen-an 級庵 , Chia-hsien 稼軒 . B. 1720, d. 1772; from Wu-chin, Kiangsu; court-painter; flowers, landscapes. (CP, VII, AL, 311.)

The Li-ts'ao Hall, album leaf (?), signed, Nat. Pal. Mus., Taipei (?). CKLTMHC, V. 66.

CHIN CHÜN-MING 金俊明 , original name Kun 袞 and t. Chiu-chang 九章 , later t. Hsiao-chang 孝章 , h. Keng-an 耿庵 , Pu-mei tao-jen 不寐道人 . B. 1602; d. 1675; from Suchou, led a hermit's life after 1644; landscapes, bamboo, plum-blossoms. (CP, VII, AL, 312.)

Ink plum blossoms, inscribed, signed, dated 1668, S. M. Siu collection, Hong Kong. CK ku-hua, B. 212.

CHIN LI-YING 金禮嬴 , t. Yün-men 雲門 , h. Wu-yün 五雲 , Chao-ming-ko nei-shih 昭明閣內史 . B. 1772, d. 1807; from Shan-yin, Chekiang, lived in Ch'ien-t'ang, wife of Wang T'an; landscapes, flowers, figures, plum blossoms, Buddhist figures. (CP, VII, AL, 312.)

Kuanyin and a playing child, inscribed, signed, dated 1803. Chechiang, 91.

CHIN NUNG 金農 , t. Shou-men 壽門 , h. Tung-hsin 冬心 ,
Ku-ch'üan 古泉 , Lao-ting 老丁 , Ssu-nung 司農 and other
names. B. 1687, d. after 1764; from Hangchou; lived in Yangchou, Kiangsu; bamboo, plum-blossoms, horses, Buddhist figures, landscapes. (CP,
VII, AL, 313-314.)

> The top of a blossoming plum tree, inscribed, signed, dated at the
> age of 70 (1756), after Wang Mien, Palace Museum, Peking.
> KKPWY hua-niao, 89*; PM, 43*.
>
> A man walking with a staff, inscribed, signed, dated 1759, (AL). Li-
> tai jen-wu, 65.
>
> Chung K'uei, signed, done at age 74 (1760). Li-tai jen-wu, 64.
>
> An album of eight leaves depicting flowers, done when 75 (1761), Liao-
> ning Provincial Museum. Liao-ning, II.113 (Butterfly lily and
> rock); 114 (Narcissus).
>
> Plum tree, inscribed, signed, done when 75 (1761), Nanking Museum.
> Yang-chou pa-chia, 1.
>
> Plum blossoms, inscribed, signed, done when 76 (1762). TSYMC hua-
> hsüan, 97.
>
> An album of twelve flower studies, each leaf inscribed, signed, one
> dated 1786. CT-h Hua-hsüan.
>
> Picking caltrops, six skiffs on the water, album leaf, inscribed, sign-
> ed, Shanghai Museum. CK shu-hua, I.41; Shang-hai, 83*.
>
> Hsiang-lin sweeping, inscribed, signed, Suchou Museum. Su-chou, 81.
>
> Four album leaves, inscribed, signed, Tientsin Art Museum. T'ien-
> ching, II, 120 (Bamboo); 121 (Eggplants); 122 (Wu-t'ung tree);
> 123 (Willow and pear blossoms).
>
> Plum blossoms, poem, signed, Chang Pe-chin collection. Tien Yin
> Tang, I.99.
>
> A boat among lotus pads, album leaf, inscribed, signed. Che-chiang,
> 77.
>
> Plum blossoms fallen at the gate, album leaf, signed. Che-chiang, 78.

CHIN T'ING-PIAO 金廷標 , t. Shih-k'uei 士揆 . From
Wu-ch'eng, Chekiang; active c. 1720-1760; court-painter in the Ch'ien-
lung period; figures, landscapes, flowers. (CP, VII, AL, 314-315.)

> A scholar and a farmer, signed, Nat. Pal. Mus., Taipei, (AL). Li-
> tai jen-wu, 63.
>
> Mencius' mother moving her residence, signed, Nat. Pal. Mus.,
> Taipei, (AL). CKLTMHC, V.60.
>
> A man seated among maple-trees in the evening, signed, Nat. Pal.
> Mus., Taipei, (AL). Che-chiang, 82.
>
> A blossoming peach-tree, signed, Nat. Pal. Mus., Taipei, (AL).
> CKLTMHC, V.61.

CHOU CH'ÜAN 周荃 , t. Ching-hsiang 靜者 , h. Hua-ch'i lao-jen 花溪老人 . From Ch'ang-chou, Kiangsu; active in the early Ch'ing period; landscapes. (CP, VII, AL, 317.)

> A mountain pass, album leaf, artist's seals, Nat. Pal. Mus., Taipei, (AL). CH mei-shu, III.

CHOU HAO 周鎬 . Unrecorded. Acording to I-yüan chi-chin and CK hua: t.Tzu-ching 子京 , from Tan-t'u, Kiangsu, painted landscapes.

> Ink landscape, signed, dated 1838, Wang Yüeh-hua collection. CK hua, I.35.
> A pavilion in a mountain grove, signed, Tientsin Art Museum. I-yüan chi-chin, 54.

CHU CH'ANG 祝昌 , t. Shan-ch'ao 山嘲 . From Shu-ch'eng, Anhui; early Ch'ing period; landscapes. (CP, VII, AL, 320.)

> River and mountain scenery, handscroll, inscribed, signed, Suchou Museum. Su-chou, 64-70.

CHU CH'ENG 朱偁 , t. Meng-lu 夢廬 , h. Chio-wei 覺未 , Chio-wei-sheng 覺未生 . B. 1826, d. 1900; from Chia-hsing, Chekiang; painted flowers and birds. (M. p. 110.)

> Sparrow on a tree, album leaf, signed, Museum of History and Technology, Shanghai. CK chin-pai-nien, 34.

CHU HAN-CHIH 朱翰之 , t. Jui-wu 睿眥 , h. Ch'i-ch'u ho-shang 七處和尚 . From Nanking; 17th century. (CP, VII, AL, 320.)

> Houses on the shore of a lake, album leaf, signed, dated 1646, Nat. Pal. Mus., Taipei, (AL). CH mei-shu, III.
> A temple among sparsely-set trees, album leaf, artist's seal, Nat. Pal. Mus., Taipei, (AL). CH mei-shu, III.

CHU LUN-HAN 朱淪瀚 , t. Han-chai 涵齋 , I-hsien 亦軒 , h. I-san 一三 . B. 1680, d. 1760; from Li-ch'eng, Shantung; descendant of the Ming imperial family; nephew of Kao Ch'i-p'ei; finger painter. (CP, VII, AL, 321.)

> Empty thatched buildings in the mountains, boat by the river shore, inscribed, signed, finger painting, Tientsin Art Museum. I-yüan chi-chin, 47.

CHU SHENG 諸昇 , t. Jih-ju 日如 , h. Hsi-an 曦菴 . B. 1618, d. after 1690; from Hangchou; orchids, bamboo, stones. (CP, VII, AL, 322.)

Ink bamboo, signed, dated 1683, S. M. Siu collection, Hong Kong.
CK ku-hua, B. 225.
Bamboo in snow, two artist's seal. Che-chiang, 74.

CHU TA 朱耷 , t. Jen-wu 人屋 , h. Pa-ta shan-jen 八大山人 ,
Hsüeh-ko 雪個 , Jen-wu 人屋 , Shu-nien 書年 , Ko-shan
個山 , Shan-lü 山驢 and other names. B. 1625, d. after 1705;
a descendant of the imperial Ming family who became a monk; landscapes,
flowers, birds. (CP, VII, AL, 322-326.)

Cat, rock and lotus plants, handscroll, signed, dated 1669; Palace
Museum, Peking. P-t s-j hua-chi, 5.
Fish and ducks, handscroll, signed, dated 1689, Shanghai Museum.
WW, 1960. 7. 6, 38; 1963. 10. 21 (section).
Two peacocks on stone under a cliff, inscribed, signed, dated 1690.
Chu Ta, 3; P-t s-j hua-chi, 3.
Kingfisher on a rock, signed, dated 1692. Chu Ta, 4 (left); P-t s-j
hua-chi, 12; TSYMC hua-hsüan, 77.
Album of fifteen leaves of painting and calligraphy, seven paintings
and nine leaves of inscriptions, each painting signed, album dated
1693, Shanghai Museum. CT Shu-hua ho-ts'e, A.
Chrysanthemum in a vase, signed, dated 1694. P-t s-j hua-chi, 14.
An album of eight paintings of birds, flowers and landscapes, inscriptions by the artist, one dated 1694, Shanghai Museum, (AL).
CT Shan-shui hua-niao; WW, 1960. 7, cover (two birds).
Pa-ta shan-jen hua-ts'e miao-p'in. An album of landscapes, flowers,
birds and fishes, fifteen pictures painted in 1694, one picture
dated 1702, Sumitomo Collection, Oiso, (AL, also listed as Sixteen leaves forming an album of flowers, birds and a few landscapes). Chu Ta, 6 (Two quail under a rock); 7 (A rat on a melon);
9 (A bird on a reed); CK shu-hua, I. 33 (A cat); P-t s-j hua-chi,
1 (Two birds by a bare tree).
Riverside plants and flowers, handscroll, inscribed, signed, dated
1697, Tientsin Art Museum. I-yüan chi-chin, 25 (two sections);
T'ien-ching, II. 106-112.
A small tiger on a rock under a mugwort plant, signed, dated 1699,
Chang Ta-ch'ien collection, (AL). Chu Ta, 10; P-t s-j hua-chi, 8.
An album of calligraphy and painting, seventeen leaves, ten paintings
with seven leaves of inscriptions, each leaf signed, dated 1699,
Shanghai Museum. CT Shu-hua ho-ts'e, B.
A small album of ten leaves including two examples of the artist's
calligraphy, dated 1700, Chang Ta-ch'ien collection, (AL). P-t
s-j hua-chi, 21 (leaf 4, A quail under a reed); 22 (leaf 3, Lotus
flowers); 23 (leaf 6, A hut under old pine-trees); 24 (leaf 5, Mountain in rain).

Two small birds on a terrace under a rock with a tree, signed, dated
1700. P-t s-j hua-chi, 2.

A crow perching on a willow trunk, signed, dated 1703, Palace Museum, Peking, (AL). PM, 33*; WW, 1958.6.4.

Two ducks on a rock under a large flower-covered stone, signed,
dated 1705, (AL, Nanga Taisei, VI.105; also listed as Two mandarin ducks resting on a stone by the water ?). Chu Ta, 11.

Bare trees and rocks, album leaf, signed, Tientsin Art Museum, (AL).
T'ien-ching, I.68.

The joy of fishes swimming between rocks, signed, Chang Ta-ch'ien
collection, (AL). P-t s-j hua-chi, 4.

Two ducks; one standing on a stone under tall lotus-plants, the other
one on a big rockery, signed, Chang Ta-ch'ien collection, (AL).
P-t s-j hua-chi, 6.

Small album of eight leaves; four landscapes and four leaves of writing, all signed, Chang Ta-ch'ien collection, (AL). Chu Ta, 2
(leaf one); P-t s-j hua-chi, 27 (leaf one); 28 (leaf four).

Lan-t'ing shih-hua ts'e. Album of six landscapes after old masters,
signed, Chang Ta-ch'ien collection, (AL). P-t s-j hua-chi, 25-
26 (the fifth leaf).

Shu-hua ho-pi ts'e. Small album of eight leaves; four paintings and
four writings, each painting signed, Chang Ta-ch'ien collection,
(AL). Chu Ta, 12 (leaf three: Grey starling on a branch of bare
tree); P-t s-j hua-chi, 15 (leaf one: Magnolia); 16 (leaf three:
Grey starling on a branch of bare tree).

A heron perching on a leafless willow-trunk, album leaf, poem, signed, (AL). CK shu-hua, I.31.

A large mynah bird on the top of a rock by some bamboos, signed,
(AL). CK shu-hua, I.30.

A tall cliff by a river; dry trees on the rocky shore, signed, Chang
Pe-chin collection, (AL). Tien Yin Tang, I.86.

Landscape-studies, eight leaves forming an album, signed, (AL).
CK shu-hua, I.29 (one leaf: Two boats along a mountain shore).

A kingfisher on a rock below a lotus plant, signed, Palace Museum,
Peking. CK ku-tai, 93; KKPWY hua-niao, 72*; PM, 32*.

Banana tree and bamboo, signed, Palace Museum, Peking. CK hua,
XIX.18; PM, 40*; WW, 1961.6.37.

A duck by a rock, signed, Shanghai Museum. P-t s-j hua-chi, 11;
Shang-hai, 74*.

A fish, album leaf, signed, Shanghai Museum. Shang-hai, 75*.

A branch of bamboo, folding fan, signed, Shanghai WWPKWYH. Shan-
mien-hua, 65*.

An album of six leaves depicting birds, flowers, landscapes, Suchou
Museum. Su-chou, 46 (landscape, seal); 47 (small bird).

,An album of twelve leaves depicting birds, signed, Suchou Museum.
Su-chou, 48 (Quail on rock, two fish); 49 (Fish and rock).
A towering mountain peak, signed, Tientsin Art Museum. T'ien-
ching, I. 67.
Melons and fruits, handscroll, Tientsin Art Museum. I-yüan chi-
chin, 26.
A bird on a branch, signed, Chang Cho-jen collection. CK hua, I. 27.
A studio in the autumn mountains, handscroll, signed, Chang Pe-chin
collection. Tien Yin Tang, I. 85 (section).
Pine tree and deer, signed, Chang Pe-chin collection. Tien Yin Tang,
I. 87.
An album of eight leaves, four of landscapes, four of calligraphy, in-
scribed, signed, S. M. Siu collection, Hong Kong. CK ku-hua,
B. 220.
An album of eight leaves depicting fish, bamboo, vegetables and birds,
each leaf signed. P-t s-j Hua-ts'e, A*; P-t s-j hua-chi, 17 (Three
fish); 18 (Two gourds).
An album of eight leaves depicting birds and flowers, each leaf signed.
P-t s-j Hua-ts'e, B.
Three geese on the shore, one flying above, signed. P-t s-j hua-chi, 7.
A deer under a pine tree, bird flying above, signed. P-t s-j hua-
chi, 9.
A kingfisher on a lotus stalk, signed. P-t s-j hua-chi, 10.
A hawk on a branch. P-t s-j hua-chi, 13.
A cicada on a banana leaf, album leaf, signed. Chu Ta, 8; P-t s-j
hua-chi, 19.
Vines and the moon, album leaf. Chu Ta, 1.
An eagle on a branch stump, signed. TSYMC hua-hsüan, 74.
Fish swimming under chrysanthemums. Chu Ta, 4; TSYMC hua-
hsüan, 75.
A wild duck under tall lotus stalks, signed. TSYMC hua-hsüan, 76.
Two eagles on a tree and a rock, signed. WW, 1960.7.37.
Four magpies in an old tree and rock, signed. WW, 1961.6.6.

CHÜ CH'AO 居 巢 , t. Mei-sheng 梅 生 , h. Mei-ch'ao 梅巢 .
D. 1899; from Fan-yü, Kuangtung; painted flowers, grasses, insects,
landscapes, studied Yün Shou-p'ing. (W. I. 10; M. p. 220.)
Pink and white tree peonies, folding fan, inscribed, signed, dated
1848, after Yün Shou-p'ing. CC tso-p'in*.
White tuberoses, folding fan, inscribed, signed, dated 1848. CC tso-
p'in*.
Ink epidendrum, folding fan, signed, dated 1851. CC tso-p'in*.
Branch of pear blossoms, folding fan, inscribed, signed, dated 1853,
Ssu-wu-yang Chai collection. Kuang-tung shu-hua, 50.

Branch of lichee, folding fan, inscribed, signed, dated 1853. CC
tso-p'in*.

Two white carnations by a rock, folding fan, inscribed, signed, dated
1857. CC tso-p'in*.

Plum blossoms, folding fan, inscribed, signed, dated 1859. CC tso-
p'in*.

Two fish in waterweeds, folding fan, inscribed, signed, dated 1863.
CC tso-p'in*.

A mountain bird in a landscape, folding fan, artist's seal. CC tso-
p'in*.

Pink hibiscus, folding fan, inscribed, signed. CC tso-p'in*.

Fish swimming, folding fan, inscribed, signed. CC tso-p'in*.

Two egrets, folding fan, inscribed, signed. CC tso-p'in*.

White flower buds, folding fan, inscribed, signed. CC tso-p'in*.

A cut branch of pear blossoms, inscribed, signed, dated (characters
damaged). Kuang-tung hua-chia, 83*.

Pink and white peonies, artist's seal. Kuang-tung hua-chia, 84*.

CHÜ CH'ING 居 慶 , t. P'ei-cheng 佩 徵 , Yü-cheng 玉 徵 .
A woman, from Fan-yü, Kuangtung, late 19th-early 20th century; painted
flowers. (M. p. 220.)

Spring flowers in full bloom, folding fan, inscribed, date unclear,
Chu-p'ing-an Kuan collection. Kuang-tung shu-hua, 51.

Roses, folding fan, inscribed, signed, dated 1863, Lei collection.
Kuang-tung shu-hua, 51.

CHÜ LIEN 居 廉 , t. Shih-kang 士 剛 , h. Ku-ch'üan 古 泉 ,
Ke-shan lao-jen 隔 山 老 人 , Ke-shan ch'iao-tzu 隔 山 樵 子 ,
Lo-fu san-jen 羅 浮 散 人 . B. 1828, d. 1904; from Fan-yü, Kuang-
tung, brother of Chü Ch'ao; painted flowers, birds, grasses, insects, figures. (W.I.10; M. p. 220.)

Grasshopper and white crepe myrtle, fan, inscribed, signed, dated
1877. CL shan-mien*.

Evening fragrance: bees on a vine, fan, inscribed, signed, dated 1877.
CL shan-mien*.

Monochrome peach blossoms, fan, poem, signed, dated 1886. CL
shan-mien*.

Narcissus, fan, signed, dated 1891. CL shan-mien*.

Cicada on a flowering vine, folding fan, inscribed, signed, dated
1891. CK -c hua-ch'ung*.

Butterflies and autumn crab apple, folding fan, poem, signed, dated
1892. CK-c hua-ch'ung*.

Crab apple and swallow, fan, inscribed, signed, dated 1893. CL
shan-mien*.

Flowers, fan, inscribed, signed, dated 1894. CL shan-mien*.

Flowers wrapped in a lotus leaf, fan, signed, dated 1897, inscribed.
CL shan-mien*.

Crepe myrtle and dragonflies, folding fan, inscribed, signed, dated
1898. CK-c hua-ch'ung*.

Praying mantis holding a cicada, folding fan, inscribed, signed, dated
1898. CK-c hua-ch'ung*.

A grasshopper on a blue morning glory, fan, inscribed, signed, dated
1899. CL shan-mien*.

A locust on a flowering branch and two flying mosquitoes, fan, inscribed, signed, dated 1899. CL shan-mien*.

A large bird on a flowering branch, signed, dated 1900, Tun-fu shu-
shih collection. Kuang-tung shu-hua, 50.

Flowers of the four seasons, eight album leaves, artist's seals. CL
Erh-shih-ssu fan*; Kuang-tung hua-chia, 87*, 88* (Spring).

Cicada and bean vine, album leaf, signed. CK-c hua-ch'ung*.

Flowers, stone and praying mantis, album leaf, signed, in style of
Yü Shou-p'ing. CK-c hua-ch'ung*.

Five butterflies and pelargonium, folding fan, inscribed, signed.
CK-c hua-ch'ung*.

A frog on a grapevine trying to catch a fly, folding fan, inscribed,
signed. CK-c hua-ch'ung*.

Locust on a rosebush, fan, artist's seal. CL shan-mien*.

Rose mallow, praying mantis holding a cicada, fan, inscribed, signed.
CL shan-mien*.

Two butterflies and pelargonium, fan, inscribed, signed. CL shan-
mien*.

Flowers and insects, artist's seal. Kuang-tung hua-chia, 85*.

A mantis catching a cicada, album leaf, signed. Kuang-tung hua-
chia, 86*.

CH'ÜEH LAN 關 嵐 , t. Wen-shan 文山 or 雯山 , h. Ch'ing-
feng 晴峯 , Hsiao-lung-ming shan-jen 小龍暝山人 , Lung-
mien shan-jen 龍眠山人 . B. 1758, d. 1844; from Tung-ch'eng,
Anhui; painted landscapes, flowers, figures. (T.I.8; M. p. 707.)

Two mynahs on a red-leafed tree with chrysanthemum, signed, dated
1833, Suchou Museum. Su-chou, 97.

FA JO-CHEN 法若真 , t. Han-ju 漢儒 , h. Huang-shih 黄石 .
B. 1613, d. 1696; from Chiao-chou, Shantung; landscapes. (CP, VII, AL,
327.)

Misty mountain landscape, inscribed, signed, done when 77 (1689),
Liao-ning Provincial Museum. Liao-ning, II.94.

FAN CH'I 樊圻 , t. Hui-kung 會公 and Hsia-kung 洽公 .
B. 1616, d. after 1694; from Nanking, one of the "Eight Masters of Nanking"; landscapes, figures, flowers. (CP, VII, AL, 327-328.)

> River landscape, handscroll, inscribed, signed, dated 1657, Liao-
> ning Provincial Museum. Liao-ning, II. 91-92.
> Fishermen on a willow stream, handscroll, several inscriptions (re-
> production too faint to read), Palace Museum, Peking, (AL, A
> fishing village?). WW, 1966.4.45.
> Flower studies in kung-pi style, an album of twelve leaves, signed,
> dated 1682, Cheng Te-k'un collection, Cambridge, (AL). Mu-
> fei, opposite p. 34 (Lotus); before p. 35 (Plum blossoms).
> Narcissus, camellia flowers and plum blossoms, signed, dated 1683,
> poem by Kung Hsien, Tientsin Art Museum, (AL). I-yüan chi-
> chin, 38; T'ien-ching, II. 96.

FAN YÜN 樊雲 , t. Ch'ing-jo 青若 . From Nanking; son of
Fan Ch'i; early 18th century. (CP, VII, AL, 328.)

> An angler on the river, a village in a grove, folding fan, signed, dated
> ting-chou (1697 or 1757), Hui Hsiao-t'ung collection. Shan-mien
> chi-chin, 15*.

FANG HSÜN 方薰 , t. Lan-ti 蘭坻 , h. Lan-shih 蘭士 ,
Ch'ang-ch'ing 長青 and other names. B. 1736, d. 1799; from Shih-
men, Chekiang; author of Shan-ching-chü lun-hua; painted landscapes,
flowers and birds. (CP, VII, AL, 329.)

> Gentleman and retinue returning home, handscroll, inscribed, sign-
> ed, Tientsin Art Museum. T'ien-ching, II. 148-149.
> Landscape after Lu Kuang: river shore and mountain spires, signed,
> Cheng Te-k'un collection, Cambridge. Mu-fei, opposite p. 56.
> Bamboo and epidendrum by a rock, inscribed, signed. Che-chiang, 84.

FANG I-CHIH 方以智 , t. Ch'ang-kung 昌公 , h. Lu-ch'i
鹿起, Chih-k'o 智可 , Mi-chih 密之 and other names. From
T'ung-ch'eng, Anhui; chin-shih in 1640; at the fall of the Ming he became
a monk, named Hung-chih 弘智 , t. Wu-k'o 無可 , h. Yao-ti 藥地
; painted landscapes. (CP, VII, AL, 329.)

> An album of landscapes, eight leaves, each signed, some inscribed,
> Cheng Te-k'un collection, Cambridge, (AL). Mu-fei, between
> pp. 26-27 (two leaves).

FANG SHIH-SHU 方士庶 , t. Tun-yüan 道遠 , h. Huan-shan
環山 , Hsiao-shih tao-jen 小獅道人 . B. 1692, d. 1751;
from Hsieh-hsien, Anhui; pupil of Huang Ting; landscapes. (CP, VII,
AL, 330.)

Walking with a staff among streams and mountains, inscribed, signed, dated 1736, Tientsin Art Museum. T'ien-ching, II. 118.
Landscape with a man on a bridge and terraced mountain tops, inscribed, signed, Suchou Museum. Su-chou, 86.

FANG TA-YU 方大猷　, t. Ou-yü 歐餘　, h. Yen-lan 奄藍
and Yün-sheng 允升 . B. 1596, d. 1677; from Wu-ch'eng, Chekiang;
Governor of Shantung in the Ch'ing period; painted landscapes. (CP, VII,
AL, 330-331.)
A pavilion on a ledge, curving mountains over the river, signed, dated
1670, Suchou Museum. Su-chou, 39.

FEI TAN-HSÜ 費丹旭　, t. Yü-t'iao 子苕　, h. Hsiao-lou
晓樓 , Huan-ch'i 環溪 . B. 1802, d. 1850; from Wu-ch'eng,
Chekiang; painter of landscapes, figures. (CP, VII, AL, 331-332.)
Illustration to <u>Hung-lou Meng</u>, fan, one of twelve illustrations done
in 1825. Fei Tan-hsü, 14.
Men and ladies playing music in the E-yüan Garden, signed, dated
1831, (AL). FH-l p'in, 3; Fei Tan-hsü, 1.
Gentlemen composing poetry in a pavilion, servants, handscroll,
signed, dated 1832, Chekiang WWKLWYH. FH-l p'in, 4-5.
The Tung-hsüan Poetry Society, gentlemen in a garden, handscroll,
signed, dated 1832, Chekiang WWKLWYH. Che-chiang, 94-95;
FH-l p'in, 6-15; Fei Tan-hsü, 2-3.
A gentleman and a lady in a garden studio, handscroll, inscribed,
signed, dated 1833. Fei Tan-hsü, 4.
Portrait of a man in a round window, inscribed, signed, dated 1837,
Palace Museum, Peking. FH-l p'in, 16-17.
Portrait of a gentleman on a path to a rustic hut, handscroll, dated
1841, Chekiang Museum. FH-l p'in, 18-19.
Portrait of a standing man holding a fan, signed, dated 1842. Fei
Tan-hsü, 5.
Portrait of Liu Hsi-hai in a pavilion by a stream, handscroll, in-
scribed, signed, dated 1842, Shanghai WWPKWYH. FH-l p'in,
20-21.
Portrait of Chiang Kuang-yü seated by a stone table; a standing lady,
handscroll, signed, dated 1843, Chiang Lu-t'ao collection, Hai-
ning. FH-l p'in, 22-23.
Portrait of Hsü Lien-shu, album leaf, dated 1844, Ch'ien Ching-t'ang
collection, Hai-ning. FH-l p'in, 24 (detail).
An album of twelve leaves depicting ladies in seasonal landscapes,
artist's seals on each leaf, last leaf signed, dated 1846. FH-l
Shih-nü.

A gentleman seated on a stone under a pine, a servant with a staff,
inscribed, signed, dated 1846, Ch'ien Ching-t'ang collection,
Hai-ning. FH-1 p'in, 25-26.

River snowscape, album leaf, inscribed, signed, dated 1848. Fei
Tan-hsü, 11.

A woman in a red cloak holding plum blossoms and standing on a
snowy bridge, folding fan, signed, dated 1848, Shanghai WWPKWYH.
Shan-mien-hua, 100*.

A lady standing on a snowy bridge, signed, dated 1849. Fei Tan-hsü,
10.

Three figures, one seated, one standing, one child, a landscape, two
handscrolls, signed, dated 1849, Chekiang Museum. FH-1 p'in,
27-30; Fei Tan-hsü, 6.

Liu Chi teaching the Classics, handscroll, signed, dated 1849, Wen-
chou WWKLWYH. FH-1 p'in, 31-32; Fei Tan-hsü, 7.

Portrait of a gentleman with a staff, signed, dated 1849, four inscriptions, Hsü collection, Shanghai. FH-1 p'in, 33.

A lady with a fan, signed, Shanghai Museum, (AL). Fei Tan-hsü, 9;
Shang-hai, 92*.

Portrait of Chu Hsiung seated on a stone under a willow, a servant
with a broom, Ch'ien Ching-t'ang collection, Hai-ning. FH-1
p'in, 1, 2.

A lady rolling up a window blind, album leaf, inscribed. Fei Tan-
hsü, 8.

Autumn flowers, inscribed, signed. Fei Tan-hsü, 12.

Han Ch'i with flowers in his hat, three other gentlemen and two servants in a garden, inscribed, signed. Fei Tan-hsü, 15.

FU MEI 傅眉 , t. Shou-mao 壽髦 or 壽毛 , h. Chü-ling
竹嶺 , Hsiao-nieh-ch'ang 小蘗禪 or 小蘗禪 , Wo-
tao-jen 我道人 , Mi-tao-jen 糜道人 , Mei-tao-jen
眉道人 , Hsü-nan 須罗 , Te-mao 德髦 . B. 1628, d.
1683; from Yang-chü, Shansi; son of Fu Shan. (Q. I. 1; U. II. 2; M. p. 513.)

Four album leaves depicting landscapes, each signed, Tientsin Art
Museum. T'ien-ching, I. 57-60.

FU SHAN 傅山 , t. Ch'ing-chu 青主 , h. Se-lu 嗇廬 ,
Kung-chih-t'o 公之它 , Jen-chung 仁仲 , Liu-ch'ih
六持 , Sui-li 隨厲 and other names. B. 1602, d. 1683; from T'ai-
yüan, Shansi; a student of Taoism, landscapes. (CP, VII, AL, 332-333.)

An album of eight leaves depicting landscapes, each leaf signed, last
leaf dated 1655, Cheng Te-k'un collection, Cambridge. Mu-fei,
before p. 25 (two leaves).

Thatched hut in the mountains, illustration to a poem by Tu Fu, inscribed, signed, dated 1666, (AL, Bridges and a pavilion built
on poles in a stream at the foot of a mountain?). FS hua-chi, 3*.

Waterfall and cypress, two inscriptions by the artist, signed, dated
1676. FS hua-chi, 6*.

Waterfall and cypress, two inscriptions by the artist, signed, dated
1676. FS shu-hua, 26.

A duck on a bank, album leaf, signed, done when 78 (1679). FS shu-
hua, 24.

A pavilion in bleak mountains, album leaf, signed, Tientsin Art Museum. FS hua-chi, 22*; T'ien-ching, I. 55.

Misty rapids at night, album leaf, inscribed, signed, Tientsin Art
Museum. FS hua-chi, 23*; T'ien-ching, I. 54.

Covered veranda under a waterfall, album leaf, inscribed, signed,
Tientsin Art Museum. FS hua-chi, 24*; I-yüan chi-chin, 22;
T'ien-ching, I. 56.

Hibiscus and willow, album leaf, artist's seal, Tientsin Art Museum.
FS hua-chi, 25*; T'ien-ching, I. 53.

Bamboo in wind and rain, inscribed, signed, S. M. Siu collection, Hong
Kong. CK ku-hua, B. 218.

Pine trees and thornbush, inscribed, signed. FS hua-chi, 1*.

Pavilion in the mountains by waterfalls, inscribed, signed. FS hua-
chi, 2*.

Bamboo and juniper behind a rock, inscribed, signed. FS hua-chi, 4*.

A gnarled pine by the Eastern Sea, inscribed. FS hua-chi, 5*.

Bamboo in wind, signed. FS hua-chi, 7*.

Six album leaves depicting landscapes, each accompanied by a leaf
of calligraphy signed by the artist. FS hua-chi, 8-13*.

Four album leaves depicting landscapes, each with artist's seal and
accompanied by a poem signed by the artist. FS hua-chi, 14-17*.

Four album leaves depicting landscapes, sealed or signed. FS hua-
chi, 18-21*.

Trees on a river bank, folding fan, inscribed, signed. FS hua-chi, 26.

Cypresses along a mountain path, folding fan, signed. FS hua-chi, 27*.

Old trees, after Hsia Kuei, folding fan, inscribed, signed. FS hua-
chi, 28*.

Pines in a wintry valley, folding fan, inscribed, signed. FS hua-chi,
29*.

Evening rain in mountains and streams, folding fan, inscribed, signed. FS hua-chi, 30*.

Houses by a stream, tall mountains, inscribed, signed. FS shu-hua,
18.

A mountain valley, inscribed, signed. FS shu-hua, 19.

Pines and stony mountains, inscribed, signed. FS shu-hua, 20.
Fishing scene, album leaf, inscribed, signed. FS shu-hua, 21.
A house by a stream, album leaf, inscribed, signed. FS shu-hua, 22.
Pavilion on a cliff, album leaf, inscribed, signed. FS shu-hua, 23.
A frog, album leaf, artist's seal. FS shu-hua, 25.

FU WEN 傅雯 , t. Tzu-lai 紫來 , h. K'ai-t'ing 凱亭 .
From Kuang-ning, Manchuria, 18th century; finger-painter, imitated Kao
Ch'i-p'ei. (CP, VII, AL, 333.)
> A cowherd on a water buffalo, inscribed, Tientsin Art Museum. I-
> yüan chi-chin, 52.

HAN JUNG-KUANG 韓榮光 , t. Hsiang-ho 祥河 , h. Chu-
ch'uan 珠船 . From Po-lo, Kuangtung; chü-jen in 1828; poet.
(W. I. 8.)
> Two gentlemen reminiscing in a mountain pavilion, inscribed, signed,
> dated 1839. Kuang-tung hua-chia, 75*.
> Scholar in a pavilion in a grove, Chu-p'ing-an Kuan collection. Kuang-
> tung shu-hua, 39.

HO CH'ING-T'AI 賀清泰 , Louis de Poirot. B. 1735, d. 1814;
a French Jesuit missionary who served in the imperial observatory and
as a court painter; birds, animals. (CP, VII, AL, 334.)
> A white eagle, signed, dated 1785, Nat. Pal. Mus., Taipei, (AL).
> CKLTMHC, V. 59.

HO CHUNG 何翀 , h. Tan-shan 丹山 , Tan-shan lao-jen
丹山老人 , Ch'i-shih-erh-feng shan-jen 七十二峯山人 ,
Yen-ch'iao lao-jen 煙橋老人 . From Nan-hai, Kuangtung;
mid-19th century; painted birds and flowers after Hua Yen. (W.I.10; M.
p. 135.)
> Mynah on willow and hibiscus, signed, dated 1859. Kuang-tung hua-
> chia, 90*.
> Ducklings swimming under plum blossoms and bamboo, inscribed,
> signed, dated 1872, after Hua Yen. Kuang-tung hua-chia, 91*.
> Two gentlemen conversing under trees, signed, dated 1873. Kuang-
> tung hua-chia, 89*.

HO I 赫頤 or 赫奕 , h. Tan-shih 澹士 . A Manchu;
active c. 1700; high official; pupil of Wang Yüan-ch'i. (CP, VII, AL, 334.)
> Empty pavilion on a promontory, distant mountains, inscribed, sign-
> ed, dated 1717, Liao-ning Provincial Museum. Liao-ning, II.104.

HSI KANG 奚 岡 , t. Ch'un-chang 純 章 , h. T'ieh-sheng 鐵 生 , Meng-ch'üan wai-shih 蒙 泉 外 史 and other names. B. 1746, d. 1803; from Ch'ien-t'ang, Chekiang; poet, calligrapher, painted landscapes, flowers. (CP, VII, AL, 335-336.)

> Crepe myrtle and gardenia, inscribed, signed, dated 1796, Palace Museum, Peking. KKPWY hua-niao, 94*.
>
> A grove of bare trees by a winding stream; gathering crows, poem, signed, (AL). Che-chiang, 86.
>
> River landscape, after Huang Kung-wang, inscribed, signed, Liaoning Provincial Museum, (AL). Liao-ning, II. 120.
>
> Four album leaves depicting landscapes, four leaves of calligraphy, signed, Tientsin Art Museum. T'ien-ching, II. 142-145.

HSIAO CH'EN 蕭 晨 , t. Ling-hsi 靈 曦 , h. Chung-su 中素 . From Yang-chou, Kiangsu; active c. 1680-1710; landscapes, figures, snowscapes, (CP, VII, AL, 337.)

> Landscape in snow, signed, Nat. Pal. Mus., Taipei, (AL). CKLTMHC, V. 41.
>
> Going to plant millet by the river, inscribed, signed. Ch'ing-jen-hua*.

HSIAO YÜN-TS'UNG 蕭 雲 從 , t. Ch'ih-mu 尺 木 , h. Wumen tao-jen 無 悶 道 人 , Chung-shan lao-jen 鍾 山 老 人 . B. 1596, d. 1673; from Wu-hu, Anhui; poet, landscapes. (CP, VII, AL, 337-338.)

> Walking with a staff in a sparse grove in the mountains, inscribed, signed, dated 1648, Tientsin Art Museum. T'ien-ching, II. 84.
>
> The long road to Szechuan, handscroll, inscribed, signed, dated 1649, Cheng Te-k'un collection, Cambridge, (AL). Mu-fei, before p. 19.
>
> Thatched hut under pines and bamboo on a rocky shore, folding fan, poem, dated 1650 (the painting apparently done before this date), Shanghai WWPKWYH. Shan-mien-hua, 55*.
>
> One-thousand peaks and ten-thousand valleys, handscroll, poem, signed, dated 1658, Liao-ning Provincial Museum. Liao-ning, II. 79-81.
>
> Landscape, handscroll, inscribed, signed, in the style of Ni Tsan, (AL). HC-m Shan-shui.

HSIEH CH'ENG 謝 成 , t. Chung-mei 仲 美 . B. 1612, d. 1666; from Chiang-ning, Kiangsu; painted landscapes, portraits, birds and flowers. (M. p. 705.)

> River valley with pines and buildings, album leaf, Nat. Pal. Mus., Taipei. CH mei-shu, III.

HSIEH KUAN-SHENG 謝 觀 生 , t. T'ui-ku 退 谷 , h. Wu-yang shan-jen 五 羊 山 人 , Wu-yang san-jen 五 羊 散 人
From Nan-hai, Kuangtung; active c. 1796-1820; younger brother of Hsieh Lan-sheng; painted landscapes, birds, flowers. (W.I.6; M. p. 707.)

> A man crossing a bridge toward a walled pavilion, boats on the river, folding fan, inscribed, signed, dated 1834, Ma Chi-tsu collection. Kuang-tung shu-hua, 39.
>
> Two men in a lotus-pond pavilion, album leaf, inscribed, signed. Kuang-tung hua-chia, 48*.

HSIEH LAN-SHENG 謝 蘭 生 , t. P'ei-shih 佩 士 , h. Li-p'u 理 浦 or 圃 . B. 1760, d. 1831; from Nan-hai, Kuangtung; poet and calligrapher. (CP, VII, AL, 338.)

> Album of landscapes, eight leaves, each signed, last dated 1826, Cheng Te-k'un collection, Cambridge, (AL). Mu-fei, between pp. 58-59 (two leaves).
>
> Empty pavilions under trees along reedy shore, two lines of poem from Tu Fu, signed, dated 1830, Ho Man-an collection. Kuang-tung shu-hua, 35.
>
> River valley landscape after Wang Meng, album leaf, inscribed, signed. Kuang-tung hua-chia, 46*.
>
> A scholar standing under a vine-filled pine tree, mountain and river scenery, poem, signed. Kuang-tung hua-chia, 47*.

HSIEH PIN 謝 彬 , t. Wen-hou 文 候 . B. 1602, d. after 1680; from Ch'ang-shu, Kiangsu; figures, pupil of Tseng Ch'ing. (CP, VII, AL, 338.)

> Portrait of Chu Yüan, signed, dated 1638. Che-chiang, 66.

HSIEH P'U 謝 璞 or 樸 , t. Kuang-ch'in 廣 勤 . From Suchou; painted landscapes. (M. p. 706.)

> Copy of Ch'iu Ying's painting of a lady sewing, two servants and a child, signed, dated keng-yin (1650 or 1710), colophon by Yü Chih-ting dated (in error?) 1703, Suchou Museum. Su-chou, 75.

HSIEH SUI 謝 遂 . Court-painter, active c. 1770; figures. (CP, VII, AL, 338.)

> Palace buildings in snow, signed, dated 1777, Nat. Pal. Mus., Taipei, (AL). CKLTMHC, V. 72.
>
> Foreign envoy with tribute bearers, handscroll, Nat. Pal. Mus., Taipei. CCAT, pl. 24* (section).

HSIEH SUN 謝 蓀 . From Chiang-ning, Kiangsu, active c. 1679; one of the "Eight Masters of Nanking"; landscapes. (CP, VII, AL, 338.)

A lotus blossom and leaves, album leaf, signed, dated 1679, Palace
Museum, Peking, (AL). KKPWY hua-niao, 68*.

HSIUNG CHING-HSING 熊景星 , t. Po-ching 伯晴 , h. Ti-
an 滌庵 , Ti-chiang 笛江 or 荻江 , Ti-tao-jen 滌道人 ,
Lao-ching 老晴 , Po-ch'eng 伯澄 . B. 1791, d. 1856, from
Nan-hai, Kuangtung, poet and calligrapher, painted landscapes, flowers
and bamboo. (W.I.8; M. p. 603.)
> Fishing boat under willows, inscribed, signed. Huang Shih-hsüan
> collection. Kuang-tung shu-hua, 47.
> Trees in cloudy mountains, album leaf, inscribed, signed. Kuang-
> tung hua-chia, 58*.

HSÜ FANG 徐枋 , t. Chao-fa 昭法 , h. Ssu-chai 俟齋 ,
Ch'in-yü shan-jen 秦餘山人 . B. 1622, d. 1694; from Suchou,
lived in retirement and great poverty after 1644; poet; painted landscapes.
(CP, VII, AL, 339.)
> Nine <u>ling-chih</u> on a rock, inscribed, signed, dated 1642, S.M. Siu
> collection, Hong Kong. CK ku-hua, B.214.
> Reminiscing in a pavilion, inscribed, signed, dated 1652, Chang Pe-
> chin collection. Tien Yin Tang, I.84.
> The bridge at Tiger Hill, signed, Suchou Museum. Su-chou, 33.
> Teng-wei Mountain, inscribed, signed, S.M. Siu collection, Hong
> Kong. CK ku-hua, B.215.

HSÜ I 徐嶧 , t. T'ung-hua 桐華 . From Hangchou; active
during the Ch'ien-lung period (1736-1795); painted landscapes, figures,
flowers and birds. (T.I.10; M. p. 366.)
> Two birds on a crab apple branch, folding fan, inscribed, signed,
> Shanghai WWPKWYH. Shan-mien-hua, 96*.

HSÜ-KU 虛谷 , family name Chu 朱 . B. 1824, d. 1896;
from Yangchou, Kiangsu; fought against the T'ai-p'ing rebels c. 1850,
became a monk; flowers, fruits. (CP, VII, AL, 339.)
> Red fish and wisteria reflections, inscribed, signed, dated 1835,
> Palace Museum, Peking. PM, 35*.
> Hollyhocks, peaches and loquats, signed, dated 1877, Palace Museum,
> Peking. KKPWY hua-niao, 96*.
> Squirrel on a willow branch, inscribed, signed, dated 1892, Suchou
> Museum. Su-chou, 116.
> Three mynahs on willow branches, inscribed, done when 72 (1895),
> Palace Museum, Peking. CK chin-pai-nien, 31*.
> Four album leaves depicting chrysanthemums, fish, narcissus, two
> squirrels on willow branches, each leaf inscribed, last one signed,

Palace Museum, Peking. CK chin-pai-nien, 29-30.

Fruits, inscribed, signed, Palace Museum, Peking. CK chin-pai-nien, 33.

Flowers and fruits, four album leaves, three with seals, one signed. H-k Hua-kuo*.

HSÜ MEI 徐玫 , t. Ts'ai-jo 采若 , h. Hua-wu 華塢 . From Suchou; active c. 1700; figures, birds, flowers. (CP, VII, AL, 339.)
> Peach blossoms, willow, birds and fish, signed, birds by Hsü, rest of painting by Yang Chin, Yü Yüan, Wang Yün, Wu Chih and Ku Fang, colophon by Wang Hui, Palace Museum, Peking. KKPWY hua-niao, 77*.

HSÜ PIN 許濱 , t. Ku-yang 谷陽 , h. Chiang-men 江門 . From Tan-yang, Kiangsu, active c. 1733. (CP, VII, AL, 339.)
> Two ducks under peach and willow trees, inscribed, signed, dated 1750, done with Hua Yen, Suchou Museum. Su-chou, 83.

HSÜ T'AI 徐泰 , t. Chieh-p'ing 階平 , h. Chih-yüan 枳園 . Figures and landscapes, followed Tai Chin. (CP, VII, AL, 339-340.)
> A lady washing the inkstone by a garden rock under a banana plant, signed, done with Lan Ying whose inscription is dated 1659, Tientsin Art Museum, (AL). I-yüan chi-chin, 17; T'ien-ching, II. 71.
> Portrait of Shao Mi, landscape by Lan Ying, inscribed, Palace Museum, Peking. CK hua, XVIII. 19; PM, 29*.

HSÜ YANG 徐揚 , t. Yün-t'ing 雲亭 . From Suchou; court-painter c. 1760; landscapes, figures, flowers, birds. (CP, VII, AL, 340.)
> Two swallows flying around a pear-tree, signed, Nat. Pal. Mus., Taipei, (AL). CKLTMHC, V. 62.
> Ink manufacture, Nat. Pal. Mus., Taipei. CCAT, pl. 133 (section).
> The flourishing city, handscroll. WW, 1960. 1. 1.

HSÜEH HSÜAN 薛宣 , t. Ch'en-ling 辰令 , h. Shui-t'ien chü-shih 水田居士 . From Chia-shan, Chekiang; active 1700-1732; pupil of Wang Chien, landscapes. (CP, VII, AL, 341.)
> A man in a pavilion enjoying the snowscape, one of twelve album leaves, signed, dated 1691, Liao-ning Provincial Museum. Liao-ning, II. 96.

HU HSI-KUEI 胡錫珪 , t. San-ch'iao 三橋 . From Ch'ang-chou, Kiangsu, active c. 1874-1883; pai-miao figures. (CP, VII, AL, 341.)
> Two illustrations of opera scenes, inscribed, artist's seals, Fan Shao-yün collection, Shanghai. CK chin-pai-nien, 26.

HU YÜAN 胡遠 , t. Kung-shou 公壽 , h. Shou-hao 瘦鶴 ,
Heng-hsüeh shan-min 橫雪山民 . B. 1823, d. 1886; from Hua-t'ing,
Kiangsu, moved to Shanghai in 1861; calligrapher; landscapes, plum-blos-
soms. (CP, VII, AL, 342.)

> An album of scenes of Wu-hsing, twelve leaves, each inscribed, last
> dated 1850, Cheng Te-k'un collection, Cambridge, (AL). Mu-
> fei, between pp. 64-65 (two leaves).
> A hut along the river, inscribed, signed, dated 1877, Palace Museum,
> Peking. CK chin-pai-nien, 27.

HUA LING 華淩 . Unrecorded. According to Su-chou , p. 12, he
was the son of Hua Yen, t. Sheng-wu 繩武 , chü-jen in 1760.

> Lady arranging her hair before a mirror, after Chou Wen-chü, in-
> scribed, signed, dated 1788, Suchou Museum. Su-chou, 84.

HUA YEN 華喦 , t. Ch'iu-yo 秋岳 , h. Hsin-lo shan-jen 新
羅山人 . B. 1682, d. 1765; from Fukien, lived in Yang-chou
and Hangchou; poet, calligrapher; painted flowers, birds, figures, landscapes. (CP, VII, AL, 343-345.)

> A gentleman seated by a stream, a servant with a pan of lichees, hand-
> scroll, inscribed, signed, dated 1707, Liao-ning Provincial Mu-
> seum. Liao-ning, II.105.
> Three gentlemen under a wu-t'ung tree, signed, dated 1727. H-l s-j
> hua-chi, 13.
> Portrait of the owner of the T'ung-hua Retreat, figure by Ting Kao,
> background by Huang Ts'ou, crane by Hua Yen, dated 1732 in an
> inscription by Hsü T'ung-li, Palace Museum, Peking. CK hua,
> X.16.
> Crested mynah and willow tree, inscribed, signed, dated 1735, Chang
> Pe-chin collection. Tien Yin Tang, I.96.
> Mountains in snow, inscribed, signed, dated 1736. H-l s-j hua-chi,17.
> Two orange-headed birds on a bare branch, bamboo and stone, fold-
> ing fan, inscribed, signed, dated 1742, Shanghai WWPKWYH.
> Shan-mien-hua, 90*.
> An album of eight leaves depicting flowers and birds, each leaf inscri-
> bed and sealed, last leaf signed, dated 1743, Palace Museum,
> Peking. HY Hua-niao*.
> A parrot on a branch of wu-t'ung tree, inscribed, signed, dated 1746.
> H-l s-j hua-chi, 3*; TSYMC hua-hsüan, 92*.
> A pheasant on an autumn branch, two sparrows below, signed, dated
> 1746. H-l s-j hua-chi, 9.
> Ink bamboo by rock, inscribed, signed, dated 1748. H-l s-j hua-chi,14.
> Feasting on a Spring Night in the Peach and Pear Garden, inscribed,
> signed, dated 1748, Tientsin Art Museum. I-yüan chi-chin, 48.

Two mandarin ducks under a flowering peach-tree, poem, signed,
dated 1748, Tientsin Art Museum, (AL). T'ien-ching, I. 85.

An album of twelve leaves depicting landscapes, figures, birds, flowers, insects, dated 1749, Palace Museum, Peking. HY Tsa-hua.

Various birds in a juniper tree, signed, dated 1749, Shanghai WWPK-
WYH. CK hua, XI. 17; H-l s-j hua-chi, 16.

Children playing while schoolmaster dozes, signed, dated 1749. H-l
s-j hua-chi, 42; TSYMC hua-hsüan, 93.

Two ducks under peach and willow trees, inscribed, signed, dated
1750, done with Hsü Pin, Suchou Museum. Su-chou, 83.

Fighting sparrows, chrysanthemums and bamboo, signed, dated 1750.
H-l s-j hua-chi, 2*.

An album of twelve landscape paintings, inscribed, one dated 1751,
(AL). H-l s-j hua-chi, 37-39 (three leaves); 40* (one leaf); 41*
(one leaf).

Carp, inscribed, signed, dated 1751. H-l s-j hua-chi, 24*.

A seated woman playing a p'i-p'a, poem, signed, dated 1751. H-l s-j
hua-chi, 19.

Cassia garden, figures and pavilions, inscribed, signed, dated 1751.
H-l s-j hua-chi, 15.

Eight mynahs in a thicket, signed, dated 1752. H-l s-j hua-chi, 12.

Cranes in a pine-tree, signed, dated 1754, (AL). H-l s-j hua-chi, 1.

Two cranes under vine-covered pine, signed, dated 1754. H-l s-j
hua-chi, 11.

Two mandarin ducks under lotus, inscribed, signed, done when 73
(1754). H-l s-j hua-chi, 5.

Landscape with an empty pavilion and an arched bridge, signed, dated
at the age of 74 (1755). H-l s-j hua-chi, 4.

A bird on the branch of a rose-bush, inscribed, signed, Palace Museum, Peking (AL). KKPWY hua-niao, 83*.

Two album leaves of birds and flowers, both inscribed and sealed,
Palace Museum, Peking. KKPWY hua-niao, 81-82*.

An eagle on a maple tree, signed, Palace Museum, Peking. PM, 34*.

Parrot on a branch, stone, bamboo and chrysanthemum, inscribed,
signed, Liao-ning Provincial Museum. Liao-ning, II. 106.

A parrot on a branch of autumn leaves, inscribed, signed, Shanghai
Museum. Shang-hai, 82*.

A thrush on a red-leafed tree, bamboo, folding fan, inscribed, signed, after Huang Ch'üan, Shanghai WWPKWYH. Shan-mien-hua,
89*.

Bird on a bare willow, poem, signed, Tientsin Art Museum. T'ien-
ching, I. 84.

Two swallows on a willow branch, signed, Tientsin Art Museum.
T'ien-ching, II. 119.

Squirrels on a branch, inscribed, Hsü Shih-hsüeh collection. CK
hua, I. 33.

A man leading a camel in snow-covered mountains, signed. CK ku-
tai, 97.

Children swinging, poem, signed. H-l s-j hua-chi, 6.

Rugged mountains and trees, poem, signed. H-l s-j hua-chi, 7.

Two fighting sparrows, one in a vine-entwined tree, signed. H-l s-j
hua-chi, 8; TSYMC hua-hsüan, 95.

Two men in a mountain studio, inscribed, signed. H-l s-j hua-chi, 10.

Bird on a pine branch, bamboo, poem, signed. H-l s-j hua-chi, 18.

Two gentlemen under cypress tree, portrait of Ch'en Chung-tzu, inscribed, signed. H-l s-j hua-chi, 20-21.

A hawk on a bare branch, album leaf. H-l s-j hua-chi, 22.

Two phoenix on a wu-t'ung tree, signed. H-l s-j hua-chi, 23.

A crow splashing in water, a bird on a willow branch, album leaf,
inscribed. H-l s-j hua-chi, 25*.

Two dragonflies on bamboo, album leaf, artist's seal. H-l s-j hua-
chi, 26*.

Insects on the ground, vines around bamboo, album leaf, inscribed,
artist's seal. H-l s-j hua-chi, 27*.

Four ducks swimming under flower branch and rock, album leaf, artist's seal. H-l s-j hua-chi, 28*.

A white-eye on a branch, album leaf, inscribed. H-l s-j hua-chi, 29*.

Two crabs, album leaf, artist's seal. H-l s-j hua-chi, 30.

Fishes, album leaf, artist's seal. H-l s-j hua-chi, 31.

Narcissus by a rock, poem, album leaf. H-l s-j hua-chi, 32.

A swallow on a willow branch, one swallow flying, album leaf, artist's
seal. H-l s-j hua-chi, 33.

Three album leaves depicting birds and flowers, each leaf with inscription and artist's seal, possibly belonging to the same album.
H-l s-j hua-chi, 34-36.

An album of ten leaves depicting birds, each leaf with artist's seal.
H-l s-j Ling-mao*.

Lantern Festival, handscroll. Li-tai jen-wu, 68 (section).

A bird singing on an autumn branch, inscribed, signed. TSYMC hua-
hsüan, 94.

HUANG HSIANG-CHIEN 黃向聖 , t. Tuan-mu 端木 . B. 1609,
d. 1673; from Ch'ang-shu, Kiangsu; landscapes. (CP, VII, AL, 346.)

An album of twelve leaves illustrating views of Yünnan, inscribed,
signed, dated 1656, Suchou Museum. Su-chou, 42 (one leaf).

Szechuan mountain scenery, folding fan, inscribed, signed, Shanghai
WWPKWYH. Shan-mien-hua, 58*.

A walled village next to a waterfall high among mountain crags, in-
　　scribed, signed, Suchou Museum. Su-chou, 41.
A tall mountain peak, a man on a ledge, boats, pagoda and village
　　roofs, inscribed, signed, Tientsin Art Museum. T'ien-ching, I. 62.

HUANG I 黄 易 , t. Ta-i 大 易 , h. Hsiao-sung 小 松 . B.
1744, d. 1801; from Hangchou; archaeologist and seal-engraver; painted
landscapes and flowers. (CP, VII, AL, 346-347.)
　　Sprays of plum-blossoms in a vase, poem, signed, (AL). Che-chiang,
　　　　85.
　　Four album leaves, each of landscape, each accompanied by calligra-
　　　　phy, inscribed, one signed, Tientsin Art Museum. T'ien-ching,
　　　　II. 146-147.

HUANG KUO-LAN 黄 國 蘭 , h. Yang-ch'eng nü-shih 羊 城 女 士 .
A woman, studied Chang Ju-chih. (W. I. 12.)
　　Landscape, inscribed, dated (indistinct), Chu-p'ing-an Kuan collection.
　　　　Kuang-tung shu-hua, 48.

HUANG P'EI-FANG 黄 培 芳 , t. Tzu-shih 子 實 , h. Hsiang-
shih 香 石 , Ao-yo shan-jen 粵 嶽 山 人 . B. 1777, d. 1859;
from Hsiang-shan, Kuangtung; painted landscapes after Wang Fu. (W. I. 6;
M. p. 548.)
　　The Liang Spring on Mt. Lo-fu, album leaf, signed, dated 1815, Wang
　　　　Hsiang-lu collection. Kuang-tung shu-hua, 36.
　　Pavilions and teashops on the Pearl River, album leaf, inscribed,
　　　　signed, dated 1850. Kuang-tung hua-chia, 52*.
　　Cottages in a bamboo grove, inscribed, Chu-p'ing-an Kuan collection.
　　　　Kuang-tung shu-hua, 31.

HUANG PI 黄 壁 , t. Hsiao-ch'ih 小 癡 . From Ch'ao-chou,
Kuangtung, c. 1720; calligraphy and landscapes after Wu Chen. (CP, VII,
AL, 347-348.)
　　Boats being towed up the river, inscribed, signed. Kuang-tung hua-
　　　　chia, 34*.
　　A scholar enjoying the snow from a pavilion, poem, signed. Kuang-
　　　　tung hua-chia, 35*.

HUANG SHEN 黄 慎 , t. Kung-mou 恭 懋 , h. Ying-p'iao 癭 瓢 .
B. 1687, d. 1766; from Fukien, lived in Yangchou, Kiangsu; landscapes,
figures. For dates see Ku Lin-wen, Yang-chou pa-chia shih-liao, (Shang-
hai, 1962). (CP, VII, AL, 348-349.)
　　Ink chrysanthemums, inscribed, signed, dated 1728, Palace Museum,
　　　　Peking. KKPWY hua-niao, 90*.

Portrait of T'ao Ch'ien, signed, dated 1752, Chang Pe-chin collection. Tien Yin Tang, I.97.

Two ducks swimming under flowers and rice plants, signed, dated
1757, Cheng Te-k'un collection, Cambridge. Mu-fei, before
p. 53.

An old man and a servant gazing at a dwarf plum tree, inscribed, signed, Nanking Museum. Yang-chou pa-chia, 7.

Two ducks, album leaf, signed, Nanking Museum. Yang-chou pa-
chia, 9.

Persimmon, inscribed, signed, Shanghai Museum. Shang-hai, 84*.

A returning cowherd on a buffalo, inscribed, signed, Tientsin Art
Museum. T'ien-ching, II.124.

Fu Sheng transmitting the Classics, Tientsin Art Museum. I-yüan chi-
chin, 49.

Wild geese, poem, signed, Chang Pe-chin collection. Tien Yin Tang,
I.98.

An old man with a basket of flowers, inscribed, signed. Li-tai jen-
wu, 66; TSYMC hua-hsüan, 99*.

HUANG TING 黄 鼎 , t. Tsun-ku 尊 古 , h. K'uang-t'ing 曠亭 ,
Tu-wang-k'o 獨往客 and other names. B. 1660, d. 1730; from
Ch'ang-shu, Kiangsu; landscapes. (CP, VII, AL, 349-350.)

Old trees along water, folding fan, signed, dated 1713, Shanghai WWP-
KWYH. Shan-mien-hua, 85*.

River-view in Ni Tsan's style, signed, dated 1715, Nat. Pal. Mus.,
Taipei, (AL). CKLTMHC, V.38.

Landscape after a Yüan master, signed, dated 1729; Cheng Te-k'un
collection, Cambridge. Mu-fei, before p. 49.

Homestead at the foot of steep mountains in autumn, after Wang Meng,
artist's seals, Nat. Pal. Mus., Taipei, (AL). CKLTMHC, V.39.

HUANG TS'OU 黄 湊 , t. Cheng-ch'uan 正 川 , h. Shan-yao 山
曜 . From Yangchou; active during the late 17th-early 18th century;
landscapes. (M. p. 548.)

Portrait of the owner of the T'ung-hua Retreat. Figure by Ting Kao,
background by Huang, crane by Hua Yen, dated 1732 in an inscription by Hsü T'ung-li, Palace Museum, Peking. CK hua, X.16.

HUANG YÜAN-CHIEH 黄 媛 介 ., t. Chieh-ling 介 令 or 皆令 .
From Chia-hsing, Chekiang, a woman, active c. 1598-1645, lived in Hang-
chou; poet, calligrapher, landscapes in the Wu Chen manner. (N.5; Q.I.3;
M. p. 545.)

Landscape, album leaf, signed, dated 1591, Tientsin Art Museum.
T'ien-ching, I.48.

HUNG-JEN 弘 仁 , the priest-name of Chiang T'ao 江 韜 , t.
Chien-chiang 漸 江 , h. Mei-hua ku-na 梅 花 古 衲 . B.
1610, d. 1663; from Hsieh-hsien, Anhui; became a priest at the fall of the
Ming dynasty; one of the "Four Masters of Anhui". (CP, VII, AL, 351-
352.)

    A blossoming plum tree, poem, signed, dated 1626, Cheng Te-k'un
        collection, Cambridge. Mu-fei, before p. 31.

    Album of eight landscapes, one signed and dated 1657, (AL). Hung-
        jen K'un-ts'an, 1-3 (three leaves).

    A pavilion behind three twisted pines and a plum tree, high mountain
        ranges, signed, dated 1658. Hung-jen K'un-ts'an, 4; TSYMC
        hua-hsüan, 72.

    A house and a small bamboo grove on a small ledge under pine and
        bare trees, inscribed, signed, dated 1659, Tientsin Art Museum.
        T'ien-ching, II. 113.

    High cliffs by a river; bare trees and a small pavilion, signed, dated
        1660, (AL). Hung-jen K'un-ts'an, 6.

    A pavilion under trees, signed, dated 1661, Chang Pe-chin collection.
        Tien Yin Tang, I. 70.

    Sketches of rocks and trees, eight album leaves, last leaf signed,
        dated 1662, Cheng Te-k'un collection, Cambridge, (AL). Mu-
        fei, opposite p. 32 (two leaves).

    Landscape of Huang-shan, handscroll, dated 1671, S. M. Siu collec-
        tion, Hong Kong. CK ku-hua, B. 224.

    An album of fifty landscapes, inscriptions and seals of the artist, (AL).
        Hung-jen K'un-ts'an, 8-9 (two leaves).

    Steep cliffs with bare trees and waterfall, poem, signed, (AL). Hung-
        jen K'un-ts'an, 7.

    Steep cliffs and spires with angular pine trees, inscribed, signed,
        Shanghai Museum. CK shu-hua, I. 38; Hung-jen K'un-ts'an, 5;
        Shang-hai, 71*.

    Four landscape album leaves, artist's seals, Tientsin Art Museum.
        T'ien-ching, I. 63-66.

    Buildings and trees along a stream, a mountain bluff, Tientsin Art
        Museum. I-yüan chi-chin, 24.

    Retreat on a mountainside, inscribed, signed, Li Ch'u-li collection.
        CK hua, II. 12.

    Plum blossoms, poem, signed, colophon by Tseng Yin. Hung-jen
        K'un-ts'an, 10.

    Landscape, boat by a shore, album leaf, inscribed. WW, 1958. 8. 56.

I CHING-T'AO 易 景 陶 , t. K'un-shan 崑 山 or Chün-shan
君 山 . From Ho-shan, Kuangtung; painted mules and figures.
(W. II.)

Travellers on foot and muleback, inscribed, signed, dated <u>mou-shen</u>, Chu-p'ing-an Kuan collection. Kuang-tung shu-hua, 48.

I K'O-CHUNG 儀克中 , t. Hsieh-i 協 一 , h. Mo-nung 墨 農 . B. 1793, d. 1834; from Shansi, moved to Fan-yü, Kuangtung, poet, landscapes after Wang Hui. (W.I.8; M. p. 624.)

Figure seated on a rock, poem, signed, dated 1817, five colophons, Ho Man-an collection. Kuang-tung shu-hua, 33.

JEN HSIUNG 任熊 , t. Wei-ch'ang 渭長 . B. 1820, d. 1864; from Hsiao-shan, Chekiang; landscapes, flowers, figures, birds. (CP, VII, AL, 354.)

Portrait of Ting Lan-shu, signed, dated 1856, (AL, <u>Nanga Taisei</u>, VII.203). Che-chiang, 97.

A lady standing behind a garden stone, signed, dated 1857, Tientsin Art Museum. I-yüan chi-chin, 55*.

Nine illustrations to poems by Yao Hsieh, album leaves, a line of poetry and artist's seal on each leaf, Palace Museum, Peking. CK chin-pai-nien, 6-11 (7*); KKPWY hua-niao, 95* (one leaf).

A pensive lady holding a mirror, illustration to a poem, inscribed, signed, Suchou Museum. Su-chou, 115.

Plum and crane on rocks, inscribed. Ch'ing-jen-hua*.

Rustic entertainment, inscribed, seal. CK ku-tai, 103.

JEN HSÜN 任薰 , t. Fu-ch'ang 阜長 . B. 1835, d. 1893; from Hsiao-shan, Chekiang; younger brother of Jen Hsiung; flowers. (CP, VII, AL, 354.)

Seven album leaves depicting birds and flowers and landscapes, after T'ang and Sung masters, leaves inscribed, signed, one dated 1879, possibly all part of same album, Kiangsu Provincial Museum. CK chin-pai-nien 12, 15-16, 13*.

Two ladies reading by a table by a screen, album leaf, artist's seal, Tientsin Art Museum. I-yüan chi-chin, 56.

A bird on a flowering tree, folding fan, inscribed, signed. Che-chiang, 100.

JEN I 任頤 , t. Po-nien 伯年 . B. 1840, d. 1896; from Shan-yin, Chekiang; birds, flowers, figures, imitated Ch'en Hung-shou. (CP, VII, AL, 354.)

Portrait of Sha-fu at age thirty-nine, inscribed, dated 1862, Kiangsu Provincial Museum. CK chin-pai-nien, 19.

Offering auspicious flowers, signed, dated 1872. JP-n hua-chi, 10*.

Buddhist meditation, signed, dated 1872. JP-n hua-chi, 52*; JP-n hua-hsüan, 3*.

Three men in a boat going past a cliff, folding fan, inscribed, signed, dated 1872. JP-n hua-chi, 67.

Narcissus and the heavenly bamboo, signed, dated 1872. JP-n hua-chi, 140.

Three swallows flying among twisted vines, signed, dated 1872. JP-n hua-ts'e, B*.

Two mynahs on banana tree, rose bush below, signed, dated 1872. JP-n hua-ts'e, B*.

Epidendrum and morning glories, fan, signed, dated 1873. JP-n hua-chi, 151.

Three herons among leaves, folding fan, signed, dated 1873. JP-n hua-chi, 157.

Three chickens on rocks, folding fan, signed, dated 1873. JP-n hua-chi, 159.

Chung K'uei, signed, dated 1874. JP-n hua-chi, 12.

Bird and flowers, folding fan, signed, dated 1874. JP-n hua-chi, 163.

T'ang Kao-tsu shooting at the peacock screen, signed, dated 1877. JP-n hua-chi, 5*.

Portrait of a gentleman reading, inscribed, signed, dated 1877. JP-n hua-chi, 65.

Birds on a stone by a stream, bamboo and flowers, signed, dated 1877. JP-n hua-chi, 93.

Narcissi, folding fan, signed, dated 1877. JP-n hua-chi, 155.

Bird on a rock, flowers and grasses, folding fan, signed, dated 1877. JP-n hua-chi, 164.

Scholar on muleback, fan, signed, dated 1879. JP-n hua-chi, 60*; JP-n hua-hsüan, 4*.

A pair of ducks on a shore, signed, dated 1879. JP-n hua-chi, 109.

Mynah on a peach branch, fan, inscribed, signed, dated 1879. JP-n hua-chi, 150.

White-head and hibiscus, fan, signed, inscribed, dated 1879. JP-n hua-chi, 161.

Two of the Eight Immortals, signed, dated 1880. JP-n hua-chi, 7.

Chung K'uei, signed, dated 1880. JP-n hua-chi, 13.

A scholar looking at a waterfall, handscroll, signed, dated 1880. JP-n'hua-chi, 71.

Bird on a blossoming peach branch, fan, inscribed, signed, dated 1880. JP-n hua-chi, 153*.

Portrait of a gentleman seated on a bamboo bench and holding a closed fan, signed, dated 1880. JP-n hua-ts'e, B*.

Travellers, inscribed, signed, dated 1880, Chinese Artists Association. CK chin-pai-nien, 19.

Woman and crane under a plum tree, signed, dated 1881. JP-n hua-chi, 4.

Three children and one adult, signed, dated 1881. JP-n hua-chi, 11.

Chung K'uei, signed, dated 1881. JP-n hua-chi, 15.

A lady leaning on a garden wall, folding fan, inscribed, signed, dated 1881. JP-n hua-chi, 69.

Two birds on a wu-t'ung branch, folding fan, signed, dated 1881. JP-n hua-chi, 165.

Two ducks behind lotus blossoms and leaves, signed, dated 1881. JP-n hua-ts'e, B*.

Three mynahs on a willow branch, signed, dated 1881. JP-n hua-ts'e, B*.

Two cranes and banana trees, signed, dated 1881. JP-n hua-ts'e, B*.

Two white-heads flying by a needle-like rock surrounded by berry plants, signed, dated 1882, Palace Museum, Peking. KKPWY hua-niao, 99*.

Two sparrows and tree peony, inscribed, signed, dated 1882. JP-n hua-chi, 88.

Two pheasants under banana tree, signed, dated 1882. JP-n hua-chi, 111.

Chickens resting under loquat tree, signed, dated 1882, inscribed. JP-n hua-chi, 113*.

Banana plant and "snowball", inscribed, signed, dated 1882. JP-n hua-chi, 120*.

Two birds on blossoming tree in late spring, inscribed, signed, dated 1882. JP-n hua-chi, 127.

Quail on rock under tall tree, inscribed, signed, dated 1882. JP-n hua-chi, 146.

Parrot on blossoming branch, folding fan, inscribed, signed, dated 1882. JP-n hua-chi, 162.

Epidendrum and fungus by a rock, inscribed, signed, dated 1882. JP-n hua-ts'e, B*.

Su Wu herding sheep, signed, dated 1883, Palace Museum, Peking. CK hua, XV. 16; JP-n hua-chi, 2.

Scholar and servant on bridge under large tree, strange rocks, fan, inscribed, signed, dated 1883. JP-n hua-chi, 62.

Two ducks under lotus leaves, inscribed, signed, dated 1883. JP-n hua-chi, 82*; JP-n hua-hsüan, 6*.

Still life: vase of wisteria, lamp, scroll, ink slab, water dropper, inscribed, signed, dated 1883. JP-n hua-chi, 92.

Two ducks, signed, inscribed, dated 1883. JP-n hua-chi, 128.

Two swallows on blossoming branch, folding fan, inscribed, signed, dated 1883. JP-n hua-chi, 156.

Chick in a rockery, folding fan, inscribed, signed, dated 1883. JP-n hua-chi, 166.

Two pheasants amid flowers and bamboo, signed, dated 1883. JP-n hua-niao*.

Three ducks in a lotus pond, signed, dated 1883. JP-n hua-ts'e, B*.

Two orange-throated birds on fruiting peach branch, signed, dated 1883. JP-n hua-ts'e, B*.

A woman leaning on a window ledge looking at plum blossoms, signed, dated 1884, Liao-ning Provincial Museum. Liao-ning, II. 122.

Man standing on a bank under bamboo, two geese, signed, dated 1884. JP-n hua-chi, 30.

A pair of ducks in water under lotus plants, signed, dated 1884. JP-n hua-chi, 136.

A cat seated under sparrow-filled loquat tree, signed, dated 1884. JP-n hua-chi, 145.

Lotus and egrets, inscribed, signed, dated 1884. JP-n hua-niao*.

Four birds and crab apple tree, signed, dated 1884. JP-n hua-niao*.

Bird on a rock under orange-colored blossoms and lilies, signed, dated 1884. JP-n hua-niao*.

Ni Tsan's servant washing the wu-t'ung tree, signed, dated 1884. JP-n hua-ts'e, B*.

A man washing his feet in a stream, album leaf, inscribed, signed, dated 1885, Palace Museum, Peking. CK chin-pai-nien, 20.

A man and servant in snow, signed, dated 1885, Shanghai Museum. Shang-hai, 94*.

Portrait of the artist's wife's grandparents, inscribed, signed, dated 1885, Chinese Artists Association. CK hua, II. 15; JP-n hua-chi, 64.

A man and a mule watching flying geese, inscribed, signed, dated 1885. JP-n hua-chi, 39.

Saddling a horse, album leaf, inscribed, signed, dated 1885. JP-n hua-chi, 49.

Fisherman in a boat, album leaf, inscribed, signed, dated 1885. JP-n hua-chi, 50.

Gentleman and servant on a bridge, album leaf, inscribed, signed, dated 1885. JP-n hua-chi, 57.

Cormorant fishing, album leaf, signed, dated 1885. JP-n hua-chi, 58.

Boy with broom on rustic bridge, album leaf, inscribed, signed, dated 1885. JP-n hua-chi, 80.

Man worshipping, a servant with a ch'in, album leaf, inscribed, signed, dated 1885. JP-n hua-chi, 73; JP-n k'o-t'u*.

Two men eating by a wall, album leaf, inscribed, signed, dated 1885. JP-n hua-chi, 74.

Two figures, illustration to the Shih-chi, album leaf, inscribed, signed, dated 1885. JP-n hua-chi, 75; JP-n k'o-t'u*.

Rain pelting pear blossoms into a doorway, album leaf, inscribed,
  signed, dated 1885. JP-n hua-chi, 76; JP-n k'o-t'u*.
A woman in a thatched hut under a tree, album leaf, inscribed, signed,
  dated 1885. JP-n hua-chi, 77.
Two figures on a bridge at the base of a cliff, album leaf, inscribed,
  signed, dated 1885, in the style of Ting Yün-p'eng. JP-n hua-
  chi, 78; JP-n k'o-t'u*.
Shrimp and vegetables, inscribed, signed, dated 1885. JP-n hua-
  chi, 107.
Four swallows flying above wisteria and rock, inscribed, signed,
  dated 1885. JP-n hua-chi, 112.
Two swallows flying above plum blossoms, signed, dated 1885. JP-n
  hua-chi, 119*.
Flying birds, flowering plant and stone, inscribed, signed, dated 1885.
  JP-n hua-chi, 122.
Swallows flying above foliage and rock, inscribed, signed, dated 1885.
  JP-n hua-chi, 137*; JP-n hua-hsüan, 10*.
Two Immortals and deer, signed, dated 1885. JP-n hua-ts'e, B*.
Three cranes in water by rock and wisteria, signed, dated 1885.
  JP-n hua-ts'e, B*.
Four swallows flying over blossom-covered water, album leaf, signed,
  dated 1885. JP-n ts'ao-ch'ung*.
Three catfish strung on a branch, a basket of clams, album leaf, sign-
  ed, dated 1885. JP-n ts'ao-ch'ung*.
A man in a pavilion built over a stream, inscribed, signed, dated
  1885. JP-n k'o-t'u*.
An album of eight leaves depicting birds and flowers, each leaf inscri-
  bed and/or signed, one leaf dated 1885, two leaves dated 1886.
  JP-n Hua-ts'e, A*.
Hsiao-hung softly singing as the artist plays the flute, a man and a
  lady in a boat under a pine, signed, dated 1886. JP-n hua-chi, 34.
Peach Blossom Spring, signed, dated 1886. JP-n hua-chi, 35.
Lin P'u and his "plum-tree wife and crane son", inscribed, signed,
  dated 1886. JP-n hua-chi, 37*.
Two gentlemen on a bridge under trees, signed, dated 1886. JP-n
  hua-chi, 38*.
A scholar holding an inkstone, inscribed, signed, dated 1886. JP-n
  hua-chi, 51*; JP-n hua-hsüan, 3*.
Six crows on a rock above blossoming branches, inscribed, signed,
  dated 1886. JP-n hua-chi, 89.
Still life: stone, jar of scrolls, books, images, spray of wisteria,
  inscribed, signed, dated 1886. JP-n hua-chi, 91.
Four swallows flying around prunus, album leaf, signed, dated 1886.
  JP-n hua-chi, 102.

Portrait of Kao Yung, inscribed, signed, dated 1887, Palace Museum, Peking. CK hua, XVIII. 19.

Man and woman with a tiger, album leaf, signed, dated 1887. JP-n hua-chi, 53.

Two parrots on red maple, dated 1887. JP-n hua-chi, 98*; JP-n hua-hsüan, 7*.

Two crested birds on plum blossom branch, signed, dated 1887. JP-n hua-chi, 103*.

Duck sleeping under melon vine, signed, dated 1887. JP-n hua-chi, 106*.

Nü Kua melting stones, signed, dated 1888. JP-n hua-chi, 1*; JP-n hua-hsüan, 1*.

A man and two horses standing under bare trees, signed, dated 1888. JP-n hua-chi, 20.

A boy standing in a boat by willows, inscribed, signed, dated 1888. JP-n hua-chi, 40.

Man on a donkey in a landscape, folding fan, inscribed, signed, dated 1888. JP-n hua-chi, 70.

Three bulbuls in a thicket, inscribed, signed, dated, 1888. JP-n hua-chi, 83.

A crow on a rock under willows, signed, dated 1888. JP-n hua-chi, 129.

Monkey trainer, inscribed, signed, dated 1888. Li-tai jen-wu, 72; TSYMC hua-hsüan, 107.

Liu Ling in his deer cart, signed, dated 1889. JP-n hua-chi, 18.

Lao Tzu arriving from the East, signed, dated 1889. JP-n hua-chi, 19.

A man and a horse in a misty grove, signed, dated 1889. JP-n hua-chi, 21.

Two figures in a landscape, fan, signed, dated 1889. JP-n hua-chi, 63*; JP-n hua-hsüan, 5*.

Wisteria and four partridges, inscribed, signed, dated 1889. JP-n hua-chi, 86.

Nine egrets along a reedy shore, inscribed, signed, dated 1889. JP-n hua-chi, 115.

Two birds on a willow branch, inscribed, signed, dated 1889. JP-n hua-chi, 116.

A crane standing below a pine tree, inscribed, signed, dated 1889. JP-n hua-chi, 117.

Chicks and hen under rock and plant, signed, dated 1889. JP-n hua-chi, 124.

A pair of mandarin ducks under reeds, inscribed, signed, dated 1889. CK hua, IV. 11*.

Three men in a boat, a servant poling, fan, inscribed, signed, dated 1890, Kiangsu Provincial Museum. CK chin-pai-nien, 23.

Two birds on a bare branch of a fruit tree, inscribed, signed, dated
1890. JP-n hua-chi, 95*.

Three geese swimming in a willow stream, signed, dated 1890. JP-n
hua-chi, 125*; JP-n hua-hsüan, 8*.

Two birds on a cliff above flowering creeper, inscribed, signed, dated
1890. JP-n hua-chi, 130.

A kingfisher on wisteria, signed, dated 1890. JP-n hua-chi, 131*;
JP-n hua-hsüan, 9*.

A bird pecking below wisteria, signed, dated 1890. JP-n hua-chi,
132*; JP-n hua-hsüan, 9*.

Six ducks swimming among reeds and plants, signed, dated 1890.
JP-n hua-chi, 135.

Hen and chickens under loquat branch, signed, dated 1890. JP-n
hua-chi, 141.

A bird singing under red flowering shrub, signed, dated 1890. JP- n
hua-chi, 143*.

Two herdboys, two water buffalo and two geese, signed, dated 1890.
JP-n hua-ts'e, B*.

Climbing vines, signed, dated 1890. CK ku-tai, 102.

A pine tree, signed, dated 1891, Tientsin Art Museum. I-yüan chi-
chin, 57.

A mule rider going over a hill, signed, dated 1891, Chinese Artists
Association. CK chin-pai-nien, 24.

Chickens under coir palm, signed, dated 1891, Chinese Artists Association. CK chin-pai-nien, 25.

Chung K'uei, signed, dated 1891. JP-n hua-chi, 14.

Music on Eastern Mountain, signed, dated 1891. JP-n hua-chi, 16.

Hsü Yu washing his ears, signed, dated 1891. JP-n hua-chi, 26.

Two ladies in boats near willow bank, signed, dated 1891, colophon
by Hsü Pei-hung. JP-n hua-chi, 28*.

Resting under the pines, signed, dated 1891. JP-n hua-chi, 36.

Banana leaves, sparrows and plum blossoms, inscribed, signed,
dated 1891. JP-n hua-chi, 84.

Two cranes and loquats, inscribed, signed, dated 1891. JP-n hua-
chi, 85.

Two quail under tree peonies, inscribed, signed, dated 1891. JP-n
hua-chi, 142.

Two sparrows on a red-leafed branch, one sparrow flying, signed,
dated 1891. JP-n hua-ts'e, B*.

Two chickens and tree peony, signed, dated 1891. JP-n hua-ts'e, B*.

Su Shih and a lady under a pine tree, signed, dated 1892. JP-n hua-
chi, 23.

Ducks on a rock under wisteria, inscribed, signed, dated 1892. JP-n
hua-chi, 87*.

Two swallows on a wisteria vine, signed, dated 1892. JP-n hua-chi, 94.

Ducks swimming through reeds, inscribed, signed, dated 1892. JP-n hua-chi, 110.

A sparrow on a twisted pine, signed, dated 1892. JP-n hua-chi, 121.

Quail and banana tree, signed, inscribed, dated 1892. JP-n hua-chi, 123.

Two sparrows flying above bamboo and rock, inscribed, signed, dated 1892. JP-n hua-chi, 134.

A lady seated on a rock playing with a child, signed, dated 1892. JP-n hua-ts'e, B*.

Two chicks and morning glory, signed, dated 1892. Ch'ing-jen-hua*.

Changing stones into sheep, signed, dated 1893. JP-n hua-chi, 24.

Spring breeze, scholar on horseback, servant following, signed, dated 1893. JP-n hua-chi, 25.

Chicken under melon vine, inscribed, signed, dated 1893. JP-n hua-chi, 90*.

Four sparrows on wisteria and rock, signed, dated 1893. JP-n hua-ts'e, B*.

Listening to the flute under the pines, signed, dated 1894. JP-n hua-chi, 22*; JP-n hua-hsüan, 2*.

A cat, fan, inscribed, signed, dated 1895. JP-n hua-chi, 154.

A peacock, signed, Palace Museum, Peking. KKPWY hua-niao, 98*.

Mynah on a willow branch, album leaf, inscribed, signed, Palace Museum, Peking. CK chin-pai-nien, 20.

Quail under red leaves, album leaf, inscribed, signed, Palace Museum, Peking. CK chin-pai-nien, 21*.

A lotus, fan, inscribed, signed, Kiangsu Provincial Museum. JP-n hua-chi, 152; CK chin-pai-nien, 23.

Immortals' birthday congratulations, twelve paintings. JP-n hua-chi, 3.

Two of Eight Immortals, signed. JP-n hua-chi, 6.

Two of Eight Immortals, signed. JP-n hua-chi, 8.

Two of the Eight Immortals, signed. JP-n hua-chi, 9.

Music on the Eastern Mountain. JP-n hua-chi, 17*.

Lady with a fan beneath a wu-t'ung tree, artist's seal. JP-n hua-chi, 27*.

A man seated beneath a tree, two chickens and some chicks, signed. JP-n hua-chi, 29.

Mi Fei, colophon by Hsü Pei-hung. JP-n hua-chi, 31.

Hsi Shih. JP-n hua-chi, 32.

Hsiao-hung softly singing as the artist plays the flute; a man and a lady in a boat under a pine. JP-n hua-chi, 33.

A scholar seated in a chair under trees, album leaf, signed. JP-n hua-chi, 41.

A man holding a fan seated on a bank above a rock and flowering bush, album leaf. JP-n hua-chi, 42.

A man resting on a rock behind bamboo stalks, album leaf, signed. JP-n hua-chi, 43.

Fisherman in a boat moored at the bank, snow scene, album leaf, signed. JP-n hua-chi, 44.

Scholar leaning on a rock below two bare trees, album leaf, signed. JP-n hua-chi, 45.

A lady holding a p'i-p'a, seated on a stool in front of bamboo, album leaf, signed. JP-n hua-chi, 46.

A boy walking on a path in wind, album leaf, signed. JP-n hua-chi, 47.

A scholar seeking shelter from snow in a thatched hut, album leaf, signed. JP-n hua-chi, 48.

A man seated on a slanting rock, album leaf, signed. JP-n hua-chi, 54.

Two scholars reading, album leaf, signed. JP-n hua-chi, 55.

Two musicians, album leaf, signed. JP-n hua-chi, 56.

A boy poling a boat near the shore, fan, inscribed, signed. JP-n hua-chi, 59.

Two men reading under a tree, fan, inscribed, signed. JP-n hua-chi, 61.

A woman leaning on a rock under a blossoming tree, colophon by Hsü Pei-hung. JP-n hua-chi, 66.

Lady writing in a garden pavilion, folding fan, inscribed, signed. JP-n hua-chi, 68*.

A man with his hat blown off by the wind, inscribed, signed. JP-n hua-chi, 72.

Verandas in craggy mountains, album leaf, inscribed. JP-n hua-chi, 79; JP-n k'o-t'u*.

Rock and trees in a stream, album leaf, inscribed, signed. JP-n hua-chi, 81; JP-n k'o-t'u*.

Narcissus, signed. JP-n hua-chi, 96.

Two swallows on a leafy branch, inscribed, signed. JP-n hua-chi, 97.

Flying sparrow and day lily, signed. JP-n hua-chi, 99.

Two fowl and plants, signed. JP-n hua-chi, 100.

A bird flying above berry bush and rock, album leaf, signed. JP-n hua-chi, 101.

A rooster on a rock, signed. JP-n hua-chi, 104.

Two dogs by a basket of vegetables, signed. JP-n hua-chi, 105.

Swimming fish, album leaf, signed. JP-n hua-chi, 108.

Two ducks swimming under blossoming tree, signed. JP-n hua-chi, 114*.

A crane on a pine tree branch, signed. JP-n hua-chi, 118.

Three birds under autumn lotus plants, inscribed, signed. JP-n hua-chi, 126*; JP-n hua-hsüan, 8*.

A bird perched on a branch behind a banana tree. JP-n hua-chi, 133.

Three chickens under a plant with red fruit. JP-n hua-chi, 138*; JP-n hua-hsüan, 10*.

Duck and lotus on moonlit night, artist's seal, JP-n hua-chi, 139.

Narcissus and camellias, inscribed, signed. JP-n hua-chi, 144*.

Water buffalo and calf, colophon by Hsü Pei-hung. JP-n hua-chi, 147.

Three sheep, signed. JP-n hua-chi, 148.

Bird on a blossoming branch, fan, inscribed, signed. JP-n hua-chi, 149.

Peacock among tree peonies, folding fan, inscribed, signed. JP-n hua-chi, 158.

A duck under white lotus, folding fan, signed. JP-n hua-chi, 160*.

A man in a boat returning in wind and rain, signed. JP-n hua-ts'e, B*.

Three chickens on a rock, wisteria, signed. JP-n hua-ts'e, B*.

Two chicks under a sunflower plant, signed. JP-n hua-ts'e, B*.

Bulbuls on a tree stump behind lotus blossoms, signed. JP-n hua-ts'e, B*.

Morning glories by a fence, album leaf, signed. JP-n ts'ao-ch'ung*.

Two birds on a willow branch, album leaf, signed. JP-n ts'ao-ch'ung*.

A spider on a web in a peavine, album leaf, signed. JP-n ts'ao-ch'ung*.

A grasshopper by a rock and pink flowers, album leaf, signed. JP-n ts'ao-ch'ung*.

Three chicks by green plants, album leaf, signed. JP-n ts'ao-ch'ung*.

A bird flying toward its nest, album leaf, signed. JP-n ts'ao-ch'ung*.

A man shading his eyes and gazing between two trees, wind blowing, artist's seal. JP-n k'o-t'u*.

Portrait of Wu Ch'ang-shih, two inscriptions. Che-chiang, 101.

Two birds on branches of cherry tree, album leaf, signed. Che-chiang, 102.

Three friends seated at side of a table, inscribed, two colophons. Li-tai jen-wu, 71.

JEN YÜ 任 豫 , t. Li-fan 立 凡 , h. Hsiao-hsiao an-chu-jen 瀟 瀟 庵 主 人 . B. 1853, d. 1901; son of Jen Hsiung; painted flowers, birds, figures, landscapes. (M. p. 87.)

Snowy spring landscape, inscribed, Kiangsu Provincial Museum. CK chin-pai-nien, 17*.

KAI CH'I 改 琦 , t. Po-yün 伯 蘊 , h. Hsiang-po 香 白 , Ch'i-hsiang 七 鄉 , Yü-hu wai-shih 玉 壺 外 史 and other names. B. 1774, d. 1829; his ancestors were from Sinkiang, settled in Sung-chiang, Kiangsu; poet; figures, landscapes, flowers, bamboo. (CP, VII, AL, 354-355.)

A man in a boat under blossoming trees, folding fan, signed, dated 1820, Shanghai WWPKWYH. Shan-mien-hua, 99*.

KAN SHIH-T'IAO 甘 士 調 , h. Feng-chi shan-jen 鳳 磯 山 人 . From Liao-yang, Manchuria, active during the K'ang-hsi era (1662-1722), a finger-painter. (M. p. 69.)

Hibiscus and wild duck, signed, dated 1716, Liao-ning Provincial Museum. Liao-ning, II. 109.

KAN T'IEN-CH'UNG 甘 天 寵 , t. Cheng-p'an 正 蟠 , h. Ch'ai-ho 儕 鶴 , Po-shih shan-jen 白 石 山 人 . From Hsin-hui, Kuang-tung, active c. 1770, painted lotus, waterbirds. (W. I. 3.)

A bird on a flat stone under lotus, signed, Cheng Te-k'un collection, Cambridge. Mu-fei, opposite p. 58.

A bird on a rock under reeds, signed, T'ang T'ien-ju collection. Kuang-tung shu-hua, 28.

An egret under lotus, signed. Kuang-tung hua-chia, 37*.

K'ANG T'AO 康 濤 , t. Shih-chou 石 舟 , h. T'ien-tu lao-jen 天 篤 老 人 , Mao-hsin lao-jen 茆 心 老 人 , and other names. From Ch'ien-t'ang, Chekiang, active c. 1726-1755; landscapes, flowers, figures, birds. (CP, VII, AL, 355.)

After the bath, inscribed, signed, Tientsin Art Museum. I-yüan chi-chin, 45*.

KAO CH'I-P'EI 高 其 佩 , t. Wei-chih 葦 之 , h. Ch'ieh-yüan 且 園 , Nan-ts'un 南 村 , Ch'ang-po shan-jen 長 白 山 人 and other names. B. 1672, d. 1734; from Liao-yang, Manchuria; a finger-painter; landscape, figures, flowers, birds. (CP, VII, AL, 355-357.)

Birds under a hibiscus plant, signed, dated 1703, Chang Pe-chin collection. Tien Yin Tang, I. 94.

An album of eight leaves depicting aquatic animals and scenes, last leaf signed, dated 1712, Nanking Museum (?). KC-p Hua-ts'e.

Chung K'uei, poem, signed, colophon dated 1728, finger-painting, (AL). Li-tai jen-wu, 67.

Waterfall on Lu-shan, signed, finger-painting, Nat. Pal. Mus., Tai-pei, (AL). CKLTMHC, V. 44.

A praying mantis on rice stalks, inscribed, artist's seals, finger painting, Palace Museum, Peking. KKPWY hua-niao, 79*.

A man on horseback going hunting, signed, finger-painting, Liao-
ning Provincial Museum. Liao-ning, II. 107.
Two album leaves of aquatic scenes, both inscribed, Tientsin Art
Museum. T'ien-ching, I. 82-83.
A man on a horse in winter, album leaf, inscribed, Tientsin Art Mu-
seum. I-yüan chi-chin, 42.
A hawk chasing sparrows, signed, Chang Pe-chin collection. Tien
Yin Tang, I. 95.
Landscape, fishermen, scholar on path, signed, finger-painting,
Cheng Te-k'un collection, Cambridge. Mu-fei, opposite p. 52.
A man at the top of a high mountain peak, folding fan, inscribed, sign-
ed, Hui Hsiao-t'ung collection. Shan-mien chi-chin, 14*.
Crabapple blossoms, folding fan, inscribed, signed, Hui Hsiao-t'ung
collection. Shan-mien chi-chin, 19*.
A praying mantis on a broken tree trunk, album leaf, artist's seal,
finger-painting. TSYMC hua-hsüan, 91.

KAO FENG-HAN 高鳳瀚 , t. Hsi-yüan 西園 , h. Nan-ts'un
南邨 , Nan-fu lao-jen 南阜老人 , Kuei-yün lao-jen
歸雲老人 , Hou Shang-tso-sheng 後尚左生 and
other names. B. 1683, d. 1748; from Chiao-chou, Shantung; calligrapher;
painted landscapes, flowers. (CP, VII, AL, 357-358.)
Chrysanthemums, bamboo and plants by rocks, inscribed, signed,
dated 1720, Suchou Museum. Su-chou, 80.
A thatched hut in a plum-tree garden, signed, inscribed, dated 1723.
Kao Feng-han, 2.
Broad view of countryside with peach and pear trees, inscribed, sign-
ed, dated 1723. Kao Feng-han, 3.
Pines by a waterfall, inscribed, signed, dated 1724. Kao Feng-han, 4.
Peony shrubs and rock, inscribed, signed, dated 1725, Liao-ning
Provincial Museum. Liao-ning, II. 111.
Peonies in moonlight, inscribed, signed, dated 1726. Kao Feng-han, 5.
Peonies, inscribed, signed, dated 1737. Kao Feng-han, 6.
A seated man, handscroll, signed, dated 1738, colophon by Cheng
Hsieh. Kao Feng-han, 1.
Portraits of Kao Feng-han and Lu Ya-yü in a garden pavilion, two
other figures, done by Kao, Lu Yin and Kuang Sung-ts'en, dated
1738. Kao Feng-han, 8.
A man on a promontory, departing boat, geese flying above the marsh,
signed, dated 1741. Kao Feng-han, 9.
Plum trees by a rock, two inscriptions by the artist, one dated 1741.
Kao Feng-han, 10.
Twisted plum tree on a rock, poem, signed, dated 1745. Kao Feng-
han, 14.

A flock of crows in an old tree, handscroll, inscribed, signed, dated
1745. Kao Feng-han, 13.

Autumn chrysanthemums, handscroll, inscribed, signed, dated 1746.
Kao Feng-han, 15.

Crows flocking to an old grove of trees, signed, dated 1748. Kao
Feng-han, 16.

The Western Pavilion, an illustration to a poem, album leaf, inscribed.
Kao Feng-han, 7.

Banana plants in the moonlight, signed. Kao Feng-han, 11.

Peonies by a tall rock, signed. Kao Feng-han, 12.

KAO HSIANG 高翔 , t. Feng-kang 鳳岡 , h. Hsi-t'ang
西唐 , Shan-lin wai-ch'en 山林外臣 and other names.
B. 1688, d. c. 1753; from Yangchou, Kiangsu; a friend of Tao-chi; poet,
one of the "Eight Eccentrics of Yangchou"; plum-blossoms. For dates
see Ku Lin-wen, Yang-chou pa-chia shih-liao, (Shanghai, 1962). (CP, VII,
AL, 359.)

Pomegranate blossoms, inscribed, signed, dated 1742, Nanking Museum. Yang-chou pa-chia, 11.

A small album of landscape-studies, inscribed, signed, Shanghai Museum, (AL). Shang-hai, 88* (eighth leaf).

An album of ten landscape paintings, one leaf inscribed and signed,
Cheng Te-k'un collection, Cambridge, (AL). Mu-fei, between
pp. 54-55 (2 leaves).

Four landscape album leaves, two signed, Tientsin Art Museum.
T'ien-ching, II.125-128.

A man on a promontory, a mountain estate and misty mountains, poem,
signed. TSYMC hua-hsüan, 96.

KAO SHIH-CH'I 高士奇 , t. Tan-jen 澹人 , h. Chiang-
ts'un 江村 . B. 1645, d. 1704; from Ch'ien-t'ang, Chekiang; connoisseur, collector, author of Chiang-ts'un hsiao-hsia lu and Keng-tzu
hsiao-hsia lu. (CP, VII, AL, 359.)

Bamboo, rock and day lily, inscribed, signed, dated 1676, in the
style of Huang Ch'üan, Chang Pe-chin collection. Tien Yin Tang,
I. 89.

KAO TS'EN 高岑 , t. Wei-sheng 蔚生 , h. Shan-ch'ang
善長 . From Hangchou, lived in Nanking; active c. 1670; one of the
"Eight Masters of Nanking"; landscapes, flowers. (CP, VII, AL, 359-360.)

A villa in a pine grove, high mountains, poem, signed, dated 1673,
Tientsin Art Museum. T'ien-ching, I. 78.

Autumn mountain landscape, handscroll, signed, dated 1675, Liao-
ning Provincial Museum. Liao-ning, II. 89-90.

Landscape, after Fan K'uan's "Autumn mountains and dense grove",
signed, (AL). Che-chiang, 73.

KAO YEN 高儼 , t. Wang-kung 望公 . From Hsin-hui,
Kuangtung; active c. 1616-1687; poet, calligrapher. (CP, VII, AL, 360.)
Riverscape, handscroll, inscribed, signed, dated 1661, Ho Hsien
collection. Kuang-tung shu-hua, 20.
Buildings on a cliff overhanging the river, signed, dated 1666, (AL).
Kuang-tung hua-chia, 21*.
A scholar reading in a pavilion by a misty waterfall, inscribed, signed.
Kuang-tung hua-chia, 19*.
A man with a staff on a mountain stairway, signed. Kuang-tung hua-
chia, 20*.
A man with a staff walking toward a pavilion, waterfall at left, signed.
Kuang-tung hua-chia, 22*.
A waterfall high in the mountains, signed. Kuang-tung hua-chia, 23*.

K'O YU-CHEN 柯有榛 , t. Yün-hsü 雲廬 , h. Li-mu
shan-jen 里木山人 . From Nan-hai, Kuangtung; active in the
mid-19th century; painted landscapes, flowers, birds, figures. (W.I.9.)
Four paintings, copies of ghosts by Lo P'ing, each painting inscribed,
Ssu-wu-yang Chai collection. Kuang-tung shu-hua, 49.

KU FANG 顧昉 , t. Jo-chou 若周 , h. Jih-fang 日方 ,
Keng-yün 耕雲 , Wan-kao 晚皋 . From Hua-t'ing,
Kiangsu; active c. 1700; pupil of Wang Hui; landscapes. (CP, VII, AL,
361.)
Peach blossoms, willow, birds and fish, signed, colophon by Wang
Hui dated 1693; water plants by Ku, rest of painting by Yang Chin,
Yü Yüan, Hsü Mei, Wu Chih and Wang Yün, Palace Museum, Pe-
king. KKPWY hua-niao, 77*.
Two men in a pavilion watching a waterfall, folding fan, poem, signed,
dated 1707, Shanghai WWPKWYH. Shan-mien-hua, 84*.

KU LO 顧洛 , t. Yü-men 禹門 , h. Hsi-mei 西梅 .
B. 1762, d. after 1837; from Hangchou; painted figures, landscapes. (CP,
VII, AL, 362.)
The Elegant Gathering in the Western Garden, handscroll, signed. Li-
tai jen-wu, 69.

KU TA-SHEN 顧大申 , original name Ku Yung 顧鏞 ,
t. Chen-chih 震雉 , h. Chien-shan 見山 . From Hua-t'ing,
Kiangsu; chin-shih in 1652; landscapes. (CP, VII, AL, 363.)

Mountains with cottages in autumn, inscribed, signed, dated 1652,
Nat. Pal. Mus., Taipei, (AL). CKLTMHC, V.6.
Four landscape album leaves, one inscribed, signed, dated 1666, Tien-
tsin Art Museum. T'ien-ching, II.92-95.

KU TSAI-MEI 顧在湄 . Unidentified.
A temple in the autumn mountains, album leaf, one of a six leaf album,
inscribed, artist's seal, Liao-ning Provincial Museum. Liao-
ning, II.110.

KU YIN 顧殷 , t. Yü-kung 禹功 . From Suchou, active
c. 1680, landscapes. (CP, VII, AL, 363-364.)
Chrysanthemum and stone, folding fan, poem, signed, dated chia-wu
1654 or 1714, Hui Hsiao-t'ung collection. Shan-mien chi-chin,
20*.

KU YÜN 顧澐 , t. Jo-p'o 若波 . B. 1835, d. 1896; from Su-
chou, went as an envoy to Japan; landscapes. (CP, VII, AL, 364.)
Massed peaks and green rivers, inscribed, signed, Palace Museum,
Peking. CK chin-pai-nien, 49.

KUAN HUAI 關槐 , t. Chin-hsien 晉軒 . From Hang-
chou; chin-shih in 1789, a Han-lin member; studied landscape painting
with Tung Kao. (CP, VII, AL, 365.)
Travellers on a bridge in the mountains, signed. Che-chiang, 87.

KUANG SUNG-TS'EN 匡松岑 . Unidentified, 18th century.
Portraits of Kao Feng-han and Lu Ya-yü in a garden pavilion, two
other figures, done by Kuang, Kao Feng-han and Lu Yin in 1738.
Kao Feng-han, 8.

K'UN-TS'AN 髡殘 , family name Liu 劉 , t. Shih-ch'i
石谿 , Chieh-ch'iu 介邱 , h. Pai-t'u 白禿 , Ts'an-tao-jen
殘道人 and other names. From Wu-ling, Hunan; active during
the last half of the 17th century; entered a Buddhist order of the Ch'an
school; served as abbot of the Niu-shou Monastery near Nanking; painted
landscapes. (CP, VII, AL, 365-367.)
Boating on a stream, handscroll, signed, dated 1660, Chang Pe-chin
collection. Tien Yin Tang, I.71.
A man in a rustic hut in a grove, pine-clad mountains, inscribed,
signed, dated 1661, Tientsin Art Museum. I-yüan chi-chin, 27;
T'ien-ching, II.114.
Buildings on a mountain terrace, cottages by a high river bank, fish-

ermen on the river, inscribed, signed, dated 1661. Hung-jen
K'un-ts'an, 4.

River winding between hills; misty atmosphere, old trees and cottages,
poem, dated 1663, Palace Museum, Peking, (AL). CK hua, XIX. 19;
PM, 14*.

A narrow path winding between the crevassed rocks, inscribed, dated
1663, Shanghai Museum, (AL). Hung-jen K'un-ts'an, 3; Shanghai, 70*; WW, 1958. 8. 54.

A deeply crevassed ravine with circling mist and rushing water, inscribed, signed, dated 1664, Palace Museum, Peking (?), (AL?).
CK ku-tai, 91.

The Pao-en Temple on a high mountain terrace, inscribed, dated 1664,
K. Sumitomo collection, Oiso, (AL). Hung-jen K'un-ts'an, 2.

River between two mountain slopes, album leaf, inscribed, signed;
Snowscape, album leaf, inscribed, signed, dated 1666, done for
Ch'ing-chi ta-chü-shih. Hung-jen K'un-ts'an, 6, 7.

A river winding between steep hills, a man in the foreground fishing,
poem, signed, dated 1667, (AL). Hung-jen K'un-ts'an, 5.

An album of ten leaves: landscape studies, mountain views, possibly
from Huang-shan, dated 1670, (AL). Hung-jen K'un-ts'an, 8
(one leaf).

Willow beside a lake, a fisherman in a boat, album leaf, signed, Nat.
Pal. Mus. , Taipei, (AL). CH mei-shu, III.

Landscape after Wang Meng, album leaf, inscribed, signed, Nat. Pal.
Mus. , Taipei, (AL). CH mei-shu, III.

Bodhidharma seated in meditation facing a cliff, handscroll, artist's
seal, K. Sumitomo collection, Oiso, (AL). CK shu-hua, I. 37;
Hung-jen K'un-ts'an, 10.

A village on a mountain cliff, inscribed, signed, Palace Museum,
Peking. WW, 1966. 4. 46.

A man with a staff on a bridge, inscribed, signed, Suchou Museum.
Su-chou, 44.

River landscpae with pavilions built over the water, mountain landscape with waterfall and temple roofs, handscroll, Suchou Museum. Su-chou, 45.

A man seated in a tile-roofed pavilion beneath a willow, mountain
landscape, inscribed, signed. Hung-jen K'un-ts'an, 1; TSYMC
hua-hsüan, 73.

Two men seated on a ledge watching rapids, pavilion and curving verandah on a mountain. Hung-jen K'un-ts'an, 9.

KUNG HSIEN 龔　賢　, t. Pan-ch'ien 半 千 , h. Yeh-i 野 遺 .
D. 1689; from K'un-shan, Kiangsu, lived in Nanking, one of the "Eight
Masters of Nanking"; landscapes. (CP, VII, AL, 368-370.)

Landscape after Chü-jan, inscribed, signed, dated 1643, Cheng Te-k'un collection, Cambridge. Mu-fei, between pp. 44-45.

Landscape with a row of trees in the foreground, album leaf, artist's seal, dated 1669, Nat. Pal. Mus., Taipei, (AL). CH mei-shu, III.

Eleven double album leaves representing landscapes; some after Sung masters; some after Yüan masters, colophon by the painter dated 1671, Nelson Gallery of Art, Kansas City, (AL). CK shu-hua, I. 40 (leaf five); Kung Hsien, 15 (one leaf).

Eight landscapes, album, the last leaf signed, dated 1681, colophon by Cha Shih-piao, (AL). Kung Hsien, 6, 17 (two leaves).

A misty valley, signed, dated 1684, Chang Pe-chin collection, (AL). Tien Yin Tang, I. 82.

Clusters of trees, thatched huts, spring waterfall, poem, signed, dated 1684, Liao-ning Provincial Museum. Liao-ning, II. 93.

Two huts in a thicket on rocky mountain side, inscribed, signed, dated 1685, colophon by Kao Shih-ch'i, Shanghai Museum. Kung Hsien, 13; Shang-hai, 68*.

Sixteen landscape-studies with poems and colophons by the painter, dated 1688, (AL). Kung Hsien, 8, 14 (two leaves).

Misty rocks by a river, a temple on the peak, handscroll, signed, Palace Museum, Peking, (AL). WW, 1966. 4. 42.

Mountain ranges and trees in mist, signed, (AL). Kung Hsien, 18.

A river landscape with bare trees, album leaf, (AL). Kung Hsien, 12.

A thatched hut on a spit of land, river view, folding fan, signed, Shang-hai WWPKWYH. Shan-mien-hua, 62*.

Landscape after Li Ch'eng, album leaf, inscribed, signed, Tientsin Art Museum. I-yüan chi-chin, 37*.

A pavilion in the mountains, poem, signed, Chang Pe-chin collection. Tien Yin Tang, I. 83.

A thatched hut in a grove, folding fan, inscribed, signed, Hui Hsiao-t'ung collection. Shan-mien chi-chin, 12*.

Huts and trees below hills, inscribed, signed, Li I-mang collection. CK hua, I. 28.

Landscape, handscroll, inscribed, signed, S. M. Siu collection, Hong Kong. CK ku-hua, B. 235.

Album of landscapes and calligraphy, S. M. Siu collection, Hong Kong. CK ku-hua, B. 236 (three leaves).

Landscape album leaves, probably from various albums. Kung Hsien, 1-5, 7, 9-11, 16.

Trees by a river, album leaf, inscribed. TSYMC hua-hsüan, 68.

K'UNG PO-MING 孔 伯 明 . From Nan-hai, Kuangtung; landscapes; probably active in the 17th century. (W. I. 1.)

Gentlemen at a wine party under blossoming peach and pear trees,
album leaf, inscribed, signed, dated <u>ting-ch'ou</u>. Kuang-tung
hua-chia, 24*.

The Seven Sages of the Bamboo Grove, album leaf, artist's seals.
Kuang-tung hua-chia, 25*.

The Nymph of the Lo River, Kuang collection, Nan-hai. Kuang-tung
shu-hua, 27.

KUO SHIH 郭適 , t. Lo-chao 樂郊 or Chao-min 郊民 .
From Shun-te, Kuangtung; late 18th century; painted flowers, peonies,
and birds. (W. I. 5; M. p. 400.)

Peonies and peach blossoms, inscribed, signed, dated 1756 or 1816,
Tun-fu shu-shih collection. Kuang-tung shu-hua, 32.

A dove on a branch, album leaf, inscribed, signed. Kuang-tung hua-
chia, 44*.

LAI CHING 賴鏡 , t. Meng-jung 孟容 , h. Pai-shui shan-
jen 白水山人 . From Nan-hai, Kuangtung; 17th century; became a monk at the fall of the Ming, called Shen-tu 深度 ; poet,
calligrapher; painted in the style of Shen Chou. (M. p. 669.)

River scene, group of spare trees in foreground, mountain background,
inscribed, Ma Chi-tso collection. Kuang-tung shu-hua, 21.

A man seated on a promontory looking at swirling mists, signed.
Kuang-tung hua-chia, 15*.

LAN MENG 藍孟 , t. Tz'u-kung 次公 and I-yü 亦輿 .
From Hangchou; active c. 1680; son of Lan Ying; landscapes. (CP, VII,
AL, 370.)

A mountain grotto, a boat approaching a shore where two men converse, inscribed, signed, dated 1663. Che-chiang, 70.

LAN SHEN 藍深 , t. Hsieh-ch'ing 謝青 . From Hangchou;
active c. 1658-1674; son of Lan Meng. (CP, VII, AL, 371.)

Two birds and autumn flowers, inscribed, signed, Palace Museum,
Peking. KKPWY hua-niao, 69*.

LANG SHIH-NING 郎世寧 or Giuseppe Castiglione. B. 1688,
d. 1766, an Italian, came to China in 1715; served as a painter in the palace; horses. (CP, VII, AL, 371-372.)

Auspicious plants in a vase, signed, dated 1723, Nat. Pal. Mus.,
Taipei. 300 M., 278*; CKLTMHC, V. 56.

The hundred horses, handscroll, dated 1728, Nat. Pal. Mus., Taipei,
(AL). CKLTMHC, V. 54.

Eight horses on the river-shore, signed, poem by Ch'ien-lung, Nat.
Pal. Mus., Taipei, (AL). 300 M., 287.

A dog under flowers, signed, Nat. Pal. Mus., Taipei. 300 M., 288.

Peonies, roses and fungus by rocks, signed, Nat. Pal. Mus., Taipei.
CH ming-hua*.

Eight horses and two grooms under misty willows, Nat. Pal. Mus.,
Taipei. CH mei-shu, III; CKLTSHH.

A white monkey, signed, Nat. Pal. Mus., Taipei. CKLTMHC, V. 55.

An album of sixteen leaves representing flowers, last leaf signed,
Nat. Pal. Mus., Taipei. 300 M., 279-286 (eight leaves);
CKLTMHC, V. 57 (two leaves).

An album of flowers, Nat. Pal. Mus., Taipei. CKLTMHC, V. 58
(two leaves).

Pine tree and pigeons, signed, Chang Pe-chin collection. Tien Yin
Tang, I. 100.

LAO CHENG 勞 澂 , t. Tsai-tzu 在 茲 , h. Lin-wu shan-
jen 林 屋 山 人 . From Ch'ang-chou, Kiangsu; active c. 1698;
spent his last years near Lake Tung-t'ing; landscapes. (CP, VII, AL, 372.)

A fisherman in a boat on a marshy river, signed, dated ping-tzu, Tientsin Art Museum. T'ien-ching, I. 81.

LI CH'I 黎 奇 , t. Wen-lu 問 廬 . From Shun-te, Kuangtung,
active during the Ch'ien-lung era (1736-1795); painted oxen. (W. I. 3; M.
p. 630.)

An ox and a herdboy under a tree, signed, Huang Wen collection.
Kuang-tung shu-hua, 34.

LI CHIEN 黎 簡 , t. Chien-min 簡 民 , Wei-ts'ai 未 裁 ,
h. Erh-ch'iao 二 樵 . B. 1747, d. 1799; from Shun-te, Kuangtung;
landscapes. (CP, VII, AL, 372.)

Su Tung-p'o examining an ink stone, inscribed, dated 1781, artist's
seals, Tun-fu shih-shu collection. Kuang-tung shu-hua, 30.

A man meditating in a pavilion below sharp peaks, inscribed, signed,
dated 1782. Kuang-tung hua-chia, 40*.

A man walking with a staff on a mountain path, inscribed, signed,
dated 1784. Kuang-tung hua-chia, 41*.

An empty pavilion on rock overlooking a far river vista, inscribed,
signed, dated 1785, Tun-fu shu-shih collection. Kuang-tung shu-
hua, 30.

Mist and rain in summer mountains, inscribed, signed, dated 1793,
in the style of Tung Yüan. Kuang-tung hua-chia, 39*.

Hibiscus cove, inscribed, poem, dated 1794. Kuang-tung hua-chia,
42*.

Two landscape sketches done for Li Nan-chien, inscribed, signed,
numerous inscriptions, Ma Pin-fu collection. Kuang-tung shu-
hua, 31.
Listening to the fisherman's flute on the autumn river, inscribed,
signed. Kuang-tung hua-chia, 43*.

LI FANG-YING 李方膺 , t. Ch'iu-chung 虬仲 , h. Ch'ing-chiang,
晴江 , Ch'iu-ch'ih 秋池 . B. 1695, d. 1754; from T'ung-
chou, Kiangsu; painted pine-trees, bamboo, epidendrums and chrysanthe-
mums in the hsieh-i manner. (CP, VII, AL, 373.)
Flowering plants, inscribed, signed, dated 1736, Nanking Museum.
Yang-chou pa-chia, 29.
Various flowers, plants, fish, handscroll, inscribed, signed, dated
1744, Tientsin Art Museum. T'ien-ching, II. 130-134.
Bamboo in wind, inscribed, signed, dated 1751, Nanking Museum.
Yang-chou pa-chia, 27.
Narcissi, album leaf, signed, Palace Museum, Peking. KKPWY hua-
niao, 92*.
Plum blossoms, inscribed, signed, Shanghai Museum. Shang-hai, 86*.
Ink lotus, signed. TSYMC hua-hsüan, 104.

LI HENG 李亨 , t. Chung-jen 仲仁 . From Wu-wei, Anhui;
painted landscapes, bird, flowers, fish. (M. p. 204.)
Riverside plants and frog. WW, 1964.3.17.

LI HSIANG-FENG 李象豐 , t. Chao-sheng 昭生 . From
Nan-hai, Kuangtung; chü-jen in 1657; poet; landscapes. (W.I.3.)
A mountain pavilion in winter, signed, dated 1667. Kuang-tung hua-
chia, 26*.

LI K'UEI 李魁 , t. Tou-shan 斗山 , h. Ch'ing-k'uei
tao-jen 青藜道人 . From Nan-hai, Kuangtung; active c.
1851-1907; landscapes. (W.I.10.)
A scholar under a red-leafed tree, inscribed, signed, dated 1897.
Kuang-tung hua-chia, 78*.
Landscapes, inscriptions, Li Fan-fu collection. Kuang-tung shu-hua,
48.
Travellers through green mountains, album leaf, inscribed, signed.
Kuang-tung hua-chia, 79*.
A scholar looking at a waterfall, inscribed, signed. Kuang-tung hua-
chia, 80*.

LI KUO-CHI 李果吉 , t. Chi-liu 吉六 . From Hsiang-
shan, Kuangtung; 17th century; painted landscapes, bamboo and stones in

Yüan styles, also worked in Mi style. (W.I.3)

> Ink bamboo and stone, signed, dated 1660 (?). Kuang-tung hua-chia, 29*.
>
> Pavilion along a mountain stream, signed, dated 1669 (?). Kuang-tung hua-chia, 28*.

LI SHAN 李鱓 , t. Tsung-yang 宗揚 , h. Fu-t'ang 復堂 and other names. D. 1762; from Yangchou, Kiangsu; chü-jen in 1711; birds and flowers, influenced by Lin Liang and Kao Ch'i-p'ei. (CP, VII, AL, 374-375.)

> Autumn hibiscus, inscribed, signed, dated 1726, Tientsin Art Museum. I-yüan chi-chin, 51.
>
> Flowers by a rock, inscribed, signed, dated 1727, Nanking Museum. Yang-chou pa-chia, 25.
>
> An old pine-tree and climbing plants, inscribed, signed, dated 1730, Palace Museum, Peking, (AL). CK ku-tai, 101.
>
> A vase of flowers and a basket of narcissus, inscribed, signed, dated 1733, Tientsin Art Museum. T'ien-ching, II.135.
>
> Two cut chrysanthemums, inscribed, signed, dated 1737, Suchou Museum. Su-chou, 82.
>
> Eight leaf album of flowers, fruits, insects, each leaf inscribed, signed, several dated 1740, Chinese History Museum. LS Hua-hui*.
>
> Album of eight leaves depicting flowers, fish, trees, last leaf signed, dated 1740, Palace Museum, Peking. LS ts'e-yeh; KKPWY hua-niao, 88* (leaf six); PM, 44* (leaf seven); 45* (leaf five).
>
> A duck bathing, signed, dated 1752, Cheng Te-K'un collection, Cambridge. Mu-fei, between pp. 52-53.
>
> Spring flowers, poem, signed, dated 1754, Shanghai Museum, (AL). Shang-hai, 89*.
>
> Banana tree, rock and day lily, inscribed, signed, Nanking Museum. Yang-chou pa-chia, 23.
>
> Banana tree and bamboo, inscribed, signed. TSYMC hua-hsüan, 103.

LI SHIH-CHO 李世倬 , t. Han-chang 漢章 , h. Ku-chai 穀齋 , Ch'ing-tsai chü-shih 清在居士 and other names. From San-han, Southern Korea; court-painter c. 1750; studied landscape-painting with Wang Hui and Ma I, figures, flowers, birds. (CP, VII, AL, 375-376.)

> A woman feeding pigs, inscribed, signed, Tientsin Art Museum. I-yüan chi-chin, 46.

LI TAN-LIN 李丹麟 , t. Hsing-ko 星閣 . From Kuei-shan, Kuangtung; late 19th century; flowers, figures. (W.II.)

One hundred quail, handscroll, signed, dated 1896, many colophons, Ssu-wu-yang Chai collection. Kuang-tung shu-hua, 52.

LI TSUNG-WAN 勵宗萬 , t. Tzu-ta 子大 , h. I-yüan 衣園 , Chu-ch'i 竹溪 , Chu-chi chü-shih 竹谿居士 , Tzu-ta 滋大 . B. 1705, d. 1759; from Ching-hai, Hopei; calligrapher; painted landscapes. (U. II. 2; M. p. 689.)

Lan-t'ing cup-floating, folding fan, signed, after Wen Cheng-ming, Shanghai WWPKWYH. Shan-mien-hua, 92*.

LI WAN-SHENG 李皖生 . Unidentified.

A gentleman and a lady seated in a garden listening to a flautist, handscroll, done with Yen Chan and Ch'en Hung-shou, made for Ho T'ien-chang, Suchou Museum. Su-chou, 32.

LI YÜ 李育 , t. Mei-sheng 梅生 , h. Chu-hsi 竹西 . B. 1843, d. after 1904; from Yangchou, Kiangsu; flowers, trees and stones. (CP, VII, AL, 377.)

Album of bird and flower paintings, in the style of Hua Yen, ten leaves, some inscribed, last leaf signed, dated 1893, Cheng Te-k'un collection, Cambridge, (AL). Mu-fei, between pp. 62-63 (two leaves).

LI YÜAN 李勉 , t. Hsiao-ts'un 嘯村 . From Anhui, lived in Yangchou; painted landscapes, flowers and birds. (T. I. 1; M. p. 207.)

Flowers, inscribed, signed, dated chia-tzu, Suchou Museum. Su-chou, 89.

LIANG AI-JU 梁藹如 , t. Yüan-wen 遠文 , h. Ch'ing-ai 青崖 . B. 1769; from Shun-te, Kuangtung; chin-shih 1814; painted landscapes. (W. I. 6.)

A scholar in a country pavilion in summer, inscribed, signed, dated 1828. Kuang-tung hua-chia, 55*.

LIANG CH'EN 梁琛 , t. Hsien-t'ing 獻廷 . From Shun-te, Kuangtung; active c. 1821-1874; painted bamboo. (W. I. 10.)

Bamboo, rock and banana, inscribed, signed, dated 1849. Kuang-tung hua-chia, 77*.

LIANG CHIU-T'U 梁九圖 , t. Fu-ts'ao 福草 , h. Shih-erh-shih shan-jen 十二石山人 . From Shun-te, Kuangtung; active c. 1821-1850; nephew of Liang Ai-ju; painted epidendrum. (W. I. 6.)

Epidendrum, inscribed, signed, dated 1877, Ssu-wu-yang Chai collection. Kuang-tung shu-hua, 40.

LIANG HENG 梁亨 . Unidentified.
    Liang Heng looking for the list of successful candidates in the exam-
       ination, handscroll, Nat. Pal. Mus., Taipei. CCAT, pl. 133(section).

LIANG LIEN 梁槤 , t. Ch'i-fu 器甫 , H. Han-t'ang chü-shih
寒塘居士 , T'ieh-ch'uan tao-jen 鐵船道人 , T'ieh-
ch'iao tao-jen 鐵橋道人 . B. 1628, d. 1673; from Shun-
te, Kuangtung; painted landscapes. (W.I.2.)
    Two men in a pavilion on the Lo-fu Mountains in summer, signed, dated
       1663. Kuang-tung hua-chia, 27*.

LIANG YÜAN-CHU 梁元柱 , t. Chung-yü 仲玉 and Sen-
lang 森琅 . B. 1581, d. 1628; from Shun-te, Kuangtung; painted
bamboo and rocks. (W.I.2.)
    Two stalks of bamboo on a slope in the wind, inscribed, signed, dated
       1624. Kuang-tung hua-chia, 10*.

LIN LAN 林藍 . Unrecorded. According to Che-chiang, p. 15:
b. 1818, d. 1847; t. Tsai-lin 在麟 , h. Pi-jen 璧人 and
Ch'in-ch'ih chu-jen 琴池主人 ; from T'ai-chou, Chekiang;
painted bamboo and epidendrum.
    Bamboo and rock, signed, dated 1841. Che-chiang, 96.

LIU YEN-CHUNG 劉彥沖 , t. Yung-chih 詠之 or
泳之 , h. Liang-ho-tzu 梁壑子 . B. 1820, d. 1870;
from Szechuan, moved to Suchou; poet; painted figures, landscapes, flowers. (T.II; M. p. 664.)
    A villa by a riverside, handscroll, signed, dated 1844, Suchou Mu-
       seum. Su-chou, 113.

LIU YIN 柳隱 , t. Ju-shih 如是 . B. 1618, d. 1664;
from Wu-chiang, Kiangsu; wife of the poet Ch'ien Ch'ien-i; flowers, birds,
landscapes. (CP, VII, AL, 378.)
    Willows on a dyke, handscroll, signed, colophon by Ch'ien Ch'ien-i,
       Tientsin Art Museum. T'ien-ching, I.46-47.

LIU YÜ 柳遇 , t. Hsien-ch'i 仙期 . From Suchou,
active c. 1700; figures after Ch'iu Ying, flowers. (CP, VII, AL, 378.)
    Opium flowers, signed, Nat. Pal. Mus., Taipei, (AL). CKLTMHC,
       V.43.

LO AN-HSIEN 羅岸先 , t. Teng-tao 登道 , h. San-feng
三峯 , Yeh-hang 野航 , Yeh-fang 也方 . From

Fan-yü, Kuangtung; active c. 1850-1900; painted landscapes, flowers, figures. (W.I.10.)

> River scene with pagoda, inscribed, signed, dated 1874. Kuang-tung hua-chia, 92*.
>
> Travellers under pines along a river, folding fan, inscribed, signed, dated 1875, in the Wang Hui manner, Chu-p'ing-an Kuan collection. Kuang-tung shu-hua, 53.

LO MU 羅 牧 , t. Fan-niu 飯 牛 , h. Yün-an 雲 菴 . B. 1622, d. after 1706; from Ning-tu, lived in Nan-ch'ang, Kiangsi; poet, calligrapher; painted landscapes, founder of the Kiangsi School. (CP, VII, AL, 379.)

> Lin-ho hsiao-su t'u. Desolate forest and mountains, poem, signed, dated 1704, Nat. Pal. Mus., Taipei, (AL). CKLTMHC, V.7.

LO P'ING 羅 聘 , t. Tan-fu 遯 夫 , h. Liang-feng 兩峯 , Hua-chih-ssu seng 花 之 寺 僧 . B. 1733, d. 1799; from Hsieh-hsien, Anhui, lived in Yang-chou, Kiangsu; student of Ch'an Buddhism; plum-blossoms, orchids, bamboos, Buddhist and Taoist figures; pupil of Chin Nung. (CP, VII, AL, 379-381.)

> Portrait of Chin Nung, colophon by Chin Nung dated 1760, an inscription dated 1762, Liu Ching-chi collection. CK hua, I.34; TSYMC hua-hsüan, 102.
>
> Portrait of the Buddhist Monk T'an, inscribed, signed, dated 1763, Suchou Museum. Su-chou, 87.
>
> A lichee tree, two inscriptions by the artist, one signed and dated 1774, Palace Museum, Peking. KKPWY hua-niao, 93*.
>
> Epidendrum-plants, an album of ten leaves, each leaf with poem and signature, last leaf dated 1777, finger paintings, Cheng Te-k'un collection, Cambridge, (AL). Mu-fei, between pp. 54-55 (two leaves).
>
> Autumn epidendrum and rock, poem, signed, dated 1794, Nanking Museum. Yang-chou pa-chia, 3.
>
> Plum blossoms, folding fan, inscribed, signed, dated 1797, Shanghai WWPKWYH. Shan-mien-hua, 95*.
>
> Bamboo growing beside rocks, poem, signed, Shanghai Museum, (AL). Shang-hai, 91*.
>
> Wasps and brambles; dragonfly and poppy, two album leaves, both inscribed and signed, Palace Museum, Peking. PM, 46*, 47*.
>
> Album of twelve leaves of landscapes and figures, each leaf inscribed, most with lines from Chin Nung, last leaf signed, Palace Museum, Peking. LP Jen-wu.
>
> A man meditating in a bamboo grove hut, signed, Suchou Museum. Su-chou, 88.

Bamboo and bare tree, inscribed, artist's seal, after Wu Chen; a
man on a bridge, inscribed, poem by Chin Nung, two album leaves,
Tientsin Art Museum. T'ien-ching, II. 137-138.
Two bamboo and stone, inscribed, signed. TSYMC hua-hsüan, 101.

LO YANG 羅 陽　　　, t. Chien-ku 健谷　　. From Shun-te,
Kuangtung, lived c. 1796-1850; landscapes; studied Lan Ying and Sung and
Yüan masters. (W.I.7; M. p. 725.)
　　Landscape after Wen Cheng-ming, inscribed, signed, dated 1849.
　　　　Kuang-tung hua-chia, 71*.
　　Landscape after Wu Chen, inscribed, signed, Chu-p'ing-an Kuan col-
　　　　lection. Kuang-tung shu-hua, 40.

LU TAO-HUAI 陸道淮　　　, t. Shang-yu 上遊　　. From
Chia-ting, Kiangsu; active c. 1700; pupil of Wu Li; landscapes. (CP, VII,
AL, 382.)
　　Cranes standing in the top of a pine tree, one flying crane, signed,
　　　　colophon by Wu Sung, Cheng Te-k'un collection, Cambridge. Mu-
　　　　fei, opposite p. 50.

LU YIN 陸 音　. Unidentified, 18th century.
　　Portraits of Kao Feng-han and Lu Ya-yü in a garden pavilion, two
　　　　other figures, done by Lu, Kao Feng-han and Kuang Sung-ts'en,
　　　　dated 1738. Kao Feng-han, 8.

LU YÜAN 陸 遠　　　, t. Ching-chih 静致　　. From Suchou;
active c. 1665-1694; painted landscapes. (CP, VII, AL, 382-383.)
　　Landscape after Huang Kung-wang, signed, dated chi-ch'ou 1649 (?),
　　　　Suchou Museum. Su-chou, 63.

LÜ HSIANG 呂翔　　, t. Tzu-yü 子羽　　, h. Yin-lan 隱嵐　.
From Shun-te, Kuangtung, late 18th-early 19th century; painted flowers,
fruits. (W.I.6; M. p. 125.)
　　The Liang Spring on the Lo-fu Mountain, album leaf, inscribed, sign-
　　　　ed, Wang Hsing-lu collection. Kuang-tung shu-hua, 36.
　　A scholar reading, another scholar seated by a stream, a servant
　　　　with books, signed. Kuang-tung hua-chia, 56*.

LÜ HSÜEH 呂 學　　, t. Shih-min 時敏　, h. Hai-shan 海山　.
From Wu-ch'eng, Chekiang, active c. 1670; figures, animals, landscapes.
(CP, VII, AL, 383.)
　　Peach Blossom Spring, signed. Che-chiang, 75.

274

LÜ HUAN-CH'ENG 呂煥成　　, t. Chi-wen 吉文　. B. 1630,
d. after 1705; from Yü-yao, Chekiang; figures, flowers, landscapes in
the style of Lo Mu. (CP, VII, AL, 383.)
>Servant sweeping snow, two children in a house, the master approach-
>ing, folding fan, signed, dated 1659 (or 1719), Hui Hsiao-t'ung
>collection. Shan-mien chi-chin, 10*.
>River landscape at dawn with travellers, signed, dated 1698, Piacen-
>tini collection, Tokyo, (AL). Che-chiang, 72.

LÜ TS'AI 呂村　, t. Hsiao-yin 小隱　. From Shun-te,
Kuangtung, son of Lü Hsiang, late 19th century; landscapes. (W.I.6.)
>An empty pavilion in the mountains, building high among slanted
>cliffs, inscribed, signed, Li Tsu-yu collection. Kuang-tung
>shu-hua, 43.
>Autumn mountains, cloudy landscape, inscribed, signed. Kuang-
>tung hua-chia, 72*.

MA SHIH-PAN 馬師班　, h. Sung-chao nü-shih 誦昭女士
B. 1777; a woman, from Wu-hsi; poetess; married to a member of the
Yang family; painted landscapes. (M. p. 341.)
>A village by the river, a man fishing in a boat, handscroll, inscribed,
>signed, Suchou Museum. Su-chou, 93-94.

MA YÜAN-YÜ 馬元馭　, t. Fu-hsi 扶義　, h. Ch'i-hsia
棲霞　, T'ien-yü shan-jan 天虞山人　. B. 1669,
d. 1722; from Ch'ang-shu, Kiangsu; pupil of Yün Shou-p'ing. (CP, VII,
AL, 384.)
>A bird on a willow branch, folding fan, signed, dated 1703, Shang-
>hai WWPKWYH. Shan-mien-hua, 86*.
>A branch of loquat, after Shen Chou, inscribed, signed, dated 1705,
>Palace Museum, Peking. KKPWY hua-niao, 78*.

MAO CHI-K'O 毛際可　, t. Hui-hou 會溪　, h. Hao-fang
鶴舫　, Sung-kao tao-jen 松皋道人　. B. 1633, d. 1708;
from Sui-an, Chekiang; chin-shih in 1658; poet, landscapes in Mi style.
(R.2; M. p. 20.)
>Pine tree and rock, inscribed, signed, dated 1681. Che-chiang, 69.

MAO CH'I-LING 毛奇齡　, t. Ta-k'o 大可　, h. Hsi-ho
西河　, Ch'u-ch'ing 初晴　and other names. B. 1623, d.
1716; from Hsiao-shan, Chekiang; scholar, painted plum blossoms. (CP,
VII, AL, 384.)
>Two mule riders in a fog-obscured landscape, inscribed, signed, done
>when 74 (1696). Che-chiang, 67.

MAO LIN 茅 麐 , t. T'ien-shih 天 石 . From Wu-hsing, Chekiang; poet, painted landscapes. (Q.II.1; M. p. 266.)

>   Portrait, a gentleman seated at a table in a garden, a maid-servant
>   bringing books, handscroll. Li-tai jen-wu, 70.

MEI CH'ING 梅 清 , t. Yüan-kung 淵 公 or 遠 公 ,
h. Ch'ü-shan 瞿 山 , Hsüeh-lu 雪 廬 , Lao-ch'ü-fan-fu
老 瞿 凡 父 and other names. B. 1623, d. 1697; from Hsüan-
ch'eng, Anhui; poet; painted landscapes, pine trees. (CP; VII, AL, 385-
386.)

>   A man and servant with a ch'in on a bridge on way to pavilion in moun-
>   tains, album leaf, inscribed, signed, dated 1659, Tientsin Art
>   Museum. I-yüan chi-chin, 23.
>   Mei Ch'ü-shan Hsüan-ch'eng sheng-lan hua-ts'e, sixteen album leaves
>   representing famous places, the last dated 1679, J. D. Ch'en
>   collection, Hong Kong, (AL). MC-s hua-chi, 4-6 (three leaves).
>   A tall pine tree by a rockery, signed, dated 1689, (AL). MC-s hua-
>   chi, 3.
>   An album of ten paintings of Huang-shan, dated 1692, Palace Museum,
>   Peking. MC Huang-shan.
>   Nineteen sketches from Huang-shan, Anhui; some with poems or colo-
>   phons by the artist, last leaf inscribed, painted when the artist
>   was 71, 1693, Shanghai Museum, (AL). MC-s hua-chi, 13-14,
>   27-42 (eighteen leaves); Shang-hai, 72* (one leaf).
>   The Po-chien Mountain, inscribed, signed, dated 1693. MC-s hua-
>   chi, 1.
>   Studies of fantastic rocks and peaks on Huang-shan, ten album leaves,
>   each with poem and signature, last dated 1694, Cheng Te-k'un
>   collection, Cambridge, (AL). Mu-fei, opposite, p. 38; before
>   p. 39 (two leaves).
>   Eight album leaves, some after old masters, possibly from the same
>   album, most inscribed and signed, one dated 1695. MC-s hua-chi,
>   19-26; TSYMC hua-hsüan, 69 (one leaf).
>   Four album leaves of landscapes, each leaf signed, one dated 1695,
>   possibly all from the same album. MC-s hua-chi, 15-18.
>   The thousand peaks of Hsi-hai, rock pinnacles and large cliff, signed,
>   dated 1695, Tientsin Art Museum. T'ien-ching, II.85.
>   Two scholars viewing a waterfall, poem, signed, (AL). MC-s hua-
>   chi, 2.
>   The T'ien-tu Peak, a scholar on a path to a pavilion; slender peak in
>   layers of mist, poem, signed, Liao-ning Provincial Museum.
>   Liao-ning, II.95.
>   An album of twelve landscapes after old masters, each leaf inscribed
>   and with artist's seals, twelve leaves of calligraphy by various

people, Shanghai Museum. MC Fang-ku.

A hermitage in rain, signed, after Kuo Hsi, Chang Pe-chin collection. Tien Yin Tang, I. 88.

Boating at Yün-men, after Wang Meng, poem, signed, Cheng Te-k'un collection, Cambridge. Mu-fei, opposite p. 36.

Six album leaves depicting famous scenic spots on Huang-shan (?), some signed or inscribed, possibly from the same album. MC-s hua-chi, 7-12.

Four album leaves depicting landscapes, possibly from the same album, three leaves inscribed and signed, one leaf inscribed and with artist's seal. MC-s hua-chi, 43-46.

A hermit in a cave, album leaf, inscribed, signed. CK shu-hua, I. 28.

MEI KENG 梅庚 , t. Ou-ch'ang 耦長 , Tzu-ch'ang 子長 , h. Hsüeh-p'ing 雪坪 and T'ing-shan-weng 聽山 翁 . From Hsüan-ch'eng, Anhui; chü-jen in 1681; brother of Mei Ch'ing; landscapes, flowers. (CP, VII, AL, 386.)

Four album leaves depicting landscapes, three with artist's seals, one signed, dated 1684, Tientsin Art Museum. T'ien-ching, II. 86-89.

MING-CHUNG 明中 , t. Ta-heng 大恆 , h. Yin-hsü 慇虛 and other names. From T'ung-hsiang, Chekiang; a priest; active c. 1750-1780. (CP, VII, AL, 387.)

A villa and a garden by a willow-lined shore, album leaf, inscribed, signed, dated 1744. Che-chiang, 81.

A man by a round window, a river view, album leaf, one of four, inscribed, signed, Liao-ning Provincial Museum. Liao-ning, II. 115.

NI JEN-CHI 倪仁吉 , t. Hsin-hui 心惠 . A woman, from I-wu, Chekiang; late 17th century; married into the Wu family; painted landscapes. (Q. I. 3; M. p. 316.)

A lady holding a fan, inscribed, signed, dated 1670. Che-chiang, 68.

NIU SHIH-HUI 牛石慧 . Unrecorded in standard biographical works; supposedly the brother of Chu Ta; active late Ming and early Ch'ing. (CP, VII, AL, 388.)

A hen and two chicks, signed, K. Sumitomo collection, Oiso, (AL). CK shu-hua, I. 39.

A cat, signed. WW, 1960. 7. 41.

P'AN KUNG-SHOU 潘恭壽 , t. Shen-fu 慎夫 , h. Lien-ch'ao 蓮巢 . B. 1741, d. 1794; from Tan-t'u, Kiangsu; landscapes, flowers. (CP, VII, AL, 388-389.)

An empty boat by a willow bank, illustration to a poem by Liu Yung, inscribed, signed, dated 1787, colophon by Wang Wen-chih, Tien-tsin Art Museum. T'ien-ching, II. 139.

A lady leaning on a rock by banana plants, artist's seal, colophon by Wang Wen-chih, Liao-ning Provincial Museum. Liao-ning,II. 119.

PAO CHÜN 鮑 俊　t. Tsung-yüan 宗 垣　, h. I-ch'ing 逸 卿 , Shih-ch'i 石 溪 , Shih-ch'i-sheng 石 谿生 . B. 1797; chin-shih in 1823; from Hsiang-shan, Kuangtung; Han-lin member; poet; painted plum and bamboo. (W.I.9.)

A branch of ink bamboo, inscribed, signed, dated 1846, Tun-fu shu-shih collection. Kuang-tung shu-hua, 46.

P'ENG JUI-HSÜAN 彭 睿 壎　, t. Kung-ch'ui 公 吹 , h. Chu-pen 竹 本 . From Shun-te, Kuangtung; became a recluse at the fall of the Ming dynasty, known as Lung-chiang ts'un-liao 龍 江 村 獠 ; calligrapher; painted bamboo and epidendrum. (W.I.2.)

Bamboo and epidendrum by rocks, signed, Han-ching Chai collection. Kuang-tung shu-hua, 14.

Tall bamboo and mist, inscribed, signed, Ho Man-an collection. Kuang-tung shu-hua, 15.

Bamboo and epidendrum on rocks, signed. Kuang-tung hua-chia, 13*.

PIEN SHOU-MIN 邊 壽民　or Wei-ch'i 維 騏 , t. I-kung 頤 公 , h. Chien-seng 漸 僧 , Wei-chien chü-shih 葦 間 居 士 . From Huai-an, Kiangsu, active c. 1725-1747; flowers and birds, particularly wild geese in p'o-mo manner. (CP, VII, AL, 390.)

A flying goose, one goose on the water with river plants, signed, dated 1732, Palace Museum, Peking. KKPWY hua-niao, 86*.

Three geese in reeds, one flying, folding fan, poem, signed, dated 1738, Shanghai WWPKWYH. Shan-mien-hua, 88*.

An album of paintings of various subjects, twelve leaves, inscribed or signed, one leaf dated 1752, Cheng Te-k'un collection, Cambridge, (AL). Mu-fei, between pp. 56-57 (two leaves).

PIEN WEN-YÜ 卞 文 瑜　, t. Jun-fu 潤 甫 , h. Fu-po 浮 白 . From Suchou, active c. 1620-1670, one of the "Nine Friends in Painting"; pupil of Tung Ch'i-ch'ang; landscapes. (CP, VII, AL, 390-391.)

A man in a boat, trees on hills by the river, folding fan, signed, dated 1632, Shanghai WWPKWYH. Shan-mien-hua, 40*.

Two men in a mountain pavilion, signed, dated 1633, Tientsin Art Museum. T'ien-ching, II. 69.

P'U-HO 普 荷　　or T'ung-ho 通 荷　, h. Tan-tang 擔 當 .
A priest whose original name was T'ang T'ai 唐 泰　, t. Ta-lai
大 來 . B. 1593, d. 1683; from P'u-ning, Yünnan; pupil of Tung Ch'i-
ch'ang, did landscapes in the manner of Ni Tsan. (CP, VII, AL, 391.)

> Landscape, a man on a bridge, mountains and waterfalls in background,
> signed, colophon by Tao-chi dated 1642, Li Ch'u-li collection.
> T-t shu-hua, 23.

> Landscape scroll painted for Pi-ch'uan, handscroll, signed T'ang T'ai,
> inscribed, dated 1643, Liang-chiang Culture Hall. T-t shu-hua,
> 15-16.

> Landscape, Palace Museum, Peking. WW, 1961.2.40.

> Colored landscape, handscroll, inscribed, signed, Liang-chiang Cul-
> ture Hall. T-t shu-hua, 56-57.

> An album of landscape painting and calligraphy, six leaves of each,
> fourth leaf signed, Yünnan Provincial Museum. T-t shu-hua, 20-
> 22.

> A man crossing a bridge, near pines, distant mountains, signed, in
> Yüan style, Yünnan Provincial Museum. T-t shu-hua, 24.

> A man and a servant on a river bank, man pointing across river to
> pavilion, inscribed, signed, Yünnan Provincial Museum. T-t
> shu-hua, 25.

> A scholar in a pavilion, a boy with a staff, signed, Yünnan Provincial
> Museum. T-t shu-hua, 26.

> Travellers on foot and horseback crossing bridges toward a city, in-
> scribed, signed, Yünnan Provincial Museum. T-t shu-hua, 26.

> Two men in a boat under willows, temple in misty mountains, inscrib-
> ed, signed, Yünnan Provincial Museum. T-t shu-hua, 27.

> Two scholars standing on a bank near a bridge, inscribed, signed,
> Yünnan Provincial Museum. T-t shu-hua, 29.

> Two scholars sitting on a river bank, travellers on a bridge, signed,
> Yünnan Provincial Museum. T-t shu-hua, 30.

> An album of fourteen leaves depicting winter on a thousand peaks,
> done in old master styles, each leaf inscribed and sealed, Yünnan
> Provincial Museum. T-t shu-hua, 31-38.

> Album of twenty leaves, ten paintings illustrating poems by T'ao Ch'ien,
> ten leaves of calligraphy, each poem signed, Yünnan Provincial
> Museum. T-t shu-hua, 39-50.

> Landscape, handscroll, signed, Yünnan Provincial Museum. T-t shu-
> hua, 53-55.

> A thousand miles of Yünnan scenery, handscroll, inscribed, signed,
> Yünnan Provincial Museum. T-t shu-hua, 58-59.

> An album of ten rough landscape sketches, each leaf with artist's seal,
> Yünnan Provincial Museum. T-t shu-hua, 60-64.

An album of sixteen landscapes, each leaf signed, some inscribed,
artist's inscription at end, Ch'en Shu-t'ung collection. T-t ts'e-
yeh.

An album of six leaves of landscape painting and calligraphy, last page
of calligraphy signed, Ch'en Yüan collection. T-t shu-hua, 50-
52.

Landscape, handscroll, inscribed, signed, Kao Yün-hua collection.
T-t shu-hua, 17-19.

A servant approaching a bridge, two scholars on a cliff above, inscribed, signed, Kao Yün-hua collection. T-t shu-hua, 27.

A man sitting on a rock near a stream, a pavilion in the background,
signed, Li Ch'u-li collection. T-t shu-hua, 28.

P'U HUA 蒲 華 , originally named Ch'eng 成 , t. Chu-ying
竹英 and Tso-ying 作英 , h. Hsü-shan wai-shih 胥山外史
B. 1834, d. 1911; from Chia-hsing, Chekiang, moved to Shang-hai; painted
landscapes, bamboo and flowers. (M. p. 598.)

Lotus, inscribed, signed, dated 1850, Shanghai WWKLWYH. CK
chin-pai-nien, 48.

The Shao-p'ing-hua Studio, signed, dated 1894. Che-chiang, 99.

SHA FU 沙馥 , t. Shan-ch'un 山春 . B. 1831, d. 1906; from
Suchou; painted figures and flowers. (M. p. 115.)

Plum blossoms and sparrow, album leaf, inscribed, signed, dated
1890, Kiangsu Provincial Museum. CK chin-pai-nien, 46.

Epidendrum, album leaf, artist's seal, Kiangsu Provincial Museum.
CK chin-pai-nien, 46.

Kingfisher and flowers, album leaf, Kiangsu Provincial Museum. CK
chin-pai-nien, 47.

Lotus and dragonflies, album leaf, artist's seal, Kiangsu Provincial
Museum. CK chin-pai-nien, 47.

SHANG-JUI 上睿 , t. Hsün-chün 尋濬 or Ching-jui 瀞睿 ,
h. Mu-ts'un 目存 , P'u-shih-tzu 蒲室子 . From
Suchou, active c. 1700-1720; a priest; pupil of Wang Hui; painted landscapes. (CP, VII, AL, 391-392.)

Two men in a house in snowy mountains, inscribed, signed, dated
1622, Tientsin Art Museum. T'ien-ching, II.116.

SHANG-KUAN CH'ING 上官清 . From Ting-chou, Fukien. (M. p. 6.)

A fishing village by the river, high mountains, two lines of poetry,
signed, Cheng Te-k'un collection, Cambridge. Mu-fei, opposite
p. 70.

SHEN CH'ÜAN 沈 銓 , t. Heng-chai 衡 齋 , h. Nan-p'in
南 蘋 . B. 1682, d. c. 1780; from Wu-hsing, Chekiang, lived in Naga-
saki 1731-1733; painted animals, flowers and birds. (CP, VII, AL, 393-
394.)

> Two deer on the bank of a river, inscribed, signed, dated 1746, Su-
> chou Museum, (AL). Su-chou, 77.
> Two birds in a blossoming peach-tree, signed, dated 1753, (AL).
> Che-chiang, 80.
> Two cranes near a stream under pine, plum and bamboo, signed,
> dated 1759, Palace Museum, Peking. KKPWY hua-niao, 84*.
> Two cranes on a large rock under a pine, signed, dated 1759. TSYMC
> hua-hsüan, 90.

SHEN HAO 沈 灝 , t. Lang-ch'ien 朗 倩 , h. Shih-t'ien
石 天 . B. 1586, d. after 1661; from Suchou, poet, author of Hua
chü; painted landscapes. (CP, VII, AL, 394.)

> Two landscape album leaves, both inscribed, one with artist's seal,
> Tientsin Art Museum. T'ien-ching, I. 38-39.

SHEN SHIH-CHIEH 沈 士 杰 . Unidentified. Perhaps Shen San-
chieh 沈 三 傑 , t. Hui-yün 惠 云 . (M. p. 153.)

> Epidendrum and stone, signed, Tientsin Art Museum. I-yüan chi-
> chin, 53.

SHEN TSUNG-CH'IEN 沈 宗 騫 , t. Hsi-yüan 熙 遠 , h.
Chieh-chou 芥 舟 and other names. From Wu-ch'eng, Chekiang;
active c. 1770-1817; landscapes, portraits; author of Chieh-chou hsüeh-
hua pien. (CP, VII, AL, 395.)

> A man and a boy seated under pines near a stream, handscroll, signed,
> dated 1758, Suchou Museum. Su-chou, 90.
> A gentleman seated under bamboo, river shore on right, handscroll,
> signed, dated 1766, Liao-ning Provincial Museum. Liao-ning,
> II. 117.
> Trees and rocks in front of a mountain peak, inscribed, artist's seals.
> Che-chiang, 83.

SHEN YÜAN 沈 源 . A court-painter c. 1745; figures. (CP, VII,
AL, 396.)

> An imperial skating-party at Pei-hai in Peking, poem by Ch'ien-lung
> dated 1746, Nat. Pal. Mus., Taipei, (AL). CKLTMHC, V. 71.

SHENG TAN 盛 丹 , t. Po-han 伯 含 . From Nanking; ac-
tive c. 1640; landscapes; followed Huang Kung-wang. (CP, VII, AL, 396.)

A boat sailing past a high cliff, album leaf, artist's seal, Nat. Pal.
  Mus., Taipei, (AL). CH mei-shu, III.
Landscape with pointed hills and many houses, album leaf, artist's
  seal, Nat. Pal. Mus., Taipei, (AL). CH mei-shu, III.

SHU KU-CH'ING 舒國卿   . A portrait artist. (M. p. 506.)
Portrait of the artist Wang Hsin-i, handscroll, signed, dated 1641,
  done with Chang Hung, three colophons, Tientsin Art Museum.
  T'ien-ching, II. 70.

SSU-MA CHUNG 司馬鍾   , t. Hsiu-ku 繡谷   . From Nan-
king; lived c. 1800-1860; painted flowers and birds. (CP, VII, AL, 397.)
A pair of birds in an old pine, screen panel, inscribed, signed, dated
  1853, Liao-ning Provincial Museum. Liao-ning, II. 121.

SU CH'ANG-CH'UN 蘇長春   , t. Jen-shan 仁山   , h. Ch'i-
tsu 七祖   , Hsi-hsia 棲霞   , Yin-shan 甯姍   , Ching-
fu 靜甫 , P'u-ti-tsai-sheng-shen-tsun-che-jen-ch'an 菩提再
生身尊者魰濴   . B. 1814, from Shun-te, Kuangtung;
painted figures. (W. II.)
Eight Immortals, inscribed, signed, Canton Museum. CK chin-pai-
  nien, 38; Kuang-tung hua-chia, 66*.
A lady holding flowers and a scroll, accompanied by a servant, inscribed, signed, Canton Museum. CK chin-pai-nien, 39; Kuang-
  tung hua-chia, 68*.
Three figures in a bamboo grove, high river view, Li Fan-fu collection. Kuang-tung shu-hua, 41.
Six Immortals, inscribed, signed (?), Li Fan-fu collection. Kuang-
  tung hua-chia, 70*; Kuang-tung shu-hua, 42.
Su Wu tending sheep, inscribed, signed. Kuang-tung hua-chia, 67*.
River landscape, signed. Kuang-tung hua-chia, 69*.

SU LIU-P'ENG 蘇六朋   , t. Chen-ch'in 枕琴   , h.
Nan-shui ts'un-lao 南水村佬   , Tsen-tao-jen 怎道人   ,
Tsen-shu 怎叔   , Hsiao-weng 笑翁   . From Shun-te,
Kuangtung; lived c. 1821-1851; figures in Yüan style. (W. I. 10; M. p. 732.)
Two gentlemen playing chess in the mountains, inscribed, signed,
  dated 1837, Canton Museum. CK chin-pai-nien, 37*; Kuang-tung
  hua-chia, 59*.
A man drinking wine and reading, handscroll, inscribed, signed, dated
  1841, Li Ch'i-yen collection. Kuang-tung shu-hua, 45.
The Lo-fu Mountain, inscribed, signed, dated 1845, Canton Museum.
  CK chin-pai-nien, 35; Kuang-tung hua-chia, 61*.

Fishermen on the river, poem, signed, dated 1845, in the style of
Wang Wei. Kuang-tung hua-chia, 63*.

Travellers fording a stream, inscribed, signed, dated 1855. Kuang-
tung hua-chia, 64*.

Playing the ch'in and the yüan, album leaf, inscribed, signed, dated
1856. Kuang-tung hua-chia, 65*.

Seven riders going through a wintry mountain pass, signed, dated 1858.
Kuang-tung hua-chia, 62*.

Canton during the T'ai-p'ing Rebellion, handscroll, Han-ching Chai
collection. Kuang-tung shu-hua, 44.

Lady Wen-chi, inscribed, signed, Ssu-wu-yang Chai collection. Kuang-
tung shu-hua, 45.

Bodhidharma on a reed, signed. Kuang-tung hua-chia, 60*.

SUNG FU　宋 賦　. Unidentified.

Camellia and mynah, album leaf, signed, part of album made for
Erh-hsiao, Liao-ning, II. 76.

TAI HSI　戴 熙　, t. Shun-shih　醇 士　, h. Yü-an 榆 菴 .
B. 1801, d. 1860; from Ch'ien-t'ang, Chekiang; Han-lin member, Vice-
president of the Board of Justice, writer; landscapes in style of Wang Hui.
(CP, VII, AL, 399-401.)

The upper portion of large pine-trees with intertwined branches, inscribed, signed, dated 1840, Cheng Te-k'un collection, Cambridge,
(AL). Mu-fei, opposite p. 60.

Three men walking on a dyke, a village on the left, album leaf, inscribed, signed, dated 1843. Che-chiang, 93.

A small grove in front of distant river and mountain view, inscribed,
signed, Tientsin Art Museum. T'ien-ching, II. 151.

Misty mountains, album leaf (?). WW, 1964. 3. 8 (two versions).

TAI PEN-HSIAO　戴 本 孝　, t. Wu-chan 務 旃 , h. Ying-a
鷹 阿　. B. 1611, d. after 1691; from Hsiu-ning, Anhui;
landscapes after the Yüan masters. (CP, VII, AL, 401-402.)

Stone stairs leading between two pavilions high in the mountains, folding fan; signed, dated 1690, Shanghai WWPKWYH. Shan-mien-
hua, 61*.

An empty pavilion in a wintry grove, inscribed, signed, dated 1690,
Tientsin Art Museum. T'ien-ching, II. 91.

The Lien Pavilion, album leaf, inscribed. WW, 1963. 6, pl. 3, no. 1.

TAN CHUNG-KUANG　笪 重 光　, t. Tsai-hsin 在 辛 , h.
I-sou 逸 叟　, I-kuang 逸 光　, Sao-yeh tao-jen 掃 葉 道 人　,
Chiang-shang wai-shih 江 上 外 史　 and other names. B. 1623, d.

1692; from Tan-t'u, Kiangsu; calligrapher; landscapes; author of <u>Hua ch'üan.</u> (CP, VII, AL, 402.)

> Steep mountain and misty valley, poem, signed, dated 1684, Cheng Te-k'un collection, Cambridge, (AL). Mu-fei, opposite p. 40.
>
> A man in a boat under leafless willow, poem, signed, dated 1710, done in the style of Tao-chi, Liao-ning Provincial Museum. Liao-ning, II. 101.

T'ANG I-FEN 湯貽汾 , t. Jo-i 若儀 , h. Yü-sheng 雨生 . B. 1778, d. 1853; from Wu-chin, Kiangsu; poet, calligrapher, author; landscapes, plum-blossoms, pine-trees. (CP, VII, AL, 403.)

> Buildings along river banks, album leaf, signed, dated 1830. TSYMC hua-hsüan, 105.
>
> A rustic hut in a bamboo grove, handscroll, inscribed, signed, dated 1851, Suchou Museum. Su-chou, 111-112.
>
> Playing the <u>ch'in</u> in a house in a secluded bamboo and chrysanthemum garden, inscribed, signed, two colophons, Tientsin Art Museum. T'ien-ching, II. 150.

T'ANG KUANG 唐光 , t. Yü-kuang 于光 and Tzu-chin 子晉 B. 1626, d. 1690; from P'i-ling, Kiangsu. (M. p. 328.)

> Pink lotus, signed, dated 1671, colophons by Wang Shih-min, Yün Shou-p'ing and others, Palace Museum, Peking. KKPWY hua-niao, 71*.
>
> Lotus plants, inscribed, Shanghai Museum. WW, 1963.10.27.

T'ANG TAI 唐岱 , t. Yü-tung 毓東 , h. Ching-yen 靜巖 and Mo-chuang 默莊 . B. 1673, d. after 1752; a Manchu, pupil of Wang Yüan-ch'i. (CP, VII, AL, 404.)

> A monkey trying to capture the moon's reflection, folding fan, poem, inscribed, signed, Shanghai WWPKWYH. Shan-mien-hua, 93*.

TAO-CHI 道濟 , t. Shih-t'ao 石濤 , h. Ta-ti-tzu 大滌子 , Ch'ing-hsiang ch'en-jen 清湘陳人 , K'u-kua ho-shang 苦瓜和尚 and other names. B. 1641, d. c. 1720; from Ching-chiang near Wu-chou in Kuangsi; a descendant of the imperial Ming family, became a monk; landscapes, flowers, orchids, bamboo, author of <u>Hua-yü lu.</u> (CP, VII, AL, 405-412.)

> Reading the Li Sao, album leaf, inscribed, signed, dated 1657. WW, 1962.12.6.
>
> An album of ten leaves depicting landscapes, some signed, one dated 1666, Suchou Museum. Su-chou, 55-57 (three leaves).

A man seated on the edge of a scrub and bamboo covered mountain gully, inscribed, signed, dated 1667, other inscriptions dated 1686 and 1697. S-t hua-chi, 68.

A mountain rising from a mist-filled grove, signed, dated 1669, Tientsin Art Museum. T'ien-ching, I. 69.

Two herb-gatherers on a path under twisted pines, signed, dated 1673. S-t hua-chi, 65.

Four leaves from a six leaf album depicting landscapes, one leaf dated 1673. S-t hua-chi, 36-39.

Ink bamboo, inscribed, signed, dated 1676, S. M. Siu collection, Hong Kong. CK ku-hua, B. 223.

Landscape for Fei-t'ao, inscribed, signed, dated 1679, Private collection, New York, S-t hua-chi, 7.

Spare trees on a river bank, a man standing by a little boat, inscribed, signed, dated 1682, Chang Ta-ch'ien collection, (AL). S-t miao-p'in, 1.

A small album of ten leaves: Landscape-studies, all with inscriptions, the fifth, sixth and ninth dated 1682, Chang Ta-ch'ien collection, (AL). S-t miao-p'in, 9-16.

An album of landscapes, five leaves, each inscribed and signed, one dated 1683. S-t hua-chi, 8-12.

Wan-tien o-mo. Sections of mountains with luxurious growth and buildings, handscroll, inscribed, signed, dated 1685, Suchou Museum, (AL). Su-chou, 51-54.

Epidendrum and bamboo, album leaf, inscribed, signed, dated 1685. S-t hua-chi, 52.

Playing a ch'in in a pavilion by the river, inscribed, signed, dated 1686, J. D. Ch'en collection, Hong Kong. S-t hua-chi, 4.

Fine rain and twisted pine, inscribed, signed, dated 1687, Shanghai Museum. Shang-hai, 80*; S-t Hsi-yü *.

P'eng-lai Mountain, covered with ling-chih, rising out of high waves, poem, signed, dated 1687. S-t hua-chi, 6.

An album of eight landscapes, artist's seal on each leaf, seven leaves inscribed and signed, leaves dated 1690 and 1693, Canton Art Museum. S-t Shan-shui ts'e-yeh*.

Two landscape album leaves, each inscribed, signed, one dated 1690. S-t hua-chi, 42-43.

A man in a hut in misty mountains, inscribed, signed, dated 1690. S-t hua-chi, 13.

Bamboos and epidendrums, signed, poem dated 1691, stones by Wang Yüan-ch'i, signed, Nat. Pal. Mus., Taipei, (AL). 300 M., 289; CCAT, pl. 120; KKCP, I. 10; CKLTMHC, V. 11.

A man in pavilion near a bridge under a towering mountain, inscribed, signed, dated 1693. S-t hua-chi, 5.

Resting in a rowing-boat on the Feng River, inscribed, signed, dated 1693, painted for Wu of Hui-chou, Chang Ta-ch'ien collection, (AL). S-t miao-p'in, 2.

An album of landscape-studies in the p'o-mo style, consisting of ten leaves, inscription by artist on last leaf dated 1695, Chang Ta-ch'ien collection, (AL). S-t miao-p'in, 17-20, 23-28.

Ch'ing-hsiang lao-jen shu-hua k'ao, album of landscapes and other subjects, the last representing a man imprisoned in a tree, dated 1696, Palace Museum, Peking, (AL). C-h Shu-hua.

Three men in a pavilion under obscuring mists, inscribed, signed, dated 1698, Private collection, New York. S-t hua-chi, 3.

Landscape, a man in a boat among reeds, a man in a pavilion under pines, a village along the river and a high mountain peak, poem, signed, dated 1699. S-t Shan-shui*.

A gnarled plum branch, inscribed, signed, dated 1699. S-t hua-chi, 63.

An album of twelve paintings, ten landscapes, two bird and flower, signed, dated 1700, Palace Museum, Peking. T-c Hua-ts'e.

Three scholars in mountains, five boats on a river, folding fan, inscribed, signed, dated 1700, Shanghai WWPKWYH. Shan-mien-hua, 66*.

A praying mantis on a gourd, inscribed, signed, dated 1700. S-t hua-chi, 50.

Peaks rising through the mist, rushing streams, sparse trees, inscribed, signed, dated 1701, Worcester Art Museum, (AL). S-t hua-chi, 21.

Listening to the spring, a scholar in a pavilion behind a huge rock, inscribed, signed, dated 1701. S-t T'ing-ch'üan*; TSYMC hua-hsüan, 78.

Landscape after "Crazy Mi", a man in a boat near a pavilion on a rock, inscribed, signed, dated 1701. S-t Fang Mi Tien*.

An open pavilion by the stream, a tall pine tree in the foreground, after Ni Tsan, inscribed, signed, dated 1702, Chang Ta-ch'ien collection, (AL). S-t miao-p'in, 5.

The ancestral tombs of the Fei family, handscroll, inscribed, signed, dated 1702, Musée Guimet, Paris, (AL). CK shu-hua, I. 37.

Four album leaves illustrating poems by Huang Yen-lü, each leaf inscribed, signed, one dated 1702, Private collection, Hong Kong. S-t hua-chi, 22-25.

An illustration to a poem by Su Shih, two men in a thatched hut, misty willow bank with bridge, album leaf, inscribed, dated 1703, from an album of nine leaves, Abe collection, Ōsaka Museum. CK shu-hua, I. 36*.

Nine landscapes from an album of twelve called Ta-ti-tzu shan-shui ts'e, one dated 1703, Museum of Fine Arts, Boston, (AL). S-t hua-chi, 19 (one leaf).

San-chüeh t'u, combination of three beauties, (painting, poetry, cal-ligraphy), a small landscape, inscribed, signed, dated 1705, Chang Ta-ch'ien collection, (AL). S-t miao-p'in, 6.

An album of ten leaves depicting flowers, each leaf inscribed and signed, one dated 1707 or 1717, Private collection, U.S.A. S-t hua-chi, 53-58 (six leaves).

A man in a boat on a mountain river between large rocks, handscroll, inscribed, signed, painted for Shu-weng, Palace Museum, Peking, (AL). CK hua, VI. 17.

Autumn in Wei-yang (Yangchou), inscribed, signed, Nanking Museum (?), (AL). S-t hua-chi, 17.

Mountains and pines, after Kuo Chung-shu, poem, signed, (AL). S-t hua-chi, 16.

Autumn landscape after rain, poem and inscription, Chang Ta-ch'ien collection, (AL). S-t hua-chi, 1.

A lotus plant, poem, signed, Finlayson collection, Toronto, (AL, also listed as Lotus). S-t hua-chi, 62.

A man seated in a thatched hut at the foot of Lu-shan, poem, signed, Chang Ta-ch'ien collection, (AL). S-t miao-p'in, 3.

Drunk in the autumn grove, three inscriptions by the artist, John M. Crawford collection, New York, (AL). S-t miao-p'in, 4.

Bamboos and epidendrums by a rock in the wind, poem, Private collec-tion, New York, (AL). S-t hua-chi, 64; NPM Quarterly, I. 4, pl. 20.

Pine-grove in wind at the foot of a mountain, an old man fishing in the stream, signed, Chang Ta-ch'ien collection, (AL). S-t miao-p'in, 7.

River landscape in ink, several sailing boats on the water and a pavil-ion under two trees, handscroll, inscribed, signed, Chang Ta-ch'ien collection, (AL). S-t miao-p'in, 8.

T'ao Yüan-ming holding a chrysanthemum flower, the fifth leaf of an album of eight leaves representing studies of flowers, bamboo, banana-leaves and figures, Chang Ta-ch'ien collection, (AL). S-t hua-chi, 66.

The first two leaves of an album of eight leaves of landscape studies illustrating poems of the Sung and Yüan period, inscribed, Chang Ta-ch'ien collection, (AL). S-t miao-p'in, 21-22.

Chrysanthemum and banana leaves, inscribed, signed, Palace Museum, Peking. KKPWY hua-niao, 76*.

Toward the pond, a scholar with a staff on a path, inscribed, signed, Palace Museum, Peking. CK hua, XIX. 18; PM, 18*.

A hamlet between cliffs, album leaf, two lines of poetry, signed, Palace Museum, Peking. PM, 19*.

Lotus blossoms, poem, Palace Museum, Peking. PM, 42*; WW, 1958. 6. 5.

Huang-shan, a man in a boat beneath mountains, poem, signed, Liaoning Provincial Museum. Liao-ning, II. 97.

Two men in a pavilion built over a waterfall, inscribed, signed, Shanghai Museum. CK hua, I. 29; Shang-hai, 79*; TSYMC hua-hsüan, 80.

An album of eight leaves depicting fruits and vegetables, inscribed, signed, Shanghai Museum. T-c Su-kuo*.

Two men fishing from a bridge, folding fan, inscribed, signed, Shanghai WWPKWYH. Shan-mien-hua, 67*.

Three men walking through misty landscape toward a temple, folding fan, inscribed, signed, Shanghai WWPKWYH. Shan-mien-hua, 68*.

Pine, plum, epidendrum, bamboo, narcissus and cypress in a vase, signed, Suchou Museum. Su-chou, 50.

A man in a building over rapids, fantastic mountain peaks and twisted pines, inscribed, signed, Tientsin Art Museum. T'ien-ching, II. 115.

Two men conversing on a river bank near a village, inscribed, signed, Tientsin Art Museum. I-yüan chi-chin, 28.

A fisherman in a boat among reeds, misty mountains, album leaf, artist's seal, Tientsin Art Museum. I-yüan chi-chin, 29*.

Reminiscences of Ch'in-huai, one leaf of an eight leaf album of landscapes, last leaf signed, Cleveland Museum of Art. NPM Quarterly, I. 2, pl. XXXIV.

An album of eight landscapes, each inscribed and signed, S. M. Siu collection, Hong Kong. CK ku-hua, B. 221 (four leaves):

Ink bamboo with background by Wang Yüan-ch'i, inscribed, signed, S. M. Siu collection, Hong Kong. CK ku-hua, B. 222.

Bamboo, inscribed. CK hua, VIII. 17.

A scholar and a servant holding a tub of chrysanthemums in the courtyard of a country villa, inscribed, signed. CK ku-tai, 94.

A man standing in front of a mountain hermitage, inscribed, signed. CK shu-hua, I. 32.

Loquat, album leaf, inscribed. CK shu-hua, I. 34.

Old trees, bamboo and rocks, album leaf, inscribed. CK shu-hua, I. 35.

A man sitting on a cliff watching a waterfall, inscribed, signed. S-t hua-chi, 2.

A man poling a boat past a tree-lined bank, inscribed, signed. S-t
hua-chi, 14.

Scene of Hua-shan, a hut among steep angular cliffs, inscribed, signed.
S-t hua-chi, 15.

Mist and pine-covered rock with pavilions, inscribed. S-t hua-chi, 18.

A man on a pavilion balcony looking over a valley, inscribed, signed.
S-t hua-chi, 20.

Four landscape album leaves, two inscribed, two signed. S-t hua-
chi, 26-29.

Six landscape album leaves, all inscribed, some with artist's seal.
S-t hua-chi, 30-35.

Two men by the shore looking across a river, handscroll, inscribed,
signed. S-t hua-chi, 40.

A boat in a cloudy sea, album leaf, inscribed, signed. CK shu-hua,
I. 34; S-t hua-chi, 41.

Two landscape album leaves, each inscribed. S-t hua-chi, 44-45.

Two landscape album leaves, both inscribed. S-t hua-chi, 46-47.

Two landscape album leaves, illustrations to T'ang poems, each inscribed, signed. S-t hua-chi, 48-49.

A lotus in a vase, album leaf, inscribed, signed. S-t hua-chi, 51.

Two album leaves depicting fruits and vegetables, both signed, one
inscribed. S-t hua-chi, 59-60.

Bamboo and plum growing from a rock, inscribed, signed. S-t hua-
chi, 61.

A boy leaning on a bent tree, bamboo and stream, inscribed. S-t
hua-chi, 67 .

Dwelling in the Hua-yang Mountains, inscribed, signed. S-t Hua-
yang*.

Pink lotus, inscribed, signed. TSYMC hua-hsüan, 79.

A man reading in a boat, handscroll of figures and landscapes, inscribed. WW, 1962.12.6.

A man on a donkey, handscroll, inscribed. WW, 1962.12.7.

A man under a pine, two monkeys, inscribed. WW, 1962.12.7.

Two men on marshy land in the mountains, inscribed, signed. WW,
1963.4, inside front cover.

Two landscape album leaves. WW, 1964.3.22.

TENG JU-CH'IUNG 鄧如瓊　　　　, t. Shih-chih 石芝　　.
From Nan-hai, Kuangtung; lived c. 1821-1851; painted landscapes.
(W.I.10.)

Landscape, inscribed, signed, dated 1841, Fei I-min collection.
Kuang-tung shu-hua, 46.

TING KAO 丁皋 , t. Ho-chou 鶴洲 . From Chen-chiang, Kiangsu; son of Ting Hsin-ju; 18th century; painted portraits. (M. p. 4.)

Portrait of the owner of the T'ung-hua Retreat, figure by Ting, background by Huang Ts'ou, crane by Hua Yen, colophon by Hsü T'ung-li dated 1732, Palace Museum, Peking. CK hua, X. 16.

TING KUAN-P'ENG 丁觀鵬 . Court-painter c. 1750-1760; Buddhist and Taoist figures after Ting Yün-p'eng. (CP, VII, AL, 412.)

Fishermen in snow, after a Sung master, signed, dated 1747, Nat. Pal. Mus., Taipei, (AL). CKLTMHC, V. 68.

Seven poets passing the T'ung-kuan Gate, signed, after Han Huang, colophon dated 1748, Nat. Pal. Mus., Taipei, (AL). CKLTMHC, V. 67.

Butterflies and bleeding-hearts, folding fan, signed, Hui Hsiao-t'ung collection. Shan-mien chi-chin, 17*.

TS'AI CHIA 蔡嘉 , t. Sung-yüan 松原 . From Tan-yang, Kiangsu; lived c. 1680-1760; landscapes, figures. (CP, VII, AL, 413.)

An album of twelve leaves depicting landscapes, signed, dated 1719 or 1779, Suchou Museum. Su-chou, 78-79 (two leaves).

A man in a pavilion, a departing guest on a bridge, an empty pavilion in distant mountains, inscribed, signed, dated 1752, Tientsin Art Museum. T'ien-ching, II. 117.

TS'AO YÜAN 曹垣 , t. Hsing-tzu 星子 . From Hang-chou; late 17th century; painted figures, landscapes, birds and flowers. (M. p. 405.)

A mountain pass covered with snow, signed, dated 1683, Chang Pe-chin collection. Tien Yin Tang, I. 90.

TSOU CHE 鄒喆 , t. Fang-lu 方魯 . B. 1636, d. c. 1708; from Suchou, lived in Nanking; one of the "Eight Masters of Nanking"; landscapes, trees and flowers. (CP, VII, AL, 414-415.)

A house at the foot of hills, a stream in the foreground, inscribed, signed, dated 1707, Shanghai Museum, (AL). Shang-hai, 69*.

TSOU I-KUEI 鄒一桂 , t. Yüan-pao 原褒 , h. Hsiao-shan 小山 . B. 1686, d. 1772; from Wu-hsi, Kiangsu; court-painter, flowers, portraits, landscapes; author of Hsiao-shan hua-p'u. (CP, VII, AL, 415-416.)

The P'an Shan Mountain, signed, dated 1752, Nat. Pal. Mus., Taipei, (AL.) CKLTMHC, V. 52.

Spring flowers and autumn fruits, signed, poem by Ch'ien-lung dated
1753, Nat. Pal. Mus., Taipei, (AL). CKLTMHC, V. 49.
Branch of apricot blossoms and white roses, signed, dated 1766, Pal-
ace Museum, Peking. KKPWY hua-niao, 85*.
Roses and wisterias, signed, Nat. Pal. Mus., Taipei, (AL). CKLTMHC,
V. 50.
Pink peach blossoms and white pear blossoms, signed, Nat. Pal. Mus.,
Taipei, (AL). CKLTMHC, V. 51.
Various flowers, folding fan, signed, Shanghai WWPKWYH. Shan-
mien-hua, 91*.

TSUNG-CH'IN 宗欽 . Unidentified.
Landscape, looking at snow-covered plum blossoms, album leaf, one
of twelve done in antique style, signed, dated kuei-ssu, 1713 (?),
Liao-ning Provincial Museum. Liao-ning, II. 108.

T'U CHO 屠卓 , t. Meng-chao 孟昭 , h. Ch'in-wu 琴鵑
and Ch'ien-yüan 潛園 . B. 1781, d. 1828, from Ch'ien-t'ang,
Chekiang; landscapes. (CP, VII, AL, 416.)
Landscape made for Nan-ya, inscribed, signed, dated 1813, Suchou
Museum. Su-chou, 110.

TUNG PANG-TA 董邦達 , t. Fu-ts'un 孚存 , h. Tung-
shan 東山 . B. 1699, d. 1769; from Fu-yang, Chekiang; land-
scapes. (CP, VII, AL, 417-418.)
Landscape, dated 1731, S. M. Siu collection, Hong Kong. CK ku-hua,
B. 238.
The K'uang and Lu Mountains, after Ching Hao, signed, poem by
Ch'ien-lung dated 1747, Nat. Pal. Mus., Taipei, (AL). Che-
chiang, 79.
Hermits' cottages on a clear day, after Tung Yüan, signed, Nat. Pal.
Mus., Taipei, (AL). CKLTMHC, V. 48.
Landscape after Wang Meng, signed, Nat. Pal. Mus., Taipei.
CKLTMHC, V. 47.

WANG CH'EN 王宸 , t. Tzu-ning 紫凝 , h. P'eng-hsin
蓬心 , Liu-tung chü-shih 柳東居士 and other
names. B. 1720, d. 1797; from T'ai-ts'ang, Kiangsu; great-grandson of
Wang Yüan-ch'i; landscapes after the Yüan masters. (CP, VII, AL, 420.)
Huts by a river in the mountains, inscribed, signed, dated 1787, done
for Hsiao-shan, Suchou Museum. Su-chou, 91.
Red trees in an autumn landscape, folding fan, inscribed, dated 1791,
Shanghai WWPKWYH. Shan-mien-hua, 94*.

WANG CHIEN 王 鑑 , t. Yüan-chao 圓 照 , h. Hsiang-pi
湘碧 , Lien-chou 廉 州 , Jan-hsiang an-chu 染香菴主
and other names. B. 1598, d. 1677; from T'ai-ts'ang, Kiangsu; one of
the "Four Wangs" and one of the "Nine Friends in Painting". (CP, VII,
AL, 421-423.)

> Four album leaves, landscapes after Tung Yüan, Huang Kung-wang,
> Wang Meng and Ni Tsan, the last dated 1660, Nat. Pal. Mus.,
> Taipei. CH mei-shu, III; CKLTSHH (landscape after Tung Yüan).
> River and mountains, handscroll, signed, dated 1664, in the style of
> Chao Ling-jang, Chang Pe-chin collection. Tien Yin Tang, I. 69.
> Mountain landscape with pavilions and village, signed, dated, 1668,
> after Huang Kung-wang, Tientsin Art Museum. I-yüan chi-chin,
> 31; T'ien-ching, I. 70.
> Mountain landscape, man and servant on stone stairs, signed, dated
> 1669. TSYMC hua-hsüan, 67.
> Landscape after Wu Chen, signed, dated 1669, Cheng Te-k'un collec-
> tion, Cambridge. Mu-fei, opposite p. 24.
> Landscape after Wu Chen, signed, dated 1669, Tientsin Art Museum.
> T'ien-ching, I. 71.
> Landscape after Huang Kung-wang, signed, dated 1670, Liao-ning
> Provincial Museum. Liao-ning, II. 88.
> A fisherman in a boat approaching the shore, heavy mists, folding
> fan, inscribed, signed, dated 1673, after Chao Meng-fu, Shang-
> hai WWPKWYH. Shan-mien-hua, 56*.
> Misty peaks, after Huang Kung-wang, signed, dated 1675, Nat. Pal.
> Mus., Taipei, (AL). CKLTMHC, V. 1.
> River village in spring mists, folding fan, signed, dated 1677, after
> Chao Ling-jang, Shanghai WWPKWYH. Shan-mien-hua, 57*.
> Autumn mountains, after Wang Meng, signed, two lines of poetry,
> Nat. Pal. Mus., Taipei, (AL). 300 M., 256*.
> Landscape after Huang Kung-wang, inscribed, signed, Nat. Pal. Mus.,
> Taipei. 300 M., 257; CAT, 107.
> Landscape after Huang Kung-wang, signed, Nat. Pal. Mus., Taipei.
> CCAT, pl. 17*.
> Landscape after the three Chaos, inscribed, signed, Shanghai Museum.
> Shang-hai, 67*.
> Landscape after Chü-jan, poem, signed, Tientsin Art Museum. T'ien-
> ching, II. 99.

WANG HOU-LAI 汪 後 來 , t. Po-an 白 岸 , h. Lu-kang
鹿 岡 . B. 1678; originally lived in Anhui, when young moved to
Fan-yü, Kuangtung; poet; painted in the style of Hung-jen; author of Lu-
kang hua-shih 鹿 岡 畫 史 . (W. I. 3; M. p. 140.)

A man in a boat under tall cliffs in autumn, inscribed, signed, dated
1721. Kuang-tung hua-chia, 30*.

Scene in the Lo-fu Mountains, two men by a river, inscribed, signed.
Kuang-tung hua-chia, 31*.

WANG HUI 王 翬 , t. Shih-ku 石 谷 , h. Keng-yen san-jen
耕 煙 散 人 , Ch'ing-hui chu-jen 清 暉 主 人 , Chien-
men ch'iao-k'o 劍 門 樵 客 and other names. B. 1632,
d. 1717; from Ch'ang-shu, Kiangsu; one of the "Four Wangs" and founder
of the Yü-shan school. (CP, VII, AL, 425-432.)

Herding buffalo in cloudy mountains, inscribed, signed, dated 1669,
colophons by Wang Shih-min and others. TSYMC hua-hsüan, 87*.

Landscape, signed, colophons by Wang Shih-min and Yün Shou-p'ing
both dated 1670, Nat. Pal. Mus., Taipei, (AL). 300 M., 258*;
CH mei-shu, III; CKLTMHC, V.18.

A twelve leaf album of flowers and landscapes, the flowers by Yün
Shou-p'ing, dated 1672, Nat. Pal. Mus., Taipei. 300 M., 269-
272 (four of the six landscapes); (CAT, 110).

Clouds and mists among cliffs, inscribed, signed, dated 1672, colophon by Yün Shou-p'ing, Shanghai Museum. Shang-hai, 76*.

A mountain gorge with rushing water and bridge, after Wang Meng,
signed, dated 1673, Palace Museum, Peking, (AL). CK ku-tai,
96.

A high peak, after Fang Ts'ung-i, signed, dated 1678, Nat. Pal. Mus.,
Taipei, (AL). CKLTMHC, V.20.

Travellers on donkey-back and in boats, misty mountain valley, signed,
dated 1679, Tientsin Art Museum. T'ien-ching, I.72.

Overgrown hills, after Chü-jan, signed, dated 1680, Nat. Pal. Mus.,
Taipei, (AL). CKLTMHC, V.21.

An album of twelve leaves of landscapes after Sung and Yüan masters,
one dated 1681, Nat. Pal. Mus., Taipei. CH mei-shu, III (three
leaves, landscapes after Li Ch'eng, Chao Ling-jang, Wang Wei);
CKLTSHH (one leaf, landscape after Wang Wei).

Mists and rain in summer mountains, inscribed, signed, dated 1681,
Tientsin Art Museum. I-yüan chi-chin, 32.

Four leaves of a twelve leaf album of landscapes of Yu-shan, done
when 53 years old (1684). Wang Shih-ku, 2-5.

Copy of Huang Kung-wang's Fu-ch'un Mountains, handscroll, inscribed, signed, dated 1686, Liao-ning Provincial Museum. Liao-
ning, II.98-99.

Travellers in streams and mountains, after Fan K'uan, handscroll,
dated 1688. Wang Shih-ku, 6-7 (sections).

A wintry grove, signed, dated 1690. Nat. Pal. Mus., Taipei.
CKLTMHC, V.22.

Mountain hermitage, signed, dated 1692, Chang Pe-chin collection.
Tien Yin Tang, I.91.

Reading in the mountain in autumn, after Wang Meng, signed, inscribed, dated 1692, Nat. Pal. Mus., Taipei, (AL). CKLTMHC, V.23.

Peaks and valleys, illustration to a T'ang poem, signed, dated 1693,
Nat. Pal. Mus., Taipei, (AL). CAT, 108; CKLTMHC, V.24.

An album of eight landscapes after old masters, leaves inscribed,
one signed, one dated 1696, Suchou Museum. Su-chou, 58, 59
(two leaves).

Drinking tea, after Tung Ch'i-ch'ang, poem, signed, dated 1696,
Nat. Pal. Mus., Taipei, (AL). CKLTMHC, V.25.

Selling fish in the snowy mountains, poem, signed, dated 1698, after
Li Ch'eng. TWYMC hua-hsüan, 86; Wang Shih-ku, 8.

Peach blossoms and a mandarin duck, bamboo by Wang Hui, rest of
painting by Wang Yün, after Lu Chih, signed, dated 1700, Nat.
Pal. Mus., Taipei, (AL). CKLTMHC, V.28.

Trees in summer, after Chao Meng-fu, signed, dated 1700, Nat. Pal.
Mus., Taipei, (AL). CKLTMHC, V.26.

Cattle on a wooded plain, inscribed, signed, dated 1701, Nat. Pal.
Mus., Taipei. 300 M., 261.

Conversing on a bridge, poem, signed, dated 1703, Chang Pe-chin
collection. Tien Yin Tang, I.92.

Landscape, inscribed, signed, dated 1703, S.M. Siu collection, Hong
Kong. CK ku-hua, B.234.

A lake village at evening, folding fan, signed, dated 1704, Shanghai
WWPKWYH. Shan-mien-hua, 69*.

Awaiting the ferry at the foot of mountains, after Tung Yüan, handscroll, inscribed, signed, dated 1704, Tientsin Art Museum.
T'ien-ching, II.100-102.

Landscape album, four leaves, signed, one dated 1704, S.M. Siu
collection, Hong Kong. CK ku-hua, B.233.

Buildings in a mountain gorge, in the style of Wang Meng, poem,
signed, dated 1707, Mu Yün-hua collection. CK hua, I.30.

Man in a thatched pavilion under bamboo and pine, after Ts'ao Chih-
po, inscribed, signed, dated 1708. Wang Shih-ku, 9.

Misty willows at West Lake, inscribed, signed, dated 1710. Wang
Shih-ku, 10.

A view over a bay, many small buildings, called "Spring in Chiang-
nan", inscribed, signed, dated 1711, (AL). Wang Shih-ku, 11.

Landscape after Li Ch'eng, inscribed, signed, dated 1712, Nat. Pal.
Mus., Taipei. 300 M., 259; CKLTMHC, V.27.

A flight of birds on an autumn evening, two friends drinking in a pavilion, signed, dated 1712, poem of T'ang Yin, Palace Museum,
Peking. PM, 15*; WW, 1958.6.6.

A misty river, men in boats collecting water-chestnuts, after Wang
    Shen, inscribed, signed, dated 1714, (AL). Wang Shih-ku, 12.

Dwelling in the mountains, a country estate by a misty river, inscrib-
    ed, signed, dated 1715. Wang Shih-ku, 13.

A fishing fleet on a mountain river, inscribed, signed, dated 1715.
    Wang Shih-ku, 14.

Dwelling in snowy mountains, after Wang Wei, inscribed, signed,
    dated 1715. Wang Shih-ku, 15.

Watching the tidal bore, after Emperor Hui-tsung, inscribed, signed,
    dated 1717. Wang Shih-ku, 16.

Autumn forest, two artist's seals, Nat. Pal. Mus., Taipei. 300 M.,
    260; CCAT, pl. 121.

Copy of Li Ch'eng's "Clearing after snow in the mountains", album
    leaf, inscribed, signed, Nat. Pal. Mus., Taipei. CH mei-shu,
    III.

Ten-thousand gullies, the wind in the pines, inscribed, signed, after
    Huang Kung-wang, Nat. Pal. Mus., Taipei. CKLTMHC, V. 19.

Winter in Kiangsu, two album leaves, inscribed, Palace Museum,
    Peking. PM, 16*, 17*.

Mist among willow trees, folding fan, poem, signed, in the manner
    of Hui-ch'ung, illustration to a T'ang poem, Shanghai WWPKWYH.
    Shan-mien-hua, 70*.

Landscape after Tung Yüan, signed, three colophons, Suchou Museum.
    Su-chou, 60.

Four album leaves, landscapes after old masters, each leaf with
    artist's seal, Tientsin Art Museum. T'ien-ching, I. 73-76.

Landscape after Ching Hao, album leaf, artist's seal. Wang Shih-ku, 1.

Emperor K'ang-hsi's progress to the south, handscroll. Wang Shih-
    ku, 17-19 (sections).

Reading in the Lu Mountain, signed, dated (reproduction blurred).
    WW, 1958. 6. 37.

An album of ten landscapes after old masters, each inscribed and
    with artist's seal. WS-k Hua-hsüan.

WANG LI 王 禮 , t. Ch'iu-yen 秋 言 , h. Ch'iu-tao-jen
秋道人 , Kua-chi-sheng 蝸寄生 . B. 1813, d. 1879;
from Wu-chiang, Kiangsu; painted figures, studied Ch'en Hung-shou.
(T. II; M. p. 63.)

    A girl inside a moon-door playing a p'i-p'a, Suchou Museum. Su-
    chou, 114.

WANG SHIH-MIN 王 時 敏 , t. Hsün-chih 遜 之 , h. Yen-
k'o 煙 客 , Hsi-lu lao-jen 西廬老人 , Hsi-t'ien
chu-jen 西田主人 and other names. B. 1592, d. 1680;

from T'ai-ts'ang, one of the "Four Wangs" and one of the "Nine Friends in Painting". (CP, VII, AL, 434-436.)

> Three album leaves depicting landscapes, one signed, dated 1658, Nat. Pal. Mus., Taipei. CH mei-shu, III (three leaves); CKLTSHH (one leaf).

> A scholar in a pavilion under trees by a stream, cloudy valley and misty streams, inscribed, signed, dated 1658, in the manner of Huang Kung-wang, Shanghai Museum. Shang-hai, 66*.

> Landscape painted for Wang Hui, signed, dated 1666, colophon by Wang Chien, (AL). TSYMC hua-hsüan, 66.

> Stream and village in the mountains, folding fan, signed, dated 1669, Shanghai WWPKWYH. Shan-mien-hua, 53*.

> Landscape after Huang Kung-wang, signed, colophon dated 1670, Nat. Pal. Mus., Taipei, (AL). 300 M., 255; CH mei-shu, III.

> Mountain landscape, two cranes in a courtyard, a scholar on a bridge, signed, dated 1671, Nat. Pal. Mus., Taipei. CCAT, 119.

> Peaks and trees in mountain mists, signed, dated 1672, after Huang Kuang-wang, Nat. Pal. Mus., Taipei. 300 M., 254; CAT, 106.

> Boat on the river, a village among spring willows, folding fan, signed, dated 1678, Shanghai WWPKWYH. Shan-mien-hua, 54*.

> Eggplant and bamboo, inscribed, signed, in the manner of Wen Cheng-ming, Tientsin Art Museum. T'ien-ching, II. 98.

> Landscape, signed, Tientsin Art Museum. I-yüan chi-chin, 30.

WANG SHIH-SHEN 汪 士 慎 , t. Chin-jen 近 人 , h. Ch'ao-lin 巢 林 , Ch'i-tung wai-shih 漢東外史 , and other names. B. 1686, d. 1759, from Anhui, lived in Yangchou, Kiangsu; friend of Chin Nung and Hua Yen; painted narcissi and plum blossoms. (CP, VII, AL 436-437; for dates see Ku Lin-wen, Yang-chou pa-chia shih-liao, Shanghai, 1962.)

> Ink epidendrum, inscribed, signed, dated 1735, after P'u-ming, Tientsin Art Museum. T'ien-ching, II. 129.

> Branch of flowering plum, dated 1736, colophon by Lo P'ing, Nanking Museum. Yang-chou pa-chia, 5.

> Epidendrum and bamboo, inscribed, signed, dated 1740, Shanghai Museum. Shang-hai, 87*.

> Trumpet creeper, album leaf, inscribed, artist's seal, Palace Museum, Peking. KKPWY hua-niao, 87*.

> A man seated on a riverbank, inscribed, signed, after Tao-chi, Canton Museum. TSYMC hua-hsüan, 100.

WANG SHU-KU 王 樹 穀 , t. Yüan-feng 原 豐 , h. Wu-wo 無 我 and Lu-kung 鹿 公 . B. 1649, d. after 1731, from Hangchou; painted figures, followed Ch'en Hung-shou. (CP, VII, AL, 437.)

Two bamboo, old tree and rock, album leaf, inscribed, signed, dated
1724. Che-chiang, 71.

WANG TZU-YÜAN 王 子 元 , t. T'ai-yü 台 宇 . From Suchou,
17th century; painted flowers. (M. p. 47.)
Plum, pine, cypress, narcissus by a stream, done with Liu Yüan-ch'i,
Sheng Mao-hua, Ch'en Chia-yen and Wang Chung-li, dated 1625,
Tientsin Art Museum. T'ien-ching, II. 61.

WANG WU 王 武 , t. Ch'in-chung 勤 中 , h. Wang-an 忘 菴 .
B. 1632, d. 1690; from Suchou; collector and connoisseur; painted flowers,
birds, landscapes. (CP, VII, AL, 438.)
Two pigeons under apricot blossoms, inscribed, signed, dated 1662,
Tientsin Art Museum. I-yüan chi-chin, 35.
Enjoying chrysanthemums in a mountain pavilion, inscribed, signed,
dated 1667, Nat. Pal. Mus., Taipei, (AL). CKLTMHC, V. 8.
Chrysanthemum and bamboo, folding fan, poem, signed, dated 1676,
Hui Hsiao-t'ung collection. Shan-mien chi-chin, 21*.
Narcissi growing by an eroded rock, inscribed, signed, dated 1678,
Suchou Museum. Su-chou, 62.
Peonies, folding fan, poem, signed, dated 1680, Shanghai WWPKWYH.
Shan-mien-hua, 74*.
Narcissi and the t'ien-chu plant, signed, dated 1683, Nat. Pal. Mus.,
Taipei, (AL). CKLTMHC, V. 9.
Birds and flowers, poem, signed, dated 1685, Nat. Pal. Mus., Tai-
pei, (AL). CKLTMHC, V. 10.
A bulbul on a pine, bamboos and plum blossoms, inscribed, signed,
dated 1689, Palace Museum, Peking. KKPWY hua-niao, 73*.
A crane and a pair of ducks by a stream, moon reflected in the water,
inscribed, signed, dated 1689. TSYMC hua-hsüan, 81.
Butterfly and autumn flowers, folding fan, inscribed, signed, Shanghai
WWPKWYH. Shan-mien-hua, 75*.

WANG WU-T'IEN 王 無 忝 , t. Su-yeh 夙 夜 . From Meng-
chin, Honan; chin-shih in 1670; painted landscapes. (CP, VII, AL, 438.)
Two of four album leaves depicting landscapes, both inscribed, one
after Tung Yüan, one after Wu Chen, last dated 1664; two more
paintings in album by Wang, plus four by Ch'en T'eng-kuei, Liao-
ning Provincial Museum. Liao-ning, II. 82-83.

WANG YÜ 王 昱 , t. Jih-ch'u 日 初 , h. Tung-chuang 東 莊
and other names. From T'ai-ts'ang, Kiangsu; active c. 1680-1729; a
nephew of Wang Yüan-ch'i; author of Tung-chuang lun-hua; landscapes.
(CP, VII, AL, 439.)

Landscape after Huang Kung-wang, signed, dated 1750, Tientsin Art
Museum. T'ien-ching, I. 88.

WANG YÜAN-CH'I 王原祁 , t. Mao-ching 茂京 , h. Lu-t'ai
麓臺 , Hsi-lu hou-jen 西廬後人 and other names.
B. 1642, d. 1715; from T'ai-ts'ang, Kiangsu; grandson of Wang Shih-chen;
one of the "Four Wangs"; landscapes. (CP, VII, AL, 439-443.)

Pavilion and trees, river views, misty mountains, signed, dated 1675,
Cheng Te-k'un collection, Cambridge. Mu-fei, before p. 45.

Bamboos and stones, the bamboos by Tao-chi, dated 1691, the stones
by Wang Yüan-ch'i, signed, Nat. Pal. Mus., Taipei, (AL). 300
M., 289; CCAT, pl. 120; CKLTMHC, V. 11; KKCP, I. 10.

The Fu-ch'un Mountains, after Huang Kung-wang, inscribed, signed,
dated 1693, Suchou Museum, (AL ?). Su-chou, 71.

Autumn colors on the Hua Mountain, inscribed, signed, dated 1693,
Nat. Pal. Mus., Taipei. 300 M., 275*; CKLTMHC, V. 29.

Summer landscape after Wang Meng, signed, dated 1694, Nat. Pal.
Mus., Taipei. 300 M., 276.

Cloudy landscape, inscribed, signed, dated 1696, after Kao K'o-kung,
Shanghai Museum. Shang-hai, 81*.

Landscape after Huang Kung-wang, poem, inscribed, signed, dated
1698, Nat. Pal. Mus., Taipei. CKLTMHC, V. 31.

Four landscapes from an album of sixteen leaves after Sung and Yüan
masters, leaves all inscribed, some with artist's seals, some
dated 1698, Nat. Pal. Mus., Taipei. CH mei-shu, III (landscapes
after Wang Wei, Fan K'uan, Kao K'o-kung, Ni Tsan); CKLTSHH,
(one leaf, landscape after Ni Tsan).

Landscape in the style of Wang Meng, signed, dated 1699, Nat. Pal.
Mus., Taipei. NPM Bulletin, II. 3, p. 16.

Landscape after Li Ch'eng, handscroll, signed, dated 1699, Nat. Pal.
Mus., Taipei, (AL). CKLTMHC, V. 32.

A poetry-filled painting, inscribed, signed, dated 1700, Nat. Pal.
Mus., Taipei. CKLTMHC, V. 33; NPM Bulletin II. 4, p. 15 (detail).

An album of six leaves, copies of Sung and Yüan landscapes, album
dated 1701, Liao-ning Provincial Museum. Liao-ning, II. 100
(two leaves: one after Wu Chen, the other, part of Huang Kung-
wang's Fu-ch'un Mountains).

Pavilions and towers on the Mountain of the Immortals, after Chao
Meng-fu, signed, dated 1702, Nat. Pal. Mus., Taipei, (AL).
CKLTMHC, V. 34.

Mountains and a broad stream in autumn, after Huang Kung-wang,
signed, dated 1702, Nat. Pal. Mus., Taipei, (AL). CH mei-
shu, III.

Village by a river, mountain terraces in the background, dedicated
to Wang Hui, signed, dated 1703, (AL). TSYMC hua-hsüan, 88.

Landscape after Wu Chen, inscribed, signed, dated 1706, Suchou Museum. Su-chou, 72.

Autumn landscape after Huang Kung-wang, dated 1707, Nat. Pal. Mus.,
Taipei. CAT, 112.

Landscape after Huang Kung-wang, artist's seals, dated 1708, Tientsin Art Museum. T'ien-ching, I. 77.

Landscape after Huang Kung-wang, dated 1711, Nat. Pal. Mus., Taipei. NPM Bulletin, II. 4, p. 10.

Landscape after Huang Kung-wang, inscribed, signed, dated 1712,
Tientsin Art Museum. T'ien-ching, II. 103.

Mountains in autumn, after Huang Kung-wang, inscribed, signed,
done at age 72 (1713), Nat. Pal. Mus., Taipei, (AL). CKLTMHC,
V. 35.

Summer mountains, after Huang Kung-wang, inscribed, signed, dated
1713, Tientsin Art Museum. I-yüan chi-chin, 33.

Landscape after Huang Kung-wang, inscribed, signed, dated 1714,
at the age of 73, Suchou Museum. Su-chou, 73.

A thatched hut and misty trees, signed, dated 1715, Nat. Pal. Mus.,
Taipei. CKLTMHC, V. 36; NPM Bulletin, II. 4, p. 13.

Floating mist on distant mountain, signed, Nat. Pal. Mus., Taipei,
(AL). 300 M., 277; CKLTMHC, V. 30.

Streams flowing out from cloudy mountains, signed, Nat. Pal. Mus.,
Taipei, (AL). CKLTMHC, V. 37.

Cloudy spring mountains, signed, Nat. Pal. Mus., Taipei. CH mei-
shu, III; CH ming-hua*.

Mountain village in clouds, folding fan, signed, Shanghai WWPKWYH.
Shan-mien-hua, 81*.

White clouds in green mountains, folding fan, signed, Shanghai WWP-
KWYH. Shan-mien-hua, 82*.

Ink bamboo by Tao-chi, background by Wang Yüan-ch'i, inscribed
and signed by Tao-chi, S. M. Siu collection, Hong Kong. CK ku-
hua, B. 222.

WANG YÜAN-CH'U 王 元 初 , t. Tzu-yai 紫 崖 . Landscapes
in the manner of Huang Kung-wang. (CP, VII, AL, 443.)

Landscape with lakeside buildings, album leaf, signed, dated 1655,
Nat. Pal. Mus., Taipei, (AL). CH mei-shu, III.

WANG YÜN 王 雲 , t. Han-tsao 漢 藻 , h. Ch'ing-ch'ih
清 癡 . B. 1652, d. c. 1735, from Kao-yu, Kiangsu; figures, landscapes. (CP, VII, AL, 443.)

Boat on the river, cloudy mountains, signed, dated 1724, Tientsin
Art Museum. I-yüan chi-chin, 36.

A mandarin duck and peach-blossoms, after Lu Chih, bamboos by
Wang Hui, dated 1700, poem by Wang Yün, Nat. Pal. Mus., Taipei, (AL). CKLTMHC, V.28.

Landscape, artist's seal, Nat. Pal. Mus., Taipei, (AL). CKLTMHC,
V.42.

Peach blossoms, willow, birds and fish, a bird by Wang Yün, rest of
painting by Yang Chin, Yü Yüan, Hsü Mei, Wu Chih, and Ku Fang,
signed by all six artists, colophon by Wang Hui, Palace Museum,
Peking. KKPWY hua-niao, 77*.

WEI P'AO 魏 龀 , t. Fo-tsun 浮 尊 , h. Hao-jan-tzu 嗥虎
然 子 . From Ch'ang-shu, early 18th century, lived in Suchou as
a Taoist at the Yüan-miao Temple; a poet and musician; studied landscape
with Huang Ting. (M. p. 713.)

River pavilion and mountain colors, after Ni Tsan, inscribed, signed,
dated 1740, Suchou Museum. Su-chou, 92.

WEN TIEN 文 點 , t. Yü-yeh 與 也 , h. Nan-yün shan-
ch'iao 南 雲 山 樵 . B. 1633, d. 1704; a descendant of Wen
Cheng-ming; landscapes, pines, bamboo. (CP, VII, AL, 444.)

A guest arriving at a mountain study, folding fan, inscribed, signed,
dated 1695, painted for Wen-ts'an, Shanghai WWPKWYH. Shan-
mien-hua, 80*.

WEN TING 文 鼎 , t. Hsüeh-k'uang 學 匡 , h. Hou-shan
後山 . B. 1766, d. 1852; from Hsiu-shui, Chekiang; collector, connoisseur; landscapes, pines, stones, followed Wen Cheng-ming. (CP, VII,
AL, 444.)

The Ten-acre Hibiscus Hall, a boy fishing in a large lotus pond, signed,
dated 1821. Che-chiang, 89.

WEN TOU 文 斗 , t. K'uei-ping 魁 柄 h. Pai-yün 白 雲 .
From Nan-hai, Kuangtung; 18th century, died at age 93; poet, chess-player,
painter. (W.I.3; M. p. 19.)

Day lily, rocks and branch, signed. Kuang-tung hua-chia, 36*.

WU CHIA-YU 吳 嘉 猷 or Wu Yu 吳 猷 , t. Yu-ju
友 如 . From Yüan-ho, moved to Shanghai; active c. 1850-1910;
painted figures, ladies, landscapes, flowers, birds, insects, fish. (M.
p. 180.)

Children playing, signed, dated 1878, Shanghai WWKLWYH. CK chin-
pai-nien, 54.

WU CHIH 吳芷 , t. Ai-an 艾庵 . From Wu-chiang, Kiangsu; lived during the second half of the 17th century; painted flowers. (U.II.2; M. p. 166.)

Peach blossoms, willow, birds and fish, fish by Wu Chih, rest of painting by Yang Chin, Yü Yüan, Wang Yün, Hsü Mei, and Ku Fang, signed by all six artists, colophon by Wang Hui, Palace Museum, Peking. KKPWY hua-niao, 77*.

WU HSÜ 吳旭 , t. Tzu-sheng 子升 . From Hsi-hsien, Anhui; painted landscapes, figures and portraits. (M. p. 171.)

Ten gentlemen enjoying the moon, folding fan, signed, dated (unclear), Hui Hsiao-t'ung collection. Shan-mien chi-chin, 16*.

WU HSÜEH-TSAO 伍學藻 , t. Yung-yün 用蘊 . From Shun-te, Kuangtung; late 19th century; painted figures, flowers and fruits. (W.I.8.)

Branches of lichee, inscribed, signed. Kuang-tung hua-chia, 82*.

WU HUNG 吳宏 , t. Yüan-tu 遠度 , h. Chu-shih 竹史 . From Chin-ch'i, Kiangsi, lived in Nanking; active c. 1670-1780; one of the "Eight Masters of Nanking"; painted landscapes. (CP, VII, AL, 445-446.)

Landscape after Li Ch'eng, a rustic homestead in a grove, inscribed, signed, Tientsin Art Museum. I-yüan chi-chin, 39.

Landscape with pavilion, waterfall and covered bridge, signed, Tientsin Art Museum. I-yüan chi-chin, 40; T'ien-ching, II.97.

WU JUI-LUNG 伍瑞隆 , t. Kuo-k'ai 國開 and T'ieh-shan 鐵山 , h. Chiu-ai shan-jen 鳩艾山人 , K'ai-kuo 開國 . B. 1585, d. 1673; from Hsiang-shan, Kuangtung; friend of Ch'en Hung-shou and Chou Liang-kung; calligrapher; painted peonies, bamboo and epidendrum. (W.I.2; M. p. 85.)

Peonies, signed, dated 1642. Kuang-tung hua-chia, 11*.

WU JUNG-KUANG 吳榮光 , t. Po-jung 伯榮 , h. Ho-wu 荷屋 , K'o-an 可盦 , Shih-yün shan-jen 石雲山人 and other names. B. 1773, d. 1843; from Nan-hai, Kuangtung; poet, calligrapher; painted landscapes, birds and flowers. (CP, VII, AL, 446.)

Workers in the rice paddies, inscribed, signed, dated 1840. Kuang-tung hua-chia, 51*.

Portrait of Wu Hsiu-tzu, inscribed, Chu Hsing-chai collection. Kuang-tung shu-hua, 32.

WU KU-HSIANG 吳穀祥 , t. Ch'iu-neng 秋農 h. Ch'iu-pu lao-nung 秋圃老農 . B. 1848, d. 1903, from Chia-hsing, Chekiang; landscapes after Wen Cheng-ming and Shen Chou. (M. p. 181.)

> Farewell scene, men in a boat under a willow, signed, dated 1901,
> a series of matched rhyme farewell poems inscribed at the top,
> Shanghai Museum. CK chin-pai-nien, 55.

WU LI 吳歷 , t. Yü-shan 漁山 , h. Mo-ching 墨井 .
B. 1632, d. 1718, from Ch'ang-shu, Kiangsu; landscapes after Huang Kung-wang; became a Christian in 1682, served as a missionary in Chia-ting, Kiangsu, buried in the Jesuit cemetery in Shanghai. (CP, VII, AL, 446-449.)

> Birds flying over spring landscape, folding fan, poem, signed, dated
> 1669, after Chao Ling-jang, Shanghai WWPKWYH. Shan-mien-hua, 72*.
> The P'i-p'a Hsing, handscroll, signed, dated 1672, Shanghai Museum.
> CK hua, II. 14; Wu Li, 1-4.
> Palaces on the Mountains of the Immortals, inscribed, signed, dated
> 1675. TSYMC hua-hsüan, 82*.
> Plum blossoms on green hills, heavy mists, two cranes on a path,
> folding fan, inscribed, signed, dated 1675, Shanghai WWPKWYH.
> Shan-mien-hua, 73*.
> A lake in spring, after Chao Ta-nien, signed, poem, dated 1676,
> Shanghai Museum, (AL). CK ku-tai, 95; Shang-hai, 77*; Wu Li,
> 5*.
> Pavilion on a plum blossom mountain, signed, dated 1678, Nat. Pal.
> Mus., Taipei. 300 M., 273; CKLTMHC, V. 12.
> Scholars enjoying the summer breeze in open garden pavilions, hand-
> scroll, poem, signed, dated 1679, (AL). Wu Li, 6-9.
> Autumn landscape with spare trees, rushing water and houseboats on
> the river, handscroll, two inscriptions by the artist, one dated
> 1681, Shanghai Museum, (AL). Wu Li, 10.
> Autumn landscape, towering mountain peak and winding river valley,
> inscribed, signed, dated 1702. Wu Li, 11.
> A flock of birds over a willow bank, signed, dated 1702. WW, 1958.
> 8. 54.
> Landscape after Wu Chen, inscribed, signed, Nat. Pal. Mus., Taipei,
> (AL). 300 M., 274; CH mei-shu, III (four leaves); CKLTMHC, V. 13.
> Ten album leaves: landscapes after Sung and Yüan masters, colophon
> by Wang Tsuan, Nat. Pal. Mus., Taipei, (AL). CAT, 111 (one
> leaf); CH mei-shu, (four leaves); CCAT, pl. 19* (one leaf);
> CKLTMHC, V. 14 (two leaves); CKLTSHH (one leaf).

Clearing after rain in summer mountains, inscribed, signed, after
Wu Chen, (AL, Summer mountains after rain, after Wu Chen?).
Wu Li, 14.

Bamboo growing beside a rock, two lines of poetry, signed, (AL).
Wu Li, 15.

Landscape after Ni Tsan, inscribed, signed, Liao-ning Provincial
Museum. Liao-ning, II. 103.

Mountain village, villas by a shore, distant pagoda, folding fan, inscribed, signed, Shanghai WWPKWYH. Shan-mien-hua, 71*.

Bamboo and rock, inscribed, signed, Tientsin Art Museum. T'ien-
ching, II. 105.

Village in a mountain ravine, inscribed, signed. TSYMC hua-hsüan,
83.

Mountain hamlet, inscribed, signed, in the style of Wang Meng. Wu
Li, 12.

Autumn landscape, after an old master, inscribed, signed. Wu Li,
13.

The Huai-yung Hall, album leaf (?), signed. Wu Li, 16.

WU PO-HOU 吴 博 厚 , h. Pu-chai 補 齋 . From Sung-
chiang, Kiangsu, moved to Suchou; lived in the mid and late 18th century;
painted flowers and birds, insects, fish. (T. I. 4; M. p. 171.)

A crane flying above a fishing boat on the river, signed, dated 1760,
Suchou Museum. Su-chou, 104.

WU TAN 吴 丹 , t. Chung-po 東 白 . From Nanking, active c. 1672-1689; landscapes. (CP, VII, AL, 450.)

A mountain village, signed, dated 1701 or 1641, Chang Hsiao-pin
collection. CK hua, I. 32.

WU WEI-YEH 吴 偉 業 , t. Chün-kung 駿 公 , h. Mei-
ts'un 梅 邨 . B. 1609, d. 1671; from T'ai-ts'ang, Kiangsu; poet.
(CP, VII, AL, 451.)

Spare trees and mountain temples, folding fan, signed, dated 1656,
Shanghai WWPKWYH. Shan-mien-hua, 60*.

River landscape, album leaf, signed, dated 1658, Nat. Pal. Mus.,
Taipei, (AL). CH mei-shu, III.

WU YING-CHEN 吴 應 貞 , t. Han-wu 含 五 . A woman,
from Wu-chiang, Kiangsu; lived during the K'ang-hsi period (1662-1722);
flowers, portraits. (CP, VII, AL, 452.)

Lotus flowers rising above the water, signed, dated 1720, Palace Museum, Peking, (AL). KKPWY hua-niao, 80*.

WU YÜN 吴雪 , t. Yeh-ma 野馬 and Ch'iu-nan 秋南 .
From Hsieh-hsien, Anhui, 16th century, poet, landscape painter. (CP,
VII, AL, 452.)

Traveller on muleback on a riverside path, a flock of birds settling
in bare trees, album leaf, signed, dated 1598, fourth leaf of an
album made for Erh-hsiao, Liao-ning Provincial Museum. Liao-
ning, II.75.

YANG CHIN 楊晉 , t. Tzu-hao 子鶴 , h. Hsi-t'ing 西亭 .
B. 1644, d. 1728, from Ch'ang-shu, Kiangsu; pupil of Wang Hui. (CP,
VII, AL, 452-453.)

A pair of ducks under wisteria, folding fan, signed, dated 1707, Hui
Hsiao-t'ung collection. Shan-mien chi-chin, 18*.
An ox under a willow tree, folding fan, poem, signed, dated 1717,
Shanghai WWPKWYH. Shan-mien-hua, 83*.
A cow-herd, poem, signed, dated 1724, Nat. Pal. Mus., Taipei,
(AL). CKLTMHC, V.40.
Peach blossoms, willow, birds and fish, peach blossoms done by
Yang Chin, rest of painting done by Yü Yüan, Wang Yün, Hsü
Mei, Wu Chih and Ku Fang, signed by all six artists, colophon
by Wang Hui, Palace Museum, Peking. KKPWY hua-niao, 77*.

YAO WEN-HAN 姚文瀚 . A court-painter in the Ch'ien-lung
period, active c. 1760. (CP, VII, AL, 454.)

New Year's Day in the palace, done in cooperation with Chang Tsung-
tsang and Chang Hao, Nat. Pal. Mus., Taipei (?). CKLTMHC,
V.64, 65.

YEH HSIN 葉欣 , t. Jung-mu 榮木 . From Hua-t'ing,
Kiangsu, lived in Nanking; active c. 1670; one of the "Eight Masters of
Nanking"; landscapes. (CP, VII, AL, 455.)

Two men standing on a high rock, another man approaching, album
leaf, artist's seal, Nat. Pal. Mus., Taipei, (AL). CH mei-
shu, III.
Two lanterns on a rocky ridge, a stream below, album leaf, artist's
seal, Nat. Pal. Mus., Taipei, (AL). CH mei-shu, III.

YEH YÜ 葉雨 , t. Jun-chih 潤之 . Painted landscapes in
the manner of Li Shih-ta. (M. p. 577.)

Scholar and servant at foot of a bridge looking at a waterfall, album
leaf, inscribed, signed, dated 1598, leaf five of an album made
for Erh-hsiao, Liao-ning Provincial Museum. Liao-ning, II.77.

YEN CHAN 嚴 湛 , t. Shui-tzu 水 子 . From Shan-yin, Chekiang; active c. 1661; figures, studied Ch'en Hung-shou. (M. p. 728.)
> A gentleman and a lady seated in a garden listening to a flautist, hand-
> scroll, done with Ch'en Hung-shou and Li Wan-sheng, made for
> Ho T'ien-chang, Suchou Museum. Su-chou, 32.

YEN LUN 嚴 倫 , t. Lun-chieh 倫 皆 , h. Shih-ch'iao
石 樵 . From Shun-te, Kuangtung; lived c. 1796-1850; poet; painted
landscapes in Mi style. (W.I.5; M. p. 729.)
> River scenery in cold weather, inscribed, signed. Kuang-tung hua-
> chia, 45*.

YEN SHENG-SUN 嚴 繩 孫 , t. Sun-yu 孫 友 , h. Kou-wu
yen-ssu 勾 吳 嚴 四 . B. 1623, d. 1702; from Wu-hsi,
Kiangsu; scholar, poet; landscapes, figures, flowers, birds. (CP, VII,
AL, 456.)
> Houses at the foot of a mountain, album leaf, signed, Nat. Pal. Mus.,
> Taipei, (AL). CH mei-shu, III.

YING PAO 瑛 寶 , t. Meng-ch'an 夢 禪 , h. Chien-an
間 菴 . A Manchu; active c. 1800; landscapes, flowers, finger-
painting. (CP, VII, AL, 457.)
> A temple in autumn mountains, folding fan, poem, signed, dated 1798,
> Hui Hsiao-t'ung collection. Shan-mien chi-chin, 13*.

YU TSO-CHIH 游 作 之 , t. Ying-ku 鷹 谷 . From Nan-
hai, Kuangtung; mid-19th century; landscapes. (W.I.9; M. p. 502.)
> Landscape, handscroll, inscribed, Li Hsia-wen collection. Kuang-
> tung shu-hua, 46.

YÜ CHIH-TING 禹 之 鼎 , t. Shang-chi 上 吉 or 尚 吉 ,
h. Shen-chai 慎 齋 . B. 1647, d. after 1709, from Yangchou,
Kiangsu; court-painter in the K'ang-hsi era. (CP, VII, AL, 457-458.)
> Landscape after Wu Chen, signed, dated 1675, Cheng Te-k'un collec-
> tion, Cambridge. Mu-fei, opposite p. 46.
> Feeding crows, inscribed, signed, dated 1695. Li-tai jen-wu, 61.
> Landscape after Wang Meng, signed, dated 1700, Suchou Museum.
> Su-chou, 74.
> Boating at evening on the autumn river, inscribed, signed, dated
> 1710, Tientsin Art Museum. T'ien-ching, I.79.
> A woman seated under a banana-plant, inscribed, Palace Museum,
> Peking, (AL). Li-tai jen-wu, 62.
> Cha Tan-yüan writing the Classics, handscroll, signed. TSYMC hua-
> hsüan, 89.

YÜ HSING 余 省　　　　, t. Tseng-san 曾 三　　　, h. Lu-t'ing
魯 亭　　. From Ch'ang-shu, Kiangsu; served in the palace during
the Ch'ien-lung era (1736-1795); flowers and birds. (CP, VII, AL, 458-
459.)

　　Two mynahs in a pine tree, signed, dated 1757. CK hua, V. 17.
　　Flowers and birds, signed, Nat. Pal. Mus., Taipei (?),(AL).
　　　CKLTMHC, V. 70.

YÜ LIEN-CHOU 俞 蓮 洲　　　. Unidentified.
　　Flowers and insects, two album leaves, Huang Chou collection. CK
　　　hua, IX. 15.

YÜ YÜAN 虞 沅　　　, t. Wan-chih 畹 之　　or Han-chih 翰之　　.
From Yangchou, lived in Ch'ang-shu, Kiangsu; active c. 1715; pupil of
Wang Hui; flowers and birds. (CP, VII, AL, 459.)
　　Peach blossoms, willow, birds and fish, willow painted by Yü Yüan,
　　　rest of painting by Yang Chin, Wang Yün, Hsü Mei, Wu Chih and
　　　Ku Fang, signed by all six artists, colophon by Wang Hui, Pal-
　　　ace Museum, Peking. KKPWY hua-niao, 77*.

YÜAN CHIANG 袁 江　　　, t. Wen-t'ao 文 濤　　　. From Chiang-
tu, Kiangsu; court-painter during the Yung-cheng era (1723-1735). (CP,
VII, AL, 459-460.)
　　Spring at the riverside pavilion, inscribed, signed, dated 1704, in
　　　the manner of Kuo Chung-shu, Shanghai Museum. Shang-hai,
　　　90*.
　　Pavilions in the Eastern Mountains, artist's seals, Palace Museum,
　　　Peking. CK hua, XIV. 14.

YÜAN HSÜEH 袁 雪　　, t. Wo-sheng 臥 生　　. From Suchou;
early Ch'ing period; seal-engraver. (CP, VII, AL, 460.)
　　Gentlemen playing chess in a riverside pavilion, signed, dated 1720,
　　　Tientsin Art Museum. I-yüan chi-chin, 44.

YÜAN TENG-TAO 袁登道　　or Tao-teng 道 登　　, t. Tao-sheng
道 生　　, h. Ch'iang-ming 強 名　　. From Tung-kuan,
Kuangtung; active c. 1640; poet; landscapes after Wang Meng and Mi Fei.
(O. 5; W. I. 1; M. p. 322.)
　　A waterfall deep in misty mountains, poem, signed, dated 1640.
　　　Kuang-tung hua-chia, 14*.
　　Willows and boats in a wind storm, inscribed, Wang Hsiang-lu collec-
　　　tion. Kuang-tung shu-hua, 21.

YÜAN YAO 袁 耀 . From Chiang-tu, Kiangsu; active c. 1744-
1755; employed at the court, nephew of Yüan Chiang. (CP, VII, AL, 460-
461.)

    The Islands of the Immortals, signed, dated 1708. CK hua, VII.16.

    Pavilions on cliffs over a stormy sea, signed, dated 1739. CK ku-
tai, 98.

    Three goats, signed, dated 1741, Ch'in Chung-wen collection. CK
hua, II.13.

    Autumn moon over the Han Palace, two people on a terrace, signed,
possibly dated (reproduction blurred), Palace Museum, Peking.
WW, 1966.4.46.

    Autumn moon over the Han Palace, inscribed, signed, Tientsin Art
Museum. I-yüan chi-chin, 43.

    Autumn moon over the Dew Terrace, signed, Hu P'ei-heng collection.
CK hua, I.31*.

YÜN HSI 允 禧 , Prince Shen 慎郡王 , h. Tzu-ch'iung
tao-jen 紫 瓊道人 . Twenty-first son of the emperor
K'ang-hsi; landscapes. (CP, VII, AL, 461.)

    Summer mountains, inscribed, signed, two colophons, Tientsin Art
Museum. T'ien-ching, I.87.

YÜN SHOU-P'ING 惲壽平 , original name Yün Ko 惲 格 ,
t. Cheng-shu 正 叔 , h. Nan-t'ien 南 田 , Yün-ch'i wai-
shih 雲溪外史 , Po-yün wai-shih 白 雲外史 ,
Tung-yüan ts'ao-i 東 園 艸衣 and other names. B. 1633,
d. 1690; from Wu-chin, Kiangsu; painted flowers and landscapes. (CP,
VII, AL, 462-466.)

    Pine and cypress, signed, dated 1666, Tientsin Art Museum. T'ien-
ching, II.104.

    The Fu-ch'un Mountains, in the manner of Huang Kung-wang, hand-
scroll, signed, dated 1670, (AL?). TSYMC hua-hsüan, 85.

    Album of six flower studies and six landscapes, flowers by Yün Shou-
p'ing, landscapes by Wang Hui, dated 1672, Nat. Pal. Mus.,
Taipei. CAT, 110 (one leaf); 300 M., 265-268 (four leaves).

    An old cedar on the Yü-hsü Mountain, inscribed, signed, dated 1673,
Nat. Pal. Mus., Taipei, (AL). CH mei-shu, III; CKLTMHC,
V.16.

    Fallen blossoms and swimming fish, poem, signed, dated 1675, after
Liu Ts'ai, Shanghai Museum. Shang-hai, 78*.

    Fishes among seaweed, folding fan, inscribed, signed, dated 1675,
Shanghai WWPKWYH. Shan-mien-hua, 77*.

    An album of five bird and flower paintings and five landscape paintings,
the last leaf depicting travellers in the mountains, a man on

muleback followed by his servant, after Tung Yüan, dated 1675, Palace Museum, Peking, (AL, other leaves in <u>Nanga Taisei,</u> II. 165; IV. 74; V. 167; VI. 123). YS-p Hua-ts'e; KKPWY hua-niao, 74* (one leaf).

Landscape after Tung and Chü, poem, signed, dated 1678, Nat. Pal. Mus., Taipei, (AL). 300 M., 263; CAT, 109.

The Five Pure Things, inscribed, signed, dated 1681, Nat. Pal. Mus., Taipei, (AL). 300 M., 262.

Scholar's cottage among trees, river landscape, poems by the artist, signed, dated 1682, Nat. Pal. Mus., Taipei, (AL). CKLTMHC, V. 17.

Wisteria, folding fan, poem, signed, dated 1682, Shanghai WWPKWYH. Shan-mien-hua, 78*.

The Five Purities, inscribed, signed, dated 1684, S. M. Siu collection, Hong Kong. CK ku-hua, B. 226.

A branch of cherries, folding fan, poem, signed, dated 1686, after a Sung master, Shanghai WWPKWYH. Shan-mien-hua, 79*.

An album of ten landscapes, some after old masters, signed, dated 1687, Nat. Pal. Mus., Taipei. 300 M., 264 (Bamboo after Kuan Tao-sheng); CH mei-shu, III (Bamboo after Kuan Tao-sheng; Cloudy mountains after Mi Fei); CKLTSHH (Cloudy mountains after Mi Fei).

Landscape, handscroll, signed, dated 1687, S. M. Siu collection, Hong Kong. CK ku-hua, B. 231.

Autumn flowers, inscribed, signed, dated 1688, S. M. Siu collection, Hong Kong. CK ku-hua, B. 229.

Landscapes after old masters, four album leaves, one dated 1689, S. M. Siu collection, Hong Kong. CK ku-hua, B. 232.

Flowers, poem, signed, Nat. Pal. Mus., Taipei, (AL). CH ming-hua*.

Trees and bamboos, after Ni Tsan, two colophons, signed, Nat. Pal. Mus., Taipei, (AL). CKLTMHC, V. 15.

Long branches of a blossoming peach-tree, inscribed, signed, in the style of T'ang Yin, Palace Museum, Peking, (AL). KKPWY hua-niao, 75*.

Recluse in a bamboo hut, after Chao Meng-fu, album leaf, inscribed, artist's seals, Nat. Pal. Mus., Taipei. CH mei-shu, III.

Flowers, a ten leaf album after old masters, Nat. Pal. Mus., Taipei. CCAT, pl. 18* (one leaf).

Flowering pear tree, album leaf, inscribed, signed, Palace Museum, Peking. PM, 41*.

Pavilion in the mountains, fishing village, boats along the river shore, inscribed, Liao-ning Provincial Museum. Liao-ning, II. 102.

Poppies, folding fan, inscribed, signed, Shanghai WWPKWYH. Shan-
mien-hua, 76*.

Copy of Wang Meng's Summer mountains, inscribed, signed, Suchou
Museum. Su-chou, 61.

Lotus flower, album leaf, Tientsin Art Museum. I-yüan chi-chin, 34.

Two small birds under flowering shrub and rice stalks, poem, signed,
Cheng Te-k'un collection, Cambridge. Mu-fei, opposite p. 44.

Plum blossoms and hibiscus, two inscriptions, signed, S.M. Siu collection, Hong Kong. CK ku-hua, B.227.

Landscape, bamboo and other subjects, four of eight album leaves,
inscribed, S.M. Siu collection, Hong Kong. CK ku-hua, B.228.

Flowers, four leaves of a twelve leaf album, each leaf inscribed and
signed, S.M. Siu collection, Hong Kong. CK ku-hua, B.230.

An album of eight flower paintings, seven leaves inscribed. YN-t
Hua-hui*.

Fish among aquatic plants, branches of willow, album leaf. CK ku-
tai, 92.

Pine, plum, bamboo in moonlight with rock and water, signed, in
Yüan style. TSYMC hua-hsüan, 84.

The Lien Pavilion, album leaf, signed. WW, 1963.6, pl. 3, no. 2.

Flowers, folding fan, signed, dated (reproduction blurred). WW,
1963.10.20.

YUNG HSING 永 瑆 , Prince Ch'eng 成 親 王 , h. Ching-
ch'üan 鏡 泉 and Shao-han 少 厂 . B. 1752, d. 1823, eleventh
son of emperor Ch'ien-lung; calligrapher. (CP, VII, AL, 466.)

Epidendrum, handscroll, inscribed, Suchou Museum. Su-chou, 95-96.

Anonymous paintings of the Ch'ing Period

Portrait of Chu Ta. WW, 1960.7.inside back cover.

Portrait of Chu Ta. WW, 1960.7.36.

Portrait of Niu Shih-hui. WW, 1960.7.41.

The empress feeding silkworms, Nat. Pal. Mus., Taipei. CCAT,
pl. 24*.

Ploughing and weaving, album leaves, Nat. Pal. Mus., Taipei. CCAT,
pl. 134 (section).

Children playing at New Year's. Ch'ing-jen-hua*.

The Ta-kuan Garden. WW, 1963.6.

MICHIGAN PAPERS IN CHINESE STUDIES

No. 1: "The Chinese Economy, 1912-1949" by Albert Feuerwerker. (April 1968)

No. 2: "The Cultural Revolution: 1967 in Review" by Michel Oksenberg, Carl Riskin, Robert Scalapino, and Ezra Vogel. (July 1968)

No. 3: "Two Studies in Chinese Literature" by Li Chi and Dale Johnson. (November 1968)

No. 4: "Early Communist China: Two Studies" by Ronald Suleski and Daniel Bays. (February 1969)

No. 5: "The Chinese Economy, ca. 1870-1911" by Albert Feuerwerker. (April 1969)

No. 6: "Chinese Paintings in Chinese Publications, 1956-1968: An Annotated Bibliography and An Index to the Paintings" by E. J. Laing. (August 1969) -- Special Issue - $ 3. 50 --

Price: $ 1. 50 (US) each
(excluding Special Issues)

Available from:

Center for Chinese Studies
The University of Michigan
Lane Hall
Ann Arbor, Michigan 48104
U.S.A.

www.ingramcontent.com/pod-product-compliance
Lightning Source LLC
Chambersburg PA
CBHW030250290526
45785CB00001B/29